LINEAGES OF STATE FRAGILITY

Western African Studies

Willing Migrants
Soninke Labor Diasporas, 1848–1960
FRAN OIS MANCHUELLE

El Dorado in West Africa
The Gold-Mining Frontier, African Labor, and
Colonial Capitalism in the Gold Coast, 1875–1900
RAYMOND E. DUMETT

Nkrumah & the Chiefs
The Politics of Chieftaincy in Ghana, 1951–60
RICHARD RATHBONE

Ghanaian Popular Fiction
'Thrilling Discoveries in Conjugal Life' & Other
Tales
STEPHANIE NEWELL

Paths of Accommodation
Muslim Societies and French Colonial Authorities
in Senegal and Mauritania, 1880–1920
DAVID ROBINSON

West African Challenge to Empire
Culture and History in the Volta-Bani
Anticolonial War
MAHIR ŞAUL AND PATRICK ROYER

Between the Sea & the Lagoon
An Eco-social History of the Anlo of Southeastern
Ghana, c. 1850 to Recent Times
EMMANUEL AKYEAMPONG

'Civil Disorder is the Disease of Ibadan'
Chieftaincy and Civic Culture in a Yoruba City
RUTH WATSON

*Smugglers, Secessionists, and Loyal Citizens on the
Ghana-Togo Frontier*
PAUL NUGENT

Eurafricans in Western Africa
Commerce, Social Status, Gender, and Religious
Observance from the
Sixteenth to the Eighteenth Century
GEORGE E. BROOKS

*Lineages of State Fragility**
Rural Civil Society in Guinea-Bissau
JOSHUA B. FORREST

*'Kola is God's Gift'**
Agricultural Production, Export Initiatives & the
Kola Industry in Asante
& and the Gold Coast, c. 1820–1950
EDMUND ABAKA

*Fighting the Slave Trade**
West African Strategies
SYLVIANE A. DIOUF

*Slavery and Reform in West Africa**
Toward Emancipation in Nineteenth-Century
Senegal and the Gold Coast
TREVOR R. GETZ

*Ouidah**
The Social History of a West African Slaving "Port,"
1727–1892
ROBIN LAW

*forthcoming

Lineages of State Fragility

Rural Civil Society in Guinea-Bissau

JOSHUA B. FORREST

Ohio University Press
ATHENS

James Currey
OXFORD

James Currey Ltd
73 Botley Road
Oxford OX2 0BS

Ohio University Press
Scott Quadrangle
Athens, Ohio 45701

British Library Cataloging in Publication Data is available
ISBN-0-85255-496-6 (James Currey, cloth)

Library of Congress Cataloging-in-Publication Data
Forrest, Joshua.
 Lineages of state fragility : rural civil society in Guinea-Bissau / Joshua B. Forrest.
  p. cm. — (Western African studies)
 Includes bibliographical references and index.
 ISBN 0-8214-1490-9 (alk. paper)
  1. Civil society—Guinea-Bissau. 2. Sociology, Rural—Guinea-Bissau. 3. Political
 stability—Guinea-Bissau. 4. Legitimacy of governments—Guinea-Bissau. I. Title.
 II. Series.

JQ3681.A591F67 2003
300'.96657'091734—dc21

                                                          2002044809

Contents

PART 4
WAR AND THE POSTCOLONIAL STATE

Maps

Preface

MY INTEREST IN THE HISTORICAL evolution of state and civil society in Guinea-Bissau was stimulated during the course of research trips to Guinea-Bissau in 1982–83.[1] As I was investigating political conflicts occurring at various levels of the political system, it became clear to me that the disjuncture between the central state and rural civil society and the enduring power of rural social formations required an explanation that lay considerably further back in time than the postcolonial period. This, in turn, led me to focus on archival research at the two principal holdings of original documents related to Guinea-Bissauan history: the Arquivo Histórico Ultramarino (AHU) in Lisbon and the Archives Nationales de Sénégal (ANS) in Dakar. The principal ideas developed in this book are based on primary documents and other written source material obtained from these archives. At the same time, recent historical and anthropological studies have added significantly to our understanding of the relations between the state and rural civil society.

This work is not intended to represent a comprehensive history of Guinea-Bissau.[2] My purpose here is to suggest that one significant and overlooked aspect of Guinea-Bissau's political evolution was the continuing ability of rural civil society to evade or thwart state power. I identify some of the social formations and praetorian achievements—representing historical lineages traceable back to precolonial times—that account for civil-societal strength in that country. Thus, in order to account for the social origins of state weakness in Guinea-Bissau, I probe, in particular, experiences of rural civil society that are significant socially, politically, and militarily. Other important aspects of Guinea-Bissauan history will necessarily be left for a later generation of researchers to pursue; it is indeed hoped that this work will help to stimulate further scholarly interest in aspects of the historical evolution of this intriguing Lusophone nation.

NOTE ON DOCUMENTS

To facilitate use of this book by the English-language reader wishing to peruse citations within the notes, the titles of most Portuguese-language and French-language documents from the AHU and the ANS have been translated into English. Letters and correspondence materials that lack an author are indicated by the description [unsigned] and identified by document number or title; documents without an author, title, or document number are indicated by date, box *(caixa)* number, and, where available, file *(pasta)* number and/or archival section number. All AHU documents are from the Guiné division of the archive.

NOTE ON NOMENCLATURE

Portuguese administrators and French observers invented, guessed at, and frequently altered the names by which they called certain African peoples in precolonial Guinea-Bissau. Some of these labels are inaccurate in the sense that they do not reveal the name that a given group of people called themselves by; for example, Balanta, instead of Brassa or Bejaa; Fula Forros, instead of Fulbe-ribê. The name Fuloo, or Fula, derives from a Mandinka appellation adopted by the Portuguese and contrasts with the name that the Fulbe call themselves—Fulbe, or Pullo.[3] A potpourri of ethnolinguistic appellations emerged by the early twentieth century, leading to confusion in nomenclatural references used in documents and reports.

Insofar as is practicable, the indigenous names are used in this study (i.e., Fulbe-ribê, Fulbe-djiábê).[4] But in some cases, more generally utilized names are relied on (i.e., Balanta, Papel, Mandjack), rather than referring to dozens of more localized ethnonyms, in order to offer nomenclatural coherence through the text.

—◦—

Throughout the book, the term *Guinea,* unless otherwise specified, refers to Portuguese Guinea. Occasional references are made to French Guinea and Guinea-Conakry, but *Guinea* standing alone refers to the Portuguese colony.

Acknowledgments

THE LIST OF THOSE WHO CONTRIBUTED to the processes involved in researching, writing, revising, and publishing this book is long, and only a brief selection can be provided here; to the many whose names do not appear, I sincerely apologize.

I very much appreciate the time spent by Philip J. Havik, Walter Hawthorne, Crawford Young, and Michael Schatzberg in critically reading early drafts. A profuse and continuing exchange of ideas and commentary with Philip J. Havik over ten years crucially influenced my thinking about Guinea-Bissauan politics, history, state, and society. Philip also provided continuous personal and professional support for my efforts at writing, and I am grateful for his informative corrections, encyclopedic knowledge, detailed and voluminous replies, and unusually thoughtful suggestions. An intensively shared campus venue with Walter Hawthorne initiated our highly rewarding scholarly and personal relationship; I thank him deeply, both for his ongoing encouragement (even insistence) that this study be completed and for his highly informed, wise, and enormously helpful commentary. I am especially grateful for his insightful explanations in our many exchanges. Intellectual and personal discourses with Mustafah Dhada and my friendship with him have similarly proven enormously beneficial; I have profited immensely from ongoing intellectual and personal exchanges with him regarding Guinea-Bissau. I appreciate his charm, creative enthusiasm, and distinctive intellectual erudition. I am further indebted to Carlos Cardoso, a well-respected Guinea-Bissauan scholar with whom I have discussed and debated political developments in his country since we met in the early 1980s. I am also grateful to Richard Lobban for introducing me to the field of Guinea-Bissauan anthropology at an early, formative moment; I learned much from him through our coauthorship of a 1988 reference work.

Shirley Washington guided my first political appreciation of key problems in Guinea-Bissauan state building; I very much want to acknowledge her personal support. Eve Crowley's friendship, sharp intellectualism, and helpfulness are highly valued; her medical assistance proved essential to my being able to complete the field research from which the ideas for this study sprang. Fred M. Hayward and Crawford Young each provided unending encouragement and advice at multiple stages of my Guinea-Bissau research. And Walker Connor's energetic scholarly acumen and insight into ethnic behavior have been greatly appreciated.

I am especially grateful to the librarians at Lisbon's Arquivo Histórico Ultramarino and Dakar's Archives National de Sénégal for their generous practical help and for their granting me access to boxes of dusty archival records that were often held together with aged drawstring. A Fulbright-Hayes research grant helped to make possible the archival work as well as prior field research. A generous Kukin Fellowship from the Harvard Academy for International and Area Studies made possible invaluable writing time, and my interaction with senior and junior scholars there, especially Henry Rosovsky, Sam Huntington, Kiren Chaudhry, Dru Gladney, and Greg Noble, helped to sharpen my ideas regarding state/ethnic relations and institutional fragility. I also want to express my appreciation to the late Myron Weiner of MIT for inviting me to participate in meetings of the Joint Society for Political Development, where I benefited from debates on state behavior and policy dysfunction.

Although many scholars, especially those named above, contributed to various aspects of the way I think about Guinea-Bissau, all responsibility for the analysis presented below and for any errors in judgment, reasoning, or fact is mine.

I would very much like to acknowledge the technical map-making production assistance of Ed Antczak of Northern Cartographics (map 2); Wendy Mann of the University of Pittsburgh (maps 1 and 3); and Jackie Belden Hawthorne (map 4). The author assumes full responsibility for any errors remaining in the maps.

Finally, I would like to acknowledge the unyielding support and patience of my mother, Rima Turkel, father, Morton Forrest, and the wonderful people they are married to, Stan Turkel (to my mother) and Vicki Sudhalter (to my father). Their collective generosity of spirit has been boundless.

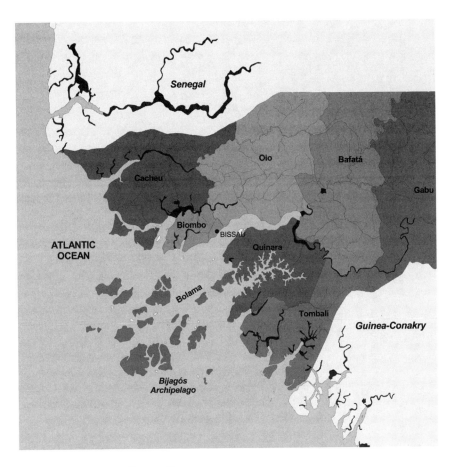

MAP 1 CONTEMPORARY GUINEA-BISSAU

Source: Africa Data Sampler. World Resources Institute in collaboration with World Conservation Monitoring Centre and PADCO, Inc., Washington, D.C. 1995.

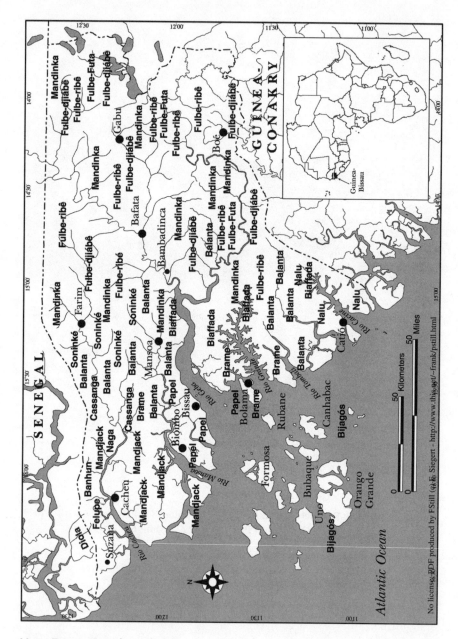

Map 2 Ethnic *Chão* (Lands)

This is an approximation only: Frequent migrations led to alteration of some chão over time; also, dispersal of some groups throughout multiple regions resulted in pluri-ethnic villages.

Sources: Derived from maps in Luis António de Carvalho Viegas, *Guiné Portuguesa,* vol. 3 (Lisbon: Freitas Mega, 1940), inserts at end of volume; ethnic charts in José Manuel de Braga Dias, "Mudança socio-cultural na Guiné Portuguesa" (Ph.D. diss., Universidade Técnica de Lisboa, 1974), 70–71, 112–13.

Introduction

The Origins of State Fragility

IN THIS BOOK I EMPHASIZE THE domestic, internal, precolonial, and colonial origins of state fragility in the West African nation of Guinea-Bissau (formerly, Portuguese Guinea). In doing so, I seek to carve out a unique perspective in analyzing weak states and civil societies in colonial-era and contemporary Africa—in particular, in Portuguese-speaking Africa. My approach underlines the importance of tracing the historical lineages of state weakness, which I argue is linked to patterns of indigenous rural civil-societal development in the precolonial and colonial eras. Such a focus is crucial to appreciating the evolution of "strong" domestic forces in explaining state fragility. As this study emphasizes the centuries-long social roots of rural civil-societal strength and governmental policy failure, and of state/rural civil society conflict, I offer an especially historically focused perspective on the study of contemporary African politics.

In doing so, I suggest that examining precolonial and colonial politics makes it possible to better understand why contemporary Guinea-Bissau is characterized by a widening state/rural civil society gap, by continuing political disarray, periodic warfare, and economic dislocation. I acknowledge the significance of the international political economy in shaping the nature of colonial states—in particular, the contour of relations between metropolitan Portugal and its African colonies. To be sure, Portugal's own relative underdevelopment and low level of industrialization played a crucial role in explaining the lack of developmental progress in its African colonies.[1] At the same time, however, an overemphasis on European imperialism in the study of Portuguese-speaking Africa has tended unduly to marginalize the domestic, indigenous side of the colonialist equation. I suggest that a full understanding of African state fragility can be obtained only by investigating the domestic rural origins of adaptable, potent, and enduring social formations.

1

Thus, while taking into account the macrolevel context of metropolitan Portugal's relative "backwardness," I argue that the specific dynamics and contour of the relations between the state and rural civil society in Guinea-Bissau over the course of many centuries significantly shaped and structured the emergence of a weak state during the colonial and postcolonial periods. In order to advance this argument, I trace the evolution of the political, social, and military aspects of the central state and of rural power arrangements in Guinea-Bissau. The central themes presented here collectively suggest that the emergence of state debility in Guinea-Bissau reflects a lengthy, historically "embedded" evolution of rural civil-societal strength.

Rural Civil Society

Analytically, this book "historicizes" the study of nonstate spheres, encompassing a wide range of political and social activities and organizations and conceptualizing them as precursors to a strong rural civil society. The main point of the study is that the basis of Guinea-Bissau's weak state is to be found precisely in the precolonial and colonial lineages of its rural-based civil societies. Thus, my focus is the generation of patterns of rural-based political and social behavior that endured through the precolonial centuries and reappeared consistently during the colonial and postcolonial periods, despite significant changes and adaptive, strategic shifts. This approach necessitates an analytic turn toward "deep history," buttressed by historical, anthropological, and sociological empirical evidence — one focused on rural zones, where approximately 70 percent of Africans continue to live and where the main sources of social and political power are located.

In these regards, in order to attain insight into the policy capacity of African states, I follow Patrick Chabal's advice to concentrate on "low politics" (i.e., popular politics) rather than the "high politics" of the central government.[2] At the same time, I suggest a broadening of the classical conceptualization of "civil society," which typically refers to urban-based, centrally located, well-organized, visible institutions, to include a wide range of rural-based social formations whose potency is less visible to the unaware observer. Some of these rural-based social institutions may be virtually clandestine in nature, but they are the loci in which rural people invest their time, energies, resources, and political loyalties and often serve as the central nexus of rural political authority.[3] In this book, I suggest that a rural civil society — characterized by rural-based social institutions that, having developed over the course of centuries, have become entrenched in the lifeblood of local society—can prove an enduring impediment to state building, while, at the same time, making possible a substantial degree of local-level autonomy and regional self-empowerment.

This argument lends support to the work of Joel Migdal, who has noted that weak, or soft, states are most likely to emerge where social structures are characterized by a "weblike" complexity marked by a high degree of political fragmentation and pluralism, which contributes to the ability of "social organizations" to function separately from state institutions.[4] For Migdal, it is the "tenacious and resilient" nature of weblike social forces that has effectively inhibited the ability of weak states to carry out their policies.[5] As a consequence, the state is unable to implement its policy agenda effectively and fails to incorporate the citizenry into government-controlled institutions or state-managed political mobilization efforts. Weak states do not achieve the status of sovereign political authority in a national domain, and they cannot extract sufficient resources from domestic markets to meet the state's institution-building requirements. Migdal usefully points out that the diffusion of power among (particularly rural) social organizations should become a key focus of investigation of the sources of state weakness.[6]

This perspective most notably finds its parallel in Africanist literature in the work of Naomi Chazan, who suggests that national-scale policy failure in Africa reflects, in part, the ability of nonstate spheres to withstand attempts at state hegemony. Chazan points out that these nonstate social spheres can serve as bases for peasant activities that provide enduring social strength to African social formations.[7] From this perspective, it is important to examine political processes "from the bottom up" and to research "specific social constellations" at the local level.[8] As both Migdal and Chazan have observed, it is these more subterranean, peasant-controlled social spheres that have served as key bases for a "strong" rural politics, offering significant protection to the countryside against the hegemonic control efforts of the central state. Like Migdal, Chazan underlines the utility of examining power centers located in the less-visible niches of social formations precisely because they help to explain why African states have been unable to achieve their goals.[9]

Embracing a parallel perspective, Martin Doornbos urges research into "the non-state sphere" in Africa to investigate the "political space" created by social and religious protests, liberation fronts, and revitalization movements.[10] Doornbos observes in particular the expansion of nonstate infrastructures at the grassroots level, including "potentially autonomous institutions" such as mutual-aid societies, farmers' organizations, religious and cultural bodies, "and many other informal and traditional groupings such as the Ghanaian *asafo* companies, fraternities, and kinship associations."[11] Doornbos has also called attention to state breakdown in eastern Africa and the emergence of local and regional groups and networks as "autonomous, 'non-state' forms of social organisation."[12] In support of such an approach, Elke Zuern has recently argued that the concept of "civil society" ought to be expanded to incorporate "a very broad range of human associations" located in the public sphere "between the household and the state" — one that includes "forms of co-operation for mutual benefit," such as ethnic associations and village groupings.[13]

Chazan et al. refer to nonstate spheres and autonomous networks as representing "popular conflicts" that form part of the "deep politics" of postcolonial Africa. They write: "Territorially defined and physically removed from official power centers, local communities do control some resources and usually have evolved their own political institutions based on shared norms. Although they cannot exercise a full exit option, they carve out their own independent niches in certain spheres."[14]

From a different perspective, Jean-François Bayart has observed the extent to which "popular actions" have undermined and reduced the scope of the state in Africa. He includes as examples "the creation of theocratic communities outside state control," as well as revolts, the refusal to grow certain crops, migrations, religious revivals, informal exchanges, and various types of "sabotage of the instruments of political control."[15] Bayart concludes that "subordinated social groups have not been as passive as they are thought to be" and that state domination has often been challenged by social forces that have been "ill-contained."[16] Bayart's assertion that "Africa's cultural diversity" has acted as "a constraint on central power"[17] approximates Migdal's thesis regarding the ability of weblike social structures to weaken central states. Bayart calls attention to "strong local autonomy,"[18] which is similar to Chazan's depiction of autonomous social forces emerging in rural and urban communities.

In a particularly probing study, Jane Guyer examines the "spatial dimensions" of civil society in order to underline the extent to which chieftaincies in Nigeria and elsewhere reach beyond their formal boundaries and localities to incorporate multiple power sources within far-reaching networks. These networks may be considered to represent a unique aspect of civil society in Africa wherein chiefly power and influence were built upon people's political devotion and investment of their resources from a wide geographic span and from multiple hierarchical levels. This allowed "officeholders" in traditional authority systems to build up extensive power structures that were not controlled or sanctioned by the colonial state but nonetheless may be considered part of a civil society that is polycentric, fractal, and defined by overlapping, flexible organizational boundaries.[19]

More generally, this book incorporates and builds upon the perspectives articulated above through an analysis of the social and historical basis of autonomy within a polycentric rural civil society defined by weblike social structures, with local as well as widely dispersed social constellations. In doing so, I adhere to the term *social formations,* rather than Migdal's *social organizations* or Zuern's *human associations,* because *formations* implies, consistently with Guyer's perspective, an especially ebb-and-flow character, enduring yet adaptable, inclusivistic, and malleable. Persistent, historically "deep" but evolving social formations represent a variegated diffusion of rural power nodes that help us to better appreciate the achievements of Guinea-Bissau's spheres of civil-societal strength, particularly in regard to carving out substantial social autonomy in rural areas. This book suggests not merely that rural social constructions are part of civil society but that they may be conceptualized to represent its core, considering that they embody the locus of power and resource accumulation in much of Africa, articulated in various and changing ways over the course of centuries.

Overall, then, this book emphasizes the internal evolution of rural-based social strength. But at the same time, it is crucial to understand state fragility from the political-science perspectives of problems in pursuing political penetration and in asserting political hegemony.

LOCAL POWER AND COLONIAL POLITICAL CAPACITY

In order to appreciate the evolution of relations between state and rural civil society in Guinea-Bissau with particular regard to the allocation of power at the local level, it is crucial to examine the central government's effort to pursue what James Coleman has termed the "political penetration" of social forces by state institutions.[20] This concept refers to the degree of comprehensiveness of the state's social reach—a powerful state being capable of determining the flow of political relations and the contour of social power at the microlevel of society. B. Guy Peters suggests that a strong state with a high degree of "extensiveness" is able to develop a central policy apparatus through which political leaders can effectively coordinate and implement national-scale policy processes.[21]

In comparative studies of present-day Africa, this concept of political penetration has been utilized to suggest that contemporary African states have been impeded in their quest to achieve a sovereign policy capacity and political pre-dominance, especially in the rural areas.[22] Most African central states have not been able to mold local power structures within rural civil society so to coincide with the state's interests, and therefore national policies cannot be universally implemented at the local level.[23] As Jeffrey Herbst's recent study of power in African states makes clear, central governments have failed to consolidate their authority beyond centralized core urban areas.[24] In Goran Hyden's terms, a soft state is fundamentally lacking in the structural or institutional ability to enforce its policy decisions in order to shape society according to its policy preferences and to carry out its national plans.[25] My task in this book is to help explain why, in the case of Guinea-Bissau, this has been so. I suggest that a full explanation necessitates reference to the historical genesis of strong social formations and the patterns of power within rural civil society.

Crawford Young's recent analysis of the colonial origins of Africa's state crisis and Mahmood Mamdani's investigation of the power relations between state and localities provide useful guides to the study of state building during the colonial period.[26] However, I suggest that the present analysis of Guinea-Bissau diverges to a considerable degree from the models of colonial/postcolo-nial linkage presented in their work. Young describes the contemporary African state as "a purposive agent of history" that embodies the past as "a reservoir of instructive experience."[27] Young indicates that the contemporary state crisis in Africa is to a large extent the consequence of inheriting the colonial state's telos as a *bula matari,* or rock crusher.[28] In other words, the authoritarian, force-based nature of postcolonial African states originated in the heavy reliance on sheer coercion to build up colonial state institutions and to carry out the imperatives of state building. In some colonial states, colonial authority remained to some extent "precarious" in that its authority continued to rest essentially on the threat of force,[29] but in general, argues Young, "the construction of hegemony had produced comprehensive subjugation of African society."[30] By about the time of World War I, he asserts, in most of Africa rural colonial officials and compliant chiefs followed centrally mandated rules, the resistance option had been effectively supplanted, and the state began to assert "a powerful hold on subject society";[31] moreover, during the interwar years, that hegemony was consolidated and colonial state rule was "thoroughly institutionalized."[32]

The recent study of colonial power by Mamdani supports this analysis. Mam-dani argues that colonial control became largely characterized by a type of "de-centralized despotism" through which state builders relied on traditional chiefs at the local level to carry out their exploitative policies coercively.[33] He suggests that local chiefs became increasingly alienated from the villagers they subjugated and repressed, inflicting harsh taxation and forced-labor policies, but in doing so they helped to assure a strong level of colonial-state domination over the peasantry.[34]

The studies by Young and Mamdani are particularly useful for understanding state growth in those cases where powerful and effective bureaucracies did emerge or where colonial control was consolidated through a hierarchical system of "fused" political, economic, and social power implemented by chiefs at the village level. However, the image of comprehensive domination suggested by Young and Mamdani does not coincide with the success of some rural civil societies in sustaining a relatively large spectrum of resistance activities through the colonial durée. In the present study, I explain that the origins of state softness lie not only in the manner of colonial state construction but also in the character of the rural social formations over which the state sought domination. In the case of Guinea-Bissau, it is not so much that the hard colonial state became transformed into the soft postcolonial state, but rather that the colonial state was essentially itself a fragile state—despite its eventual ability to extract and accumulate capital—that was internally fractured by corruption and relied preeminently on terror to assure its security and sovereignty.[35] In these terms, the "transition" was not so much hard-to-soft as soft-to-soft.

Relatively weak African colonial states such as Guinea-Bissau performed the "essential elements of state logic" (i.e., of policy making and implementation) poorly, and they had great difficulty consistently assuring their own "security"; they were unable to achieve "hegemony," or social and political domination, over rural civil society.[36] Attention to the dynamics of political and social life at the community level reveals that a wider range of colonial states stood on more fragile legs than has generally been assumed. Part of the reason for the emergence of weak states in various parts of postcolonial Africa in many cases reflects the enduring strengths and adaptability of rural social structures.

In this respect, this book differs sharply from the approach adopted by Herbst in his recent analysis of the limitations of African state power.[37] Extending prior discussions of state softness,[38] Herbst asserts that state failure to project administrative power outward from core urban settings in part reflected state leaders' political attitudes and pattern of elite decision making and in part reflected obstructive geographic factors. He argues that it was precolonial leaders' unwillingness to consolidate central state power throughout their territorial domains, along with the difficult topographical terrain, that lay the foundation for weak states in the colonial and postcolonial periods, resulting in highly circumscribed political geographies of state power.[39]

The conceptual problem there is that while Mamdani's and Young's analyses do not adequately recognize the limited character of colonial state power, Herbst's study fails to provide adequate attention and historical responsibility to social actors and structures within the African rural heartland—territory that he dismissively terms as the "hinterland."[40] In this book, by contrast, I include but go beyond state leaders' attitudes and incentives to probe the dynamic evolution of rural civil society and the way in which rural social structures, political activists, interethnic alliances, and potent rural-based military forces posed complex roadblocks to the builders of central state power. In doing so (and in contrast to Young, Mamdani, and Herbst), I assert interepochal linkages among the precolonial, colonial, and postcolonial periods with specific regard to the vibrancy, malleability, and assertiveness of rural civil society.

Victor Azarya has helped to lay the analytic groundwork for such a perspective by underlining the link between colonial and postcolonial Africa in terms of focusing on the "continuing gap between state and society" in both epochs. He argues that in some parts of Africa (such as Chad, Niger, and Sudan), the notion of "disengagement" actually misrepresents social continuities, because this term inaccurately implies that social actors had been "engaged" or "incorporated" into state-controlled social spheres during the colonial period.[41] Azarya highlights the continuing process of social disengagement through both periods in certain parts of Africa and suggests that the task for the policy analyst, in light of such continuities, is to "pay more attention to how a given society lives beyond the scope of state capabilities."[42] My investigation into the historical nexus of rural social and political spheres does precisely that with specific regard to Guinea-Bissau.

In doing so, I suggest that the Portuguese colonial state in Guinea-Bissau was unable to achieve meaningful and effective incorporation of the rural populace into the state's social or economic policy spheres (in Young's, Mamdani's, or Hyden's senses). As occurred elsewhere in the rural areas of African colonies, the relative isolation of state officials promoted a certain arbitrariness in the effort to carry out the hegemony imperative since each official relied on "situational strategies" and "a large range of initiative" to assure the subjugation of the peasantry under his charge.[43] However, I shall make clear that despite this relatively wide latitude of rulership, in Portuguese Guinea the rural populace not only found ways of circumventing colonial state officials but also built up alternative spheres of political and social authority and of economic activity that served as social counterforces to power.

That is why I refer to the four decades that followed the military conquest of rural Guinea[44] as the "settled" colonial period,[45] rather than adopting Young's notion of a period of state "institutionalization." In doing so, I emphasize, consistently with Herbst's analysis, the relative incompleteness of the hegemonic superstructure created to rule over rural Guinean society.[46] However, it is crucial to appreciate the variability of the power arrangements between state and rural civil society in differing parts of Africa; thus, I argue that the colonial state in Portuguese Guinea was unable to attain the degree of effective social control that had been achieved by some of its west, central, and southern African counterparts.[47] Attempts at a Lusitanian version of southern Africa's decentralized despotism (meaning, in Guinea-Bissau, the appointment of Fulbe—and, to a lesser extent, collaborative Biaffada and Mandinka—chiefs to rule over provinces dominated by other ethnic groups) were not successful. In contrast to the destruction of rural civil society in parts of southern and eastern Africa (per Mamdani), Guinea-Bissau's peasants found numerous ways of "avoiding" the state centralist administrative structure, of locating alternative trade circuits, and of strengthening their own social and civil-societal institutions—including the recreation of alternative authority sources such as age-based decision-making forums and social spheres of activity controlled by nonstate actors that originated in precolonial times (e.g., shrine-based societies).

This does not mean that the state in Portuguese Guinea was unable to accomplish any official task: during the relatively brief settled colonial period, annual taxes were collected and forced-labor parties were occasionally organized. However, sending a tax-collection police force out through the countryside once a year and putting together an occasional work party is not equivalent to establishing a tightly monitored hierarchy of control by the colonial state over indigenous, village-level production, trading flows, and the reorganization of labor—as occurred in the "fused power" village structures described by Mamdani and Young. In Guinea-Bissau, in contrast to other colonial states, political penetration and social domination were in effect "blocked"—not (as Herbst argues) by leaders' lack of incentive to pursue hegemonic politics or by the existence of mountain passes, rivers, or other geographic structures,[48] but by the emergence of vibrant, adaptive, locally embedded social institutions located outside the administrative rubric of the national government and its appointees.

The relative uniqueness of Guinea-Bissau's experience and the extent to which it diverges from many of its colonial counterparts deserves emphasis. To be sure, in much of Africa during the 1890s and early 1900s (i.e., the initial period of colonial state construction), state hegemony remained fragile, assured only by "a skeletonal grid of territorial administration" and by occasional displays of its coercive capacity.[49] During this early phase, state administration consisted at best of a string of far-flung outposts staffed by a handful of officials, interpreters, and soldiers and was only intermittently sustained by contacts from the capital city. According to Young, by the end of this construction phase (normally by 1910), the basic infrastructure for state building had in fact been established in most of the continent; the routinization of violence had ended, "basic order" was established, and colonial officials restructured social institutions so as to assure a rising revenue flow.[50]

However, in contrast to this schema, I argue that in the case of Portuguese Guinea, the transition from construction to institutionalization was incompletely realized. The routinization of societal subordination lagged significantly behind the more "institutionalized" colonies. In these regards, a brief comparative look at the case of the Belgian Congo helps to clarify Portuguese Guinea's distinctiveness. Both the Belgian Congo and Portuguese Guinea were characterized by heterogenous rural societies that complicated the achievement of political and social hegemony. In both colonies, a mixture of "administrative" and "domination" strategies was employed, including the cultivation of chiefly rule in traditionally hierarchical areas as well as the effort to employ more direct methods of supervision where chiefs were regarded with suspicion.[51] In both cases (although more extensively in Guinea-Bissau), administrative inadequacies were such that the colonialists had no choice but to rely on African auxiliary chiefs to rule over those areas that lacked indigenous chiefs, and this helped to underline the relative fragility of state domination. Tom Callaghy has analyzed the Belgian Congo as having imposed a relatively superficial administrative structure over the rural areas, using a "coverover" strategy based on prefectures that did not enjoy a deep hegemony within peasant communities.[52] Similarly, I will argue that the hegemony of the Portuguese Guinean state remained at best superficially imposed.

However, this aspect of the Congo-Guinean parallel must be placed in proper perspective; the superficial character of the colonial state was manifested far more dramatically in Portuguese Guinea than it was in the case of the Belgian Congo. The demands that the colonial state superstructure was able to impose on peasants in the Belgian Congo were in substantial excess of those placed on the peasants of Portuguese Guinea. And the extent of peasant avoidance and the creation of peasant spheres of alternative authority in Guinea notably exceeded those in the Congolese case. Here again, it is crucial to peer closely into the dynamic evolution of rural social formations in order to appreciate differential results in the implementation of the state's hegemonic mandate.

Overall, it may be suggested that the case of Guinea-Bissau, today as during the colonial era, represents the high end of a continuum of policy paralysis and state softness; at the same time, the findings here—and, to a greater extent, the general approach adopted—bear significantly on the general study of relations between civil society and the state in Africa. This work demonstrates the general utility of tracing the social lineages of rural power to better understand the domestic sources of state fragility. In doing so, I suggest that a focus on the historical origins of weblike social formations and rural civil society in Africa may reveal significant aspects of the sources of policy paralysis elsewhere on the continent, despite the relative uniqueness of Portuguese Guinea's dénouement.

At the same time, in analyzing the dynamics of state incapacity, it is important to observe that one consequence of policy dysfunctionality is state actors' often frantic, desperate search for a mechanism of political domination. In Portuguese Guinea, I argue that this search in fact led to the introduction of state terror.

STATE TERROR AND STATE FRAGILITY

Indeed, precisely because of the relative weakness of the colonial state's infrastructure, its policy difficulties, and its failure to establish its political authority within the countryside, during two important historical episodes the Portuguese colonial state in Guinea turned to an overt policy of state terror in an effort to fulfill its security function—that is, to assure its political sovereignty throughout the Guinean would-be nation. The first episode was the 1913–15 conquest of the interior; the second was the 1962–74 war against the movement for national liberation. In both cases, massive violence was used by the state against defenseless civilians in an overt effort to terrorize the peasant population into submission.

How can a colonial state that we here characterize as relatively "weak," or "soft," possibly carry out a "terror"-based strategy of rule? What could be the connection between a strong rural civil society, a fragile national state, and the use of state terror? My argument is that it was precisely the inability of the state to carry out its security and hegemony functions by more "normal" or peaceful means that pushed the Lusophone state builders in Guinea—who were fully determined to consolidate state sovereignty throughout their claimed territory— to turn to state terror to carry out their goals. It was because the Portuguese were operating "from a position of weakness" that they relied so heavily on "brutality," or ultraviolence.[53] I conceptualize the 1913–15 and 1962–74 wars against the civilian populace as "state terrorist" violence because of the methods of cruelty employed against the unarmed civilian populace.

Here we must observe that the colonialists in Portuguese Guinea were not alone in their reliance on massive state violence to secure political sovereignty. Most other colonial powers relied on similar means at some point in the conquest period to assure the "pacification" of the interior of their respective colonies. As Young has demonstrated, "punitive expeditions" characterized by the "burning of villages," the carrying out of various "barbarities," and the destruction of sacred symbols of African power were frequent.[54] Crowder has similarly underlined the burning of villages by the British in Sierra Leone and the forced enslavement and the killing of women and children by the French in Western Sudan.[55]

It may well prove helpful for scholars to reconsider this period of colonial "conquest" in much of Africa as having been characterized by the widespread use of state terror in the senses depicted above. At the same time, however, I would suggest that the extent and viciousness of state-sanctioned violence used against the peasantry of the Guinean interior represents an extreme version of most "pacification" military assaults carried out against resistant African societies. Moreover, whereas in most of sub-Saharan Africa this conquest phase was completed by 1900,[56] in Portuguese Guinea violent resistance continued for nearly two decades after that date.

Conceptually, we may note that few analyses of African state building have employed a "state terror" analytic perspective. Several studies do note the use of terror in present-day Africa—for example, Ibrahima K. Sundiata's analysis of Macias's personal reign of terror in Equatorial Guinea and Rhoda Howard's argument that Moi's regime in Kenya in the 1980s was heading toward a terror-based strategy of rule.[57] In addition, the suppression of black Christians in Mauritania in the 1980s has been interpreted as a "campaign of terror."[58] However, none of these analyses places the *colonial-era* use of terror at the forefront of their analytic frameworks.[59]

In this book, especially in chapter 5, I suggest that the massive use of violence by the colonial state in Portuguese Guinea during the 1910s and the 1960s constitutes state terror in the sense of the term as used in examinations of terror-based regimes in Latin America, Central America, Nazi Germany, Stalinist Russia, and Eastern Europe[60]—that is, the use of massive violence by a government against unarmed citizens to achieve total political domination. As Stohl and Lopez suggest, state terrorism is "the purposeful act or threat of violence to create fear and/or compliant behavior in a victim and/or audience."[61] Schmid's definition of state terrorism is particularly useful: it refers to "patterned and persistent atrocities by state or state-sponsored actors" in which the government "goes beyond the legitimate use of violence" and includes "deliberate attacks on civilians, . . . secret torture, and massacres."[62] Schmid also notes that state terrorism is "a method of rule whereby some groups of people are victimized with great brutality . . . by the state or state-supported actors, so that others who have reason to identify with those murdered will despair, obey or comply."[63] Bushnell et al. suggest that the terror-based state aims to create a "culture of terror" in which "people are numbed into subservience" through the use or threat of massive violence.[64]

It is important to emphasize that analysts of state terror have typically linked the emergence of institutionalized large-scale violence with a particularly weak state. Indeed, Bushnell et al. argue that state terror is especially likely to emerge when government institutions become marked by "disarray" and ill-trained civil servants weakly committed to the public service; when ethnic factors complicate the relations between state and society; and when the state becomes especially dependent on a foreign power.[65] A study of state terror in Latin America similarly suggests that terrorist strategies are utilized by government leaders as survival mechanisms of weak regimes when political institutions become "incoherent" and institute erratic, ineffective policy programs.[66] I argue below that it was precisely because of the relatively brittle character of its "stateness" that the colonial government in Portuguese Guinea turned to a policy of national-scale terror in order to attain political sovereignty (in the 1910s) and, later (in the 1960s), to retain its rulership. Reliance on a methodological campaign of terror by the Portuguese colonialists in Guinea reflected a perception by state leaders that no other options were available, considering the inability to achieve domination over the Guinean interior by treaties, through economic exchanges, or other means.[67]

Thus, in analyzing the historical basis on which the colonial state in Portuguese Guinea was constructed, I suggest that state building in that colony was distinctively characterized by a heavy reliance on massive anticivilian violence during key historical moments. Even during the "settled" colonial period, the colonial state relied on authoritarian control measures that often developed into extreme violence, thus perpetuating the "terror"-oriented culture on which its rule was based. This zero-sum logic of rulership was a logical consequence of the failure to establish enduring linkages with the key power structures of rural civil society (in Young's terms, it reflected the inability to carry out the hegemony imperative effectively).

Despite this state violence, in Guinea-Bissau both before and after the 1913–15 conquest, rural social formations were able to mobilize an impressive praetorian response and retained the integrity and autonomy of most social and political spheres. Through the forty-year settled colonial period, social formations in the countryside proved capable, by various means, of fending off or deflecting many of the colonial state's hegemonic thrusts (see below). To be sure, from the 1930s to the 1950s, taxes were collected on a fairly consistent basis, and forced-labor gangs assured that some roads and public buildings were constructed. However, these measures were applied inconsistently and only in certain locations, and they did not collectively result in the coercive incorporation of cultivators into a colonially controlled national economic trade structure.

Thus, producers retained control over land tenure and land use, and clandestine rural markets operated so as to severely limit the extent of both internal economic change and institutional state building. The Guinea-Bissauan countryside was in fact marked by extensive peasant avoidance of state tax collectors, internal migration, self-sufficiency with regard to food crops, the sale or barter exchange of items on hidden marketing circuits, a widespread refusal to cooperate with officials in regard to economic policies, as well as extensive levels of external trade across the porous Senegalese border that was invisible to Portuguese colonial officials. All of these activities helped to serve as independent financial sources of relative economic autonomy for many rural communities, and in doing so they deprived the state of much-needed resources, assured a fundamentally disarticulated economy, and hindered the potential for statecentric economic development. At the same time, community-based political power structures and indigenous sources of authority proved more influential, at the local level, than the stooled chiefs appointed by the state. Reliance on co-opted indigenous representatives of the state did not have the desired effect since these local leaders lacked popular respect in most regions, and the state largely was unable to reinforce appointed chiefs' decisions on a consistent basis. The variegated nature of rural civil society was in fact characterized by locally generated political structures and social formations that represented viable popular alternatives to government-sanctioned authorities.

By the 1960s, the extent of peasant autonomy contributed to villagers' ability to provide widespread support to the growing nationalist movement for independence. More particularly, the de facto decentralization of political and social structures politically facilitated peasants' capacity to choose to ally with the rebels. This, in turn, helped make it possible for the nationalists to mobilize the rural populace and, eventually, to outbattle the colonialists. In this sense, the return to a policy of state terror had backfired, with extensive popular support for the violent anticolonial movement assuring the military success of the rebels, which in turn eventually helped to provoke the abandonment of Guinea by the Portuguese.

SOCIAL FORMATIONS, ALLIANCES, AND PRAETORIAN SOCIAL MEMORY

It is precisely in reflection of the crucial role played by rural civil society in help-ing to assure state fragility through the colonial era and in helping to determine the outcome of the nationalist war that it is so important to investigate the his-torical evolution of rural social forces. Here it is vital to refer back not merely to the nature of the Portuguese-African encounter, but also to precolonial indige-nous social institutions, locally rooted communities, empire formation, military experiences, regional spirit deities, and, especially, interethnic exchanges and cooperation. These represent the historical antecedents of rural civil-societal strength and the origins of modern social formations. By the time of the emer-gence of the colonial state, spheres of political, social, and economic activity had been carved out that lay outside the rubric of the colonial state, and they would remain so after independence.

In some cases, these alternative fields of power and social formations were specific to a locality or communal group, but this did not prohibit a robust set of political, military, and economic exchanges with other rural communities. Thus, the same communities that displayed strong, ethnically based attachments to cer-tain territorial locales commonly decided to forego ethnic exclusivity in ex-change for interethnic alliances when they were faced with external challenges. In this way, political mobilization often assumed relatively fluid forms. For ex-ample, I suggest that different sets of chiefs from Fulbe-djiábê, Fulbe-ribê, Mandinka, and Biaffada ethnic backgrounds formed common alliances through-out the latter portions of the nineteenth century, as did ordinary members of de-centralized societies such as the Balanta, Papel, Oinka, and Bijagós groups, with particular alliances depending on changing macropolitical circumstances.

We will also see that chiefs and peasants from various groups made political choices that were largely pragmatically based, rather than ethnically based, dur-ing the 1960s–70s struggle for national liberation. I contend that the particular nature of rural civil society within each community, especially regarding their varying political structures, helped to determine the direction of political deci-sion making during the war for national independence. The idiosyncratic ways that communities evolved, despite their belonging to the same ethnic group, re-sulted in differing types of leadership structures from one community to the next and therefore produced differing political choices during the liberation struggle. Thus, decisions regarding which side to support tended to reflect the character of rural civil society rather than ethnic identity per se.

On this theme of ethnic flexibility, it is important to emphasize the role of multiethnic alliances in appreciating the sources of rural civil society's capacity for praetorian mobilization. Historians have tended to discount the role of multi-ethnic alliances in understanding the military resistance by rural African communities in Guinea-Bissau to Lusitanian-led armies of conquest. René Pélissier, for example, underemphasizes these alliances and the extent of supraethnic coordination, remarking that, along with an "absence of charismatic chiefs" and a lack of a "community of interest," the indigenous peoples of Guinea-Bissau were characterized by an absence of interethnic coordination of political and military affairs.[68] Similarly, Peter Karibe Mendy, in his study of primary anticolonial resistance in Guinea-Bissau, underlines the extent of warfare between Portuguese and Africans but does not stress the degree of military cooperation between groups.[69]

According to these perspectives, it was not until the recent national-liberation struggle that common military fronts were forged by Guineans. However, as I make clear in chapters 2, 3, and 4, the local peoples of Guinea-Bissau did form large-scale alliances among widespread villages of common ethnic origin (intra-ethnic collaboration) as well as multiethnic alliances. This alliance forming helps to account for the effectiveness of rural civil society in countering Luso-colonial attacks. Prior to the conquest-period battles, and throughout the precolonial period, multiple alliances had been created among chiefs hailing from different locational and ethnic origins. Thus, the ethnic commitment to defend specific territories among the Balanta, Papel, Mandjack, and others did not prohibit active and frequent involvement in common interethnic military fronts. At the same time, the ruling families of the powerful Gabu kingdom represented intermarriages among Mandinka, Fulbe, and Banhun elites; the kingdom functioned as a "decentralized hegemony" in which Mandinka, Banhun, Biaffada, Diola, Fulbe, and other groups were able to mobilize and coordinate their forces effectively.[70]

In these respects, a search for the social origins of state weakness can reveal significant, previously unappreciated nuclei of rural praetorian strength. Indeed, through those lengthy precolonial centuries, the armies organized and trained by the military and political leaderships of various Papel, Mandjack, Balanta, and Biaffada societies, of the Fuladu empire as well as of the Gabu kingdom, were often better organized than their Portuguese counterparts, were commonly better trained, and sometimes had access to technologically superior weaponry. This remained the case through the first decade of the twentieth century. Thus, for most of the period stretching from 1879, when the Portuguese began to launch full-scale invasion attacks on the countryside with the intent of conquest, up until 1913, most African chiefs, groups, and allied forces who fought the Portuguese troops and their African allies defeated them. The period from 1800 to 1912—eleven decades—was in fact a time of great military success for rural civil society in Guinea-Bissau.[71] During this period, colonial troops were repeatedly humiliated, beaten, diseased, and frustrated in vain efforts to subdue various chieftainships and anti-Portuguese African forces.

To some extent, these military successes against Portuguese armies were reflective of a general pattern of indigenous military success against European armies prior to the introduction of superior military technology in the late 1800s (particularly the Gatling and Maxim guns).[72] The fact is that African resistance against European expansion has generally been overlooked, largely as a consequence of what appeared to be the "ultimate" outcome of European victory. In much of the continent, resistance proved significant for two or three decades, as African armies took advantage of their superior numbers, knowledge of local terrain, rapid mobility relative to the slow-footed Europeans (who had to transport heavy equipment), and their ability to purchase weapons from illegal traders.[73] As a result, African fighters slowed or even set back the advance of the Europeans in central Nigeria, Western Sudan, Ivory Coast, Sierra Leone, Ghana, southern Guinea, Mali, and Mauritania.[74]

A particularly interesting aspect of this resistance was that "segmentary societies" often proved especially effective in battling the Europeans because they tended to resort to guerrilla warfare, which was difficult for European standing armies to overcome.[75] In Guinea-Bissau, we shall see that groups with acephalous political traditions proved especially adept at guerrilla-style confrontations. However, a number of centralized kingships throughout sub-Saharan Africa, such as the Temne (Sierra Leone), the Ijebu kingship (Nigeria), the Sarakole (western Sudan), the Sokoto Caliphate (Nigeria), the Mandingo empire of Samori (French Guinea), and the Dahomey kingdom also effectively confronted European forces through the 1880s and 1890s. Indeed, it was often the case that Europeans perceived it to be too difficult to seek to defeat centralized kingships directly and so had to take advantage of divisions within or between these kingdoms to make military progress against African resistors. This was possible precisely because African chiefs and kings did not perceive the coastally based Europeans to represent a serious military or political threat.[76] This occurred in Guinea-Bissau as well, but more slowly and with lesser effect than elsewhere. Thus, the Portuguese did not seek to defeat the Gabu or Fuladu empires but rather awaited their slow internal weakening through intersocietal warfare, a process that the Portuguese did not fully profit from until after the turn of the twentieth century.

In the following chapters, I suggest that even compared with the impressive resistance efforts of their West African counterparts, the precolonial societies of Guinea-Bissau were unusually successful in mobilizing armies that pushed back the imperial military drive. Other West African indigenous societies also developed military skills that enabled them to counter the invasive thrusts of colonial armies for a noteworthy period of time. But in Guinea-Bissau, powerful indigenous armies and a weakly endowed colonial bureaucratic infrastructure made possible an unusually long-lasting and effective anti-European war effort.[77] This helped to entrench within Guinea-Bissau's social formations a memory of praetorian success that would reemerge periodically through the colonial period, and then with dramatic impact during Portuguese colonialism's terminal phase. Indeed, this memory was reinvoked at the start of the nationalist war and would help assure that the state's reintroduction of terror policies in the 1960s would fail as rural peoples succeeded in remobilizing their military forces and made substantial progress toward defeating the colonialists.

It is important to underline the fact that the praetorian accomplishments of the indigenous communities of Guinea-Bissau on the field of battle represent a key component of the social lineages of rural strength, and hark back to indigenous military developments during the precolonial period. Through the period from the sixteenth century to the twentieth, political and military power in most of the rural areas was located in key social institutions that were usually able to keep aggressive Europeans at a relatively safe distance. The remobilization of the countryside in the 1960s was based in part on the historical continuity of interethnic patterns of praetorian coordination.

To some extent, this argument extends and supports T. O. Ranger's point that the historical basis of modern nationalism in Africa lies not so much in the mobilizational activities of an educated urban elite, but rather in a tradition of resistance established during the "primary" anticolonial wars of the period from the 1880s to the 1910s.[78] Ranger notes that in much of Africa, the separation between primary wars of resistance and the modern nationalist movements was often chronologically brief, that the historical memory of prolonged anticolonial fighting during that early resistance period remained very much alive, and that modern (1960s) nationalist leaders openly called upon those memories to induce members of different ethnic groups to cooperate in a common proindependence front.[79] Mendy's study of primary resistance in Guinea-Bissau does not link ethnic cooperation to the building of a proindependence front, but it convincingly emphasizes the nationalist struggle as representing in a general sense a continuity of Guinea-Bissau's lengthy tradition of resistance.[80]

While my argument is consistent with these points, I stretch the chronology further back in time, suggesting that many African societies were engaged in lengthy episodes of combat with one another as well as in multiethnic alliance formation throughout the precolonial period and that the historical origins of twentieth-century resistances lie in these older historical experiences. Indeed, I use the term *praetorian social memory:* I do so to suggest that this was not simply a matter of African social formations resisting European imperialism, but rather was reflective of a long-standing set of experiences of success at warfare during pre-colonial times—thus, it is more of a memory of praetorian capability, rather than a memory of "resistance" per se. I link this praetorian social memory to the deter-mination of certain communities to retain their local autonomy, reflecting a many-centuries-long social history of community based self-rulership that rural Africans have been willing to fight and die to retain, from the early precolonial period through to contemporary times. In other African rural societies as well, such as among the Shona of Zimbabwe, a continuity of military struggle against invaders became manifest during precolonial times and was extended, through spirit me-diums calling upon this ancient past, to Zimbabwe's anticolonial struggle.[81]

In Guinea-Bissau, the continuity of this praetorian social memory and multi-ethnic alliance making helped to set the historical stage for the military success of the nationalist liberation struggle: it can therefore be considered a key social factor in the emergence of anticolonial nationalism. Although the strategic, or-ganizational, and international success of the nationalist movement may in part be attributed to Amílcar Cabral and other key leaders of the PAIGC (the Afri-can Party for the Independence of Guinea-Bissau and Cape Verde), I argue that it was a history of interethnic cooperation on and off the field of battle that, in effect, established favorable social conditions for the nationalist movement to become embraced by members of all of Guinea-Bissau's ethnic groups.[82] In this sense, the origins of the anticolonial nationalist struggle in Guinea-Bissau hark back to ancient practices of social interchange and military cooperation that would be reflected in the eventual formation of an autonomous, yet interlinked rural civil society and in the practice of praetorian coordination on the part of various local communities.

SOCIAL AUTONOMY, RURAL CIVIL SOCIETY, AND ETHNICITY

The preceding set of discussions enables us to suggest more precisely what is meant by autonomy with regard to social formations. In doing so, we may con-tribute to a better understanding of the ways in which rural civil society retained its relative independence in the colonial and postcolonial periods and how it has helped to determine the contours of rural political space vis-à-vis the central state.

Social autonomy may be understood as the historical evolution of political, social, religious, and economic practices and spheres of social activity that are established by local communities rather than by nation-state governments. The way in which social autonomy evolves in a given locale is determined by the nature of the continuing and changing structures of civil society and its inter-action with external forces. To the extent that local communities achieve auton-omy, they are able to undertake political decisions that are not overturned by government agencies, they are able to create social units over which external powers hold little or no influence, and they control the major portion of their own social resources. Strong civil societies may not achieve autonomy in all these respects, but to the extent that they do so, they may be considered to rep-resent powerful bulwarks against central state intervention that advance and deepen the extent of community-based rulership.

In Guinea-Bissau, as I will make clear, rural civil society derived its strength from various historical sources, including the evolution of multiethnic interrela-tions and alliances, age-based social structures, locally selected village authority systems, dynamic religiosocial formations, and a variety of rural decision-making institutions. These aspects of rural civil society have contributed significantly to the establishment of substantial social autonomy and have been manifested con-sistently over time in rural Guinea-Bissau, although the particular nature of their manifestations sometimes changes in reaction to altered circumstances and exter-nal challenges. Thus, for example, the centralized and hierarchical Fulbe, Biaf-fada, and Mandinka sociopolitical structures of the precolonial era had become considerably restructured through the twentieth century, becoming significantly more decentralized despite the efforts of colonial officials to uphold their cen-tralized nature. One consequence of this change was that it augmented the ability of community leaders to distance themselves from central state control.

The internal structures of social formations in rural Guinea-Bissau have in some cases changed markedly over time, with the degree of change depending on the particular region or community, but typically in a way that has produced a retention or deepening of local autonomy. At the same time, the enduring na-ture and versatility of certain social practices and of spheres of social and political behavior such as interethnic exchanges allow us to identify a set of characteristics of rural civil society that are particular to Guinea-Bissau's evolution of locally generated social autonomy. Overall, in consequence of the combination of the considerable durability and the relative adaptability of rural civil society, Guinea-

Bissauan communities have been able to carve out a significant latitude of self-direction that has obviated repeated efforts at statecentric domination.

Finally, as a result of the emphasis placed throughout this book on interethnic relations as serving to strengthen rural civil society and on the simultaneous endurance of locally specific commitments, it is important to make clear that the term *interethnic* is intended to suggest the extent of group interchanges and their dynamic impact on social relations. This approach stands in contrast to the use of *interethnic* to imply exchanges among "fixed," or unchanging, social entities.[83] On the contrary, it will be suggested that members of ethnic groups manifested a substantial degree of social malleability in reflection of the dynamics wrought by interethnic exchanges, despite some communities remaining relatively committed to locally grounded social institutions and practices. Most Mandjack and Balanta, for example, engaged in peaceful exchanges with members from other groups, incorporating them into their own communities through intermarriage; new members were often absorbed into the host community and adopted local practices, but in some areas this process led to the formation of new ethnic formations (such as the Oinka).[84] Religious and social sources of civil-societal strength have been characterized by relatively flexible organizational boundaries over time, rather than fitting cleanly into corporate ethnic categories. Among these are the spirit-based movements through which Guineans reconstructed new domains of political and social authority untouched by colonial overseers. Key power figures within the communities based on spirit shrines allocated meaningful real-world resources, both political and economic, that directly affected the daily lives of shrine-society members hailing from different ethnic backgrounds. This is one of many examples of the way in which cultural exchanges among ethnic groups often produced new dynamics both within and among local groups and, in doing so, strengthened and enriched rural civil society.

THE INFORMAL ECONOMIC SECTOR

One factor that contributed both to rural civil-societal strength and to central state fragility in Guinea-Bissau was the emergence, in the colonial and postcolonial periods, of an "informal" economic sector based on peasant-controlled land use and trade links. The concept of an "informal" or "second" economic sector has been developed by, among others, Daniel dos Santos (with regard to Angola) and Janet MacGaffey (with regard to the Congo). For MacGaffey, this sector involves "unmeasured, unrecorded" economic activities, income in kind that is hidden from state officials, and activities such as transborder trade, often on ancient mercantile circuits, involving food crops and other items that fetch higher prices outside the Congo and that "deprive the state of revenue."[85] Barter— frequently based on "reciprocal obligations," "mutual trust," and personal ties between producers and merchants[86]—is often the central mechanism for commodity exchange.[87] Dos Santos describes "systematic arrangements," or *esquemas,* developed in Angola under colonial rule and expanded after independence, through which a variety of producers and merchants exchange foods, clothes, meat, and other products.[88] These are so predominant in Angola that "the population devotes at least one-third of its productive time to them on an everyday basis";[89] this practice has represented a major barrier to organizing a national economy, while providing a channel of economic opportunity for those engaged in this economic sector.

In Guinea-Bissau, peasants determined their own land-use patterns and the direction of their trade sales or exchanges: a significant segment of rural economic activity remained "uncaptured" (i.e., effectively outside the rubric of state monitoring or control).[90] Despite growing levels of taxation and the establishment of "formal" trading circuits controlled by the state or by state-approved companies, most peasant economic activity in Guinea-Bissau in fact remained unmonitored and unregulated in the senses noted by MacGaffey and dos Santos; it therefore was part of the informal economic sector. As in the case of the Congo, so, too, in Guinea-Bissau the practice of intercommunity barter exchanges as well as long-distance trading networks hark back to marketing systems and exchange circuits that existed in precolonial times. In both the colonial and postcolonial periods, the predominance of "hidden" trading circuits and the accumulation of resources within rural civil society helped to assure the continuing fragility of the economic base upon which state power rested.

A general parallel may be drawn with the French colonial state established in the Middle Niger Valley during the final two decades of the nineteenth century. The French sought through treaty making as well as the use of military force to assure that the leaders of the precolonial Segu Bambara empire carried out the economic policies of the French colonialists.[91] But despite the broad political supremacy achieved by the French at the national level, they failed to control economic production, the supply of labor, or commerce.[92] Instead, a "parallel market" in cotton and cloths emerged that supplanted the state-sanctioned markets and that remained indigenously controlled.[93] As a result, the French colonial state in the Niger valley remained a fragile entity at the turn of the twentieth century. Although local resources could be extracted through sheer force, economic production and trade was not effectively controlled, and so the French colonial state may be regarded as a "weak state" during that time period.[94]

Richard L. Roberts implies that after 1905, the French colonial state in Niger would progress out of this weak-state character and become more fully entrenched through the middle decades of the twentieth century. In contrast, in this book I suggest that the colonial state in Portuguese Guinea would never quite emerge out of this weak-state status. Rather, the predominance of the informal economy and of peasant-determined production patterns prohibited a fuller exploitation of indigenously controlled resources. Like the French colonial state in Niger in the late nineteenth century, the Portuguese Guinean colonial state as well as the postcolonial state in independent Guinea-Bissau remained fragile in part because the central government failed to more effectively exploit agronomic production or rural commerce and could not intervene in village-level land-tenure arrangements.

In both the colonial and postcolonial periods, the lack of state access to substantial rural resources coincided with the previously discussed political and social limitations on state policy capacity, manifested at the most fundamental level by the inability of the central government to establish effective institutions that incorporated rural social formations into its political domain. This, in turn, reflected the ability of rural civil society to achieve and sustain its autonomy in various social, economic, political, and military spheres.

A DOMESTIC VS. INTERNATIONAL PERSPECTIVE

Finally, it is important to state clearly that although this book focuses primarily on the domestic sources of African state fragility, I do not seek to minimize the international context as an important explanatory variable. I refer here to the relative underdevelopment of Portugal itself and the administrative paucity of the Portuguese state in Lisbon (noted earlier), which has been accurately targeted by perceptive analysts as a key source, even the central source, of colonial weakness in Angola, Mozambique, and Guinea-Bissau.[95] However, I suggest that this is not the only side of the story. There is also a domestic, Africa-focused, and historically rich component to the relative failure of the colonial implantation in Portuguese Africa. To understand this analytic perspective, it is essential to peer into rural, indigenous lineages of civil-societal change and continuity. In this respect, I argue that the evolution of Guinea-Bissau's weak-state character cannot be appreciated without understanding the social context in which that state was created and sought to function.

Roberts makes a similar point in his study of French colonial development in Senegal, in which he urges a focus on localistic processes, in addition to examining the state/international conjuncture, in order to more fully understand both "the social history of rural change in Africa" and the inability of colonial administrators to fulfill their goals.[96] We may concur that it is important to recognize the colonial and international context within which relations between the domestic state and rural civil society unfold, but it is no less crucial to underline the extent to which Africa's indigenous actors were able to retain local control over key social processes.

Thus, to be sure, the origins of Portuguese Guinea's colonial state fragility can be partially traced to Portugal's weak economic position in the world economy of the nineteenth and twentieth centuries, as Lisbon proved unable to provide sufficient administrative and economic resources to its colonial projects to allow officials to carry out their hegemonic and institution-building goals. In this regard, Guinea-Bissau, and Lusophone Africa more generally, were somewhat unique within Africa, reflecting the relative economic and institutional backwardness of Portugal during the nineteenth and early-to-mid-twentieth centuries. But the origin of the colonial state's weakness in Guinea-Bissau is also in part to be found in the manner in which the precolonial states and the variations of rural civil society within the physical borders of what is now Guinea-Bissau evolved. Furthermore, investigation of the historical linkages among precolonial societies, rural social formations, and the problematics of colonial state building is crucial for an appreciation of postcolonial policy malaise. The roots of the contemporary state's inability to configure rural civil society in its preferred direction reflect, in part, the history of these precolonial/colonial/postcolonial connections.

PART I

Precolonial Polities and the Afro-European Encounter

CHAPTER I

Indigenous Polities and Intersocietal Relations in Precolonial Guinea-Bissau

THE STATE THAT WOULD EVENTUALLY be constructed in what is today Guinea-Bissau was preceded by a lengthy, complex history of indigenous empire formation and the territorial installation of some localized societies (despite forced relocations by larger kingdoms, in some cases), as well as more broadly based political kingship construction and decline. It is necessary to offer a sense of this complexity in order to gain insight into both the historical origin of a strongly entrenched rural civil society and the social context within which colonial state building would eventually take place.[1] A central point here is that, in the 1446–1890 period, despite European settlement in places along the Guinean coast and the expanding impact of oceanborne trade (especially the slave trade),[2] the political structures of African societies remained indigenously controlled, and the direction of political changes was largely set by African chiefs and empire builders. Through the period from the fifteenth to the nineteenth centuries, indigenous societies dominated the political and geographic landscape of what is today Guinea-Bissau, despite a Portuguese presence and claims of sovereignty. This fact highlights the significance of appreciating the political structures of these societies and the nature of their political interrelations (including both alliance creation and warfare).

I make clear below that many precolonial societies manifested strongly decentralized political features and a powerful commitment to local/territorial autonomy—two characteristics that would serve as bases for a strong rural civil society during the colonial era. To a large extent, these precolonial societies—most notably, Balanta, Papel, Mandjack, Felupe, and Bijagós—were marked by a particular identity, history, language, cultural traits, and other distinct social features. This would prove especially important in regard to their political mobilization when faced with external threats. It is important to stress that the defense of political autonomy was viewed as integrally linked to the protection of particular land areas (called *chão*), which were not only central to their agronomic economies, but also housed the ancestor-spirits that formed the basis of their social order. Even when translocated to a new chão (through defeat in war or in search of new farmland), people proceeded to defend their newly embraced territories with impressive military tenacity (as we shall see in chapters 2, 4, 5, and 6).

At the same time, however, these groups were characterized by intersocietal exchanges and alliance creation. In recent studies, George E. Brooks portrays extensive economic relations and trade networks in Guinea-Bissau and the Senegambia in the period from 1000 to 1630, while Carlos Lopes describes the far-reaching political linkages between the Mandinka and other groups that made possible the rise of the Gabu kingdom beginning in the thirteenth century.[3] I suggest below that many peoples, states, and empires, not only during the latter portion of those time periods, but also extending into the 1700s and 1800s, were similarly characterized by multiethnic alliances, social linkages, and political ties. Beyond the ethnically heterogenous federation of Gabu, in other kingdoms and in the acephalous societies of precolonial Guinea-Bissau, intermarriage was common, members were incorporated who hailed from diverse ethnic origins, regional market fairs brought together a broad array of buyers and sellers, and agreements and alliances were forged among far-flung communities both within and between different groups.

Indeed, despite the emergence of important conflicts, particularly at peak periods of empire expansion, most of the more locally oriented communities in precolonial Guinea-Bissau enjoyed extensive exchanges in regard to politics, trade, and culture, and intermarriages sometimes led to important changes in ethnic identity. Thus, the commitment to localistic political structures remained a defining feature of precolonial political life in some areas, but did not preclude the undertaking of significant cross-ethnic contacts and convergences. I will furthermore suggest that multiethnic relations would serve as a cornerstone of a relatively autonomous rural civil society during both the colonial and postcolonial periods.

A Brief Overview

By the 1400s, what is now Guinea-Bissau was populated primarily by animist peoples (whose date of origin varies from before A.D. 1000 to the sixteenth century), including Felupe, Biaffada, Brame/Papel, Balanta, Cassanga, Cobiana, Banhun, Cunante, Bayotte, Nalu, Mancany, and Bijagós.[4] Of these, the Brame/Papel, Felupe, Balanta, and Mancany formed part of the distinct "Bak" linguistic group,[5] who would eventually distinguish themselves by their resistance to external invasion and Islamic conversion.[6] However, their respective commitments to specific terrains did not preempt the formation of alliances with other groups, intermarriages, and the gradual construction of larger polities.

Meanwhile, Mandinka had migrated into the interior portions of precolonial Guinea-Bissau as early as the thirteenth century,[7] settling in areas that they called Cumisse (later, Farim) and Brassu (later, Oio).[8] Both these areas would eventually become part of Gabu (Kaabu, Cabú),[9] a federation of satellite states that remained predominantly Mandinka through its five-century span, although many other groups were incorporated into it. Through the late eighteenth century, some Mandinka had become Islamized,[10] but most had not.[11]

Mandinka as well as other peoples, including Mandjack, Papel, Banhun, and Cassanga, participated in regional trade fairs at which goods were exchanged among agriculturalists hailing from a broad range of ethnic and geographic backgrounds.[12] The Biaffada, Banhun, Brame, and Cassanga had established a rotating market system through which the daily market would shift to a different village for each of six consecutive days, and typically attracted thousands of producers and consumers from various locales.[13] Mandinka, Fulbe, Biaffada, and Banhun participated in caravan trade networks that drew on mercantile circuits linking coastal traders with merchants traveling across the Sahara.[14] Intersocietal trade also involved exchanges between coastal Balanta, Diola, Mandjack, and Brame producers of salt, rice, dried fish, mollusks, and palm products, as well as long-distance Mandinka merchants, who offered iron, cotton, gold, and other products.[15]

Empire building and the generalization of warfare in the interior in the eighteenth to nineteenth centuries, reflecting a variety of factors—including slave rebellions, Gabu's decline, and the rise of newly Islamized kingships—pushed some of the more animist groups (especially Balanta) toward the coastal and southern areas.[16] The most prominent example of indigenous state building at this time was the Fulbe-dominated Fuladu empire (1867–1903), which rose in part on the remnants of Gabu's collapse in 1867.[17] However, a total of approximately eighty other kingships or powerful chiefships remained influential in the area of Guinea-Bissau through the nineteenth century,[18] most notably the Basserel king-ship of the Mandjack people along the Cacheu River and the Papel kingships of greater Bissau. The remainder of Guinea-Bissau's rural communities were defined by more acephalous political structures.

Below, I provide a brief overview of Guinea-Bissau's precolonial kingdoms and decentralized societies in order to emphasize the extent of interethnic ties within a context of local indigenous territorial control, while also underlining the evolution of a strong praetorian capacity.

PAPEL-BRAME-MANDJACK ORIGIN AND KINGDOMS

Because the Papel/Brame lived directly on the coast, they were among the first peoples that European traders and sailors met in the early centuries of contact (1400s–1600s).[19] The names Papel and Brame (or Burame) were in all likeli-hood invented by Portuguese settlers from words that they heard commonly spoken.[20] From the fifteenth century and through the late eighteenth, the two names referred to the same people, although Brame would be used with de-creasing frequency.[21] The Papel inhabited most of the island of Bissau, as well as having a number of communities inland along the Cacheu River.

By the seventeenth century, the Papel king based near Bissau had managed to incorporate into a Papel-dominated "federation" a number of ethnic groups that were not of Papel origin but whose chiefs formally paid tribute to the Papel king.[22] Still, most of the leadership positions were held by Papel chiefs selected from six matrilineal clans on a rotating basis.[23] By the end of the eighteenth cen-tury, the Papel king's singular power had diminished substantially as the Papel population grew and associated chiefs proliferated. Two Papel kings emerged, one in Basserel (in what later became Cacheu region), with the other Papel king remaining on the island of Bissau.[24] Those communities loyal to the Basserel king came to be called Manjaco (English: Mandjack) by the early nineteenth cen-tury.[25] A coherent Mandjack ethnic identity did not begin to be created until the late eighteenth and early nineteenth centuries, when the Basserel kingdom grew in size and influence.[26]

Through the 1800s, the Mandjack came to assume a unique culture, political system, and religion. The Basserel kingdom expanded to include approximately forty villages by the end of the nineteenth century, making it the largest kingdom in coastal Guinea-Bissau at that time.[27] Here it is clear that the multiethnic reality of kingship building in precolonial Guinea-Bissau conflicted with Portuguese ethnic naming. Hundreds of communities of various origins located throughout coastal and north-central Guinea-Bissau were allied with the Basserel king. It was their common allegiance to this king that provoked the Portuguese to consider them all to be Mandjack. In this sense, the creation of this ethnic category may be considered to have been political in nature.

Nonetheless, most Mandjack remained principally committed to their localities and identified themselves according to specific territories. Thus, Mandjack from Caió called themselves Ba-aió, Mandjack from Calequisse called themselves Ba-lequisse, and so on.[28] However, through the 1800s, these village communities also began to assume a dual identity, with the Mandjack label reflecting their loyalty to Basserel but without subsuming their primary, localistically informed Ba-aió self-identification. This suggests the relatively malleable character of ethnic-group formation in nineteenth-century Guinea-Bissau. Still, this dual identity was a long time in genesis, and the localistic label remained the primary mode of identification: it was not until the twentieth century that most of those who lived along the Cacheu River were identifying themselves (to outsiders) as Mandjack.[29] In fact, even as late as 1930, Mandjack informants indicated to a colonial investigator that the appellation Mandjack was of recent derivation.[30] And it was not until the period of the 1950s to 1980s that *Mandjack* came to refer, essentially, to all those who inhabited Cacheu region.[31]

However, through the nineteenth century, those who were considered Mandjack did begin to manifest certain shared social, cultural, and religious characteristics, including a common allegiance to certain spiritual forces, as well as having a praetorian ability to defend the integrity of their local territorial domains. Thus, Mandjack ethnic identity bore particular geoterritorial as well as socioreligious in-group implications, despite the fact that the Basserel-allied communities upon which Mandjack identity was originally constructed initially consisted of a variety of identity groups. Mandjack identity formation proved both socially malleable and territorially specific: it incorporated people from various social and ethnic origins, but also gave rise to a broader ethnic Mandjack identification that helped to confer the right to rule over specific land areas. Both of these aspects would be repeatedly manifested in later decades: strong territorial control directed by Mandjack leaders occurred at the same time as spiritual societies incorporated people from a variety of ethnic groups who had migrated to Cacheu region.[32]

As for the Basserel kingdom, from the late eighteenth century to the end of the nineteenth, the Mandjack kingdom of Basserel was composed of not fewer than twenty-six chiefdoms in the densely populated coastal littoral.[33] Interestingly, recent research suggests that political power was less hierarchical than early Portuguese ethnographers believed.[34] In particular, the relationship between the king, chiefs, and commoners reflected a politically accountable leadership structure with the Basserel king entering into "contracts" with federated Basserel chiefs.[35] In later chapters, I make clear that this tradition of mutual leadership recognition and accountability helped form the basis of a rural civil society geared toward a political culture based on leadership cooperation and relative political autonomy. Here we may note that through much of the nineteenth century, the Portuguese continued to call those Mandjack located in the northwestern sector (between the Cacheu and Mansoa Rivers) the "Papel of the north."[36] This was because those communities (Churo, Pecau, Mata, Cacanda, Biànda, Boté, and Caboi) did not become part of the Mandjack Basserel kingdom.[37] They were loyal to a separate king at Mata and were culturally and linguistically Mandjack, but because of their affiliation with the Mata kingship they would become identified as Mandjack only after the 1910s (when the kingships began to decline).

We may also observe that the "Papel of the north" were in fact more ethnically mixed than the Portuguese realized, reflecting their incorporation of newly arrived settlers. For example, in Caboi during the period from the seventeenth to the nineteenth centuries, Mancanya and Banhun newcomers were allowed to establish founding lineage households.[38] Also, slaves who had been captured from other ethnic groups were eventually integrated into Caboi society.[39] However, despite their heterogenous social structures, by the twentieth century the "Papel of the north" were being called Mandjack by the Portuguese, and they themselves would in fact adopt that broader ethnic affiliation.

Meanwhile, within Bissau region itself, continued Papel population expansion and internal conflicts had produced a multiplication of kingships, so that by the mid-1800s, six Papel kings ruled the areas surrounding Bissau. These included the Papel kings of Bandim, Antula [or Antulla], Intim [or Antim], Tor, Safim, and Biombo.[40] In all Papel kingships, the power of the king was limited by his need to consult a council of elders as well as religious advisers (known as baloubeiros).[41]

The Papel of the Bissau area would attain a reputation as a coastal people highly competent in military affairs, particularly when it came to defending their own communities.[42] This was manifested repeatedly by the powerful defense they were able to mount against outside invaders, proving a daunting military challenge to the Portuguese through several centuries (see chapter 4).

Meanwhile, the Papel and Mandjack had each established regularized market fairs at Bandim (near Bissau) and at Basserel and elsewhere in Cacheu region, and these fairs attracted producers and traders from various parts of the coast.[43] They also continued to trade with each other (Papel-Mandjack),[44] building on a network of economic and social links that reflected a continuity of close inter-ethnic ties.

BALANTA

The Balanta, like other Bak speakers (including the Papel, Mandjack, and Brame), were among the original settlers of the lands of Guinea-Bissau.[45] Today the Balanta comprise approximately one-fourth the populace of Guinea-Bissau; they are one of the country's two largest ethnic groups.[46] According to new re-search on precolonial economic change, Balanta settlements tended to be spread over wide areas, reflecting the acephalous community and leadership structures of Balanta society and the independent nature of yam production.[47] As of ap-proximately the sixteenth century, partly reflecting external threats, partly reflecting population pressures, and partly reflecting the fact that Balanta had begun to embrace wet-rice farming as the basis of their economy and needed large, well-watered basin areas to farm, increasing numbers of Balanta migrated from the Geba Valley (between the Geba and Cacheu Rivers) to northern, southern, and (to a lesser extent) eastern parts of precolonial Guinea-Bissau.[48] At the same time, the Balanta evolved highly efficient techniques of preventing salt-filled ocean water from invading their riverine rice fields and developed a widespread reputation for their unusually large annual rice surpluses.[49]

The majority subgroup of Balanta, the Brassa, comprised 85 to 90 percent of the Balanta as a whole. The Brassa, as well as most of the smaller Balanta sub-groups such as the Batchaa and BaNaga, successfully avoided domination by centralized kingdoms and became well regarded for their fighting skills. In fact, the word *Balanta* is believed to derive from the Mandinka word *balanto*, referring to those who refuse to submit.[50]

However, in the sixteenth and seventeenth centuries, a small portion of the Balanta came under the influence of neighboring Mandinka and changed their language, customs, and religion accordingly.[51] Moreover, some Balanta women who had come into contact with Mandinka men decided to marry into Mandinka families and eventually became fully absorbed into Mandinka society. For this reason, a segment of the contemporary Mandinka of Guinea-Bissau in fact can trace their matrilineal descent to Balanta backgrounds.[52] In the nineteenth century, this practice of intermarriage between Balanta and Mandinka and cultural conversion gave rise to a separate, relatively small Balanta subgroup known as the Betxá (also called Balanta-Mané).[53] In their case, traditional Balanta culture remained dominant but syncretistically incorporated some Mandinka social practices (including the adoption of Mandinka patronyms).[54]

Still, the vast majority of the Balanta-Brassa remained committed to preserving their own customs and to fighting for their respective land areas. Periodically, and especially as of the mid-nineteenth century, many Balanta communities could not fend off attacks by the larger kingdoms, while others had grown in size and needed to find more rice-farming areas; these conditions set in motion additional waves of migration. In all these cases, they were able to preserve their distinct culture and social practices.[55] At the same time, their settlement within new areas typically resulted in cultural exchanges with residents from other groups. It was typical of the Balanta not to seek to conquer new potential areas of settlement but rather to request permission from the kings or chiefs of a new territory—controlled by Papel, Biaffada, Mandinka, Mandjack, Nalu, Cassanga, or Banhun.[56] Once settled, Balanta culture tended, over time, to become predominant, with members of these other groups being gradually absorbed into Balanta society. For example, it is today common to find Banhun and Cassanga patrilineal surnames among the Balanta-Batchaa, despite the dominance of Balanta traditions.[57]

For several centuries, Portuguese observers referred to this process of intercultural incorporation as Balantasization. More recently, however, a specialist in Balanta society, Diana Lima Handem, has argued that this is a misnomer because it implies hegemony on the part of the Balanta; rather, argues Handem, it is more accurate to describe a process of the "transculturation" between Balanta society and other groups with whom they came in contact, which included the Biaffada, Papel, Mandinka, Brame, Nalu, Banhun, Cassanga, Felupe, and Mandjack.[58] This represented more of an equal exchange and a peaceful and voluntary adoption of certain practices.

Thus, for example, the Balanta-Bungue of the southern districts adopted the Biaffada mythical figure of *kankurā*—a reincarnated spirit with a significant political function—to control the behavior of those who deviated from normal social practices. Economic and social interchanges between Balanta and Mandjack, Papel, Felupe, and Brame led to the adoption by these latter groups of the use of a Balanta farming tool known as a *kebinde* (in creole: *radi*). Exchanges similarly took place among Balanta subgroups: members of the Patche and Pete adopted the Brassa practice of *bdí*—collective celebrations through the month of July of young affianced women.[59]

These cooperative interrelations were also manifested with regard to trade, with Balanta exchanging part of their surplus agricultural produce with Papel, Biaffada, and Mandinka merchants. Balanta surplus products included yams (initially), then paddy rice, in addition to livestock; these were exchanged for finished goods such as cloths, palm oil, and iron tools.[60] Balanta commonly traveled to Bissau to enact these transactions as well as traveling to Biaffada and Brame areas further inland.

In essence, it was precisely because these contacts involved a sharing and mutual incorporation of cultural traits, reflecting the Balanta characteristic of receptivity toward other social practices, that it is more precise to speak of trans-culturation than of Balantasization.[61] Still, it was generally the case that despite these intercultural exchanges, Balanta social rules prevailed, in the sense that Balanta elders retained control of political affairs, and Balanta social and economic traditions were maintained and tended to take precedence. Thus, as this process of peaceful incorporation occurred, even though newly settled Balanta often agreed to abide by the dictates of the original group and adopted aspects of what was for them a new culture, the process of transculturation typically assured that the Balanta in effect made this new territory their own.[62]

Indeed, control of specific land areas was, and remains, central to the Balanta political and social system and, more generally, to their religious and cultural worldview.[63] Land is identified with particular village authority figures; it helps to define the legitimacy of Balanta communities not only by the living but also in regard to ancestors and spirit entities who guard over particular territorial domains.[64] At the same time, this emphasis on land (especially rice fields) coincides with a political determination to preserve their community-level autonomy.[65] An anticentralist political tradition reflects a political system characterized by participation-oriented, gerontocratically based leadership groupings, grounded in shared governance, rather than centralized kingly rule.[66] Indeed, oral traditions "speak to very local concerns," and while Balanta social and economic institutions such as age-grade societies facilitate cross-village exchanges and make possible common economic and military activities, political power is highly deconcentrated at the local level: it is "the *tabanca,* or village, which is the largest political unit."[67]

In part reflecting their strong commitment to defend their particular territories (which they considered to be their homelands); in part as a consequence of their determination to preserve their political autonomy; in part reflecting the high social prestige accorded to those with proven fighting skills; and in part reflecting their frequent involvement in war, the Balanta developed a reputation for being able to mobilize skilled and effective fighting forces. Specialized groups within Balanta society became responsible for military decision making, strategizing, and the mobilization and coordination of fighters from various villages for the purpose of defending specific territories (although decisions were generally rendered collectively, and there was no individual "war chief").[68] Over time, when challenged externally, the Balanta would demonstrate a capacity to defend their settled territories with an effectiveness that by the eighteenth century was already legendary among the peoples of Guinea-Bissau.[69] Ultimately, mobilization for military purposes served to reinforce a specifically Balanta sense of group cohesion, consolidating ties both within each community and among various Balanta communities.[70]

Thus, the Balanta have manifested two social characteristics that were in fact typical of many of the peoples of rural Guinea-Bissau: one was a strong praetorian capacity to defend their control of their territory; the other was their tendency to trade with neighboring peoples and to incorporate them through intermarriage into the local community. It is important to emphasize that this incorporative political culture was similarly reflected with regard to intraethnic ties: links among geographically dispersed Balanta villages (mentioned above with regard to military cooperation) were reinforced through cross-cutting social institutions such as age grades, marriage, and the use of agricultural labor teams.[71]

BIAFFADA KINGDOMS

Oral histories recorded in the 1940s suggest that the Biaffada (or Beafada) originated in the east of sub-Saharan Africa, migrated to Firdu (at that time including Patchana and Pakessi), and, fleeing Mandinka domination, settled in the region later known as Oio.[72] By the sixteenth and seventeenth centuries, the Biaffada had spread out over as much as one-third of the area of present-day Guinea-Bissau.[73] They wielded a notable influence on nearby peoples, including the Papel; the Biaffada king of Guinala was reputed to have bestowed upon the Papel king of Bissau his royal power in the late 1600s.[74] The Biaffada market at Guinala was particularly important as a regional trading center, attracting as many as twelve thousand Papel, Nalu, Bijagós, Mandinka, and others and serving as a key source of cloth, gold, kola, horses, cattle, wine, and foodstuffs, as well as slaves.[75] Biaffada were also adept at navigating wide expanses of the Guinean coast and inland rivers in large dugout canoes that could carry between forty and a hundred people (or the equivalent in merchandise), which enabled them to trade in kola, pepper, fish, cotton, ironware, maize, and salt with Balanta, Papel, and Mandinka.[76]

In the sixteenth and seventeenth centuries, the Biaffada living to the west of lower Geba, particularly at Gole (or Cuor) and at Mansomine, came under the influence of the Brassu (Braço) kingdom.[77] Other Biaffada were heavily influenced by the Gabu kingdom (see below). This resulted in partial assimilation of the Biaffada into Mandinka culture, which helps to explain the Biaffadas' alliance with the Mandinka against the Fulbe in the wars of the nineteenth century.[78] One observer noted that so many Biaffada were living among the Mandinka of Gabu that the populace of Gabu was in effect mixed Mandinka-Biaffada.[79] However, partial assimilation into the Mandinka world should be emphasized, as some Biaffada remained culturally distinct and animist, despite extensive Islamic preaching on the part of Muslim Mandinka holy men in Biaffada villages.

Banhun-Cassanga

Oral tradition recalls that the Banhun (or Baïnuk; or Baïnouk; or Banyun) were among the first people to reside in the areas that would later comprise the founding provinces of the kingdom of Gabu (discussed below), stretching from northern Guinea-Bissau through the Gambian valley.[80] Their blacksmiths became renowned for their iron hatchets, which took on religious meaning for a variety of peoples. Hatchets were exchanged with the Papel and the Biaffada for kola, pepper, and other products. Their trade fairs were held weekly in villages north of the Cacheu River; according to Brooks, these fairs attracted thousands of Papel, Biaffada, Bijagós, and Mandinka (some traveling long distances to reach these markets).[81] In the sixteenth century, they came to be alternately influenced by the king of Casamance and by the Mandinka kingdom of Braço (Brassu). Through their extensive social and economic interaction with the Mandinka, the Banhun of the Songrugru River intermarried with Mandinka and began a process of gradual assimilation into Mandinka culture — resulting in a severe diminution of the Banhun populace.[82] This Banhun-Mandinka mixing also gave rise to a new group known as Cassanga, which eventually asserted their political dominance over the Banhun.[83] The fact that the name of the last king of the Banhun, Nana Sira Bana Bai (in the late eighteenth century), was Mandinka suggests the intimate level of Banhun-Mandinka intersection by that time.[84]

BIJAGÓS

The people of the Bijagós Islands (the Bijagós, or Bissagós) initially inhabited portions of the coast of mainland Guinea-Bissau. They were probably forced to flee to the islands by invading Biaffada who had seized their territories.[85] In precolonial times, each of these islands was dominated by one or more monarchical groups in which women from ruling lineages played a leading part (although male chiefs served as the principal decision makers regarding war). The Bijagós became immersed in international trade and barter exchanges, developed extraordinary skills as fishermen and canoeists, and often traded with coastal peoples such as Papel, Mandjack, and Banhun, although they consistently carried out raids on coastal villages.[86] As early as 1594 and repeatedly through the 1600s and 1700s, the people of the Bijagós islands (especially Orango and Sogá) sold captured slaves to foreign vessels.[87] After the international slave trade diminished in the 1800s, the Bijagós continued to participate actively in coastal trade with other Guinean groups and in international trade involving peanuts and other items.[88]

Through 1936, the Bijagós enjoyed full political autonomy within their island communities; their military toughness assured that they would not be conquered by mainlanders or by Europeans. In their first recorded military encounter with the Portuguese, Bijagós fighters pummeled a contingent of sailors in a battle over control of Roxa isle (later called Canhabac) in 1550.[89] The Bijagós would remain free from Portuguese intervention until the Canhabac wars of 1925 and 1936.[90]

FULBE

Beginning at the end of the fifteenth century, animist, nomadic, pastoral Fulbe migrated from the Futa Jallon mountains in present-day Guinea-Conakry and from Toro in Senegal to southern Guinea-Bissau;[91] they were in search of pasture land and water for their cattle.[92] Once settled, the Fulbe groups remained subservient to the Gabu kingdom's rulers (see below); nonetheless, they achieved a high degree of economic self-sufficiency, relying on a combination of husbandry, food crop growing, and hunting.[93]

Within Fulbe society, two broad social classes gradually emerged: the Fulbe-ribê, the "free," or "ruling," Fulbe, and the Fulbe-djiábê, or "captive" Fulbe, which referred to those with slave status, many of whom worked as cloth producers.[94]

Many of the Fulbe-djiábê originally hailed from different ethnic groups (including Biaffada, Soninké, Mandinka, and others) but had been captured in war and incorporated into Fulbe society.[95]

Gradually, Gabu's ruling elites sought to gain access to the Fulbes' stored wealth (cattle, cloth, millet): increases in taxes were imposed, assured by harsh physical mistreatment.[96] By the mid-1800s, this helped to provoke the settled Fulbe to raise rebel armies against Gabu.[97] Taking advantage of the resultant instability, the Fulbe-djiábê broke free of their slave status. This warfare would lead to the rise of a new Fulbe-dominated kingdom known as Fuladu (see chapter 3), which, despite the initial predominance of the Fulbe, was marked by interethnic incorporation and political inclusivism.

The Gabu Kingdom

By far the most significant of the political entities created in the precolonial era was the Gabu kingdom.[98] Founded in the fourteenth century and reaching its height in the period from the sixteenth to the eighteenth centuries,[99] the Gabu kingdom included much of the interior land area contained within what are today Guinea-Bissau, the Gambia, and Senegal's Casamance region—an area stretching from the Gambia River to the Futa Jallon Mountains.[100]

The Gabu kingdom was largely ruled by the political elites of the Mandinka people (who predominated numerically in these regions), called *niantio* (or *ñaanco,* or *nyancho*) and who bore the name Sané (Saane), or Mané (Maane).[101] However, the kingdom came to include numerous ethnic groups, including Serer, Felupe/Diola, Cassanga, Banhun, Biaffada, and some Balanta.[102] Intermarriage was common within the kingdom, although historians are divided as to whether this led the Mandinka to adopt indigenous practices of already existing groups such as the Cassanga and Banhun or whether the latter groups came to adopt Mandinka culture. Joye Bowman and Mamadou Mané each suggest that eventually many of the previously settled peoples adopted Mandinka social and cultural practices.[103] Lopes acknowledges Mandinka absorption of some aspects of preexisting societies, but emphasizes the profound "homogenization" of culture throughout the Gabu empire.[104] According to this perspective, the influence of Mandinka overrule through the political structures and cultural impact of the Gabu kingdom produced a "Mandinguization" of dozens of local societies.[105] This process, Lopes argues, explains why 24.5 percent of current Fulbe names derive from Mandinka origin and why the word *bolanha,* originally of Mandinka origin, referring to low-lying wetlands, eventually came to be used not only by Mandinka but by all Guinea-Bissauans to refer to wet-rice fields.[106]

However, a study by Eve Crowley has pinpointed particular political and cultural practices that are specifically Banhun, Felupe/Diola, and Biaffada and that predate the arrival of the Mandinka in eastern Guinea-Bissau.[107] These include reliance on royal slaves as king's councillors and the use of a broom and red hat as regalia. Bowman has also pointed to the adoption of aspects of Biaffada culture by Mandinka society.[108] And let us recall Handem's point (noted above) regarding Balanta-Mandinka intermarriage and exchanges reflecting a "transculturation" of practices — with Balanta culture, rather than Mandinka, normally remaining dominant. All of this — contrary to Lopes's notion of "Mandinguization" — suggests that alliances and interchanges within the broadly based Gabu kingdom occurred in a way that enabled original peoples to retain their own identity and culture while also influencing and impacting Mandinka society, despite partial convergence by some groups.

Some of the initial members of the *koring* (governors of provinces) of Gabu were likely to have been not Mandinka but rather members of the first groups to have settled in this area, including Banhun, Balanta, Biaffada, and Padjadinca.[109] Founding lineages from these groups laid spiritual and historical claim to the land areas in question, but decided to ally with this new kingdom; in doing so, they managed to preserve the integrity of their respective cultural identities and internal political structures.[110] Fulbe, Soso, and Banhun lineage heads were also absorbed into the ruling families of Gabu, reflecting extensive polygamy involving Gabu's elites and their politically affiliated neighbors.[111]

Thus, despite its Mandinka origins, Gabu had embraced a multiethnic leadership from its inception, and the members of the kingdom reflected intermarriages and alliances with a number of different groups. Mutual acculturation proved inevitable; at the same time, as the koring came to form a unified ruling elite, non-Mandinka among them more readily assumed a Mandinka identity.[112] Overall, throughout the ensuing centuries, the constructive, intergroup ties that defined Gabu's social relations would represent an enduring tradition within the associated regions of the north-central areas of what are now Guinea-Bissau and the Senegambia. This was reinforced through the Gabu empire's rotating kingship (among the member provinces), a practice that had been adopted by Gabu rulers from an already existing Cassanga/Banhun tradition.[113] The resultant political and cultural syncretism reflected a mutually reinforcing, balanced, constructive evolution of intersocietal interchange.[114]

The total number of Gabu provinces, both the core and more outlying provinces, may be approximated at forty in the eighteenth century;[115] collectively, these units represented the predominant political force in northern and north-central Guinea-Bissau. Most of Gabu's provinces were ruled indirectly, with tribute paid only on occasion. Indeed, Gabu was defined to a large extent by the federated character of its political structure, rather than by a hierarchical central control over the empire's provinces. This can be effectively illustrated by a description of Gabu's military organization and preparedness. Each Gabu province had at least one *tata,* an armed fort marked by wooden palisades and raised platforms to enable soldiers to receive distant signals from neighboring provinces as well as to fire downward when challenged by invaders; most provinces also built an administrative center *(sansamo)* from which the provincial governors ruled.[116] These tatas made it possible for Gabu to respond effectively to external threats and therefore to act decisively as a federated empire, while also enhancing the political and territorial autonomy of each province by protecting its respective borders. In the nineteenth century, thirty-seven tatas formed the relatively decentralized but rapidly mobilized praetorian foundation of the Gabu kingdom.[117]

While Lopes admits of the federated nature of Gabu, calling it a "family of states," he also insists that the rulers of Gabu exercised a "decentralized hegemony" over "dominated ethnic groups" such as the coastal Papel, Balanta, Diola, Brame, and societies of the Guinean interior (including the Biaffada, Banhun, and Cassanga), producing a relatively unified and homogenous culture.[118] I would suggest, however, that this imagery of unification and domination is rather exaggerated and that the fundamental political autonomy, identity, culture, and control over territory of the groups described above is underappreciated. There is, for example, no direct evidence of Gabu ruling over coastal peoples such as the Balanta or Diola, and only a single incident of a one-time payment by a Papel king to a Gabu *mansa* (king). Moreover, within Gabu itself, political relations reflected multiethnic alliance building and social and economic exchanges.

Gabu's Economy

The various peoples within the Gabu kingdom were agriculturalists who grew their own foodstuffs and also participated in regular market fairs, both local and interregional, at which were traded a variety of produce and finished products.[119] The Mandinka were particularly renowned for their production of finely made cotton threads and cloths in hues of bright red, blue, and white, which they bartered in market fairs.[120] These fairs were defined by their social heterogeneity, participation by thousands of cultivators from different ethnic backgrounds, and specialized, long-distance traders known as *djula,* or *djila.* The djula became so proficient at obtaining diverse precious goods from distant lands that they were allowed to function with considerable mercantile independence, and during the six centuries of the kingdom's reign they developed partially autonomous circuits of trade throughout and beyond Gabu that contributed to Gabu's expansion.[121]

At the same time, however, because of their military expertise, the armies of Gabu were able to capture large numbers of slaves. Some of the slaves were Islamized and used for agricultural cultivation, while others were traded on indigenous slave-trade circuits (including those operated by the djula).[122] With the rise of the Atlantic slave trade in the sixteenth century, the Gabu kingdom was well positioned to trade with European shippers and, with the relatively high prices paid by the Europeans, the Atlantic segment of the slave trade not only increased but soon displaced most other aspects of Gabu's foreign commerce.[123] Toward the end of the seventeenth century, Gabu was exporting to European shippers some twelve thousand to fifteen thousand slaves per year.[124] Gabu's predominance over slave trading in this area of West Africa provided Gabu elites with strong bargaining power, and they were able to impose right-to-trade taxes on European merchants.[125]

Over the course of the seventeenth and eighteenth centuries, the Atlantic slave trade provoked a rise in general warfare in the Guinea-Bissau region as Gabu's rulers sought to obtain more and more slaves to sell to the European slave merchants frequenting the upper West African coast.[126] Gabu's success at warfare helped make possible a major expansion of the kingdom.[127] The monetary wealth accumulated by the rulers of Gabu through the slave trade enabled them to augment their military potency through the purchase of modern weaponry, including rifles and cannons,[128] and Europeans did not dare to challenge the Gabu kingdom militarily. Gabu-European trade was regulated and controlled by Gabu officials, with certain restrictions imposed — for example, Europeans were commonly forbidden from entering inland zones.[129]

— —

Indigenously controlled kingdoms in the interior, along with a variety of acephalous and hierarchical societies along the coast, dominated politics in the Guinea-Bissau area from ancient times through the nineteenth century. Two of the more important political and social traditions that emerged through these centuries were (1) a strong commitment to territorially based locales (despite periodic displacements) on the part of specific ethnic groups, and (2) a recurrent capacity for constructive interethnic ties, which reflected the social malleability and incorporative capacity of most groups, as well as their economic trading interests. It is crucial to emphasize the multiethnic composition of many of Guinea-Bissau's precolonial states and the extensive social relations and cooperation between—as well as within—various groups.

Thus, Gabu continually absorbed members of groups from many parts of ancient Guinea-Bissau. The Fulbe ruling groups hailed from different geographic and ethnic origins, as did their slaves. Papel kings had established ties or directly ruled over a number of different coastal communities, while many Papel and Mandjack retained strong economic and cultural links with one another despite their many-centuries-long defense of staked-out coastal territories. The Biaffada, while also successfully integrating into Balanta and Mandinka communities, strongly influenced the Papel in the early centuries. The Balanta demonstrated a profound commitment to local political autonomy and staved off external challenges, but they also constructed institutions that linked together people from their own widespread communities as well as periodically incorporating outsiders such as Mandinka.

A number of precolonially important peoples such as the Banhun and Cassanga were peacefully absorbed by surrounding groups such as the Mandjack and Mandinka through intermarriage; this indicates that intersocietal contact was in some cases so pervasive that it produced the decline of previously large, coherent groups. At the same time, intermarriage sometimes led to the formation of entirely new groups; for example, the Caboiana, of Caboi region, located east of Cacheu, originated from mixes among the Banhun, Mandjack, and Cassanga.[130] The Cunante, or Mansoanca, were a product of intermarriages between Balanta and Mandinka: they came to speak their own dialect—a combination of elements of the Balanta and Mandinka languages.[131]

These experiences of multiethnic exchange were reflected in long-standing political and economic traditions, including alliance making that sometimes produced large states as well as trade relations that provided communities with a diversity of products. All the groups discussed above participated extensively in regional economic fairs, where they obtained, mostly through barter, a broad array of foods, handicrafts, livestock, precious metals, kola, dyes, cotton, and other goods. The ability to intersect, peacefully and voluntarily, with people from other groups may be regarded as a significant source of internal social strength in rural Guinea-Bissau. This ability would constitute a central component of a strong rural civil society in the colonial and postcolonial periods.

At the same time, the military effectiveness of indigenous forces displayed repeatedly through the late nineteenth and twentieth centuries (see chapters 2 and 4) would, in part, reflect a deeply embedded praetorian social memory based on Guineans' respective military accomplishments through the course of the precolonial era. Most groups had developed a praetorian capacity to defend their political autonomy and control over local territories from attacks by opposing indigenous polities, although in some cases ambitious war makers (who might be kings or stateless groups of age-group leaders) mounted assaults on weaker peoples. At the same time, extensive alliance making and cooperation among different groups added to indigenous military strength and helped to prepare rural Guineans to be able to resist colonial armies in the late nineteenth and early twentieth centuries with unusual effectiveness. This military legacy was sustained through the colonial implantation and would contribute to the generation of an effective nationalist uprising in the 1960s.

The next chapter makes clear that during the four centuries that preceded the twentieth century, indigenous praetorian strength was such that the Portuguese would find themselves dependent on local African leaders, both along inland rivers and along the coast.

CHAPTER 2

Overview of Portuguese-African Political Relations and Warfare, 1446–1890

WHEN THE PORTUGUESE SETTLERS first arrived on the shores of "Guiné" in 1449, they entered into a relationship of dependency on local Africans that would, in effect, persist until the late nineteenth century. During that lengthy period, most of the colonialists remained largely restricted to their coastal or riverine forts, dependent on the good will of African kings and groups of leading elders. When colonial administrators initiated military campaigns against African polities, as they did with increasing frequency through the nineteenth century, they typically suffered humiliating setbacks. Rural Guineans repeatedly manifested a praetorian capacity that the Portuguese could not match. This left a four-centuries-long legacy of psychological defeatism among the would-be colonial state builders.

At the same time, however, some individual Portuguese settlers did establish a web of social and political ties with their African neighbors, in some cases resulting in peaceful relations based on mutual exchange. George E. Brooks emphasizes that the ability of African communities to incorporate Europeans into their societies reflected a strong tradition of reciprocity between village "hosts" and newly arrived "strangers"—this latter category including long-distance African traders as well as white Europeans who arrived at Guinea-Bissauan villages.[1]

In many cases, this dispersal, settlement, and incorporation of Europeans in fact led to Luso-African intermarriages, in turn producing an intimate network of social relations between settlers and local African "landlords."

This helped to assure the immersion of many of these very early Portuguese settlers *(lançados)* in local trade precisely because of their newly established kinship ties with local kings or chiefs.[2] This worked to the mutual advantage of the African leaders and "host" villagers and the European newcomers.[3] A pattern was initiated whereby these settlers made payments to kings, chiefs, and "landlord" villagers in return for the right to reside in the area and to engage in trade, and in some cases in return for the labor of local Africans.

However, as the centuries wore on, the Portuguese authorities who remained stationed in Cacheu, Bolama, Bissau, Farim, and other Guinean port towns (not the dispersed lançados) became increasingly anxious to establish Lusophone political overrule, and especially to assure Portugal's control over export-oriented trade. At the same time, European settlers in the port towns tired of their dependency on the goodwill of local African chiefs and kings and the need to make regular payments to those kings for the right to remain settled in those towns. These goals and frustrations produced waves of military campaigns by the colonialists against their African hosts. However, the military frailty of the Portuguese units assigned to Guinea meant that most Europeans would have to remain confined within particularly tiny, fort-protected settlements called *praças* or *presídios* (squares). The exceptions, to note again, were the lançados who had migrated to more isolated areas upriver because they were useful to local Africans as traders or had intermarried into a neighboring African family (but let us recall that they, too, remained dependent on the preferences of the local African rulerships).

This chapter emphasizes that the would-be colonialists in the Portuguese port towns remained subservient to African kings and chiefs during these centuries, as indicated by the continuing need to render gifts to them and by the ability of African forces to respond effectively to military and political aggression on the part of Portuguese forces.

PORTUGUESE-AFRICAN POLITICAL RELATIONS

Early recordings of Portuguese-African contact indicate that tensions mounted substantially between town-based settlers and the Africans they traded with through the mid-to-late 1600s, apparently as a consequence of misunderstandings regarding economic exchanges or trading deals gone awry. Portuguese settlers in the trading port of Cacheu were repeatedly attacked during this period; the twenty Portuguese soldiers assigned to protect the European community in Cacheu proved unable to deter those attacks.[4] Strategically, the Cacheu settlers were at a substantial disadvantage because of the vulnerability of their water supply. The settlers' fresh water was frequently either taken from them or poisoned, and by 1670 most settlers were forced to leave Cacheu. These Cacheu traders proceeded to "spread out over the entire coast of Guinea"[5] — an area essentially along the major rivers, where they established private trading farms.

Perhaps it was for this reason that Portuguese settlers along the coast of Guinea were known as lançados—"the launched ones," reflecting their having independently "thrown" themselves along the Guinean waterways.[6] However, since many of these early Portuguese settlers were Jews and other targets of the Inquisition, it is alternatively possible that the term refers to their being "launched" out of Portugal during the fifteenth- and sixteenth-century expulsions.[7] Because they were essentially on their own and were faced with large, well-armed polities controlling the coastal waters, most of these lançados sought to forge peaceful relations with their immediate neighbors. As noted above, this included intermarriage with local African women,[8] and the ensuing miscegenation produced growing numbers of mixed-race Guineans known as *mestiços* (creoles). Brooks refers to these descendants of African-Portuguese marriages as Luso-Africans, thus emphasizing the importance of their African parental linkage, with particular regard to the fact that their life chances depended to a large extent on the social ranking of their African mothers.[9]

Meanwhile, Portuguese residents of the fort towns made regular payments (of cash and valued goods) to local Papel, Mandjack, or Biaffada chiefs, which enabled them to rely on local African laborers. As these laborers remained for years within the colonial world (within the fort towns), they came to adopt many aspects of Portuguese culture and lifestyle, including Western-style clothing and the Christian religion, and it was this group that was largely responsible for the evolution of Portuguese *crioulo* (creole), which became the predominant language in the Guinean fort towns.[10] They came to be called *grumetes,* although many Portuguese chroniclers referred to them as "Christianized Africans"; they were sometimes treated as unpaid workers, but many did obtain minimal compensation. Europeans initially relied on these grumetes as boat workmen, or dockhands,[11] but later their work assignments were expanded to include a variety of economic, social, and military tasks.[12] The grumetes often served as translators and trading intermediaries among the Portuguese, the lançados, and local African communities; many of them also retained close ties with villagers.[13]

At the same time, some of the more isolated lançados near the Cacheu River were occasionally, for the purpose of marriage, offered the hand of a daughter of a local Mandjack chief.[14] This helped to consolidate social and economic ties with neighboring communities because the recipient lançado was, in return, expected to provide economic benefits to the "host" chief.[15] Moreover, the offspring of these mixed marriages served as "trade middlemen" between Africans and lançados.[16] In some instances, once the original lançado passed away, his offspring also invested some of the inherited wealth in land and cattle acquisition back in the home village.[17] This makes clear that links between Portuguese lançado settlers and local Africans were strengthened along the coast of Guinea, but in ways that assured the continued dependency of the Lusophone newcomers. And it is important to emphasize that lançados' circumference of operations was highly limited; for example, they were generally unable to extend their operations into the Gabu- and Fulbe-dominated interior.[18]

Meanwhile, despite the outbreak of periodic fighting, African-Portuguese exchanges continued to take place in the sixteenth and seventeenth centuries between coastal Papel, Mandjack, and Biaffada and Portuguese administrators in the fort towns of Cacheu, Bissau, Bafatá, Geba, Farim, and Ziguinchor. Thus, for example, in November 1687, the king of Bissau accepted the presence of missionaries among his people and even promised to defend the European fort at Bissau against any attacks by "foreigners."[19] In 1694, this Bissau king chose to have himself baptized into Christianity, and formal agreements were reached with the Portuguese regarding trade.[20] However, the king did not relieve the Portuguese of their obligatory resident tax payments.

A further indicator of peaceful exchanges was the fact that, in the sixteenth century, lançados near the Cacheu River participated in traditional oath-swearing exercises involving the sacrifice of chickens and dogs.[21] Here we may also note that three centuries later (during the 1840s), peace treaties between the Portuguese and the Mandjack of Churo and the Papel, Balanta, and Biaffada of Bissau required Portuguese participation in oath-swearing rituals involving sacrificial bloodshed and the drinking of sacred beverages.[22] Thus it is clear that during these centuries, moments of peace were established on terms essentially favorable to the neighboring African polities.

Toward Luso-African Warfare

Despite these Luso-African exchanges, it often occurred that Portuguese military administrators in the fort towns of Cacheu, Farim, Bissau, Bafatá, Geba, and Ziguinchor—out of ignorance or simply tiring of their dependency or in reaction to misunderstood trading deals—defied the requests of their African hosts and provoked armed assaults. Thus, two years following the Papel king's baptism, in August 1696, attacks by Mandinka on the settlement of Farim resulted in at least eleven European dead.[23] In that same month, the Portuguese allied with the Papel king of Intim and created a war party of approximately 170 (with two boats and seven canoes) that attacked and burned down a Mandinka village. Conflict in Farim did not end at this point. Mandjack (or Felupe) near Farim sent groups of fighting men to that *praça* to attack Europeans in November 1698.[24] Combat between European settlers in Farim and Felupe from Bayote occurred frequently during the early 1700s, with Felupe occasionally capturing one or more Europeans and charging the other Europeans a ransom for the captured parties' release or selling the captured Europeans into slavery.[25]

It is important to reemphasize that Portuguese settlers, lançados, and mestiços remained entirely vulnerable to the decisions of neighboring African kings and chiefly political rulers. Although the Europeans retained a semblance of self-rule within their protected settlements (protected by wooden palisades) and could occasionally mount a quick foray of soldiers, those soldiers usually were made to return hastily to their fort. During these early centuries, outside the palisade every aspect of life was controlled by neighboring peoples. Moreover, African kings, chiefs, and village elders dictated the terms of trade and other aspects of economic and social relations with mestiços and with Europeans.[26] Thus, for example, in 1721, António de Barros Bezerra, the *capitão-mor* (lit.: captain-major, but a term in colonial parlance referring to the head administrator) of Cacheu, observed that in Bissau, Portuguese were being "forced" to buy "inferior" slaves from the king of Bissau at "exorbitant prices."[27]

By the first decade of the eighteenth century, it was widely recognized in Lisbon that efforts to establish a fort (rather than a makeshift palisade) in Bissau were faring poorly due to continuous attacks by neighboring peoples, and in 1708 a royal decree ordered the dismantling of Bissau's partly built fort.[28] The king of Portugal had apparently decided that the cost in pesos and in soldiers' lives was not worth the sacrifice necessary to sustain the fort.[29] This concern over the potential for Luso-African violence later proved to be realistically grounded.

There is scant evidence of motivation on the part of neighboring peoples, but it is likely that local villagers' military efforts against the Portuguese were at least in part provoked by their opposition to Portuguese involvement in slave trading. Moreover, at least as early as 1733, Africans were able to obtain guns (mostly flintlocks or "dane guns") and ammunition through illegal trade and to use them against Portuguese soldiers.[30] This pattern of indigenous communities obtaining weapons through the underground arms trade and then using those weapons against the Portuguese would be repeated many times during the Lusophone presence in Guinea.

In the early 1730s, battles were fought between Europeans and indigenous communities in most of the Portuguese settlements. In 1730, local communities near the Portuguese settlement of Ziguinchor (along the Casamance River) organized military charges against the European settlement and were easily able to overpower the Portuguese soldiers there, seizing weaponry, gunpowder, and other items.[31] In 1733, in the fort town of Farim, battles between Mandinka — the people with whom Farim's Europeans typically traded — and Farim's European residents resulted in mortalities on both sides.[32] In July of the same year, again in Farim, an African military commander, Biofá, kidnapped some Christians (presumably whites) and sold them into slavery.[33]

In Cacheu, peaceful relations between Portuguese and the neighboring Balanta were reestablished in 1697, which allowed Portuguese residents there to feel relatively secure, but only if they remained within a few hundred meters of the praça. This peace with the Balanta enabled the local Portuguese commander to write to his superiors in Lisbon that the Portuguese now "dominate all the surrounding peoples."[34] He was undoubtedly all too aware of the absurdity of such a claim, but it helped to spur Lisbon's continued interest in Guinea. But in 1733 — the year of the attacks by Mandinka against Farim — fighters with guns challenged Portuguese soldiers in Cacheu "night and day."[35] A brief peace was reached between Europeans in Cacheu and neighboring Mandinka in May 1735.[36] However, sixteen years later, Africans traveling to the Cacheu praça in canoes were reported to have thieved virtually all movable European property, and widespread robbery of European traders traveling into the countryside was similarly reported.[37] The following year (1752) witnessed the "ruin" of the fortification of the praça of Cacheu, leaving the town "indefensible against the slightest invasion," Cacheu's administrator, Francisco Roque Souto-Major, wrote in a letter to the king of Portugal in March 1752.[38] In May 1763, residents of villages near Cacheu again organized war parties, successfully attacking the praça of Cacheu, where they were able to capture slaves who had been purchased by Cacheu residents.[39] And in 1774, most of the Portuguese soldiers at Cacheu were killed by attackers, who also kidnapped a number of Portuguese residents.[40] One observer noted at least four major wars between the European settlers in Cacheu and different groups of neighboring peoples in the 1770s.[41]

It is particularly noteworthy, considering Cacheu's importance as the primary Portuguese trading stronghold on the coast of Guinea, that soldiers were unable to protect the town during the seventeenth and eighteenth centuries.[42] During the century following the 1670 dispersal of Europeans from Cacheu, the Portuguese crown did not augment the number of soldiers in Guinea. The number of Portuguese troops assigned to guard Cacheu in 1670 was twenty, and it was again only twenty in 1777.[43] This helps to explain the continuing vulnerability of that praça. On 4 July of that year, these twenty soldiers were overwhelmed by large numbers of Balanta — between six and seven hundred of them. The attackers reached Cacheu's town square and broke into settlers' homes, looting the Europeans' property.[44] In 1780, Cacheu was attacked by fighters arriving in fifteen war canoes; the handful of soldiers there proved unable to repel them.[45] And in 1782, colonial soldiers again failed to defend the town of Cacheu against indigenous attackers.[46] In June of that year, the commander of Cacheu suggested that his problems reflected an inadequate number of European settlers; he also blamed the level of the soldiers' wages, which were not only paltry but arrived late: the resultant low morale had diminished the soldiers' willingness to fight.[47] In 1785 and again in 1786, the commander of Cacheu reported that Felupe from Bulor repeatedly attacked, robbed, and kidnapped the slaves of the residents of Cacheu.[48] In 1802, Cacheu was described as being under "continuous attack";[49] and in May and June 1803, fighting occurred several times.[50]

Bissau

In Bissau, Portuguese officials in the 1750s engaged in a classic colonial deceit vis-à-vis the local Papel king. On the one hand, they sought to appease him by acceding to his requests for what was in effect a residential tithe. In 1752, the Portuguese presented to King Palanca:

> One complete suit of clothes
> One other complete suit of clothes
> One long-trained gown made of green cloth
> Other clothes
> A feathered hat braided with gold
> Twelve shirts; twelve [illegible]
> Twenty-four white handkerchiefs with rose and blue stripes
> One long-bladed knife; two pairs of shoes.[51]

On the other hand, however, even as these gifts were being presented, Portuguese officials were preparing for war with this king; they wanted to reconstruct the fort of Bissau and for this purpose were requesting more shipments of weaponry and war materiel from Lisbon.[52] In January 1753, the government in Lisbon sent the man-of-war *Nossa Senhora da Estrela* to Bissau, along with three other vessels.[53] Responsibility for the fort's construction was contracted to the Lisbon-based Companhia Geral do Grão-Pará e Maranhão, which spent 147,690,763 reis on the fort. By May 1753, the fort-building effort provoked Papel attacks, however.[54] The Portuguese were again forced to accede to King Palanca's demands for a tithe and remained unable to proceed with the fort's reconstruction.[55] Twelve years later they tried again, having reached peace agreements with King Palanca. The Portuguese recognized that the project's success remained dependent on the decision making of this Papel king and they were careful to continue providing him with gifts and other payments. However, other communities not affiliated with the Papel, such as Balanta villagers, proceeded to attack the fort project. Officially named (in 1765) the fort of São-José-de-Bissau, the fort took a full decade to be (re)constructed; it was not completed until July 1775.[56] During the ten years of rebuilding, hundreds of Portuguese lives were lost, mostly to attacks by Papel and Balanta.[57]

In 1777, 190 soldiers at the fort were responsible for the protection of a civilian population of about 700 (the total included "blacks and Catholics").[58] However, the assignment to protect Bissau's residents proved more challenging than initially anticipated. On 2 June 1777, Bissau commander Inãçio Xavier Baião reported that his troops were decimated by attacking Balanta, who frequently robbed Europeans and mestiços in Bissau.[59] Also in the late 1770s, all members of the family of the governor of Bissau (excepting the governor himself) were killed by "natives," an incident that resulted in desperate pleas from Bissau to Lisbon for more assistance.[60] Clearly, the peace forged between the Portuguese and the Papel did not obtain regarding the Balanta, who presented a major threat to Bissau despite the construction of the new fort.

Other Praças

In the 1770s, the Portuguese praças not only at Cacheu and Bissau but also at Bafatá, Geba, Farim, and Ziguinchor all suffered military assaults, with 1775 being the bloodiest year.[61] In 1775 in the Farim area it was not uncommon for neighboring villagers to respond to perceived wrongs committed by settlers by kidnapping a Christianized black or a European, for whose return a ransom was demanded. The ransom was usually paid.[62] Hostilities between European settlers in Farim and neighboring Mandinka occurred throughout 1776,[63] and continued through 1779 and 1781.[64] In 1783, Farim sustained severe attacks during which Europeans were taken captive and their property was seized; these captives were sometimes sold into slavery.[65] The reaction of Farim's remaining settlers did little to reestablish peaceful relations. The residents "revenged" their losses by traveling in small boats to "two villages of the enemy, one Islamic and the other Mandinka," and setting the villages afire.[66] A letter dated 29 March 1784 states that when Governor António Sar de Araujo assumed his post, the European residents of the praça of Farim had been engaged for three years in all-out war with neighboring Mandinka, with the European residents of Cacheu providing assistance to the Farim residents when possible.[67] This war continued in 1785.[68] A 1791 note suggested that the European residents at the praça of Farim had waged war for six continuous years with neighboring Mandinka.[69]

The record regarding the other Portuguese praças during the closing decades of the eighteenth century and beginning of the nineteenth was hardly less violent. The Portuguese military commander of the praça of Geba fought a "continuing war" with its neighboring peoples in the 1770s.[70] In 1787, in the praça of Ziguinchor, five Portuguese soldiers were killed.[71] Violence recurred near the shores of the praça of Ziguinchor in October 1802, with one Portuguese soldier and several sailors being killed and a number of Portuguese citizens being captured.[72]

Meanwhile, in Bijagós, in 1792 islanders had canoed to Bolama, where they killed a number of British sailors.[73] In the nineteenth and twentieth centuries, Portuguese soldiers and their African allies would repeatedly suffer a similar fate on the Bijagós islands, as indicated in chapter 6.

The Dependency of Europeans on Gift Giving

The need for the Lusophone settlers of Bissau, Cacheu, and other praças to make regular payments to neighboring African kings merits a separate discussion. As early as the 1490s, Portuguese officials recognized that the African peoples along the western coast of Guinea could not easily be subdued by force and that therefore it made strategic sense to offer gifts to the kings. It was explicitly acknowledged that war prisoners who had been captured by African kings could be obtained "for a trinket."[74] These tributes to African kings came to be called *daxas (dattas; dachas)* and they were mandatory for any trader who wanted to settle, let alone engage in economic exchanges along the coastal waters or rivers of Guinea. In the larger settlements (fort towns), too, these daxas had to be paid, at least annually. In 1670, Lisbon specified the relatively extraordinary composition of the annual daxa being paid to the local African king: 40 quintals of cotton; 160 canisters of wine; and 569,000 reis.[75]

In the latter part of the seventeenth century, it was established in the official budgets of the towns of Bissau and Cacheu that funds would be allocated to them for distribution by Portuguese administrators as gifts to nearby kings.[76] Thus, by 1693 "daxas to the native kings" were listed as a budget item of the settlement of Cacheu; it totaled 300 reis, or 11.7 percent of Cacheu's budget.[77] By 1696, such daxas were similarly being listed for the presídio of Bissau: 260 reis, or 10.9 percent of Bissau's budget.[78] Thereafter, the king of Bissau was regularly accorded 260 Portuguese reis.[79] Historian António Carriera has calculated that government officials of Bissau and Cacheu in the early and mid-1690s paid out as daxas a total of 560 reis annually.[80] The daxa being paid to a single African king near Cacheu alone was more than 120 reis in 1707. In the first few decades of the eighteenth century, African kings, perceiving the wealth being accumulated by white traders, greatly increased the amounts they demanded as daxas. During the remainder of the 1700s, the kings of Bissau and of Cacheu were paid annual tributes totaling more than 1,000 reis, and probably more during the construction of the fort of Bissau.[81] The Portuguese continued to pay a daxa to the Papel king located at Nhacra (twenty kilometers from Bissau) through the 1850s. To travel outside Bissau, a tax of one-tenth of the value of what was being transported had to be paid to this Papel king's council—but the Portuguese were forbidden from traveling to Nhacra itself.[82]

Meanwhile, the political rulers of the Gabu kingdom imposed a tax on all settlers in their territories, including Europeans, and on any trader who ventured into a Gabu province.[83] Daxas were also paid to African kings and chiefs by foreign merchant vessels (i.e., those that were non-Portuguese: French, Dutch, English) plowing the waters of Guinea.[84] This tax was commonly paid with either brandy or tobacco.[85]

In 1815, the authorities of Cacheu failed to deliver their expected gifts: the result was large-scale attacks by neighboring peoples on the town; the resignation of the commander of the praça; and a general troop rebellion on the part of the soldiers. The Portuguese troops, out of control, repeatedly attacked and violated indigenous women living in the town, adding to the mayhem within the praça and helping to convince Portuguese authorities of the need to keep paying daxas.[86]

In 1842, at Cacheu, every time a ship docked at the port the authorities were required to pay two daxas—one each to two different local kings.[87] In 1848, the kings of Mata and Pecau, controlling the lands on which the settlement of Cacheu was located, demanded the following as daxa payments: two damask waistcoats, each braided with lace; two fancy hats with plumes; two cloth cloaks with braided sleeves; two pairs of fancy braided trousers with buckles; two pairs of shoes with buckles; two walking sticks; two pairs of long, white socks; two white shirts; two silk handkerchiefs; two chairs; brandy; gunpowder; and cloths from Cape Verde.[88] Eventually, monetary sums allocated for these daxa payments at Cacheu were incorporated into the annual budget of the Cape Verdean government.[89]

In a promulgation issued by the governor-general of Cape Verde dated 24 August 1843, it was stipulated that the daxas to the kings of the territories of Bissau, as well as of Fá and Ganjara, for the concessions granted by those kings to the Portuguese crown for the right to retain settlements there, totaled annually—in kind or in money—a value of 20,000 to 30,000 reis.[90] In 1850–51 the total paid by the officials of Bissau and Cacheu as daxas had risen to 137,000 reis.[91]

Portuguese administrators in Guinea, beginning with Honório Barreto in 1856, complained that the sums then being handed over in the daxas were too small to continue to have much impact on the local king. Thus, in 1856, the sum allocated in the colony's budget for these gifts was raised to 800,500 reis.[92] An official Portuguese government source indicated that the budget line allocated for the payment of tributes to African kings in Guinea rose again to 1,000,000 reis for FY1863/64.[93] It apparently remained at that level through the subsequent three decades.[94]

As already noted, such payments were also made by the other European settlements. Furthermore, in the 1840s, it was still the case, as it had been for decades, that a number of Felupe communities located along the Cacheu River imposed tolls on European merchants passing by.[95] Meanwhile, Biaffada living along the Geba River between the settlement of Geba and Bissau imposed unusually high tolls on European river-travel merchants, averaging about 4,000 reis per payment.[96]

Between the 1840s and the 1870s, about a hundred independent Portuguese, Cape Verdeans, mestiços, Frenchmen, Germans, and Englishmen established trading farms (*pontas* and *feitorias*) along one of Guinea's principal rivers—the Rio Grande de Bolama (also called Rio Grande de Guinala/de Bolola/de Buba), on which they principally grew groundnuts, but also palm products and foodstuffs.[97] For the right to do so—and to remain there—they were often required to pay daxas to local groups of African elders or to individual chiefs (particularly Fulbe and Biaffada). One merchant residing at Santa Cruz de Buba paid an annual tribute of 8,000 reis to the local Fulbe-Futa king, in addition to making gifts worth 4,000 reis to other Fulbe-Futa big men.[98] Those who refused to pay these tributes were occasionally beaten by the king's loyalists, and their property was confiscated. In 1879 it was still the case that European traders along the Rio Grande paid Fulbe-Futa chiefs annual gifts for the right to trade.[99] An 1885 report stated that trading-farm owner Joaquim L. Thiago "religiously" made monthly payments of 6,300 reis to indigenous chiefs.[100] In November 1899, Mandjack on the island of Pécis refused to allow the boat of German merchant Otto Schact to disembark because for six months he had not paid rent to the Pécis king.[101] In southern Catió region it was necessary for European travelers to pay a travel tax to Balanta groups in order to secure the right to pass through. This tax was being paid through the 1880s. Europeans also had to pay a similar tax to the Oinkas of Oio region as late as the 1920s.[102]

In general, until the Portuguese terror campaigns of the 1910s, and, as just noted, even later in isolated parts of Oio region, European merchants and settlers had to pay daxas to local African kings to secure their safety in most of Guinea. It was also necessary for Europeans to pay a toll in order to cross certain rivers and to pay a tax on whatever goods were being transported. Failure to pay invited the burning down of stores, farms, and warehouses, and the capture or enslavement of the owner-Europeans and of their African workers.[103] The Portuguese authorities were therefore determined, despite the Europeans' military misfortunes to date, to press on with their military efforts to reverse Portuguese dependency on local kings.

WARFARE CONTINUES: 1800–1890

The nineteenth century was marked by a rising frequency and intensity of indigenous warfare, provoked by multiple causes, among them disputes over political predominance.[104] During the first six decades of the century, these power struggles generally did not involve Europeans: the tiny European communities along the coastal rivers lacked the military capacity to interfere. At the same time, however, the momentum of antagonism between the increasingly frustrated Lusophone officials and the African communities that controlled the interior and the coast intensified through the 1860–90 period.

One factor that contributed to the ability of indigenous communities to counter Portuguese efforts was access to clandestine arms markets. The first recorded instance of such trade took place in 1856, when one observer reported the selling of weapons to Balanta by French merchants throughout the course of the Portuguese-Balanta wars of 1845–56.[105] Subsequently, during the early 1890s, the Papel chiefdoms of Safim, Bor, Antula, Enterramento, Intim, and Bandula were all fairly easily able to obtain weapons clandestinely from Cacheu, where arms were sold or bartered by Mandjack merchants.[106] In 1897, a lucrative and extensive gunrunning operation took place between the Gambia and Soninké villages in Oio province; there were multiple points of clandestine arms exchanges.[107] This ability to procure guns on hidden trading circuits helped enable rural fighters to assure that the Portuguese would not hold a weapons advantage in battle.

Cacheu

The seventeenth- and eighteenth-century wars in Cacheu did not diminish in the nineteenth century. Lusophone settlers in Cacheu fought indigenous groups of armed Baïote, Mandjack, and Felupe in 1808, 1814, 1815, throughout 1817 to 1836, and again in 1840 and 1844.[108] Typically, attacks by local groups against the town were provoked either by Portuguese reneging on trade agreements or as a consequence of the Cacheu commander's defiance of the local chiefs' authority.[109] The Cacheu fort rarely deployed more than seventy-five soldiers and several dozen grumetes, or Papel allies of the Portuguese, to defend the settlers, and more often than not these were inadequate to defeat the attackers. In 1840, a report by a Bissau-based lieutenant suggested that the military fortifications and buildings of Cacheu were in ruins and had been virtually abandoned.[110]

Cacheu's principal water source remained situated a nautical mile from the town's fort—as had been the case in the 1690s. This serious problem left the settlers constantly vulnerable.[111] Settlers desperately sought to kidnap nearby Mandjack villagers to hold as hostages when tensions were high, and when all else failed some settlers fled to more remote parts of Guinea.[112] Attacks frequently provoked mayhem within Cacheu: there were Portuguese troop rebellions and even desertions. The administrative chief—the capitão-mor—pleaded with officials in Praia, in Cape Verde, for auxiliary support, but his pleas were often unheeded.[113] After suffering a devastating defeat in 1861, a Portuguese officer in Cacheu wrote, in desperation, to a French officer in Senegal requesting French assistance.[114] In August 1862, the governor-general of Cape Verde mentioned, in correspondence, an ongoing war between the townspeople of Cacheu and the Biaffada of Badôra.[115] In 1866, Portuguese residents of Cacheu wrote that the town was now completely surrounded by "enemies."[116]

On 24 January 1871, the governor of Guinea, Alvaro Telles Caldeira, and his escort were assassinated in Cacheu by grumetes.[117] The governor of Cape Verde, Caetano Alexandre de Almeida e Albuquerque, marshaled a revenge expeditionary force in order to punish Mandjack villagers, whom the governor believed to be associated with the assassins.[118] Villages were bombarded with rifle fire by the expedition, but fourteen (of two hundred) soldiers were killed or wounded, which was considered enormously humiliating by the Portuguese.[119] Apparently this experience had an intimidating impact on the governor, for he and his men remained at Cacheu for the next several weeks, electing not to pursue and confront the Mandjack fighters. The Mandjack of Caió proceeded to attack and pillage European vessels through the 1870s and early 1880s.[120]

Like the rest of the colonial powers, the Portuguese were at that time in the process of obtaining recently invented rapid-fire weapons, which would significantly bolster their military potency. Rapid-fire weaponry was first employed in Guinea in June 1884; as Portuguese-Mandjack tensions rose in Cacheu, Governor of Guinea (as of 1881) Pedro Inaçio de Gouveia sent a military expedition of 220 soldiers to the area sporting newly obtained Snyder guns. These soldiers fared successfully in battle against some two thousand Mandjack from the villages of Cacanda, Pecau, Capo, Bijope, Bianga, and Matta-de-Cacheu. The colonialists escaped with only two killed and a dozen wounded, in contrast to heavy losses for the Mandjack.[121] However, events after 1890 would make clear that even the use of machine guns would not be sufficient to tip the balance of Luso-African warfare in favor of the Portuguese.

Bissau

In Bissau, the peace forged between the Portuguese and the Papel king, which endured from the 1760s through the 1780s, had broken down by the early 1790s,[122] leading to a state of warfare with Portuguese officials for much of the next 120 years. Throughout 1795 and 1796, the European settlement at Bissau engaged in military confrontations with what one observer at the time called "the Papel nation";[123] another wrote of "the great forces of the enemy."[124] An 1804 report makes clear that the Portuguese populace in Bissau was "almost always in the throes of war with the indigenous people of this land."[125]

Violence in Bissau recurred in April 1805, when grumetes killed a number of Mandjack who had been working as sailors and shipworkers for the Portuguese.[126] On 9 January 1809, Papel attacked and killed a soldier patrolling the fort of Bissau; they killed another soldier on 20 January and yet another in March.[127]

A Bissau military officer, Duque Collaio da Veiga Vidal, wrote that five or six indigenous kings held power in the 1820s and 1830s in the vicinity of Bissau,[128] and that they were all quite "insolent" and "insulting" to the Portuguese.[129] The most important of these was the king of Intim, who was the most "rebellious" of the Papel kings. Vidal makes clear that the governor of Guinea lacked the military force to react against the king of Intim. The consequence for Bissau was "anarchy."[130] Within Bissau, officials did not possess enforceable political or military authority. In the 1840s, most of Bissau's residents (about two thousand at that time) were actually grumetes or Papel, none of whom were particularly enamored of the Portuguese, Cape Verdeans, or mestiços. (Most of Bissau's political and business elite were by then mestiço, as was the case in the other Portuguese settlements.)[131] Authority was so lacking that, commonly, groups of armed Papel would walk around—and even enter inside—the residences of the Portuguese, Cape Verdeans, and elite mestiços, taking what they pleased.

In mid-1844, the Portuguese tried to construct a large wall, in effect to extend the fort further around the central residential area. Papel kings opposed this, and fighting broke out numerous times throughout late 1844 between Papel and the residents/merchants of Bissau.[132] By this point, the Papel kingdoms of Bissau, Bandim, Intim, Antula, Cúmere, Chafi, Bijimita, Tor, Biombo, Prabis, and Cuntum had united specifically in order to fight against the Portuguese within the fort of Bissau.[133] Conflict ensued throughout the construction period, with the wall finally being completed the third week of December. A peace pact was concluded with the kings of Bandim, Intim, and Antula on 19 December 1844. However, the killing of a slave belonging to João de Barros, a merchant, on 6 January 1845 led to heightened Papel-Portuguese and grumete-Portuguese tensions, and when Portuguese sailors destroyed some small boats belonging to grumetes who had fought the Portuguese in Bissau but then fled to Bandim, the incident led to fighting and to the retreat of the Portuguese sailors.[134] Meanwhile, on 1 August 1845, grumetes and their Papel allies began making preparations to blockade Bissau; despite the arrival of a warship from Cape Verde on 7 August, the grumetes and Papel effectively surrounded and besieged the town, preventing Bissau's 123 soldiers from leaving. The situation was not resolved until February 1846, when the governor of Bissau, Joaquim de Azevedo Alpoim, made a large payment to the king of Bandim, known to the Portuguese as Jery Napenac da Roca.[135]

Meanwhile, the Papel of Bissau formed military alliances with the Mandjack chieftainships of Jeta and Pecixe (located on the islands known by the same names) to augment their ability to confront the Portuguese.[136] This helped to fortify indigenous Papel fighting groups, especially through the 1890s and early 1900s, in battles that usually ended favorably for the Papel.

Nhacra

A peace pact was concluded with the Balanta of Nhacra on 27 June 1873,[137] but it would not be long before they would recommence their attacks on European merchant vessels traveling along the Rio Impernal (the river separating the island of Bissau from the mainland). It was not uncommon for the Balanta to mass five thousand fighters when necessary, including Balanta from Nhacra, Cuméré, and Oco, to repel colonial assaults.[138]

Here we may note that, according to Walter Hawthorne, the Balanta had developed a highly refined method of mobilizing large numbers of combatants from different villages, coordinating their attacks through the use of specialized drums, referred to as "the Balanta telephone."[139] Young men belonging to specific age-grade groupings were designated with the responsibility of organizing multi-village fighting forces through the use of these drums. This technique was developed and used by the Balanta as least as early as the 1500s. Used to raise armies during the period of the slave trade, it would be utilized repeatedly by the Balanta in defending against colonial attacks throughout the nineteenth century and during violent epochs of the twentieth century.

It may also be pointed out that Balanta armies were also commonly provided with additional support from their allies, the Papel of Antula.[140] This helped to assure the Balanta of Nhacra that they would be able to repel subsequent Portuguese attacks.[141]

Casamance

Portuguese and Cape Verdeans had settled in Ziguinchor and other parts of Casamance region in the seventeenth and eighteenth centuries. Hostilities emerged in the early and mid-1800s, culminating in a war between Balanta and the Portuguese beginning in 1845 and lasting until at least March 1856.[142] The Portuguese fared poorly, with Europeans occasionally being captured and enslaved by Balanta. Ziguinchor would remain highly vulnerable to attack until after the transfer of Casamance region from Portuguese to French control in 1886.

Bijagós

In 1856, the governor of Guinea, Honório Barreto, requested from the Portuguese Ministry of Overseas Colonies a special line in the budget of Cape Verde/Guinea for the purpose of educating the sons of the kings of the Bijagós islands of Canhabac and Orango.[143] Barreto was clearly seeking to curry favor with those kings. However, subsequent events made clear that this would have little impact and that Bijagós-Portuguese relations would only degenerate. Indeed, the Bijagós continued to attack and pilfer from European vessels.[144] The Portuguese proved unable to respond effectively to the military challenge presented by the Bijagós fighters. And they were often humiliated — in one instance, a Portuguese trade ship was enticed to visit the island, but as it arrived, the Bijagós took possession of it.[145]

Jufunco/Bolôr

The tiny settlement of Bolôr on the Cacheu River remained, in 1878, entirely at the mercy of neighboring Felupe kings, with whom, wisely, the residents had established amicable relations.[146] However, a dispute emerged (over access to trade routes) between the Felupe of Bolôr (perceived by other Felupe to be associated with the Portuguese) and the Felupe of Jufunco, Ossor, and Igim. On 21 December 1878, Felupe from Jufunco attacked and burned down much of Bolôr, including the European section.[147] In response, the governor of Guinea, António José Cabral Vieira, sent to Bolôr in December 1878 a combined force of grumetes and regular soldiers.[148] This force was attacked by fighters from Jufunco immediately upon disembarking on the shores of the Cacheu River; panic-stricken soldiers swam back to the schooner, but it became mired in the sand. A misfired (and poorly mounted) cannon fell overboard, and Jufunco's fighters ended up boarding the ship and killing all but four soldiers and the governor (who had escaped by rowboat).[149]

—▬▬—

Several themes emerge from this discussion of Luso-African political relations and warfare. First, it should be stressed that many Portuguese, particularly in the early centuries, engaged in mutually beneficial trade and social relations with local communities along the rivers, with Luso-African intermarriages being common. Second, during most of the 1446–1890 period, solitary Portuguese settlers as well as those who were concentrated in the towns remained largely at the mercy of neighboring African leaderships and needed to make regular payments — daxas — to local kings to assure their own safety. Efforts to evade those payments often resulted in violent confrontations. The small number of Lusophone soldiers at the disposal of the governor of Guinea were no match for the thousands of fighters who could be mobilized by local communities when necessary.

It is likely that most African political leaders in Guinea did not regard the Portuguese, nestled in their mini-settlements, as a major threat to their territorial sovereignty. By the late nineteenth century, most rural communities had developed enormously powerful fighting forces and were well-experienced in the art of war, as exemplified by the Balantas' effective use of war drums to mobilize large-scale forces. This praetorian capacity had been fine-tuned over centuries and remained embedded in the sociological firmament of rural Guinea-Bissau, bolstering the self-confidence of combatants from one epoch to the next and assuring them virtually total self-rule through the nineteenth century.

Third, it is important to note that some colonial towns came to be openly controlled, for months or years at a time, by armed Africans loyal to their indigenous king. Moreover, it was not uncommon for white settlers to be captured and held for a ransom or even sold into slavery. This particularly denigrating aspect of European-African relations in Guinea-Bissau would help to dramatize the lack of effective colonial authority even within (much less outside of) the settlements. Another source of humiliation for the Portuguese was the occasional cry for help sent by besieged Portuguese officers in Cacheu to the French stationed on Gorée or in Sedho. The traditional bitter jealously of the Portuguese regarding the French military meant that the situation had to have been truly desperate for such a plea to have been sent out.

Fourth, we may call attention to the ambiguous role of the grumetes. Portuguese, Cape Verdean, and mestiço settlers relied on them not only as workers but also as auxiliary soldiers. However, their loyalty could not always be counted on, and if they perceived neighboring African villagers to have been wronged by the Portuguese, they often chose to ally with those villagers. In fact, for this reason, in 1878 the governor-general of Cape Verde, emphasizing his distrust of indigenous African soldiers, sought to recruit soldiers from other Portuguese overseas colonies to serve in Guinea.[150]

Fifth, fighting initiated by the Portuguese commonly provoked African kings, chiefs, and ruling elders from different ethnic groups into military alliances. The Balanta of Nhacra formed multiple military alliances with the Papel of Antula. A variety of Papel groups joined with the Mandjack of Jeta and Pecixe to engage the Portuguese in battle. Most historians have tended to downplay such alliances,[151] but I regard them as crucial elements of indigenous politics in precolonial Guinea-Bissau, providing the basis for effective multiethnic resistance repeatedly in the 1890–1909 period. These alliances would serve to enhance the potency of rural civil society during colonial rule.

Finally, there was the extent to which the military victories of indigenous fighters, combined with Portuguese daxa payments, provided rural African communities with a sense of their own political and military strength. This point bears particular emphasis. Their superior power reinforced these communities' faith in their political and social frameworks, while also concretely allowing for change to occur largely along patterns of African intercommunity and intergroup relations, rather than becoming dependent on or subservient to European authority. This is made especially clear in chapters 3 and 4.

CHAPTER 3

African Kingdoms at War, Changing Fulbe Alliances, and Portuguese Aggression, 1840s–1910

DESPITE THE MOUNTING ANTAGONISMS between Portuguese and indigenous forces during the course of the nineteenth century, most of the resultant conflicts were confined to the immediate vicinity of the coastal and riverine port towns. The large, powerful kingdoms that dominated the interior remained almost wholly unaffected by Lusophone politico-military machinations until virtually the last decade of the nineteenth century. Until that time, there were few meaningful political contacts or military conflicts between "Portuguese" Guinea and most of the large political systems that characterized the greater portion of the Guinean countryside.

Most prominent among the kingdoms of the interior were the Gabu empire, initially founded in the fourteenth century, and the Fulbe state of Fuladu, which did not arise until the mid-nineteenth century.[1] Internal conflicts weakened Gabu through the course of the nineteenth century, followed by massive wars between Gabu and Fuladu. They are especially significant because the way in which these conflicts evolved helped to reinforce the multiethnic political culture in rural

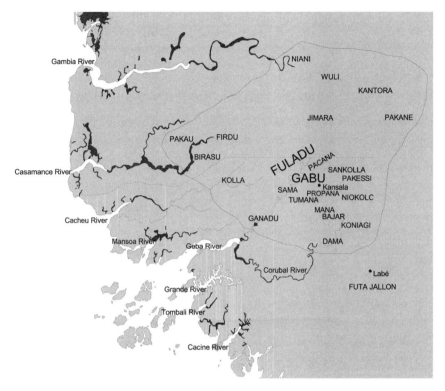

MAP 3 PRECOLONIAL GABU AND FULADU

Approximate areas of precolonial states of Gabu (15th c. to 1867) and Fuladu (1867–1903) and major affiliated provinces. Gabu included most of what became Fuladu. After Gabu's fall, Fuladu extended southward to absorb parts of former Gabu. Dotted line indicates location of colonial-era border that was later established between Senegal and Guinea-Bissau.

Sources: Derived from sketches in Mamadou Mané, "Contribution à l'histoire du Kaabu," *Bulletin de l'Institut Fondamental d'Afrique Noire* 40, no. 1 (1978): 105; and descriptions in Sékéné Mody Cissoko, "Introduction à l'histoire des Mandingues de l'Ouest," *Ethiopiques* 28, special issue (1981): 73–91. Compiled by the author.

Guinea-Bissau, while also helping to entrench social memories of praetorian success. At the same time, the dynamics of the eventual conclusion of these conflicts proved crucial in determining the strategies of conquest and of state building that the Portuguese would pursue in the twentieth century.

Below, I make clear that as federated provinces grew increasingly rebellious in the 1850s and 1860s, the Gabu empire weakened internally until finally the Fulbe invasion of Futa Jallon precipitated the downfall of Gabu in 1867.[2] The collapse of Gabu was followed by the construction of the Fulbe empire of

Fuladu, but internal discord from the 1860s to the 1890s assured that Fuladu would remain perpetually unstable and would not be able to consolidate its power.[3] During this period, the Fulbe-djiábê (Fulbe slaves, called Captive or Black Fula by the Portuguese) would carry out increasingly successful rebellions against their Fulbe-ribê (Fula Forro) masters and against the Fulbe-Futa and Fulbe-Toro allies of the Fulbe-ribê.[4]

In order to construct the new Fuladu empire, various Fulbe groups — mostly Fulbe-djiábê but also including new Fulbe-ribê allies — carried out attacks against land areas controlled by Mandinka and Biaffada chiefs previously associated with Gabu.[5] These dynamics set in motion a half-century of warfare in Guinea-Bissau (from northern Gabu to southern Forria) between 1849 and 1900,[6] and hundreds of smaller battles.[7] They were marked by intraethnic alliance making among Fulbe-djiábê communities and by the formation of pragmatic, multiethnic military fronts involving Fulbe, Mandinka, and Biaffada.

The latter portion of this chapter makes clear that during the closing stages of the nineteenth century, the Portuguese finally did begin to wield a growing impact on these internal wars. They provided military assistance to Fulbe chiefs in a concerted effort to weaken Fuladu,[8] but Fulbe power struggles continued independently of Lusophone eyes. It is essential to emphasize that throughout the greater portion of the nineteenth century, great wars unfolded in Guinea-Bissau's interior that took place outside the purview of the Europeans,[9] and that those wars were characterized, more than has been previously recognized, by multiethnic alliances and broad political collaboration.

Societal Context: The Wars of Gabu, 1849–1883

During the course of the first half of the nineteenth century, the decentralized nature of Gabu's intergovernmental relations — the fact that most of its provinces were ruled indirectly — facilitated the growing independence of the provincial rulers.[10] For a variety of reasons, the provinces began to insist on retaining most or all of their collected taxes and proved increasingly reluctant to send large numbers of troops to the Mansa Ba's general army,[11] accentuating the decline of the empire's military potency.[12]

Significantly contributing to this decline was the curtailment of the Atlantic slave trade, which reduced the income and attendant political benefits to Gabu's centralized political leadership.[13] The diminution of the externally oriented slave trade, robbing the kingship of a key source of wealth creation, strengthened the independent power of the *ñaanco* (provincial aristocratic lead-ers),[14] while the ñaanco expanded the diversity of their exchanges with djula (long-distance traders).[15] The djula also took advantage of Gabu's weakened power to strengthen their trade links to peoples theretofore subjugated to de-pendency on the Gabu kingdom; in doing so, they helped to provide those peoples with the economic means to rebel against Gabu's continuing control.

As of the mid-1840s, the center of the Gabu kingdom, represented by the provinces of Sama, Jimara, and Pacana, was unable to enforce its power upon the outer provinces.[16] Within some provinces, this new independence led to internal wars between those favoring and those opposed to continuing links to Gabu.[17] These conflicts widened when the Gabu province of Jimara obtained the military support of the powerful Fulbe kingdom of Futa Jallon (located in the mountains of the present-day Republic of Guinea) to assist Jimara in its war with the Gabu province of Wuropana.[18] Meanwhile, during the early 1850s (probably in 1850), the Gabu provinces of Sama and Pacana became engaged in a major war after Sama refused to accept Pacana's turn in the rotational swing of kingly succes-sion.[19] This war concluded in Pacana's favor, allowing its designated leader, Janke Wali Saane, to assume formal control, as king, of all of Gabu.

The defeated Mandinka of Sama sought revenge by allying with the Fulbe kingdom of Futa Jallon. Furthermore, the head of Sama province, Nkouy Maane, converted to Islam, changing his name to Mfamara Maane, in reflection of a grad-ual trend toward Islamic conversion on the part of some Mandinka aristocrats— and perhaps also to gain a strategic alliance with Fulbe Islamic leaders, particularly those ruling Futa Jallon.[20] With the number of Gabu provinces seeking alliance with Futa Jallon gradually mounting with each passing decade, reflecting grow-ing intra-Gabu schisms, it would not be long before Futa Jallon's chief strategists would decide to mount a full frontal assault on the heart of the now-weakened Gabu kingdom.[21]

One of Futa Jallon's chief incentives was religious: the determination to subdue a powerful, largely pagan empire and to convert its leaders and citizens to Islam.[22] Another factor was economic: the leaders of Futa Jallon were inter-ested in securing access to markets located at Bissau, Boke, and elsewhere along the coast, and Gabu lay between those markets and Futa Jallon.[23] The Sene-galese historian Thierno Diallo places particular emphasis on the fact that this was not so much an ethnic war—especially as the number of Mandinka allies of Fulbe-dominated Futa Jallon was growing—as a religious effort at Islamic conversion.[24] Later, when the Fulbe-djiábê rose in rebellion against Gabu's Mandinka rulers and asked for help from their ethnic Fulbe brethren in the

Futa Jallon mountains, more often than not the leaders of Futa Jallon failed to support these Fulbe-djiâbê rebels. Indeed, Futa Jallon displayed an attitude of disdain toward Fulbe-djiâbê slaves and former slaves, and this was a major reason why the Fulbe-djiâbê would have such difficulty in constructing a kingdom after Gabu collapsed.

Futa Jallon's rulers preferred to ally with those Mandinka kings who had converted to Islam. Therefore, the notion of an intraethnic alliance between Fulbe-djiâbê and royal Fulbe from Futa Jallon as a cause or even a significant factor in Futa Jallon's decision to attack Gabu must be discarded. These wars were not so much ethnic in origin as reflective of more potent religious and economic factors, which then generated multiethnic alliances between various groups of Fulbe and Mandinka.

War between the two great empires, Gabu and Futa Jallon, began in earnest in 1843, with Futa Jallon sending against Gabu's tatas, or military forts, at least one major military expedition in each of the years 1843, 1851, 1854, 1858, 1860, 1863, 1864, 1866, 1867, 1868, 1872, 1876, and 1878.[25] As a result of the conversion of a number of Gabu's provincial ñaanco to Islam, troops from Futa Jallon would be able to construct a military corridor of access to Gabu's northwestern border by the late 1840s.[26] By the midpoint of the nineteenth century, Futa Jallon had nearly encircled the Gabu heartland, but Gabu's best armies had not yet been seriously challenged.[27]

In 1854, with the concordance of Almaami Umaru Sorya, the king of Futa Jallon, soldiers under the command of Alfa Ibrahima Maúdo (head of Labé province in Futa Jallon) traveled to Ñampay, a Gabu stronghold they defeated after three days of combat.[28] Between 1858 and 1861, the Fulbe sought and obtained the alliance of Bakar Sado (Bubakar Saada), a non-Fulbe Gambian strongman,[29] and their combined forces attacked and subdued the Gabu province of Mana.[30]

In 1863, Alfa Ibrahima conducted a major military offensive and succeeded in capturing key centers of Gabu resistance, including Pirada and Tabajan.[31] Subsequently, many Fulbe-djiâbê appealed to the king of Futa Jallon to mount an all-out attack to definitively conquer Gabu, and the decision was made to seek to do so. All nine *diwan,* or provinces, of Futa Jallon were mobilized.[32] The attack force totaled approximately thirty-two thousand soldiers, including twelve thousand cavalrymen.[33] The king of Gabu at the time, Janke Wali Saane, aware of the imminent attack, assembled a defense force at his fort in Kansala that included soldiers from throughout the remainder of the Gabu empire (essentially the provinces of Pacana, Jimara, Tumana, Kantora, and Sankolla). An additional twenty-seven provinces retained formal links to the Gabu empire but did not provide troops. The total number of Gabu fighters was approximately between two and five thousand—five times fewer than the number of their Futa Jallon attackers and, compared with the giant armies mobilized by Gabu in previous decades, a very small force.[34]

Janke Wali's son Tura Saane knew that Gabu's resistance was futile, and he urged his father to order the political and military leadership of Gabu, particularly the ñaanco, to flee. When Wali refused to do so, Tura Saane fled on his own.[35] Meanwhile, Fulbe forces encircled Kansala and imposed a month-long siege. Collectors of oral sources vary as to the precise date of the military confrontation:[36] 1865, according to Mané and Cissoko; 1867, according to Cissé,[37] with Bowman and Lopes being partial to the 1867 date.[38]

As the fighting began, Gabu's defenders repulsed the first wave of assaults so effectively that Futa Jallon's forces, despite their superior numbers, became demoralized; but eventually the lack of food and munitions within Kansala took its toll. Hit-and-run assault waves by the Futa Jallon armies proved increasingly successful, and a final, massive assault overwhelmed the Gabu fighters. As this occurred, King Janke Wali and his chief advisers and leading ñaanco collectively committed suicide, destroying the entire fort of Kansala with explosives.[39] This battle is known in the Mandinka language as Turu-Bâ, meaning "the end of the seed" (derived from *turô*, seed, and *ban*, finished)[40]—that is to say, the end of Gabu as a kingdom.[41] At least two thousand Gabu soldiers and as many as eight thousand Fulbe lost their lives on that day.

For the following decade, small-scale conflicts occurred between the appointees of Futa Jallon and relatively isolated tatas in several former Gabu provinces. However, eventually these remnants of the Gabu kingdom would be dominated by chiefs who had forged alliances with Futa Jallon.

THE ORIGINS OF FULADU: REBELLION OF THE SETTLED FULBE-DJIÁBÈ

The demise of Gabu facilitated the emergence of the second principal war in the interior of Guinea-Bissau during the nineteenth century—that between the Fulbe-ribê and Fulbe-djiábê.[42] This conflict would eventually result in the establishment of the predominantly Fulbe-djiábê state of Fuladu. According to Joye Bowman, it lasted from 1867 to 1903.[43] During those decades, not only did the former slaves of the Fulbe-ribê—the Fulbe-djiábê—establish the new kingdom of Fuladu, but the larger, more powerful empire of Futa Jallon also continued to expand its political power.[44] Thus, in the 1870s and 1880s, at the height of Fuladu, a chain of Fulbe-controlled provinces, beginning in the Futa Jallon mountains, extended through much of central Guinea-Bissau and included the former Gabu provinces.[45]

The Fulbe-djiábê who created Fuladu had done so in order to create a power base against their former Mandinka ruling elites (who, despite the Kansala debacle, remained capable of raising armies), but without becoming dependent on the Fulbe-ribê nobility of Futa Jallon. The fact that the former Gabu provinces were now ruled only indirectly by Futa Jallon contributed to the ability of Fulbe-djiábê fighters to form an independent polity. But they still had to struggle militarily to do so—in some areas against their former Fulbe-ribê overlords as well as against Biaffada leaders who had allied with Fulbe-ribê—leading to widespread warfare throughout the 1870s and 1880s.[46] The large and growing informal trading networks dominated by djula traders greatly benefited the Fulbe-djiábê rebels, as they now were able to procure previously unobtainable weaponry (guns and gunpowder).[47]

The most powerful Fulbe-djiábê leader was Alfa Molo, a Bambara who fitted easily into Fulbe-djiábê society and who used impressive diplomatic skills to craft an alliance between Fulbe-djiábê and a small but growing number of Fulbe-ribê who sensed the potential for creating a new political order.[48] In addition, Molo reached out to potential allies among the Mandinka, and succeeded in securing the support of the influential chiefs Nfali Dahaba of Sumakunda and Jali Bamba Suso.[49] Molo also struck an agreement of mutual support with Tafsiru Bara, a Toucouleur marabout who provided Molo with a large company of fighters.[50] On the basis of this multiethnic political network, Molo felt confident to commence independent military operations.

First, however, Molo sought to appease Alfa Ibrahima, king of Futa Jallon, by personally making a pilgrimage to Timbo (a holy center in Futa Jallon) and converting to Islam. Ibrahima then appointed Molo as ruler of the province of Firdu, but Molo, once in place in Firdu, declared "the existence of the state of Fuladu"[51]—in effect launching the founding of his own mini-kingdom in Guinea-Bissau. Molo would then spearhead a major expansion of rebellious uprisings in former Gabu provinces where ñaanco retained some power, including Jimara, Tumana, and Kantora.[52] By 1870, Molo's combined forces of Fulbe-djiábê, Fulbe-ribê, Mandinka, Toucouleur, and Bambara had overseen military victories over Mandinka and Biaffada opponents at Jimara, Pacana, Suna, and Balmadu,[53] and by 1873 Molo's armies were in control of most areas between Firdu and the Rio Geba.[54]

THE FULBE STATES OF FORMER GABU

Despite these victories by the now-expanding state of Fuladu, some Fulbe-ribê continued to wield power over parts of the interior. Molo's military successes, however, inspired many Fulbe-djiábê who still labored as slaves to rebel and cast their arms with Fuladu.[55] In a sense then, the process of Fuladu state building was intimately linked to Fulbe-djiábê slave liberation, while at the same time generating a broader set of alliances spanning diverse identities and communities.

By 1878, Molo's forces had successfully seized control of most of the provinces of former Gabu and were able to consolidate their new Fuladu empire.[56] At this stage, Molo's de facto autonomy from Futa Jallon could no longer be tolerated by Alfa Ibrahima, who coveted the substantial natural resources and riverine access to trading ports now controlled by Fuladu.[57] Meanwhile, Molo had opened up the Fuladu empire to British traders as a means of obtaining commercial independence from Futa Jallon.

Alfa Molo did not live to see his state-building goals through to full fruition; in 1881, ill and aged, he died in what is today the village of Dandu, Guinea-Bissau.[58] At that point, Fuladu stretched from the former Gabu province of Firdu in southern Senegal through to Forria (in what is today central Guinea-Bissau).[59] Neither Alfa's son Musa Molo nor other allies and leaders of the Fulbe-djiábê would be able to reproduce Alfa's success in controlling this relatively large area, and Fuladu would not achieve full independence from Futa Jallon.[60] An internal conflict over leadership succession was eventually resolved in favor of Futa Jallon.[61] By November 1883, Musa Molo felt it necessary to sign a protectorate treaty with France, which, in effect, helped to enhance Molo's power through the remainder of the 1880s.[62]

Adding further complexity to this military drama were the Biaffada chiefs (as noted above, the Biaffada became increasingly involved in battles with Fuladu to protect themselves against Molo's ambitious state-building efforts).[63] Biaffada rulers quickly lost dominion over their lands in Forria, but they retained strongholds alongside the Rio Grande and the Rio Corubal; however, in the mid-1870s, a series of battles with troops from Futa Jallon pushed the Biaffada out of those sites as well.[64] In January and February 1884, Musa Molo took advantage of the remaining power gap in erstwhile Biaffada areas, sweeping through the banks of the Rio Grande with three thousand horsemen and riflemen and attacking remaining pockets of Biaffada resistance; in retreat, Biaffada attacked supporters of Fuladu as well as Portuguese trading farms along the Rio Grande. The resultant mayhem devastated Portuguese riverine trade through the 1880s; cattle seized from trading farms were exchanged for gunpowder through informal-sector djula traders, which further fueled the fighting capacity of Biaffada and of Fulbe-ribê groups opposed to Fuladu.[65]

Nonetheless, battle successes by Musa Molo throughout the eastern regions of Guinea-Bissau produced an expansion of Fuladu into most of former Gabu (including Sankolla and Ganadu), part of Casamance region, and the southern Gambia.[66] Molo was provided with sharpshooters and arms by the French, who viewed him (for the moment) as their ally[67]—although, eventually, Molo's growing alliance with the French would fatally compromise Fuladu's autonomy. Meanwhile, the Portuguese would remain unable to assert political control over the eastern and northern land areas that fell within Fuladu's rubric until well after the turn of the twentieth century.

PORTUGUESE AGGRESSION AND CHANGING FULBE ALLIANCES, 1879–1910

From 1830 to 1879, the Portuguese trading town of Buba had enjoyed a period of modest expansion, reflecting the impact of the groundnut-based trading farms (feitorias; pontas) along the Rio Grande. There were about thirty pontas in the 1840s, expanding to approximately seventy or eighty pontas by the 1870s.[68] These trading farms had been constructed by Europeans and Cape Verdeans, who planted groundnuts for export as well as a variety of food crops. However, by the late 1870s to early 1880s, the wars involving allies and enemies of Fuladu had begun to disrupt this groundnut production significantly. In part, the farms were attacked because they harbored workers perceived to be associated with an enemy chief. By 1881–82, pillaging of the trading caravans traveling alongside the Rio Grande in the Forria resulted in the economic decline of Buba as a trading town.[69]

Correspondence from Portuguese in Bolama attests that the wars of the interior continually threatened the safety of European traders and residents, with the colonial authorities being powerless to provide protection.[70] European merchants asked the Portuguese royal house to send adequate military forces so that they might continue to engage in "commerce, agriculture, and coastal trading" in Guinea.[71] The merchants and farmers complained of having their possessions stolen and their farms torched. Colonial commanders were determined to provide such assistance, not only to protect export-oriented riverine trade, but also for broader political reasons. In 1879, Guinea became administratively disassociated from Cape Verde and was accorded separate status as a colonial province of Portugal.[72] Guinea's newly achieved administrative status proved a significant boost to the political ambitions of Agostinho Coelho, the governor of Guinea, and, more generally, those of Portugal and those of the bureaucratic-military staff in the coastal and riverine port towns of Guinea.[73] Liberated from their administrative dependency on Cape Verde and provided with a minimal — but psychologically significant — amount of additional financial and military aid from Lisbon, Guinea's tiny staff of military-administrative appointees were especially determined to push forward with their quest for political sovereignty, with a view to achieving de facto control over the interior and the coast.[74]

But the most the colonial army could do at this point was to try to forge agreements with potentially collaborative chiefs and, where possible, to provide them with logistical support. Thus, the Portuguese began to offer protection in the town of Buba to pro-Fuladu Fulbe-djiábê fighters, allowing a number of them to settle there and to use Buba as a base for attacks against their anti-Fuladu Fulbe-ribê and Biaffada enemies.[75] This policy, initiated by Guinea's first post-separation governor, Coelho,[76] provoked counterattacks by a number of Fulbe-ribê and Biaffada forces against Fulbe-djiábê villages, as well as against Lusophone trading farms.[77]

In February 1880, Coelho signed a friendship treaty with Alfa Molo, although Molo did not demonstrate, in word or deed, any deference to the Portuguese.[78] This provoked more counterattacks by Fulbe-ribê and Biaffada against Fulbe-djiábê villages and against Portuguese trading farms. Pillaging of the trading farms along the Rio Grande now occurred with impunity, helping to cause the destruction of the groundnut trade on that river.[79]

Most treaties that had been signed were ignored by virtually all signatories.[80] The treaties could not be enforced by the Portuguese because, despite the bolstering of their troops (now numbering 150 in Buba), they lacked the firepower to patrol the countryside without suffering serious loss of life. Still, they were beginning to engage in occasional hit-and-run attacks on targeted villages. On 17 March 1881, a military unit of eighty soldiers attacked and burned down a Fulbe-ribê village. This success produced a peace treaty signed by Governor Coelho and major Fulbe-ribê powerholders in Forria on 3 July 1881 in Bolama. On the Fulbe-ribê side were Chiefs Alfa Ahmadu Sampenda, Alfa Délo, Bakar Quidali, and Mamadu Paté Bolola. A representative of Chief Alfa Ibrahima of Futa Jallon also signed.[81]

However, this treaty, called "Peace Treaty with the Fula and Forro Kings, the Fulbe-Futa of the Forriá and of Futa djalón," contained certain points that in fact underlined the superior power of the Fulbe chiefs. Historian António Carreira points out that the fifth clause of the treaty stipulated that the Fulbe chiefs must alert the Portuguese authorities whenever any of their fighters enter "the territory of Buba" in order to specify the objectives of those fighters.[82] Carreira interprets this clause as signifying de facto recognition by the Portuguese authorities of the sovereignty of the Fulbe over the entire area of Forria. By suggesting that the Fulbe should alert the authorities whenever they entered Buba, it was implied that the Fulbe were in their own territory when they were outside Buba—that is to say, when they were anywhere else in Forria. Thus the treaty implicitly recognized the de facto control of Forria by Fulbe chiefs.[83]

Commenting on this 1881 treaty, Coelho's successor, Governor Correia-Lança, expressed disgust at his predecessor's signing of a treaty that he knew could not be enforced. Indeed, this treaty was almost completely ignored by the Fulbe signatories.[84] In fact, it provided some of those chiefs with an opportunity to rearm their troops, and Portuguese political authority continued to remain unrecognized by its supposed subjects. In November 1881, the status of the Portuguese diminished further when a colonial army battalion was defeated at the hands of the Biaffada community of Jabadá on the Geba River. A dozen Portuguese riflemen and officers were killed or captured. This incident was especially injurious to the authority of the Lusophone government because they were supposed to have been acting to enforce treaty stipulations.[85] Their defeat made a mockery both of the government's claim to sovereign power and its ability to measure up to treaty obligations.

Three months later, in January 1882, the Portuguese forces at Buba regrouped, and a military unit led by Captain Carlos Maria de Sousa Ferreira Simões attacked Jabadá. Forty Biaffada defenders were killed, while two Portuguese lost their lives, twenty-three were wounded, and twenty-eight Mandinka auxiliaries were wounded. This led to a peace pact signed by Guinea's governor, Pedro Inácio de Gouveia, and the king of Jabadá, Baba Jai, on 11 February.[86] However, when a colonial force attacked the Fulbe-ribê stronghold of Gam-Suômó in mid-1882, they were soundly beaten by the Fulbe-ribê defenders, who then laid siege to European trading farms, from which they kidnapped dozens of farmworkers.[87]

Later that year, Governor Gouveia organized a fighting force of nearly 2,000 men, commanded by Lieutenant Colonel Francisco José Rosa. Consisting of 160 regular soldiers, Mandinka auxiliaries from Bolama, and Fulbe-djiábê auxiliaries from Corubal, on 28 September 1882 the force laid siege to and burned down four Fulbe-ribê villages under the authority of Chief Mamadu Paté Bolola. A month later (27 October), a representative of Chief Bolola signed a treaty with the Portuguese at Buba.[88] This treaty signaled a reversal of Portuguese support for the Fulbe-djiábé—the Portuguese now had agreed to ally with the Fulbe-ribê, if only to produce an end to the raids on the trading farms. Bowman attributes this reversal of policy to a realization by Governor Gouveia that "open Portuguese support for the Fulbe-djiábé had a detrimental effect on Portuguese enterprise."[89]

As a result of this policy shift, Fulbe-djiábé fighters aligned with Fuladu now began to attack Portuguese trading farms.[90] A subsequent attack by Dansa Demba, a Musa Molo ally, against the Portuguese town of São Belchior on the Geba River ended with the defeat of the town's defenders and the burning down of their houses.[91] This ended any potential for a Molo-Portuguese alliance, and Molo's forces then proceeded to attack Portuguese trading farms along the Geba River in a conscious effort to wipe out what remained of Buba's economy.[92] Molo's troops also seized control of the towns of Geba and Farim and helped themselves to the property and possessions of Portuguese, African, grumete, and mestiço residents and traders.[93] For the next two years (1883–85), Molo's troops enjoyed essentially free rein in the vicinity of Geba, simultaneously extracting goods from the local populace and asserting Fuladu's political supremacy.

Fuladu's predominance proved especially humiliating in light of the Berlin Accords of 1884–85, which initiated the notorious race among the European powers to establish "effective occupation" over claimed African territories. Now a sense of immediacy was implanted in the need to achieve an internal conquest of "Portuguese" Guinea.[94] Lisbon authorized an increase in funding and soldiery for Bissau's port towns, and the arrival in 1884 of the newly invented rapid-fire Snyder gun helped to make it possible for the Portuguese to pursue bolder campaigns. But the increased assistance and access to machine guns received by the colonial troops at interior locales (such as Buba) was not enough to make a definitive difference in warfare.

Thus, in pursuit of the quest to expand Lusophone political influence, Governor Paula Gomes Barboza in 1885–86 still had to rely on fragile and fleeting treaties and deals with local chiefs. He provided rifles to Fulbe-djiábé in 1886, but this merely served to provoke more intensive attacks by Fulbe-ribê and Biaffada forces against trading farms along the Rio Grande. Barboza reacted by instructing Captain Caetano Filipe de Sousa to organize a force of regular soldiers, grumete irregulars, and Fulbe-djiábé auxiliaries to attack those Biaffada who had joined forces with Fulbe-ribê against the Portuguese and who were contributing to the trading-farm decimations. The colonial attack unit marched out from Bolama in the morning of 15 January 1886, but three hours later fell under heavy fire from a group of Biaffada fighters and was forced to retreat. Captain Sousa and a Portuguese corporal were killed.[95] This, along with continued assaults by anti-Portuguese forces, assured the abandonment of virtually all the remaining trading farms and ruin for the Euro-colonial settlements of Buba and Bolôr.[96] Portuguese, Cape Verdean, mestiço, and grumete traders and farmers who scanned Guinea for other locales in which to settle found little or no improvement elsewhere.[97]

It took a Fulbe-ribê chief by the name of Umbucu (Nbuku Nyapa), whose power was rapidly increasing, to help assure that the intricate web of frequently changing alliances would function in favor of the Portuguese. Umbucu's incentive was to construct an alliance with which he could effectively confront the forces of Fuladu. To this purpose, in September 1886 Umbucu signed an accord with the Portuguese, while also consolidating a multiethnic military alliance with a number of Mandinka and Biaffada chiefs. The alliance massed a total of 4,330 Fulbe-ribê and Mandinka fighters and 170 Biaffada fighters, supported by 200 Portuguese soldiers and grumete auxiliaries.[98] A three-hour battle with Molo's men ensued at Sankolla: Molo's horsemen staged repeated attacks, but the Umbucu-Portuguese war party eventually forced Molo's fighters to flee. Molo then signed a peace treaty with the Portuguese.[99]

Historians René Pélissier and Peter Mendy point out that this grand battle represented a significant step toward Portuguese political influence in the Guinean interior.[100] Molo, however, despite the peace treaty, spent early 1887 regrouping his men, and he soon launched counterattacks against the Portuguese and Umbucu. Musa Molo's aggressiveness surprised Umbucu and the Portuguese because they had believed him to be permanently conquered upon his 1886 defeat.[101] Molo's forces expanded their influence through the late 1880s sufficiently to establish control over the trading pipeline to the Portuguese town of Farim. For the indigenous population near Farim, the inability of the Portuguese decisively to break Molo's power again confirmed the mockery of Portuguese claims of sovereignty.[102] Molo's continuing attacks on trading caravans between Farim and Firdu contributed to his rising wealth and power.

In 1890–91, Fulbe-ribê (including Chief Mamadu Paté Coiada), Biaffada, and some Mandinka leaders joined with the Portuguese to combat Molo and his various allies.[103] On 2 March 1891, Coiada's combined forces of 1,221 fighters, including 178 horsemen, joined with Captain Zacarias Lage of Geba to raze what were presumed to be pro-Molo villages along the Geba river. Cattle were stolen, women and children were kidnapped, and male defenders were killed.[104] However, no organized fighters under Molo's command were confronted and not a single pro-Molo chief was captured. Moreover, in the midst of this campaign, on 11 March 1891, Bolama sent word that part of Lage's unit was needed in Bissau to contend with a Papel uprising there, so the campaign was halted.

The armed forces of Fuladu continued to control villages in much of the Geba area. The Portuguese-allied indigenous head of Ganadu, Sambel Serandim, perished at the hands of Molo's attackers in May 1891.[105] Portuguese problems with military coordination were suggested by the fact that, despite having been forewarned about this attack by Molo himself, the Portuguese were not able to organize a counterattack to stop Molo's advance.

Eight months later, on 20 January 1892, Vasconcellos e Sá, Guinea's new governor, organized a military unit consisting of 7 officers, 170 soldiers, and more than 4,000 Biaffada and Fulbe-ribê allies. The force departed Geba the following day searching for Molo ally Mali Boiá. Under Captain Sousa Lage's direction, the military unit proceeded to burn and destroy seven villages in northeast Geba over the next two and a half weeks. The second week of March 1891, they found and defeated Boiá's forces after an eighteen-hour firefight; many of Boiá's men, however, were able to flee, and Boiá himself was not captured.[106] Moreover, the French were providing supplies and munitions, and this boosted Molo's fighting capacity and those of his allies, including Boiá.[107]

Molo's confidence had grown to the point where he was able to play diplomatic games with the Portuguese. For example, in February 1893 Molo requested authorization from the Portuguese commander at Farim to engage in attacks against Molo's enemies in that region. The request was ignored, but the Portuguese forces at Farim lacked the strength to interfere with Molo's men, who proceeded to carry out large-scale attacks on villages in Farim region through the rest of 1893.[108] Fuladu's armies also moved into the former Gabu province of Pachesi and overcame resistance from a contingent of forces from the Fulbe kingdom of Labé, which had previously controlled the province.

Meanwhile, Molo's very success—because it proved threatening to the independence of an ever-greater number of Fulbe leaders (both Fulbe-ribê and Fulbe-djiábê)—drove many of those leaders into alliance with the Portuguese. By 1900, in addition to much of the eastern portion of Portuguese Guinea, Molo had consolidated his rule over Firdu and other areas in Casamance and in the Gambia. However, his dependency on French aid and his trust of the French authorities would soon prove his undoing. In early 1903, Molo was informed that despite his years of serving French interests, French colonial commanders were apparently preparing to seize and deport him so as to assume direct French control of all of Casamance. Molo promptly fled to that part of Fuladu that was located within the British-controlled Gambia.[109] This effectively marked the end of Molo's reign as ruler of Fuladu; Molo remained in the Gambia with a corps of his followers.[110]

Meanwhile, Fuladu itself began a process of self-dismemberment, as wars in the Forria involving various groups of allied Fulbe-djiábê, Fulbe-ribê, Biaffada, and Mandinka dragged on through 1908.[111] Only then would these wars subside, essentially because Molo, the great state builder, was out of the picture and because the remaining combatants were exhausted from so many years of combat.[112] As Fuladu broke apart (beginning in 1903), the Portuguese were able to secure agreements from Fulbe chiefs,[113] and by 1908 the majority of chiefs in the area of the erstwhile state of Fuladu and the former kingdom of Gabu had agreed to sign formal treaties with colonial commanders,[114] although some refused.[115]

In the face of what were still profound military weaknesses on the part of the Portuguese, it is not fully clear why the more powerful Fulbe chiefs made the transition to colonial collaboration.[116] Once Molo's forces had departed from most of Guinea and essentially were restricted to Casamance and the Gambia River, the remaining Fulbe chiefs were militarily strong enough to have ruled over the Forria, Gabu, and Geba areas without submitting to Portuguese rule. Former colonial official António Carreira believed that the Fulbe chiefs realized that their flintlocks would likely offer an inadequate response to the machine guns and armored gunboats increasingly being used by the Portuguese in Guinea in the early 1900s.[117] However, the Fulbe chiefs were aware of the inadequate number of soldiers the Portuguese were able to rely on, and the Fulbe still controlled enough armed men to defy the colonialists effectively, had they chosen to do so. It was more probably the case, as Bowman has suggested, that these Fulbe leaders could not have anticipated the future consequences — regarding colonial state building — of allying with Portuguese military commanders.[118] At the time, there seemed little risk. This argument is especially compelling when one considers that each Fulbe chief who had expressed loyalty to the Portuguese was nonetheless able to wield full economic and political control within his own particular rural community. These chiefs commanded fighters who patrolled their respective areas and who monitored local affairs.[119] They did not perceive themselves to be "under" the authority of the Portuguese: they had merely allied with them.

In effect, then, this remained a highly nominal form of colonial authority, as the Portuguese exercised few concrete measures of political overrule. For the Fulbe chiefs, there was little cost to their pledges of loyalty to the Portuguese at that time, while their alliance with the Portuguese had helped to assure the downfall of their grand enemy, Musa Molo, and his allies.

— —

This chapter has made clear that the great precolonial, multiprovince state of Gabu, having endured for several centuries, weakened internally as a consequence of the diversification of the directional flow of political and economic resources and other changes occurring in the mid-eighteenth century. Once Gabu had been rendered more fragile, the combined forces of Fulbe from Futa Jallon and already settled Fulbe from the rebellious provinces of Gabu were able to precipitate Gabu's collapse. Meanwhile, the Portuguese remained aloof from the massive wars associated with Gabu's decline and final defeat. As was the case elsewhere in West Africa, these widening indigenous conflicts in the nineteenth century largely reflected internal changes, more than exogenous military pressures from Europeans.[120]

The expansion of Fuladu—the Fulbe-based empire built, in large part, atop the ashes of the former Gabu kingdom—represented the conquest of their former masters by former slaves who had engineered alliances with dozens of strongmen from a variety of ethnic groups. Fuladu, led by Alfa Molo and Musa Molo, enjoyed a nearly thirty-year effort at empire building. A key variable that prevented this empire's further expansion and consolidation was personal conflict between Musa Molo and his erstwhile allies: this resulted in difficulty of centralization, while external factors centered on Fuladu's widening political breach with Futa Jallon.[121]

It is instructive to compare the similarities and differences between these two great polities, Gabu and Fuladu, in precolonial Guinea-Bissau. Leaders of both empires proved capable of forging key alliances with other strongmen not only within their respective ethnic groups (intraethnic linkages) but also with chiefs and military commanders from other communal and geoterritorial backgrounds, producing a potent multiethnic polity. However, Fuladu's efforts in this regard remained somewhat limited after Alfa Molo's demise. Molo's son Musa expanded Fuladu's war-making success and attained control over a significant expanse of territory, but Fuladu would undergo repeated attacks by multiple challengers, provoking widespread and multiethnic anti-Molo alliances. By the 1890s, many Fulbe-ribê chiefs had allied with Biaffada and Mandinka chiefs to fight off Musa's empire-building efforts.

It is also important to note that the political ties between anti-Molo

Mandinka and the Fulbe rulers of Futa Jallon proved more crucial than any common ethnic solidarity between Fulbe-djiábê and Fulbe-ribê. Throughout the wars described above, the strategic interests of particular chiefs provoked multiethnic networks that assured a consistent base of challengers to Fuladu hailing from divergent communal origins.

Furthermore, Fuladu lacked the tradition and understanding of state building that had served Gabu for so many centuries. Alfa Molo and Musa Molo could not call upon a multicentury history of political overrule and empire administration that Gabu's rulers had been repeatedly able to invoke.

The way in which the precolonial African state of Gabu collapsed and the problems experienced by Fuladu would, to some extent, shape not only Portugal's conquest strategy in the early twentieth century, but also the way in which the Portuguese sought to construct a colonial state. In particular, the Portuguese sought to exploit the collapses of these African kingdoms by creating links with defeated or weakened chiefs from both former Gabu and former Fuladu. Eventually, the Portuguese would rely on those links in many aspects of colonial military activity and rural administration.

However, it should be emphasized that the Portuguese, despite their presence in several port towns, played no significant role in the great political and military events occurring in the interior and the littoral expanses prior to Gabu's demise, and for some two decades afterward.[122] It is important not to permit later events to obfuscate the fact that indigenous political alliance formations and kingdom collapses were the primary determinants of the flow of warfare through the vast portion of the nineteenth century. It was not until Fuladu was in a process of self-dismemberment that the Portuguese began more aggressively to intervene in political affairs in the Guinean interior. Until then, the African armies of Gabu and Fuladu respectively displayed such overwhelming praetorian power that the Portuguese could only observe these massive wars from afar. The political and military influence of indigenous alliances created after Fuladu's downfall determined the political fate of the interior. These facts would persist in the historical memory of rural Guineans and would later reemerge as a strand of confidence on which to base later anticolonial praetorian activities and alliances.

It is crucial to emphasize that military and political relations regarding Gabu and Fuladu evolved on quintessentially pragmatic, rather than primarily ethnic, foundations. The nonethnic nature of the political schisms described above ought to be given special emphasis. Molo had expanded Fuladu's reign by creating alliances among Fulbe-djiábê, Biaffada, some Mandinka, and some Fulbe-ribê; it was those Fulbe-djiábê, Mandinka, and Fulbe-ribê who were against

Molo that had allied themselves with the Portuguese. Thus, this division reflected a political cleavage based on pragmatic alliance creation between those for and against Molo, rather than being an ethnically defined conflict.

This focus on selective intraethnic collaboration and pragmatic interethnic alliance making thereby became further entrenched within the political culture of rural Guinea-Bissau, and it would serve as a crucial component of a strong rural civil society in subsequent decades. In the meantime, it is important to underline the fact that the Fulbe chiefs who had allied with the Portuguese would remain in de facto on-the-ground control of their territorial domains in the early 1900s, which served to further limit the extent to which Lusophone officials were able to extend and enforce their political authority in the interior. It is important to stress that the Portuguese did not achieve political or administrative control over Fulbe areas. Aside from attaining the concurrence of Fulbe (and to a lesser extent Biaffada) chiefs to fight alongside European soldiers in specific battles, those allied Fulbe chiefs continued to control political and economic life inside the regions of Forria and Gabu.

The nature of Fulbe-Lusophone collaboration tended to reinforce the structure of intracommunity autonomy within predominantly Fulbe zones. In a later chapter (chapter 9), we will see that this intracommunity Fulbe self-rulership would, during the later colonial period, facilitate the rise of locally legitimate competitors to unpopular, state-approved Fulbe chiefs.

PART 2

Vanquished State,
Terrorist State

CHAPTER 4

The Vanquished State

Multiethnic Resistance and the
Great Siege of Bissau, 1890s–1909

WE HAVE SEEN HOW THE PORTUGUESE became involved in Fuladu-related wars toward the close of the nineteenth century, accumulating a number of allies. In this chapter we turn to their military campaigns carried out against coastal and inland-riverine areas dominated by, most notably, Balanta, Papel, Mandjack, "Oinka" (the people of Oio region), and animist Biaffada.[1] Attacks were carried out in rural areas near the towns of Farim, Geba, Ziguinchor, and Cacheu, as well as in the environs of Bissau itself. These war campaigns, launched once or twice a year, typically provoked effective multiethnic alliances on the part of rural communities. Those alliances made it possible for regional indigenous forces to push the Lusophone aggressors out of Oio, Farim, and Cacheu and to keep them away from the greater portion of Bissau island.

Having secured alliances with the dominant Fulbe chiefs, the Portuguese were able to deploy thousands of Fulbe fighters as "irregulars," or "auxiliaries," by the early 1900s.[2] In the course of their operations against Musa Molo, the Portuguese also created links with a number of Biaffada and Mandinka chiefs, who now, like the Fulbe, began to provide the colonialists with auxiliary fighters. In addition, as previously noted, Portuguese auxiliary forces included significant numbers of grumetes—the Christianized Africans living in Portuguese towns who were currently working or who had previously worked for

Lusophone (Portuguese, Cape Verdean, or mestiço) employers.[3] These were generally the easiest to mobilize because they usually lived next to or very near the fort-town centers. However, again as we have seen, they often played an ambiguous role, occasionally shifting their allegiances to their relatives or friends back in their home villages.

A heavy reliance on auxiliaries was necessary because Lisbon failed to provide Bissau, Bolama, Cacheu, Farim, and the smaller fort towns of Guinea with adequate numbers of Portuguese or Cape Verdean soldiers. To help motivate their Fulbe, Mandinka, Biaffada, and grumete troops, Portuguese commanders sustained a practice already well-established by the 1890s: auxiliaries were granted the right to sack and pillage defeated villages, to confiscate all the possessions of the defeated communities, and to kidnap villagers and sell them into (local) slavery.[4]

In addition to increasingly effective deployment of such "irregular" forces, the use by the Portuguese of rapid-fire guns bolstered colonialist confidence and aggressiveness. However, the machine gun would not prove as definitive a military factor in Guinea as it did elsewhere in sub-Saharan Africa. Portuguese military units in Guinea lacked the manpower and repair capabilities necessary to make full and effective use of the new weapon, while various indigenous fighting forces often overpowered Portuguese fighters in number, or proved especially adept at rural guerrilla combat. Thus, despite rising levels of auxiliary support and access to machine guns, colonial victories during the 1890–1909 period proved occasional at best, and the majority of Portuguese military campaigns ended in disaster for the colonialists. While establishing allies in Forria and Gabu, colonial forces were unable to overcome indigenous defenders elsewhere in "Portuguese" Guinea. The ability of local fighters to secure relatively modern weaponry (rifles, ammunition) in great quantities through informal trade proved a formidable antidote to the colonial conquest efforts, enabling coastal and riverine groups, especially, to marshal large, heavily armed fighting forces. When colonial soldiers did manage to win a battle, they then typically returned immediately to Bolama or Bissau, failing to establish effective overrule of the conquered area.

The years 1907–8 represent a critical historical moment in Portugal's effort effectively to occupy the Guinean interior. Governor João Augusto de Oliveira Muzanty (appointed 1906) was determined to carry out successful large-scale war campaigns, and in fact he was able to organize and dispatch seven military campaigns in seven months—by far a record for the Portuguese in Guinea.[5] However, Lusophone political authority would be repulsed throughout the interior, with rural social formations displaying the full extent of their praetorian mobilizational capacities.

The war campaigns depicted in this chapter emphasize both the extent of the Portuguese effort to expand the reach of the colonial state and the ability of coastal peoples to form alliances to protect their domains. The two most dramatic illustrations of this occurred in the multiethnic region known as Oio, where powerful indigenous armies made effective military use of dense forest zones, and in the vicinity of Bissau itself, where Papel-Balanta forces imposed what I refer to as the Great Siege of Bissau (1907–8) and very nearly thrust the epicenter of the would-be colonial state into the sea.

Oio

In order to understand the broader social context of Portuguese military problems in Oio, it is helpful briefly to discuss the issue of Oinka identity. At some point during the nineteenth century, Portuguese administrators accepted, in the case of Oio, the name applied to that region by the former rulers of the Gabu kingdom. In addition, and more significantly, the Portuguese applied the regional designation Oinka to the people who inhabited that region, rather than identifying each of the individual ethnic groups therein, which was their usual practice.

Why did they do this in Oio, in contrast to their extensive ethnic identification efforts elsewhere in Guinea? It appears that the region had already become so ethnically intermixed by the late nineteenth century that it was simply too difficult for colonial observers to offer an ethnic accounting of the Oinka. The region was dominated by already settled and recently arrived Balanta,[6] Islamized Mandinka, and Soninké (animist Mandinka recently settled in Oio after fleeing the Fulbe/Biaffada wars in Forria and Gabu).[7] It was in large part a consequence of peaceful interethnic relations between these three groups that the Portuguese often found it easier to refer to the Oinka as a geographic people rather than to separate them out into coherent ethnic groups. (Adding to this complexity, the Balanta-BaNaga, one of the Balanta subgroups within Oio, enjoyed extensive contact with Balanta-Brassa, while Balanta-Batchaa gravitated toward the Mandinka.)[8] Indeed, the ethnic groups inhabiting the region—Balanta, Soninké, and Islamized Mandinka—functioned cooperatively in so many aspects of life (trade, intermarriage, military actions) that the Portuguese were simply unable to separate out the ethnic identities of a given village. Moreover, Portuguese colonial officials could not comprehend the notion of interethnic cooperation, much less that of ethnic malleability, so they dismissed it, or at least would not make written observations of it, instead preferring simply to lump the people of Oio together into the territorial category of Oinka (or Oinca). This was the only region where this was done.

Thus, the Oinka was a makeshift ethnoregional name for the Balanta, Islamized Mandinka, and Soninké who inhabited Oio region. All three of these groups interacted socially, economically, and politically and formed common military fronts when confronted with external challengers, including African attackers from outside the region. Thus, the Soninké worked in alliance with the already settled Balanta, forming an interethnic fighting force in the 1890s that was able to mount an effective military defense of the province against attacks by Fulbe strongmen, including Musa Molo.[9]

These interethnic military defenses of Oio proved similarly effective when the Portuguese began to launch their war campaigns. In February 1897, the Portuguese committed a large attack force to the interior of Oio;[10] the target of their assault was the Soninké.[11] Lieutenant Graça Falcão commanded a military unit that included some regular soldiers who were based in Farim, as well as about eight hundred Islamized Mandinka.[12] Across the Olossato River, Falcão ordered the launching of some explosive missiles into the village of Mindodo. This caused the villagers to flee, but in reaction to the inhumanity of the assault, it also provoked some of the Mandinka auxiliaries to turn against Falcão and to fire on him and his soldiers. In essence, these Mandinka auxiliaries created a spontaneous alliance with the Soninké villagers under attack. In the process, they killed two soldiers and wounded Falcão.[13] Falcão then ordered the company's sole machine gun to be trained on the auxiliaries; but when the machine gun jammed, Falcão and his soldiers returned promptly to Farim.[14]

Falcão subsequently recruited more auxiliaries and soldiers from Farim and Geba—mostly supporters of the procolonialist chief Mamadu Paté Coiada and of Biaffada Chief Unfali Soncó (who had been officially recognized as a chief by the Portuguese in 1895), as well as allies of a number of other Biaffada chiefs.[15] The governor of Guinea also sent Falcão two cannon boats. Falcão succeeded in building up a combined force of thousands of Fulbe, Mandinka, and Biaffada auxiliaries, and with them he entered a number of villages near Farim and demanded, by force of arms, their horses, cows, and pigs, as well as money. During this period, Falcão also rounded up sixty Oinka, selling them into slavery to his Mandinka allies, and distributed arms and ammunition to allied Fulbe and Biaffada chiefs.[16]

An enormous battle ensued in March 1897 near the Cacheu River (close to Farim), with some eight thousand colonialist auxiliaries—Fulbe, Biaffada, and

Mandinka—pitted against a nearly equivalent number of Oinka (principally Soninké).[17] The colonialists were directed by First Lieutenant Alvaro Herculano (the commander of the war boat *Flecha*) and Lieutenant Falcão.[18] The intensive fighting produced several hundred casualties on both sides, including the deaths of two Portuguese lieutenants, two sergeants, several soldiers, and a number of grumetes.[19] The result, in essence, was a stand-off.

Later that month (29 March), this showdown was reenacted. This time the colonialist forces were attacked by between five thousand and twelve thousand Oinka—Soninké, who had been joined by significant numbers of Balanta.[20] Groups of young Balanta men whose forebears had perfected a technique of intervillage communication in the early precolonial period were able to mobilize enormous fighting forces near the Cacheu River.[21] At the sight of the vast indigenous army, thousands of colonial auxiliaries deserted their commanders almost instantly, taking with them gunpowder, munitions, and supplies. Moreover, the deserters attacked the auxiliaries—a minority—who remained loyal to the Portuguese.[22] Here again, the tentative support of the African auxiliaries was dramatically displayed. When the Europeans appeared vulnerable, most of the African auxiliaries abandoned their European patrons. A similar abandonment by auxiliaries had occurred in 1891, when, at the first sign of fighting, Angolan auxiliaries deserted the Portuguese regulars near Bissau. In the Cacheu River battle, only the 150 regular Portuguese soldiers remained at the battle site, and after several hours' exchange of gunfire, they decided to head back to their war boat.[23]

In April 1897, in the month following the Cacheu River battle, the Portuguese lost another major battle against the Soninké, near Farim: two Portuguese officers, three sergeants, and fifteen soldiers were killed, along with several dozen auxiliaries. Subsequent (May–June 1897) negotiations between Guinea's governor, Pedro Ignaçio de Gouveia, and Soninké leaders—including chiefs from Gússará, Gindu, Biribão, and elsewhere—resulted in a peace accord (28 June) in which the Portuguese indicated that they would not make war on the Oinka.[24]

Thus, in Oio, the Soninké, supported by their Balanta allies, had proved capable of defeating the Portuguese and of then securing a peace in which the Portuguese in Farim agreed to desist from further encroachments into Oio. This was an extraordinary accomplishment, and it dramatized the military fragility of the would-be colonial state. The extent of interethnic support should also be emphasized. Here we may note evidence of small groups of Mandjack near Farim providing arms to Balanta and Soninké—arms that had originally been provided to these Mandjack by the Portuguese in hopes that they would be used against the Oinka.

The peace created through the Oinkas' military victories was respected by the colonial authorities for five years. Then, in April 1902, Governor Joaquim Pedro Vieira Judice Biker organized another war campaign into Oio region, fielding two military columns totaling about one hundred soldiers plus grumete auxiliaries from Geba, Farim, Cacheu, Bissau, and Bolama; an additional column of Fulbe auxiliaries was led by the Portuguese commander of Geba, Captain Almeida.[25] These forces confronted the Oinka at Bafatá and at Farim. In both cases, the Oinka used a strategy that the colonialists found impossible to overcome: Oinka fighters moved quickly away from the population centers (Bafatá and Farim), leading the colonial army into the bush, where other fighters were positioned on either side of extremely narrow paths so that they were able to shoot at the colonial soldiers as they passed by.

At other times, Oinka fighters challenged the colonialists in head-on battles, and again they proved to be a superior fighting force. In one battle, provoked by Governor Biker, the Oinka charged en groupe, and the response of the grumete and Fulbe auxiliaries was simply to flee. In this particular battle, the governor was deserted so quickly that he was left virtually in the open. The Oinka fighters, given this clear view of him, shot him in the buttocks. The Portuguese forces lost both battles.[26]

In November 1902, upon returning to Bolama from a three-month visit to Lisbon, Governor Biker received word from the Oinka that they wished to discuss a treaty: they proposed to meet the governor in Mansoa—a more or less neutral locale. The governor accepted this proposal and, after traveling by boat to the Mansoa port, disembarked and, accompanied by his doctor and an assistant, walked the one and a half hours into the town of Mansoa. Representatives of the Oinka arrived soon afterward. They agreed to pay a hut tax; however, they actually handed over only 100 reis, a tiny, nominal sum. The governor, at that point, aware that he lacked the military forces to wage a war campaign against Oio, accepted the Oinkas' payment and promised peace.[27] On the ground, this left the Oinka politically autonomous, without having to defend their terrain against Portuguese incursions and without promising fealty to Portugal.

The humiliation of this accord, combined with the deterioration of Biker's own physical health, led to his resignation as governor of Guinea in September–October 1903. He was replaced by Governor Alfredo Cardoso de Soveral Martins, who, upon assuming his post, remarked that Oio was actually a "free state . . . totally outside our influence," whose people "would be ironically surprised if they were told that their territory belongs to the dominion of Portugal."[28] Little changed over the next several years.

Bafatá Region and the Generalization of War

In 1907, the Portuguese were determined to wrest control of Bafatá region because they perceived the area to represent a potentially important farming and cash-crop zone. Within Guinea, Chief Falli Sonko (also called Unfali Soncó) was made a prime target of the Portuguese because he had, in effect, "turned" against the colonialists after having previously worked in alliance with them.[29] Governor Muzanty (who assumed the governorship in 1906) described Chief Sonko as effectively uniting many chiefdoms across a variety of Guinean ethnic groups,[30] a claim that Pélissier finds little evidence to support.[31] But the Portuguese chronicler João Barreto argued that Sonko did in fact create a multiethnic alliance—especially among local Biaffada, Mandinka, and Fulbe chiefs—to stop maritime traffic along the Geba River and to ensure that the Portuguese did not gain access to the agricultural resources of the region.[32]

Barreto noted the predilection of traders in this region to transport produce to Senegal, rather than to Bissau, and he argued that the rural communities of the area sought to protect this trading circuit against the Portuguese.[33] Moreover, correspondence from French administrators in Senegal, who were closely monitoring these events, suggested that Sonko did in fact effectively organize a coalition of African resistance—one that included his nephew Boncó Sanhá of the Islamized Biaffada and several Fulbe chiefs: Dembajai (or Dembage or Bembajá), of the Corubal; Délage (or Guelage), of Cossé; Ierobiri (or Irobiri), of Gússará; and Ansomani (or Assemam, Asmane), of Pakessi.[34] Essentially, this represented a Biaffada-Fulbe alliance, backing up a large corps of Mandinka fighters already supporting Sonko. Against them and in alliance with the colonialists were arrayed Abdulai Kassala (probably Mandinka), of Xime; Cherno Cali (Fulbe-ribê), of Forria; and Monjur (or Monjuro), a Fulbe-djiábê who had become chief of Gabu, replacing Selu Coiada (brother of Mamadu Paté Coiada).

In May 1907, a naval lieutenant, José Proença Fortes, was charged with collecting forty Snyder guns that had previously been distributed to Chief Sonko by one of Muzanty's predecessors, Judice Biker. Fortes and Sonko met on a path near to Sambel Nhanta, Sonko's village; after words were exchanged, supporters accompanying Sonko attacked Fortes and his chief aide, wounding them and forcing them to retreat. Muzanty then sent Fortes to Lisbon for recuperation; the governor lacked the resources and the soldiers to send a war party to retaliate against Sonko.[35] Meanwhile, the Fulbe-Biaffada allies attacked and burned down part of the Portuguese military post of Bambadinca, despite the defense put up by twenty-five colonial soldiers, including use of a cannon and a machine gun.[36]

The Portuguese had essentially been ousted from the entire Bafatá region and from the banks of the Geba River.[37]

A French military observer underlined the praetorian challenge that the Portuguese faced: in his estimation, between fifty thousand and sixty thousand indigenous Guineans possessed firearms.[38] Painfully aware of this context, in the wake of the disaster at Bambadinca Governor Muzanty voyaged to Portugal to bemoan the failure to "pacify" the territory and to request further assistance from the Lisbon government. Lisbon agreed to send a military column to Guinea, and did so in November 1907, along with arms, munitions, and a 131-page instruction manual on how to conquer an African colony.[39]

However, between Muzanty's departure and return, more chiefs had joined up with Sonko's forces in Bafatá region,[40] while informants (both African and European) to French observers stationed in Casamance reported that growing numbers of chiefs—in Bafatá region as elsewhere—were mobilizing their forces.[41] A French official stationed across the southern border in French Guinea noted in November 1907 that much of the eastern portion of Portuguese Guinea was under the control of these chiefs.[42] A different official added that the colony's northern sector had become "more or less anarchic."[43] A French official in Conakry received a telegram on 29 November 1907 stating that a Portuguese military command post had been surrounded by African forces; Europeans had been killed.[44]

Muzanty returned from Lisbon in late November 1907 with fifty European sailors and a gunboat, the *Don Luiz.* At the end of the month, the governor led an excursion, consisting of those sailors plus thirty local soldiers, toward Bambadinca. Chiefs Sonko, Sanhá, Dembajai, and Délage returned to their respective home villages to defend against Muzanty's forces.[45] Sonko and Sanhá's men regrouped on both banks of the Geba River, where they constructed what amounted to a booby trap: they pulled strong cables of barbed wire across the river (near the village of Sambel Nhanta), and then camouflaged the blockage. A Portuguese gunboat, the *Canhoneira Cacheu,* soon approached, firing salvos that generally were aimed toward shoreline villages.[46] Ramming the hidden cables, the gunboat soon became immobilized, after which it came under intense rifle fire from Sonko's fighters on the right bank of the river. Trapped, 106 Portuguese regulars and indigenous auxiliaries were shot dead or wounded.[47] Only the following day was the gunboat able to break free of the blockage and limp downstream.[48] Meanwhile, still in December 1907, the governor's military column found itself cut off at Xime, surrounded by Fulbe-Futa fighters and their allies. In the ensuing battle, the Portuguese column suffered a major defeat; among the casualties were 1,666 wounded African auxiliaries.[49]

A French observer noted that the "rebellion" in Bafatá region was characterized by Islamic and animist peoples making "common cause" and that the previously existing animosities among certain local chiefs had subsided under the authority of Islamic leaders such as Chief Mahfoudh.[50] As the historian Peter Mendy has pointed out, the Portuguese in Bissau and Bolama correctly perceived that the survival of the entire colonial entity of Guinea was at stake.[51] That same December (1907), they convinced the government in Lisbon to send as many as a thousand or twelve hundred troops to fight in Guinea.[52] This force immediately proceeded to Bafatá region, where on 23 December 1907 they seized and beheaded several chiefs: Thierno Demba, chief of Kassé (Kossé); Demba Dia, chief of Korobali (Corubal); Nianson Diande, chief of Paguessy (Pakessi); and other chiefs "of lesser importance."[53] This provoked a massive indigenous migration into French Guinea.[54] However, Falli Sonko and his allies remained in control of most of the region. In January 1908 a column of Portuguese troops and African auxiliaries set out to subdue the valley of the Geba River, but they met nearly immediate resistance and were devastated in battle, with about forty Portuguese regulars and one hundred to one hundred fifty auxiliaries being killed by local fighters.[55] By the end of January 1908, Governor Muzanty decided to disband the entire military column.[56]

Meanwhile, in late January, Biaffada of Quinara in the southern part of the colony, hearing news from their fleeing kinsmen about the massacres, attacked procolonialist Mandinka trade caravans near Bolama. They also attacked Portuguese and Lusophone traders in the area, effectively demanding travel taxes from anybody passing through the Quinara area. The Portuguese military chief of staff, Illidio Marinho Falcão de Castro Nazareth, then charged into Quinara with a small war party, but he was defeated by a Biaffada ambush. Two dozen colonial fighters were wounded.[57] At this point, Balanta who had recently arrived in Quinara joined with Biaffada to fight the Portuguese.[58] Since those Biaffada were considered by the Balanta to be the legitimate distributors of land in Quinara, these recently arrived Balanta were in part expressing gratefulness to their Biaffada hosts, but it is important to emphasize that they also shared a common determination to defend the area against the Portuguese invaders. Djabada, Cassiquinho, and Gandua were among the Balanta communities in Quinara that mobilized their forces in support of the Biaffada.[59]

Meanwhile, Portuguese overeagerness to defeat Sonko would eventually play to the advantage of Tono Biré, chief of Daudoum. On 4 March 1908, Biré was invited by Portuguese officials to take part in military operations in Gabu region against Sonko's forces.[60] Biré asked for arms and ammunition and was granted two shipments of rifles. However, Biré then decided not to march his men against

Sonko and instead used his new weapons to expel a Portuguese military unit from his area of Daudoum. Similarly, a Biaffada chief, Sanhá of Gam-Sanhá, had promised to support Nazareth in battle but having received weapons, instead mounted ambushes against Nazareth's men, forcing them to abandon the area.[61]

Events such as these added to the humiliation of the Portuguese in seeking to subdue Sonko. At the end of March 1908, a French official in Conakry wrote that he had just received a telegram from the administrator of Kadé to the effect that in Gabu the Portuguese were defeated "on all fronts."[62] According to additional cablegrams sent by Europeans in Kadé to French officials in Dakar on 4 March 1908, "Yolas" (Diolas) in combat against Portuguese troops, had succeeded in killing five Portuguese soldiers and their commander.[63]

That same month, a military column sent from Lisbon arrived in Bissau: it was composed of 460 European soldiers, an artillery battery, a dozen administrative officers, and a medical unit. In addition, a company of 250 auxiliary riflemen recruited from Mozambique arrived in Bissau.[64] Muzanty directed these combined forces, along with Fulbe auxiliaries, in an attack on Sonko's supporters at Cuor (Kouhor, Côro), on the right bank of the Geba River. The opposing armies fought again on 6 April 1908 at Gantourey and on 8 April at Madina. Large numbers of Mandinka and Biaffada loyalists of Sonko were reported to have fled to Oio, as Fulbe auxiliaries of the Portuguese sacked Gantourey. Part of the army, working in concert with Senegalese mercenary Abdul Injai, ravaged Madina.[65] The people of Oio welcomed the fleeing Biaffada refugees,[66] reflecting their longstanding tradition of interethnic tolerance. Governor Muzanty, in a gesture of appreciation for Injai's services, installed Injai as chief of Cuor, and Sonko was forced to provide Injai with one hundred head of cattle.[67] Meanwhile, Muzanty set up a military post at Carenque Cunda, manned by a group of Injai's horsemen and sixty soldiers from a Mozambican military company that had arrived on 8 April.[68] This was the first time that the Portuguese in Guinea were able to establish a military command post in the course of a campaign.[69] However, the range of effective occupation of this post was quite limited; for example, Biaffada fighters were seen burning Portuguese installations in Bolama, some fifteen hundred meters from the governor's palace.[70] Moreover, the following month, according to a telegram sent by a Portuguese administrator from Bissau to Dakar, the Portuguese suffered a string of military setbacks, beginning with the retreat of a Portuguese military column on the heels of attacks by Balanta forces in Oio.[71] And closer to Bissau, the Balanta of Nhacra continued, virtually at will, as they had since the 1890s, to attack and loot European boats passing nearby.[72]

Also in May 1908, the Bijagós, fighting several battles with colonial attackers, were able to repel them.[73] In the same month, Felupe in northeastern Oio similarly forced Portuguese envoys to leave their territory; Papel fighters remained in control of most of Bissau island;[74] and Biaffada forces attacked and burned European houses in Bolama, the colonial capital.[75] At virtually the same time, Mandjack in the interior of Cacheu region expelled the Portuguese from their land areas. Along the coast of Cacheu region, Mandjack had obtained modern weapons, including mortars, from underground Senegalese arms traders, and they used them to attack passing ships.[76] These Mandjack had formed an alliance with the Felupe of Jufunco (on the north bank of the Cacheu River), and this interethnic opposition presented too formidable a threat to Portuguese forces for a campaign to be considered.

A French observer writing in May 1908 noted that the Portuguese armies, which had already been ousted from half the colony, now were pushed out of most of the remaining half.[77] In official Portuguese reports sent from Bissau to Lisbon, it was stated that between 18 March and 15 May 1908, Portuguese regular soldiers suffered four dead and thirteen wounded in battle, one dead by accident, and four dead by disease, for a total of twenty-two losses.[78] The actual figures were likely higher. The military chief of staff in Bissau made clear in a report that between November 1907 and March 1908, the Portuguese military forces in Guinea suffered growing battlefield losses in Brodal, Buhor, Geba, Farim, Buba, and elsewhere.[79] This report admitted that communities in most regions refused to pay colonial taxes. Along the Geba River, Balanta fighters routed Injai and his (mostly Senegalese) mercenaries, with Injai himself being wounded, as the Balanta retained control of both shores of the Geba River.[80]

In this context, Portuguese military officers remained emphatically cynical regarding the prospects of a significant military victory in the near future, and in fact predicted failure for future war campaigns against "the savages of [Portuguese] Guinea."[81] From the point of view of Portuguese colonial officials, the most that could be done in this context was to occupy unguarded villages—for a very brief time—and to spread fear in such villages by torturing people. Thus, for example, in June 1908, the Guinean governor personally led war campaigns along the Geba River, pillaging undefended villages where possible and making a point of physically abusing civilians. As news spread, people fled their villages as the column approached, then returned after its departure and reestablished indigenous political control.[82]

By the end of June 1908, Biaffada, Mandinka, Mandjack, Balanta, and Felupe, often in multiethnic military formations, had inflicted multiple defeats upon Portuguese forces while chasing colonial functionaries and traders out of their land areas.[83] The regions of Oio, Cacheu (apart from the fort town of Cacheu it-self), and Quinara (Catió) had effectively jettisoned all aspects of a Lusophone presence. In a last-ditch effort against Oio, the Portuguese in March 1910 sent yet another large war column into the region, but, according to a Portuguese infantry captain, after approximately ten thousand Oinka had been effectively mobilized, they inflicted serious losses on the colonialists, who retreated.[84]

In those few instances in which the Portuguese achieved a military victory in a specific village, they immediately departed, and local political power was restored. But such instances were rare: indigenous political sovereignty had been effectively defended, and in some cases Lusophone settlements had been encircled and besieged.[85] By far the most dramatic of these encirclements was the Great Siege of Bissau.

The Great Siege of Bissau, 1907–1908

The Great Siege of Bissau refers to the effective military occupation of the environs of the fort town of Bissau from late 1907 to mid-1908 by indigenous anti-colonial Papel fighters in collaboration with their Balanta allies. In order to appreciate the background to this event, it is necessary briefly to recount that fighting had already occurred repeatedly between the Portuguese of Bissau and the Papel kingdoms[86]—who were often supported by Balanta and grumetes[87]—in the two decades prior to the siege. It is also important to point out that this warfare helped to provide intraethnic military unity to the major Papel kingships at Intim, Bandim, Antula, Safim, Enterramento, and Borm, whose combined forces constituted several thousand well-armed fighters.[88]

Prior to combat, many of the fighters sent their families for safekeeping to stay with the Mandjack of Cacheu, while obtaining modern guns from these same Mandjack. Thus, preparation for battle was marked by both intraethnic ties among the Papel kingships and interethnic collaboration with the Mand-jack and grumetes. These ties contributed to victories over Portuguese forces despite Portuguese access to machine guns and the back-up support of Biaffada and Fulbe auxiliaries, along with reinforcements brought in from Cape Verde and Angola.[89] For example, in December 1893, the Papel of Antula, Bandim, and Intim had made common alliance with the Papel of Safim, as well as with the Balanta of Nhacra, massing a total of about three thousand fighters.[90] Within several days, Balanta support also came from Malafo (in the area of Mansoa).[91] The colonial commanders in Bissau decided to call off their intended attack. In May 1894, Governor Sousa Lage succeeded in recruiting some seven hundred soldiers and auxiliaries and attacked Bandim and Intim, but his force was limited by resupply problems, even though these Papel centers were located only one or two kilometers from Bissau.[92] Three months later, in July 1894, the Papel of Biombo and of the isle of Jeta responded by launching, along with Balanta supporters, large-scale attacks against Bissau. Three European boats were seized from Bissau harbor.[93]

In 1903, it was still the case that no Portuguese could safely leave the confines of Bissau's walls without the express permission of the Papel kings.[94] In fact, occasional raids into the Bissau fort by Papel fighters meant that the governor could not even guarantee the safety of Europeans within Bissau's walls. Governor Muzanty carried out another war campaign in 1906, the colonialists being supported by one thousand Fulbe and Mandinka auxiliaries, but the attackers again were turned aside by Papel-Balanta resistance.[95] In September 1907, Papel kingdoms, supported by Balanta allies, massed their troops against the Bissau fort in order to prevent Portuguese troops from departing. All land exits from Bissau were cut off, rendering Bissau's European populace entirely dependent on ships traveling the Rio Geba, and communications between Bissau and other parts of the colony ceased.[96] The Papel forces were strengthened by arms obtained from grumetes who had previously gone on war campaigns on the side of the Portuguese; the grumetes, after returning home without turning the arms over to the Europeans, now decided to support the indigenous fighters. Those weapons included modern Snyder rifles and ammunition.[97]

Correspondence from December 1907 and January 1908 describes Bissau as still under an unbroken "state of siege";[98] communications between Bissau and Conakry had ceased.[99] Paul Brocard, a French colonial envoy based in Dakar who was visiting Bissau, was able to obtain a significant amount of detailed information on these events because of "emissaries" he sent to Papel villages.[100] One of these emissaries learned that the Papel chiefs wanted the French to send the *Cassard* naval ship to the harbor at Bissau to provide security for their interlocutors—so that Papel chiefs would not be seized by the Portuguese if they arrived for peace talks. Meanwhile, Brocard's go-betweens traveled to Antigne to let the chiefs know that conditions of peace would include: (1) the Papel should recognize European authority; (2) the Papel should allow their villages to be open to commerce and the free circulation (of Europeans); (3) the Papel should begin paying Portuguese colonial taxes; and (4) the Papel should hand over their guns to the Portuguese authorities, especially the Snyders. According to Brocard's emissaries, the Papel chiefs accepted all of these conditions. At that point, however, Portuguese officials insisted that the Papel chiefs pay a "war" fine of 15,000 francs within three days.[101] This was rejected by the Papel chief of Antigne.[102] In reaction, on 2 May 1908 the Portuguese closed the portals of the town of Bissau.[103] On 3 May, a Portuguese artillery unit bombarded Papel villages located near Bissau; on 4 May, a column of 791 soldiers and auxiliaries was sent out from the fort.[104]

Since the Portuguese column lacked machine guns, the Portuguese and the Papel would be almost equally matched in terms of military hardware, and the Papel fighters were quick to take advantage. After marching only 800 meters outside the fort, the column was attacked intensively by Papel riflemen hidden behind trees. At the same time, Papel swordsmen, even though facing waves of gunfire, directly charged the colonial column. The Papel killed 4 and seriously wounded 26 Portuguese soldiers.[105] Nonetheless, the column reached Intim, at which point Portuguese gunboats bombarded the villages of Intim, Bandim, and Antula from the river.[106] The colonialists, finding Intim undefended, promptly burned the village and murdered several unarmed Papel.[107] However, over the next several days, Papel guerrilla fighters carried out frequent assaults against the colonial forces. By 10–11 May, 130 Portuguese troops had been killed.[108]

On 11 May 1908, the Portuguese dug themselves in behind sand barriers at Intim, where they were then confronted by a force of between four and five thousand Papel and Balanta who had joined together to fight the column.[109] Unwilling to suffer further losses and intimidated by the Papel-Balanta fighters, the colonialists retreated to Bissau the next day. Meanwhile, the soldiers who had traveled from Lisbon the preceding month now became ill (from heat prostration, intestinal maladies, and malaria), and 125 of them returned to Portugal on 18 May 1908.[110] In every respect, this represented an enormous political and military victory for the Papel-Balanta forces of greater Bissau.

An item published in the official government journal of Portuguese Guinea on 16 May 1908 makes clear that the siege of Bissau was reestablished, with the Papel kingdoms of Intim, Bandim, and Koumtoumbe especially taking part.[111] The siege provoked Portuguese officials to forbid Europeans from allowing African residents of Bissau to enter European homes, where some had been working as house servants. All European-African communication was effectively stopped. The Europeans' level of fear was such that they did not even bury their dead in Bissau's cemetery, which was located 100 meters from the town gates, but interred them within the fort.[112] An observer noted that the colonial troops were severely demoralized.[113] In contrast, the Papel forces were proving increasingly confident and aggressive. They now fully encircled the fort of Bissau (excluding the Rio Geba port) and, each night, fired several shots at the fort's guards.[114]

At this stage, even Portuguese military officers appeared to assume that the only way to avoid being expelled from the colony would be for France to assist the Portuguese militarily. The Papel had now effectively besieged Bissau for half a year and, at the end of May 1908, were in a military position to overrun the fort and force the departure of the Europeans. A Portuguese official described in writing how soldiers assigned to defend the fort of Bissau would not be able to withstand a Papel assault,[115] a view confirmed by Séguy, a French consular agent who visited Bolama and Bissau in late May 1908. Séguy wrote from Bissau that "all the Portuguese forces that had left [Bissau] under the pretext of conquest were obliged to return after a week spent on a borderline located 1,500 meters from the town."[116] Brocard subsequently met with the governor of Guinea, and it was agreed that the French frigate *Cassard,* commanded by a Captain Boyer, would be allowed to dock at Bissau temporarily.[117] The *Cassard* arrived at the port of Bissau on the Rio Geba on 13 June 1908 and remained anchored for one month, officially to provide French citizens of Bissau with protection during the continuing siege.[118]

By this point, the Papel and Balanta forces surrounding Bissau had grown to an estimated twenty thousand, who essentially held the town at their mercy.[119] The Portuguese had only 150 soldiers defending Bissau at the time.[120] As described by Captain Boyer, the Portuguese were unable to advance "more than fifteen hundred meters outside the city, while [the Papel] circulate freely everywhere."[121] Nonetheless, the arrival of the *Cassard* was much noticed by the Papel chiefs, who very much wanted to avoid provoking the French navy into supporting the Portuguese. Thus, all nocturnal Papel attacks against the Portuguese soldiers guarding the fort of Bissau ceased. Moreover, fear that the French might join the Portuguese in a military attack led those Papel who had temporarily migrated to Casamance to cultivate peanuts, but who heard about the arrival of the *Cassard* in Bissau to hurry back to their Papel kingdoms to defend against a potential Franco-Lusophone assault.[122]

At the same time, Papel chiefs were hoping that the French would proceed to negotiate with the Portuguese for a peaceful resolution.[123] The French would, in fact, assume an intermediary role. On 16 June, Governor Muzanty, aware of the Papels' respect for the French, met with the French envoy, Brocard, and a M. Durac, an agent of the French Company of West Africa. Muzanty asked Durac to send an African envoy to the Papel chiefs. The evening of the next day, 17 June, Muzanty, told of the chiefs' willingness to negotiate a peace, apparently mistook the message to be a surrender. The morning of June 18, Muzanty departed happily for his residence in Bolama.[124] According to Brocard, by leaving before actually negotiating a peace, Muzanty in effect left further diplomatic decisions in the hands of inexperienced, midlevel functionaries. Moreover, those functionaries were influenced by a factionalized European community, significant numbers of whom were strongly interested in Muzanty's ouster as governor and who were determined to assure that Muzanty's arrangement of a surrender would fail. Their goal was to damage his standing in Lisbon's eyes and to increase the likelihood that he would be replaced.[125]

After Muzanty's departure, on the morning of 19 June, approximately six hundred Papel, led by a large contingent of chiefs, bivouacked in grumete homes lying just outside Bissau's fort.[126] On 20 June 1908, a group of twenty Papel representatives arrived at the gates of the fort of Bissau to talk with the Portuguese authorities. They were ignored. The Papel departed, but as they left they shouted a warning: the Cassard would be leaving on 22 June.[127] There was an implication that when the docked French warship left, in two days' time, the Portuguese would again be vulnerable to attack.

On that same day, the Bissau commander stood on the doorstep of the portal of the fort. Speaking in crioulo (which some Papel of Bissau understood), he asked the Papel what they desired. Papel leaders replied that they were interested in peace, but that they preferred not to enter the fort. They suggested that the commander accompany them to a Papel village to discuss the terms of peace; in response, the Portuguese simply shut the fort's portals.

On 25 June 1908, a new Bissau commander was appointed, Captain Viriato Gomes da Fonseca, who immediately ordered his sentries not to fire on any unarmed Papel. According to Brocard, this move was (ironically) perceived by the Papel to have essentially reflected the influence of the French. The Papel believed it was the influence of the Cassard—whose departure had been delayed—that made it possible to continue to negotiate with the Portuguese. Confidence in the ability of the French to assure that this more lenient policy would be maintained was reflected by the appearance of numerous Papel on the banks of the Geba River in order to fish, without apparent worry of attacks by Portuguese sentries.[128]

A week later (1 July), a large number of Papel arrived at the gate of the fort of Bissau bearing white flags. They were making a peace offering. The gate was opened and a Portuguese officer stepped outside—alone—and talked with the Papel, while at the same time sending for Fonseca, the commander. When Fonseca arrived, he invited seven of the Papel chiefs to accompany him into the fort.[129] During the talks in the fort, Fonseca responded to the chiefs by indicating that the Portuguese administration in Lisbon would have to decide whether to accept their offer, but that one condition would have to be that the Papel turn their guns over to the Portuguese. The Papel chiefs replied that they would have to discuss the question of disarmament with people from their villages.[130] In fact, the Papel chiefs were very divided on the question of disarmament, with some agreeing to turn their guns over but others remaining opposed. The village of Antula was identified as especially hostile to this proposal, with villagers suggesting that without arms they would become helpless prey.[131]

Meanwhile, Portuguese confidence was such that they prepared a written acceptance of Papel defeat for the chiefs to sign. The chiefs' refusal to sign now meant that the Portuguese bluff had been called.[132] The colonial army was in no position to engage in military action. There were only 120 trained soldiers, plus 150 auxiliaries, in the Bissau garrison, of whom about one-third were, apparently for health reasons, unable to engage in combat actively.[133] It appeared likely that the two 32 mm cannons aboard an offshore gunboat would provide little protection against a large-scale Papel attack.[134]

Suddenly, on 15 July, Governor Muzanty was recalled to Lisbon, apparently because officials there were convinced that his policies were failing. It should also be mentioned, however, that the French had utilized all measure of influence to damage Muzanty's personal reputation.[135] The Papel were overjoyed with Muzanty's departure, which they interpreted as a noteworthy victory (he would, however, resume his post as governor of Guinea several weeks afterward). Meanwhile, the *Cassard* sailed from Bissau on 16 July — one day after Muzanty's departure. Yet the siege continued, and Muzanty's return to Bissau in August would bear no notable impact. In fact, at the end of that month, negotiations between the Portuguese and the Papel ceased.[136] The resulting impasse lasted through the end of 1908: the Papel chiefs decided not to try to overrun the fort of Bissau, and the Portuguese remained too short of soldiers and military hardware to attempt a war campaign.[137]

Demise of the Governor

We have made clear that indigenous defenders of local communities achieved widespread victories over the Portuguese in Guinea-Bissau by 1908, and they were able to continue to lay claim to vast portions of their territories. In November 1908, Governor Muzanty was again recalled to Lisbon for discussion of his failure to defeat resistant communities. On 4 December 1908, he returned to Bissau from Lisbon advised by his superiors to proceed more cautiously.[138] For the next month, he remained holed up in his governor's residence at Bolama and, in line with Lisbon's directives, ordered no military actions.[139] But the Portuguese authorities needed to blame someone for Portugal's continuing humiliation in Bissau, so yet again, Muzanty was recalled — this time, permanently.[140] In effect, Muzanty's final departure on 14 January 1909 was strongly symbolic of Portugal's failures in Guinea-Bissau throughout the 1890–1909 period.

— —

Between 1890 and 1909, almost all of Guinea-Bissau remained under the political authority of local leaders. Only a few Fulbe and Biaffada allies of the Portuguese (most of them in Gabu) provided a measure of allegiance, which in any case was only occasionally and weakly manifested.[141] Militarily, in Oio and elsewhere, colonial officials were stunned to find that even their largest allied forces and best commanders were unable to defeat local fighters. When they were able to organize a coherent, large-scale, well-armed force — of Portuguese, Cape Verdean, and mestiço soldiers, alongside grumete, Fulbe, and Mandinka auxiliaries — they proved capable of winning a particular battle in a given village, but they then retreated to a coastal fort, allowing political authority to revert to indigenous hands. Portuguese embarrassment at the military setbacks peaked with the Great Siege of Bissau, in which Papel kingdoms supported by Balanta allies nearly overran the fort town. It is probable that only the arrival of the *Cassard,* a French navy vessel, made possible a continued Portuguese presence during the siege. Overall, the colonial state in "Portuguese" Guinea during the two decades analyzed in this chapter can be accurately characterized as militarily vanquished.

The chapter has also made clear that indigenous resistance to Portuguese war campaigns commonly bore a multiethnic dimension. To be sure, many of the anticolonial battles were fought on a distinctly community-specific basis, with a given village or group of villages defending its local territory; however, the multiethnic military collaboration in Guinea-Bissau was commonplace, not exceptional, particularly in regard to the larger battles. Chief Falli Sonko, for example, created an effective Biaffada-Fulbe-Mandinka alliance that produced enormous difficulties for the Portuguese; and Balanta communities located on the isle of Bissau and along the Geba River provided support troops to Papel kingdoms at various points in the Papel-led siege of Bissau, repeating a pattern of Balanta-Papel alliance formation that was operative during the 1890s. We may further recall the support provided to the Balanta by Mandjack near Farim. Another notable example was the coordinated military operations carried out by the Balanta, Soninké, and Islamized Mandinka of Oio province; the extensiveness of these interethnic collaborations is what led the Portuguese to assign to the people of that region the (geographic) name of Oinka. It is also noteworthy that the inclusion of Islamized Mandinka in this Oinka alliance represented a conjoining of Muslim and animist forces, belying the long-held Portuguese myth of a hard and fast religioethnic division between these groups in Guinea.

There was, furthermore, strong evidence of alliance making among communities who shared common ethnic origins. Intraethnic alliances of rural communities, which had repeatedly manifested in previous centuries, again effectively bore praetorian fruit. This created unending crises for the colonial authorities. The ability of rural Guineans to establish common military fronts both within and between various groups and continually to repel European invaders would not be forgotten by subsequent generations of Guineans, and it would later help to provide both a meaningful historical memory and strong social bases for the construction of an independent and autonomous rural civil society.

Chapter 4 has also made clear that the Portuguese suffered an inability to deploy weaponry markedly superior to that obtained by indigenous forces. The acquisition of modern weapons, including mortars, by local defenders had clearly augmented the risks of combat for the would-be colonial state builders. Papel kings, Oinka fighters, Balanta along the Geba river, and Mandjack in Cacheu region all managed to obtain modern-day rifles and even, occasionally, machine guns.[142] To be sure, other West African societies had also procured weapons and used them with some degree of effectiveness against invading French and British imperial armies;[143] however, Portuguese machine guns and cannons were often of poor quality; they jammed with unusual frequency. Although the Portuguese possessed more rapid-fire weaponry than their African opponents, they were in insufficient numbers to break the back of the Papel, Oinka, Balanta, and Mandjack fighting forces.

As to strategy, African military leaders commonly proved superior to Portuguese commanders, who relied on traditional Portuguese hunt-and-peck "war campaigns." A frequently repeated pattern emerged wherein Portuguese forces attacked and pillaged one or two unguarded villages only to be set upon—and defeated—by local defenders after the conclusion of the pillaging. For this reason, Oio region remained untouched by colonial authorities through the first decade of the twentieth century. In 1910, Governor Pimental complained that the wealthiest regions of Guinea, including Oio, Cacheu, and Bafatá, remained free from Portuguese colonial authority.[144] Thus, Portuguese military forces, in effect, were set at bay in "Portuguese" Guinea, with the interior under the control of local leaders to such an extent that Europeans hardly dared to venture out from towns and outposts.[145] As the second decade of the twentieth century began, the Portuguese controlled no more than one-tenth of Guinea.[146]

In conclusion, I must disagree with Pélissier when he insists that the precolonial resistance efforts were largely "rear-guard battles for fleeting micro-independences" and that "at no moment were they [the resisters] prepared to place Portuguese supremacy in question."[147] Pélissier exaggerated the purportedly "micro" and "fleeting" character of Guinean resistance. Many Papel, Balanta, Felupe, Bijagós, Soninké, and others did aim precisely to remove Portuguese officialdom from entire regions, and they often linked up various rural communities to do so. Overall, this was much more than a confluence of "rear-guard" defensive stands; the extensive interethnic alliances would, in fact, help set the stage for the emergence of a strong, interlinked rural civil society.

As the second decade of the twentieth century began, Portuguese claims to political sovereignty in Guinea appeared increasingly untenable. The resultant sense of desperation led the Portuguese to turn toward near-total reliance on an infamous Senegalese mercenary who agreed to carry out a policy of civilian-based terror. That is the subject of chapter 5.

CHAPTER 5

The Terrorist State

Conquest through Mercenary Pillage

REELING FROM MULTIPLE DEFEATS in the period from 1890 to 1909, Portuguese Guinean officials paused in their 1910–12 war-making effort. Lisbon, meanwhile, reduced its military and institutional support.[1] At the beginning of 1913, a decision was made by the Portuguese leadership in Bolama and Bissau to try once more to extend their authority out from their barricaded port towns. This time, their strategy would be to regularize and systematize the infliction of violence against unarmed villagers. To be sure, killing people who did not openly resist had been part of colonial war campaigns in the past; the policy change in 1913 reflected an effort to implement a comprehensive, village-by-village set of attacks throughout the colony. The intention was to wreak massive violence against civilians methodically in order to force the population into acceptance of Portuguese political hegemony. I call this a policy predicated on state terror because of the planned, sustained, systematic nature of extreme violence carried out by state leaders and those operating on behalf of the state.[2]

A highly experienced military officer, Captain João Teixeira Pinto, was placed in charge of this mission.[3] Pinto had achieved considerable renown in coordinating the conquest drive in Angola; he arrived in Guinea as the newly appointed Guinean military chief of staff on 23 September 1912.[4] Pinto's strategy in Guinea, in contrast to the hit-and-run war campaigns of the past, would be "to burn [down villages]; to collect taxes and to gather up [indigenously held] weapons: in a word, to inflict an exemplary punishment and to do away with the half measures of the past. A task of mercenaries working at their own pace, far from the sight of, and possible criticisms from, Bissau."[5]

It is ironic that the Guinean state now turned to a policy of official terror: a regime devoted to constitutional republicanism had just been established in Portugal itself, and the new governor of Guinea, Carlos de Almeida Pereira, was a partisan of the new values of liberal legalism—values that the Portuguese government purported to embrace. However, Portugal's weak hold over the Guinean interior was a tired embarrassment for Lusophone officialdom: the Portuguese could hardly pretend to rule a colony when its regions remained politically autonomous. Pinto would be given free rein to provide African mercenaries with the resources and the political license to embark on a village-by-village campaign of barbarism, killing and mutilating unarmed civilians. Unbridled state terror would be implemented in 1913–15 more effectively than any other public policy in the five-century history of that territory.[6]

How was Pinto able to implement this policy? He did not arrive in Bissau with a substantial column of European soldiers, or with new weaponry or new funding for the government's military adventures. He would have to rely heavily on the traditional basis of colonial war making in Guinea: indigenous allies. These included large numbers of Fulbe auxiliaries provided by allied chiefs,[7] but Pinto's new aims would necessitate going beyond simply augmenting the numbers of Fulbe fighting men.[8] His fortunes turned favorable when in November 1912 Vasco de Souza Calvet de Magalhães, the resident commander of Geba region, introduced him to the Senegalese mercenary Abdul Injai at Bafatá.[9] Injai was a self-made businessman from a Wolof-speaking area of Siné-Saloum, Senegal, who had spent much of the 1898–1912 period organizing brigands to carry out specific attacks against Guinea-Bissauans at the behest of Portuguese governors and military commanders.[10] Injai and his men, who installed themselves in a small fortified area near Geba, had developed a notorious, widespread reputation for the grotesquely brutal ways in which they pillaged undefended villages as part of various Portuguese war campaigns.[11] Pinto came to the conclusion that Injai's men were potentially capable of accomplishing what previous collaborators— and Portuguese soldiers themselves—had been unable to do, and Injai and his growing band of Senegalese mercenaries would eventually prove so effective at their mission that Pinto's war-making strategy would increasingly be defined by simply allowing Injai to carry out wave after wave of military campaigns and terror attacks.[12] Indeed, Pinto could not have sustained his military drive without Injai's forces, and he "generally preferred them to regular soldiers."[13]

Injai's mercenaries were provided with five-shot rifles by the Portuguese, whereas the Balanta were using single-shot flintlocks;[14] however, this alone would have been insufficient to break through the Balanta defenses. I suggest that the key factors in Injai's success were the battle skill of his men and their methodical, village-by-village targeting and slaughter of unarmed civilians. Pinto normally accompanied Injai on these war campaigns (along with a handful of Portuguese soldiers) and participated in the selection of the targets of operation. The Injai/Pinto unit benefited from the fact that the governors of Guinea in the 1913–15 period, beginning with Pereira, all chose to remain largely detached from military affairs. This relative freedom of operations contributed to Injai's growing power because he was able to make substantial use of his war captives: his own band of brigands, consisting mostly of Senegalese mercenaries, would be bolstered by these captives, seized from various parts of Senegal and Guinea-Bissau and forced to join his men.[15] Thus, Injai's forces grew in proportion to his battle victories. Also, the colonialists managed to convince other collaborative chiefs (such as Malam Bá and Alfa Mamadu Seilu) to help carry out war campaigns.[16]

THE DIRTY WARS BEGIN: OIO

Oio in 1912 remained, as it had previously been, essentially independent of colonial influence. The closest Portuguese outpost to Oio was established in 1909 at Bissorã, to the immediate southwest, where the colonialists were able to befriend Soninké Chief Malam Bá. But neither this Bissorã post nor the tiny military outpost established (1907) at Carenque Cunda to the east had any impact within Oio itself. In fact, the only recorded interaction between the Oinka and the Luso-European enclaves prior to the twentieth century was occasional trade carried out at Porto Mansoa and with Soller, a (first German, then French) commercial establishment whose directors paid taxes to the local Soninké and Balanta peoples.[17]

　　Pinto and Injai set about organizing a war party in March 1913 after Pinto had made an investigatory visit to the region disguised as a French commercial inspector.[18] On this war campaign, Pinto brought along several dozen regular soldiers directed by Geba administrator Calvet de Magalhães, while allowing Injai to command all the irregulars—virtually the entire war party. However, word had spread among the Oinka (Balanta, Soninké, and Mandinka) of this military expedition. The Oinka defenders had obtained rifles and gunpowder from illegal traders, and the strategists among these Oinka mapped out a strong defense.[19]

On 29 March 1913, Balanta foot soldiers dodged colonial machine-gun and cannon fire and managed to position themselves as close as thirty meters to the war party's encampment. These Balanta riflemen, supported by Soninké horsemen, sustained an attack for four hours. The Balanta fighters then pulled back and decided to seek additional recruits from Balanta villages throughout Oio, while the Soninké departed to obtain mounted reinforcements.[20] On 2 April, the now-reinforced and resupplied indigenous defenders reengaged the invaders and sustained a four-and-a half-hour firefight. In the end, however, they proved unable to withstand the firepower of the artillery and machine guns and, in retreat, they were pursued by Injai's forces, who murdered all whom they caught. Magalhães then traveled to Bafatá to enlist the support of as many Fulbe auxiliaries as possible, while Injai sent for his own reinforcements from Gole (one of Injai's bases of operation). Injai's reinforcements arrived at Porto Mansoa on 13 April, with his forces now totaling 3,000 foot soldiers and 180 horsemen.[21]

Meanwhile, Oinka fighters harassed the small colonial outpost of Bissorã (which was headed by Lieutenant Augusto José de Lima Jr.). On 14 April a small-scale attack was made against the encampment at Porto Mansoa. That same day, emissaries from nearby Balanta villages located on the northern bank of the river arrived at Porto Mansoa and inquired into conditions of peace. Pinto's response was to insist that Balanta in the region hand in their weapons and pay a full year's taxes, regardless of whether they had participated in the attacks. Some villagers decided to do so. Villages that did not send emissaries to promise submission were attacked and burned down (16 April and several days afterward) by Injai's forces.[22] Injai's unrelenting brutality wreaked on the unarmed people of those villages was characteristic of the terrorist mode of conquest that typified this Oio war campaign.

On 24 April, Injai's men diverted the attention of Oinka fighters by engaging them in small-scale combat in the woods, allowing the force commanded by Magalhães, composed largely of Fulbe recruited in Bafatá, to seize and occupy Gindu, a strategically significant Soninké village. Magalhães and his Fulbe forces were attacked later that same day by Soninké, and a twelve-hour battle ensued, toward the end of which most of the Fulbe auxiliaries fled.[23] Magalhães and his remaining troops retreated to Bananto on the Farim River; they would not reappear in action for a month.[24] Meanwhile, from 30 April to 3 May, a separate attack party besieged Balanta villages in the area of Jugudul (near the Gole military outpost). The Portuguese were surprised to find that grumetes were fighting alongside Balanta. The motivation of these grumetes was unclear: it was not known whether they were grumetes who had traveled from towns such as Farim

and Cacheu to Oio specifically to help the Balanta defense, or whether these grumetes lived in these villages and were attempting to defend and fight for their
lives and property. What was clear was that "the tacit Portuguese-grumete alliance was broken."[25] Furthermore, Injai's spies reported that Papel fighters were
helping the besieged Balanta of Oio between Porto Mansoa and Gole along the
Mansoa River. So now it was clear that a Balanta-Papel-grumete anticolonial alliance had emerged in this indigenous struggle against colonial state terror. For
all three parties in the alliance, the significance of this struggle had already
evolved into more than simply a regional Oinka territorial defense.

Nonetheless, Injai's mercenary forces were proving increasingly formidable.
They showed no mercy when arriving at undefended villages. A massive assault
on unarmed homesteads near the Mansoa River between 5 and 7 May resulted
in the murder of dozens of villagers and provoked the exodus of many Balanta
to other parts of Oio.[26]

The Great Battle of Cambajo

The operation was a nearly all-mercenary one: the Portuguese presence consisted only of Pinto and a nominal showing of ten regular soldiers. Prodded by
Pinto, in May 1913 Injai's three thousand fighters proceeded through Oio region. On 15 May, they encountered a substantial force of Soninké defenders at
the village of Cambajo. The combat that followed turned out to be one of the
most intense battles not only in the history of "Portuguese" Guinea but, according to René Pélissier, in all of Portugal's empire to date.[27] More than forty thousand cartridges were spent in the battle,[28] and the village of Cambajo, in the
end, was seized and burned. Despite this defeat, the next day (16 May) Soninké
defenders regrouped and again attacked the convoy, this time for an hour and a
half, with both sides suffering heavy losses.

The defiance of the Soninké defenders should be underlined; they would, in
fact, regroup for a third battle. However, the chief strategists among the Soninké
wisely decided to change tactics, so that rather than engaging in head-to-head
battles in major villages, they now set up numerous traps and ambushes from the
woods alongside the paths traveled by the Injai forces. Part of this guerrilla strategy also included the systematic poisoning of wells and waterholes as the invaders approached, which slowed the advance of Injai's column.[29] The column,
however, was able to obtain new supplies, including fresh water, from Fulbe auxiliaries and then proceeded to set afire the villages of Maqué and Sansabato, where
they carried out mass murders of civilians, often by hand, using knives or swords.

They continued on toward Morés;[30] along this route, Soninké riflemen concentrated intensive gunfire on Injai's forces, killing several dozen foot soldiers and horsemen. However, by 30 May Injai's men seized and burned down Morés.[31]

Soninké defenders still did not give up. On the path between Morés and Mansodé, another center of Oinka resistance, Soninké fighters dug huge pits, laid piles of tree branches, set up barricades, and laid ambushes. The advancing column was appreciably slowed, but the column was able to remain at all times within about four hours' walking distance from Porto Mansoa and could therefore continue to be resupplied with water and ammunition. Thus able to proceed, Injai's men captured Mansodé (5 June), the village's residents having put up an intensive but short-lived defense.[32]

Essentially, northern Oio had now been conquered. Between 6 and 8 June, Soninké villages and their chiefs surrendered to Injai and Pinto en masse. In contrast to what had occurred after previous expeditions, when colonialists simply departed and local chiefs regained autonomy, Injai's men spent ten days rounding up weapons (a total of 3,248 guns were seized), taking a village-by-village population census for taxation purposes, and establishing nuclei of Injai loyalists throughout the region.[33] This made possible a tax collection, which began on 17 June; approximately thirty thousand people were forced to turn over money or goods.[34]

This represented a clear-cut display of state-guided military power in Oio, the first time that Lusophone "stateness" had made itself felt at grassroots level in that region. No less importantly in terms of colonial political authority, a fortified military garrison was constructed on 24 June at Mansabá,[35] which had historically been a center of Oinka resistance. The chances that this process of state penetration would evolve into an institutionalized system of rulership were augmented when Pinto convinced Injai to remain personally at Mansabá and to assure a continuity of governance within Oio.[36]

CHURO IN CACHEU REGION

In Cacheu region, on 12 December 1913 a Portuguese official, José Nunes, was killed, along with eight aides, while traveling by canoe on the Pelundo River on a tax-collection mission in the interior (his boat was set afire by Mandjack fighters).[37] This, in itself, was not an unusual turn of events, but at this juncture it presented the governor of Guinea, Andrade Sequeira, with a special incentive to move rapidly to extend the conquest mandate to Cacheu region. A war party

(352 of Injai's men, 17 European soldiers, and several dozen grumetes and aux-iliaries) set out for the Pelundo River in Cacheu. They were rapidly confronted (2 January 1914) by a Mandjack defense force from Pelundo, Basserel, and Churo.[38] Heavy rifle fire from the Mandjack produced seven dead and twenty-eight wounded in the colonial column; the Mandjack attackers also suffered "large losses."[39]

The next day the battle was rejoined, resulting in a similar stand-off, but during the course of the fighting the colonial column captured several hundred young men (these would later serve as forced auxiliaries).[40] Over the next couple of days (3–5 January), the expedition reached Churobrique, where they burned and pillaged the village. When the column departed, a thirty-five-man detach-ment was left to set up and staff a military outpost there. Remaining Mandjack fighters in the Churo area now fought back in a more dispersed pattern, but this proved a tactical error since the Injai-Pinto forces overcame each village's defense one by one and then ransacked and burned down huts and killed unarmed vil-lagers.[41] Oral histories recorded in 1987 attest to still-vivid memories of the vi-ciousness of these murders and to the indiscriminate brutality inflicted against pregnant women and children.[42]

Some Churo peasants managed to escape when people from a nearby vil-lage (Caboi) provided canoe transports, taking them to noncombatant villages dominated by Banhun and Cassanga.[43] However, the Injai-Pinto methodology of state terror accomplished its mission of establishing colonial state rule in the Churo sector. Injai's men assisted Portuguese officials in establishing two per-manent bases in Cacheu region, at Churobrique and Canchungo.[44]

Churo's Last Stand

The defeat of Churo, a key Mandjack area within the Basserel kingdom, had significantly weakened the will of the remaining Mandjack fighters. Most of the Mandjack chiefs who had previously remained loyal to the Basserel king now opted not to wage war in defense of the kingship.[45] However, a number of Mandjack chiefs, breaking with their compatriots, remained determined to defend the territory of greater Basserel. This included the king himself. Thou-sands of resisters were mobilized, and on 18–19 March 1914, a force of some ten thousand Mandjack gathered at Brame Grande, near Basserel.[46] Spies loyal to Injai informed him of the gathering, and a military column proceeded di-rectly to confront these fighters. The battle, which was unusually bloody, even-tually tilted in favor of the invaders.[47] The Basserel king was captured by the

Injai-Pinto forces on 29 March. The military column collected 2,076 guns from Mandjack villagers.[48] The king was later deported, which marked the end of the independent political power of the kingdom of Basserel.[49] Equally crucial regarding colonial state power, a military outpost was established at Basserel. It was from there that an Injai-Pinto column swept through nearby villages, killing people and imposing a war tax.[50]

Northern Cacheu and Mansoa Region

While these battles were in progress at Churo and Basserel, the Balanta of Braia, north of the Mansoa River, attacked and destroyed a colonial military platoon comprising twenty-five men, killing three second lieutenants and fifteen indigenous auxiliaries on 5 February 1914.[51] Four days later, Balanta fighters attacked a colonial military column between Mansoa and Braia and in the first round of gunfire killed a number of European officers, four Fulbe auxiliaries, and eleven regular soldiers.[52]

Meanwhile, two of Injai's lieutenants in Mansoa, Aly Cissé and Sadio Coumba Zamara, were called upon by Portuguese officials to attack the village of Souloulou to avenge the ambush-killing of a Portuguese tax officer and indigenous auxiliaries who had sought to collect taxes in late 1913. Cissé and Zamara's forces entered Souloulou and upon finding few residents, simply burned the villagers' homes. During the return of Cissé, Zamara, and their men from Souloulou, they were attacked by a large group of well-armed Balanta. The force was decimated: Cissé, Zamara, and forty-three of their men were killed (out of a total force of seventy).[53] By May, the Injai-Pinto expedition was ready to marshal a column against Souloulou and Braia in revenge—and to complete the conquest of northern Cacheu and Mansoa region.[54] They explicitly intended to kill "the maximum number of [Balanta] men."[55] Balanta defenders, aware of the imminent arrival of the Injai-Pinto forces, concentrated their fighters along the northern bank of the Mansoa River in an area called Encheia (Incheia).[56]

Although the Balanta lived in dispersed, relatively isolated communities, they amassed as many as twenty thousand fighters. Hawthorne explains how they were able to pull together such a large force: specific age-grade groupings communicated to one another with *bomboloms* ("talking drums"), through which "they were able to transmit battle plans over great stretches of territory."[57] Certain drumbeats indicated that women and children should flee into dense forest areas, while men able to fight should prepare to join up with their comrades from other villagers. This intervillage means of communication had been used effectively since the 1500s (perhaps earlier); now, in 1914, it again provided the dispersed Balanta with a praetorian methodology of rapidly organizing a large intraethnic military force.[58]

The battle at Encheia on 20 May lasted more than eight hours.[59] The Pinto-Injai expedition, split into five attacking columns supported by machine-gun fire from war boats, eventually overcame massive Balanta resistance and thereafter proceeded to "ravage the zone between Bissorã and Braia";[60] reaching Braia on 7 June, they defeated the Balanta forces gathered there. A week later (15 June), the Balanta rallied for a third and final defense of Encheia but were overcome once more by machine-gun fire. Upon this defeat, the Balanta, reflecting their lack of centralized chieftainship, responded to Pinto's offer of peace-upon-submission in various ways: each family decided for itself whether or not to turn in its weapons and promise submission. Most decided not to, preferring immediate flight.

Finally, the Injai-Pinto forces proceeded to Nhacra, a significant Balanta settlement located near the Geba and Impernal Rivers — two busy trade routes — at the center of the rice-rich agricultural lands of Mansoa region.[61] Balanta fighters attacked the column at multiple approach points, but Injai's men punched through those defenses, ransacked Nhacra on 30 June, and established a sixteen-man garrison.[62] Four days later, Balanta from Changué outfought a seventeen-man party of Injai's horsemen that had become separated from the main contingent. The following day, Injai's forces seized and executed forty-nine unarmed, civilian Balanta from Changué village,[63] completing the process of not only subjugating Mansoa but also establishing state authority through a combination of military prowess and wanton, anticivilian terror.

THE PAPEL-PORTUGUESE WAR OF 1915

Having conquered the regions that had enjoyed the greatest degree of autonomy from the colonial state — most notably, Oio, Cacheu, and Mansoa — the colonial power knew that now the key remaining center of indigenous resistance was Bissau island. Indeed, in December 1914, the governor of Guinea, Josué de Oliveira Duque, noted to an official in Bolama that Portuguese authority on the island of Bissau was wielded only within the European fort town itself: Papel kings retained autonomous control over the rest of the island.[64]

Many mestiços and grumetes within Bissau, especially those whose personal, family, and trading ties with neighboring Papel villagers had made them all too aware that they could expect further terrorist tactics, virulently opposed the governor's planned Pinto-Injai campaign. They used every political maneuver at their disposal to prevent the campaign from taking place: they tried to provoke a rivalry between Pinto and Injai; they attempted to set Governor Duque against Pinto and to convince the minister of colonies to intervene to curtail Injai.[65] None of these efforts succeeded: the governor was determined that the conquest be completed, and that it include Bissau island.

In May 1915, Pinto communicated to the Papel chiefs that villagers were required to pay taxes. The chiefs refused.[66] Instead, Papel fighters secured more weapons from clandestine gun traders in Bafatá[67] and then positioned themselves close to Portuguese sentries and taunted them.[68] In response, according to an announcement in the Portuguese official bulletin, all communication and trading activity between Bissau town residents and the Papel were forbidden; any mestiço not found to be carrying official identification papers would be considered a "rebel"; and all mestiços living within Bissau had to present themselves to the authorities twice a day.[69]

During the first week of June, Bissau bolstered its defense forces to 150 regular troops and 200 auxiliaries.[70] A separate battalion of auxiliaries, under the command of (mostly) Fulbe chiefs, gathered at Nhacra, twenty kilometers from Bissau.[71] On 27 May, with the troops awaiting the arrival of Injai, who was to direct the anticipated rampage,[72] it was made clear for motivational purposes that the "salary" of these brigands would be the pillaging of the Papel villages that they attacked.[73] To assure that the Papel could not obtain support from Mandjack villagers to the north of Bissau, the Portuguese blockaded northern routes.[74]

The fighting began on 31 May. Cannons at the Bissau fort bombarded Papel villages 1,200 meters to the west. Papel riflemen, armed with advanced Mauser firearms, returned fire, hitting targets in the fort of Bissau. The Papel raked bullets along the greater part of the main street of Bissau, hitting house porches, rooftops, and the windowpanes of stores.[75] On 3 June, thousands of Papel fighters, along with several hundred grumete allies, took the initiative and attacked colonial auxiliaries near Intim, killing twenty, wounding seventy, and forcing the remainder to retreat. Two days later, Injai's forces attacked the Papel stronghold of Antula, while auxiliaries commanded by Mamadu Cissé and Fulbe mercenaries supported by machine-gun fire assaulted Intim and Bandim.[76] Hundreds of Papel and grumetes perished. On the colonialist side, one regular soldier and five auxiliaries were killed; there were twenty-four wounded. Intim and Bandim were seized, and Antula fell on 8 June.[77]

With Antula, Intim, and Bandim defeated, the expedition began a march on

11 June that aimed to establish Portuguese authority in every remaining village on the island. However, the resistance of Papel and grumete villagers would be no less tenacious than that of the Soninké and Balanta of Oio and the Mandjack and Balanta of Cacheu and Mansoa. On 12 June, intensive fighting at the village of Jal produced hundreds of casualties on both sides—including the wounding of Pinto by a grumete. Subsequently, hundreds of Papel civilians—women, children, and the aged—were mutilated or killed outright. At the conclusion of a 20 July battle, Injai captured, tortured, and killed Chief Cassande. (There are two versions of how it happened: his eyes were gouged, then he was buried alive; or he was decapitated after being tortured.)[78]

After the military battles, a campaign of egregious violence took place against the defenseless Papel populace from July until October.[79] During that period, Injai's mercenaries stole more than four thousand cattle, raped hundreds of Papel and grumete women, and kidnapped many Papel women and children and sold them in clandestine slave markets.[80] According to Papel who had fled to Casamance, Injai publicly executed dozens of villagers, including women and children, in each Papel community. He was said to have sliced open the bellies of pregnant women and removed the fetuses as a display of his power and cruelty.[81] His troops forcibly sequestered themselves in grumete homes.[82]

Injai and his mercenaries had been given free rein to unleash a stream of colonial state terror against the Papel and grumete people of Bissau island. It was through these methods that colonial state authority was established.

CONQUEST ACHIEVED

Between 1913 and 1915, the colonial forces carried out military operations in Cacheu region, São Domingos, Farim, Oio, Mansoa, Geba, and Gole.[83] In April 1914, a Portuguese official reported that in "Mandjack and Brame territory," despite seventy-six soldiers lost to death or injury, Portuguese rule had become established, and 24,000 escudos (out of a goal of 50,000 escudos) had been collected.[84] The great Mandjack kingdom based in Basserel, which had expanded to include some forty chiefdoms by the end of the nineteenth century, was substantially reduced and weakened as a consequence of these terror campaigns.[85] With the conquest of the Papel kingdoms in 1915, the autonomy of the final remaining centralized indigenous power structure was broken. It appeared that Lusophone colonialism had finally succeeded in establishing state sovereignty over the interior of Portuguese Guinea.

Crucial to the success of the Injai-Pinto expedition was the unbridled use of state terror. By *state terror* I refer not simply to the military defeat of armed indigenous fighters but, as noted earlier, also to the systematic killings of unarmed civilians, the massive theft of village property, the destruction of livestock, and the capturing of young men and their forced conscription as colonial auxiliaries. During 1914 and early 1915, Injai's men continuously "exterminated people, destroying, pillaging, burning everything."[86] It was common for them to enter a village, kill many of the men, rape and brutalize the women, and then sell the women and their children into slavery.[87] These actions were a key element in rendering indigenous forces unable to reply, militarily or politically, to the new politico-military assertions of state power. Injai's terror left the Guinean populace with enduring memories of unending horror, as described by witnesses decades later — in 1940,[88] the mid-1970s,[89] and the early 1980s.[90] Dramatizing the central role played by Injai in these terrorist massacres, testimonies obtained in the mid-1990s found virtually no Balanta memories of Pinto, but distinct recollections of Injai.[91] At the same time, it is crucial to emphasize that this ultraviolence was state sanctioned. Portuguese officials in fact used the term *war of extermination* in discussing Injai's actions with foreign diplomats.[92]

In contrast to previous military expeditions, the colonialists made it a priority to set up heavily armed, well-manned military outposts in the conquered areas. They thus consolidated state power in Cacheu, Oio, Mansoa, Farim, Bissorã, and Catió. State sovereignty was further enhanced by the setting up of telegraph lines that linked the outposts with Bissau. Professional clerks and tax collectors were also hired.[93]

Could the "final conquest" of the Guinean interior have been accomplished by Portuguese soldiers? According to the official Portuguese version of events, it was Pinto who had "prepared, organized, and commanded the campaigns of Mansoa and Oio in 1913, of Cacheu and against the Balantas in 1914, and of the isle of Bissau in 1915, suppressing the rebellions in the latter and pacifying the entire country."[94] With greater accuracy, Pélissier emphasizes Pinto's effective capacity to mobilize Africans against Africans.[95] To be sure, it should be underscored that Pinto's tactical success substantially hindered, and in some areas broke, the intraethnic and interethnic alliances that had helped to make possible previous indigenous military successes. However, it was not only Pinto but also, and in many areas primarily, Injai who shrewdly crafted the meticulous village-by-village "holding" strategy[96] — and who combined this with civilian mass murder. It was Injai's indigenous mercenaries and not Portuguese soldiers who, on the ground, were able to assure the success of the conquest.

Injai and his hired men did what was necessary to wreak the sustained terror capable of establishing colonial stateness in the Guinean interior. In most campaigns the Portuguese forces relied almost exclusively on Injai's fighters, sometimes along with Fulbe auxiliaries.[97] Portuguese and French observers repeatedly emphasized the overwhelming numerical superiority of Injai's forces vis-à-vis Portuguese soldiers and the central role played by Injai and his men.[98] Thus, we may conclude that Portugal's military success in the interior was made possible only by the active support of indigenous allies.[99]

Finally, it should be emphasized that it was colonial bureaucratic and military fragility that made imperative the use of state terror. Cruelty, arbitrary punishment, the burning of entire villages, and the public murder of pregnant women are the methods employed by fragile governments unable to marshal a modern army, but desperate to secure political sovereignty.

From a comparative viewpoint, it may be noted that as in Portuguese Guinea, elsewhere, too, in Africa early in the colonial period, the conquest episode witnessed barbaric acts committed by European forces. The British campaigns against Bai Bureh, a Sierra Leonean indigenous strongman, were marked by the systematic burning of villages, and in Western Sudan the French sacked towns, "killing innocent women and children and enslaving adult males."[100] In much of Africa, European sovereignty, when it was established, remained "inherently precarious," necessitating repeated demonstrations of bloody military might.[101] In some cases, such as in Bakongo areas of the Belgian Congo, this was manifested in repeated acts of state violence.[102] Still, these atrocities did not occur to the same extent or as late as in Portuguese Guinea, where (1913–15) Injai and Pinto massacred villagers throughout the rural regions. Moreover, in contrast to what occurred in Portuguese Guinea, most other colonial states did advance to a more stable assertion of hegemony—"a comprehensive apparatus of domination"—despite some scattered instances of revolt.[103] As we shall see, the Portuguese would experience great difficulty in achieving such domination and in consolidating the colonial state's security imperative.

PORTENTS OF AN INCOMPLETE CONQUEST

From 1915 to 1920, certain centers of allied indigenous power, being fully independent, lingered and threatened to railroad the Portuguese state-building project in Guinea. Oral testimonies collected later from Mandjack in Cacheu region verify that Fulbe, Wolof, and Sarakolé (i.e., colonialist "auxiliaries" operating on behalf of Injai, rather than the Portuguese themselves) ruled Cacheu region after the con-quest.[104] Duque, the governor, himself complained that the colonial army was not yet strong enough to replace Injai's men.[105]

Injai's autonomy presented a challenging policy quagmire in several ways: (1) His brutal predations against the local populace did not cease, making it more difficult for the Portuguese to establish political stability;[106] and he continued the hated (and illegal) practice of selling captives (in July 1916, for example, Injai sold on clandestine slave markets a large number of Papel children whose par-ents he and his men had recently killed).[107] (2) After the end of the major wars of conquest, Portuguese officials publicly began to accuse Injai of what they had known in private for some time: that he retained the major portion—often 100 percent—of the hut tax he collected nominally on behalf of the Portuguese colo-nial government.[108] (3) Injai controlled a significant percentage of territory: he exerted virtually independent hegemony over much of Oio region as a conse-quence of his tax-collection responsibilities (accorded to him by Pinto after the conquest) and he also held a mini-fiefdom in Bafatá region.[109] And (4) Injai failed to hand over his mercenaries' weapons to the Portuguese authorities.

Portuguese officials very much wanted to avoid confronting Injai militar-ily; they feared his forces could best them in an all-out engagement. In addi-tion, they needed his fighting men to remain at their posts, especially in Oio, where colonial officials felt that indigenous fighters could still regroup. More-over, now that the rivers and the interior of the colony had been subjugated, the colonialists needed Injai's forces to support their 1917 war effort on the last remaining enclave of sovereign indigenous political power—the Bijagós island of Canhabac.

CANHABAC, 1916–1918

Canhabac had proved difficult to vanquish in the past: its inhabitants enjoyed a "natural" defensive advantage—the dense clusters of trees that characterized the island (similar to the terrain in Oio region).[110] However, with the mainland conquered, the Portuguese could marshal their military forces for an all-out as-sault on Canhabac. In 1916, a military unit was dispatched to the Bijagós is-lands. In the initial fighting, twenty-five soldiers were killed. The remainder returned to Bissau.[111]

In April and May 1917, Colonel Coelho, the interim governor of the colony, organized a war column with regular soldiers, Fulbe, and some of Injai's men.[112]

These forces engaged in pitched battles with Canhabac defenders throughout the island between 15 May and 5 July.[113] The problem for the colonials was that they could not see their opponents, who relied on guerrilla-style fighting techniques, hiding out of sight in dense brush and firing on their enemy selectively.[114] Also, the indigenous defenders proved skilled at tracking down and shooting groups of soldiers who had strayed toward a river, seeking water, or who were trekking back to their ships for supplies.[115]

Fighting continued for months. By that September, desperate to gain the upper hand, a sub-lieutenant, Cipriano Pereira, decided to aim his cannons at population centers, including Inorei (In-Orei) and Meneque, even though few Bijagós fighters were expected to be there. The resulting loss of civilian life provoked most Canhabacers to travel by canoe to other Bijagós islands (particularly Bubaque and Galinhas).[116] However, some Canhabac fighters continued to hide out and ambush the colonialists. A November letter describes the "occupation troops" of Injai loyalist Mamadu Cissé as still actively fighting on Canhabac.[117] They were weakened by an outbreak of intestinal ailments that may have been caused by the purposeful contamination of waterholes by Canhabacers.

The Canhabacers, having suffered extensive losses in these battles, in early January 1918, formally surrendered: some of the resistance leaders were transported to Bolama for a ceremonial presentation in which they signed a treaty.[118] Afterward, the colonial forces burned half the huts and established command posts at Inorei and Meneque.[119] However, I will suggest in chapter 6 that this conquest of Canhabac would prove relatively short-lived and incomplete.

INJAI'S AUTONOMY

During the course of the Canhabac operations, Abdul Injai, based in Oio, oversaw a particularly large "tax collection"—a pruning of the economic resources that had been accumulated by villagers.[120] At that point, a military officer, Ivo de Sá Ferreira, asked Injai to curtail his excessive pilfering. Injai refused and in fact threatened to remove his forces from participation in the attack on Canhabac.[121] The issue was not further discussed during the Canhabac operation, but afterward the Portuguese felt that it was time to rein in this powerful warlord, despite the services of conquest he had performed. The fact was that state building could not proceed with Injai in autonomous control of significant swaths of Guinean territory.[122] The conquest mandate had been completed, and the colonial administration aimed to move beyond the infliction of terror as a strategy of rule.

In 1918–19, the government refused to pay Injai what had been promised to him in return for his contribution to the colony's conquest (405 horses, 8,000 francs).[123] Injai made clear that what he now wanted was to retire to a portion of Guinea and "to live in peace."[124] In other words, he was asking the Portuguese to officially grant him formal control over Oio. Injai would later tally his losses and costs as totaling 692 men killed, 328 injured, 236 horses killed, and having incurred expenses amounting to 512,050 French francs.[125] Considering these alleged sacrifices, Injai was strongly dissatisfied with the refusal of the Portuguese to accord him any compensation despite their previous promises. He adopted an increasingly hostile attitude toward the government.[126] Injai also, under a variety of pretexts, reportedly executed large numbers of Fulbe chiefs allied with the Portuguese. The governor, fearing defeat, remained reluctant to embark on an all-out confrontation.[127]

Meanwhile, relentless political pressure to disarm Injai was being placed on the Portuguese authorities by Europeans, Cape Verdeans, mestiços, and grumetes living in Bissau and by former Guinean Cape Verdeans and mestiços living in Lisbon. These groups especially abhorred Injai's ability to behave as he pleased—which continued, in 1919, to include the carrying out of raids on villages.[128] A Cape Verdean/mestiço political lobby pressed for his downfall, in large part because they felt that Injai represented an embarrassment to Portugal. Seeing in Injai's power a mark of Portugal's continuing dependency on indigenous Africans to sustain hegemony over the interior, they felt that his ongoing power-mongering humiliated the colonial state itself—an entity they aimed eventually to render more independent of the metropolis. These Cape Verdeans and mestiços hoped to control the Guinean state: greater separation from Portugal, they believed, would enable them to profit more fully from import-export trade.[129]

At the same time, according to Sherif Hamed Ben Salah, an African agent of the French governor-general in Dakar who had spent several months in 1919 with Injai's men, Injai now was aiming to expand his mini-empire into neighboring regions.[130] Frustrated by the unresponsiveness of Portuguese state officials, in May 1919 Injai and his men carried out raids on villages in Oio—raids of such brutality that masses of villagers fled to Casamance.[131] The following month, Injai told Caetano José Barbosa, the administrator of Farim, that he (Injai) was equal to Barbosa in power and stature.[132] Barbosa, appalled, then told José de Oliveira Duque, the governor of Guinea (in 1919), that he would resign were an expedition not organized to remove Injai by force.

Later that June, Governor Duque's inaction in fact provoked his own removal as governor; his replacement—Captain Henrique Alberto de Sousa Guerra—was determined to do battle. Sousa Guerra and Injai then held talks for two days (27–28 June), during which time the colonial army reinforced the post of Mancabá with light artillery and four contingents of African auxiliaries.[133] This post was located near Injai's private residence—only a few hundred meters away. At the meeting, Injai explicitly declared that he would not submit to Portuguese rule: he rearticulated a series of demands, including one for monetary compensation.[134] At this point, Sousa Guerra decided to halt discussions with Injai. About 250 regular soldiers, armed only with 160 rifles and a few cannons, were transported from Bissau to Oio by boat.[135] Injai, by contrast, was in command of approximately a thousand fighting men, each in possession of a modern rifle.[136] The unanswered question was, therefore, not so much whether Injai could defeat the Portuguese, but whether he would engage them in battle after his many years of service; it appeared that Injai did not desire a confrontation and was personally depressed at the way the Portuguese now treated him.[137]

On 19 July, tensions arose between Injai's fighters and a Portuguese contingent led by Lieutenant Alonso Figueira, stationed at Mancabá. Injai's men cut the telephone lines linking Oio, Farim, and Bolama, infuriating Figueira.[138] On 1 August, one of Injai's fighters was killed by Figueira's soldiers, and in response Injai grouped three hundred of his men in two columns near the barricade at Mancabá. The Portuguese initiated a two-hour exchange of gunfire, toward the conclusion of which Figueira and others in the colonial force were killed by Injai's riflemen.

Alerted, Captain Lima traveled to Mancabá with a contingent of troops, and during the night of 1–2 August, these troops fired more than one hundred artillery shells into Injai's encampment. On 3 August, Injai surrendered, raising a white flag and offering himself and 90 of his most loyal men to Captain Lima.[139] According to a French source and Injai's own report, Captain Lima proceeded to order the mass execution of 475 of Injai's men.[140] This massacre is not indicated in Portuguese reports. French observer Edouard Hostains inferred that Injai's near-passive response reflected the fact that Injai had anticipated that the Portuguese would not kill more than a few of his men. Also, Injai did not want to make it impossible to restore constructive relations with the Portuguese after the confrontation.[141] However, Injai may simply have lost his will to fight the colonial forces he had defended, befriended, and actively allied with for more than fifteen years. Injai apparently had the confidence that after surrender, he would eventually be restored as ruler of Oio. To Injai's astonishment, the Portuguese government in Lisbon soon decided to expel him (to Cape Verde), awarding him only a modest pension.[142]

PERSPECTIVES ON ABDUL INJAI

Injai's reputation as a brigand, cruel murderer, and state terrorist, and the renown of his mercenaries as rapists, pillagers, killers, and slave traders, had become well-established throughout "Portuguese" Guinea during the mid-1910s.
The pogroms that Injai carried out against villages in the most recalcitrant regions represented the very basis on which colonial state authority was established. However, it is important to emphasize (as the historian Joye Bowman
does) that Injai had in every case acted to enrich himself and his mercenaries,
and he did so at the expense of his role as colonial appointee.[143] Injai, remorse-
less, intended above all to establish a basis for the construction of a minor empire that would provide him with political power and an economic fortune. He
was, in fact, already succeeding in doing so.

When, to Injai's enormous surprise, the quid pro quo established between
himself and the colonialists was broken, Injai did not hesitate to present an image
of having been exploited by military officials who had broken their promises to
him.[144] But Injai's impressively articulated legal arguments, verbally transmitted
to colonial officials and later presented in a finely detailed written report,[145]
would brook no ground with the Lisbon authorities, who knew that Injai needed
to be removed from Guinea once and for all if Portuguese sovereign power and
political authority were to be firmly consolidated in that colony.

More generally, Injai dramatized the ability of a powerful and resourceful
African leader to manipulate Lusophone state weakness to his own benefit for
an unusually lengthy period of time. It is important to recall that Injai was not
outmaneuvered by superior Portuguese strategizing or firepower, whereas he
outwitted and took full advantage of colonial fragility for more than fifteen
years. He built a potent military force and a spoils-based mini-empire that
dominated local African communities to a greater extent than Portuguese authorities had been able to do in Guinea during the preceding four and a half
centuries. A balanced appreciation of Injai's political significance for Portuguese Guinea must emphasize these facts—not simply his role in making possible the establishment of Portuguese colonial state sovereignty.

POCKETS OF LINGERING RESISTANCE

Injai was not the sole challenge to Portuguese political authority during the
1915–19 period; additional pockets of resistance lingered through those years.

Most notably, in that period at least two other African chiefs had constructed networks of power that were independent of Portuguese colonial authority or influence.[146] There were also, as late as 1917, still some Islamic chiefs and marabouts, many of whom had previously migrated to Geba region from Senegal, preaching "holy war" against the Portuguese. These were watched carefully, especially by Colonel Manuel Maria Coelho, who rounded up and deported a number of them (often to São Tomé), including Naian Baldé; others remained active.[147] In April 1916, a French official reported that a large quantity of arms and munitions had been transported by clandestine traders into Portuguese Guinea from French Guinea;[148] this weapons trade greatly concerned the Portuguese.[149] An underground arms trade was also active in Farim and in Bafatá, as well as between Bissauans and Bijagós.[150] The colonial government admitted an inability to control the sale of guns and gunpowder.[151]

Arms trading helped make possible the carrying out of a series of violent challenges in different parts of the colony. In December 1916, the people of Elia (near Arame) refused to pay taxes and obtained weapons to defend against an anticipated repression (although this was not forthcoming).[152] On 3 May 1917, in Nhambalâ (north of the Cacheu River), Portuguese troops were sent to capture Baïote who attacked employees of European merchants, but when the troops were fired at by these Baïote, they retreated.[153] In July 1917, the predominantly Felupe communities of Varela, Sucujaque, and Suzana (near the Cacheu River), refused to pay the colonial hut tax; there was no Portuguese reaction.[154] In August 1919, no troops were sent against the Mandjack, who frequently harassed European merchants traveling near Cacheu.[155] And a group of Balanta fighters killed the commander of the post at Braïla, as well as seventy-one auxiliaries, but there was no Portuguese reprisal.[156]

With villagers still able to procure their own weapons, the government decided to select only the potentially more significant rebellions to repress. To be sure, macrolevel security had been attained and conquest had been achieved on a colony-wide scale, but this remained an insecure domination. Major wars seemed unlikely to explode, but Portuguese rule could not be described as hegemonic. As late as 1920, many local chiefs and ordinary peasant fighters retained or had procured weapons and had not accepted the political sovereignty of the colonial state. In chapters 6 and 9, I suggest that this would bear significantly on the ability of later rebels to rally peasant support for anticolonial actions. Despite the military conquest of 1913–15, such independent attitudes and behavior would indicate the continuing relative infirmity of colonial authority.

PART 3

The "Settled" Colonial Period

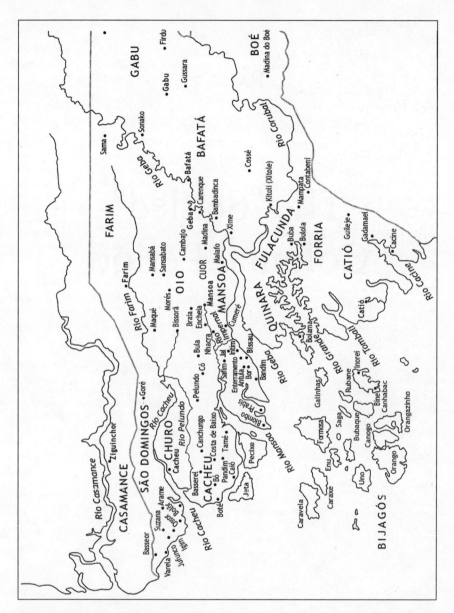

Map 4 Colonial Regions (Districts)

Most regions, villages, and rivers on this map were sites of significant military battles or political disputes on repeated occasions in the nineteenth and twentieth centuries. Casamance region was part of Portuguese Guinea until 1886.

Sources: Derived from maps in Luis António de Carvalho Viegas, *Guiné Portuguesa,* vol. 3 (Lisbon: Freitas Mega, 1940), inserts at end of volume; José Manuel de Braga Dias, "Mudança socio-cultural na Guiné Portuguesa" (Ph.D. diss., Universidade Técnica de Lisboa, 1974), 124–25, 148–49, 158–59.

CHAPTER 6

Military Resistance to State Building, 1923–1950

FOLLOWING THE MAINLAND CONQUESTS of the 1910s, the colonial state would initiate the process of consolidating colonial political and economic power more fully in the Guinean interior. Now begins what Crawford Young refers to as the "construction" phase of colonial state building.[1] As was typical in Africa, in Guinea-Bissau colonial power in this early period was entrenched largely in the capital city, in this instance Bissau, percolating outward in initially episodic fashion in the form of tax collection, road construction, and forced-labor projects.[2] An additional significant component of the state-building project in Guinea-Bissau was the effort to institute a village-level structure of "traditional" ethnic authorities—essentially chiefs who had collaborated with the Portuguese during the conquest period or chiefs who had been defeated during that period and who had subsequently aligned themselves with the centralized state rulers.

However, in this chapter and the two following I argue that—despite a degree of success in these colonial projects, especially taxation—the core indigenous political power structures either remained intact or adapted themselves to the new assertions of state authority in ways that prevented the establishment of central state overrule in the rural regions. As a result, most appointed chiefs did not rule effectively; rather, rural-based social formations retained local control and so were sociologically located in a relatively strong position vis-à-vis the central state throughout the 1923–50 period of colonial state building. In doing

127

so, these rural-based social formations may be considered to comprise a strong civil society that was able to determine the composition and direction of the major part of rural political, economic, social, and religious resources.

In this chapter, I suggest that one strategy through which rural civil society was able to defy state power was through a rekindling of the social-historical memory of praetorian success, built upon the extensive indigenous military experiences that preceded the colonial conquest. Indeed, repeated rebellions and violent challenges to the state occurred through the 1923–50 period that created a context of instability in many of the rural areas. The most dramatic examples were the 1925 and 1936 wars on the Bijagós island of Canhabac, which substantially drained state resources and manpower, but other, smaller-scale uprisings also occurred that government forces were often hard pressed to repress. Thus, while macrolevel state sovereignty existed and the colony as a whole was more orderly than during the pre-1920 and post-1960 periods of sustained, all-out generalized warfare, an important degree of rural rebelliousness nonetheless persisted during the period under discussion that exposed the fragile, profoundly tentative nature of colonial rulership (and which is why, when I use the term *"settled" colonial period,* I use quotation marks).

It is important to underline that these rebellions were important not only for appreciating the extent of state frailty but also in serving as a historical link between conquest-period resistance and the nationalist struggle of the 1960s and 1970s. The nationalist struggle is discussed in chapter 9; my point here is that the eruption of anticolonial war in the 1960s was preceded by extensive acts of rebellion through the "settled" colonial period, and those acts, in turn, provide a certain measure of continuity with the anticonquest warfare that had taken place prior to and during the first decade of the twentieth century. This link was facilitated because the reawakening of what was, in effect, a praetorian social memory in the 1920s through the 1940s and then again in the 1960s was, in each case, separated by a relatively short time period (about a decade).

Peter Karibe Mendy asserts that the various types of resistance that occurred from the 1920s through 1940s in Portuguese Guinea supports T. O. Ranger's thesis that anticolonial nationalism in the 1960s represented a "tradition of resistance" with earlier primary resistance movements.[3] Ranger had argued that in parts of Africa, nationalist leaders were able to rely on a generalized remembrance of heroic resistance efforts carried out during the primary resistance period of 1890–1910, when those modern nationalist leaders organized anticolonial movements.[4] The argument presented here differs from those of Mendy and Ranger in that while I concur with the notion of a continuity of military defiance, I argue throughout that the collective memory of praetorian capacity in fact harks back to centuries of warfare—as indicated in earlier chapters—that preceded the anticolonial primary wars, and not simply to the era of the wars of "pacification." The twentieth-century struggles, then, represent not so much a "tradition of resistance" born during the period of the European conquest, but more an extension of an ancient, precolonial praetorian local defense.

Moreover, because actual antistate violence was regularly carried out during the colonial period itself, the collective memory of praetorian capacity was in fact continually and dramatically reinforced, rather than—as Ranger suggested regarding the (mostly) East African cases he analyzed—being held in stasis and then rekindled during the modern nationalist movement. The extent of this continuity of praetorian defense during the 1923–50 period is made clear below.

REBELLION AND THE COLONIAL STATE

We may observe two distinct types of antistate violence that occurred during the years of Portuguese colonial rulership in Guinea: the Canhabac uprisings on the Bijagós archipelago, which erupted into veritable wars; and more limited, often spontaneous acts of rebellion that took place on the mainland. Here we may point out that the reaction by the colonial state to rural resistance remained unchanged from the conquest period: where possible, brute force was used to repress acts that appeared to represent antistate activity. This does not mean that the state during this colonial period was devoted to a terror-based policy to the extent that it had been during the conquest phase: to be sure, its primary attention and resources were marshaled for economic exploitation, bureaucratic expansion, and the attempted consolidation of its ethnically based leadership structure in the rural areas. But the state terror reflex remained ever-present and would be quickly revived in cases of violent rebellion. Ultimately, this reflex reflected bureaucratic frustration at colonial administrators' inability to wield a more comprehensive domination over rural civil society.

The most important sources of social disquiet that served to provoke the various acts of rural resistance in the Guinean interior and on the Bijagós were taxation and forced labor. Local uprisings or individual acts of resistance were often provoked by the brutality and rigorous beatings used while collecting local taxes.[5] To a lesser extent, some communities were determined simply to make an occasional, declarative statement, through violence, of their general disapproval of colonial-state overrule. In most cases, rebellions reflected a localistic mobilization and were typically led by popular, village-based political and military chiefs, as was the case with the Bijagós. In other parts of rural Guinea-Bissau as well, local-level leaders, especially those willing to challenge state power openly, generally emerged through identifiable social or political structures operating at the community level.

The analysis of the national-liberation struggle in chapter 9 makes clear that the longstanding practice of multiethnic military-alliance formation would be quickly reestablished once this became possible; but during the 1923–50 period macropolitical control by the colonial state made such alliances unworkable. Nonetheless, the struggle of the Canhabacers in the Bijagós was not easily contained by colonial forces; those islanders continued to fight back even in the face of the repeated waves of attack launched against them during the 1920s and 1930s.[6]

THE STATE TERROR POLICY REVIVED: WAR ON THE CANHABAC, 1925

The Bijagós are an archipelago—nine inhabited islands and several uninhabited ones. The inhabited islands are Bubaque, Canhabac, Caravela, Caraxe, Formosa, Orango, Uno, Enu, and Orangazinho.[7] As indicated earlier,[8] the Bijagós people had attained renown among European shippers for their military prowess— they had never been seriously challenged on their own islands by coastal peoples and they were able to repel Portuguese military forays in 1856, 1879, 1900, and 1908. In January 1918, following extensive fighting during the preceding year, treaties were signed and military posts were built on Canhabac island at Inorei and Bine. But tax payments from the Bijagós were still not provided.[9] The posts were eventually abandoned. Thus, the French consul in Bissau was correct to point out (1925) that the Bijagós "always refused to pay a tax" and remained "in fact independent" of colonial authority.[10] A Portuguese *chefe de posto* (local administrator) on the Bijagós island of Formosa, in a letter to the administrator of the Bijagós (who was stationed in Bissau), confirmed that the Canhabacers paid taxes only when and if they felt like it.[11]

This state of affairs provoked the Bijagós administrator to urge the governor of Guinea, Velez Caroço, to wage a new military campaign. The governor agreed and marshaled a force of about fifteen hundred men armed with half of the weaponry held by the colony.[12] The attack began on 20 April 1925; the moment the column landed, it confronted intense fire from Bijagós riflemen. The French consul to Bissau, Hostains (who based his comments on information from Fulbe chiefs who were taking part) expressed bewilderment that the commanders relied on the tactics that had proved so risky in 1917: large-scale patrols using narrow, vulnerable paths.[13] Here we may note that the island of Canhabac (which covers some 13,500 hectares, 9 km by 15 km), was geographically suited both to long-term indigenous resistance and to covert flight. The island's surface was almost entirely covered with dense forest (palm and other trees), and only very narrow paths led to villages. On these paths, it was impossible to see farther than five or six meters in any direction.[14] Canhabacer ambushers were able to fire their rifles in groups of two or three and then disperse into the forest. Furthermore, by the time the Portuguese neared a village, many of the Canhabacers of fighting age had already loaded families, livestock, and possessions into dugout canoes for transport to other islands or to French Guinea.[15] The islanders had also burned a number of villages to ensure that the Portuguese would capture virtually nothing; there would be no livestock with which to augment their food supply.

In this manner, the two colonial columns "captured" one village after another, including Ancanhe and Inhoda, finally converging at the village of Indena, the home of the Canhabac queen, Juliana, at the center of the island. There, Canhabac fighters put up a coordinated defense, and extensive battles ensued. Helped by reinforcements from Bine, the attackers eventually defeated the defenders and captured Queen Juliana and her top chiefs, all of whom were later imprisoned at Bolama.[16] Thereafter, the policy of state terror was pursued with vigor: many of the remaining villages of Canhabac were systematically burned and sacked by the colonial forces between 3 and 12 May 1925.[17] However, this operation was ended earlier than anticipated, in large part because few people remained in the villages and because of lack of food and livestock on the island.[18] On 15 May, the Portuguese-led columns returned to the mainland. The attackers had suffered twenty-two deaths and seventy-four wounded, while the losses of the Canhabacers were relatively light, reflecting their guerrilla-style tactics.[19]

Participating Fulbe chiefs made clear that the Portuguese and their African auxiliaries left Canhabac without securing the slightest indication of indigenous submission to colonial rule. In fact, even on the day of the column's departure, ambushers succeeded in killing six and wounding two soldiers traveling by small boat toward their ship.[20] Moreover, in contrast to what occurred at the conclusion of conquest episodes on the mainland, the Canhabacers did not turn in any weapons or pay taxes to the authorities.[21] The extent to which the events of 1925 represented at most a Pyrrhic victory for the Portuguese was made dramatically clear through the recurrence of a new Luso-Bijagós war in 1935–36.

THE THIRD AND "FINAL" BATTLE FOR CANHABAC, 1935–1936

The calm that enveloped Canhabac in the 1925–35 period, during which the Portuguese maintained small outposts but did not challenge de facto self-rule, endured until early 1935, when the Portuguese initiated a widening of roads extending outward from Inorei and Bine. Tensions rose. The Canhabacers correctly perceived that the road extensions represented a serious threat to their relative isolation and social and political autonomy. They were particularly aware that a central purpose of the roads was to facilitate tax collection by Portuguese soldiers.[22] However, the Canhabacers' response was delayed due to internal dissension: some villagers believed that attacks should have been carried out immediately, while others preferred a more restrained approach.[23] As in 1925, most families left by canoe for nearby islands: Orango, Orangazinho, and Enu. The Canhabac fighters were well-armed, having obtained large stocks of handmade rifles from blacksmiths on the mainland.[24] In addition, a businessman in Bolama and some European traders illicitly sold modern guns and gunpowder to the Canhabacers.[25]

On 12 November 1935, Canhabac fighters took the initiative, attacking Inorei and killing a soldier.[26] This provoked a colonial march into the dense bush. As in 1925, the Canhabac defenders avoided direct, face-to-face combat, launching guerrilla ambushes from wooded hideouts, and the Portuguese soon realized that to pursue such attacks they needed a larger military force. The entire Portuguese armed forces in Guinea, still modest in size, totaled approximately two hundred standing troops. Thus, through December 1935, the state engaged in a major recruitment drive among collaborative Fulbe, Mandinka, and Biaffada communities.[27] A Fulbe chief, Modi Aguibou, who had been imprisoned by the Portuguese for refusing to send his wives to work on road-building projects, was freed from jail and given 2,000 escudos to recruit Fulbe soldiers for military campaigns against the Canhabacers.[28] Aguibou accepted on condition that his community be exempted from taxes in 1936 and 1937. However, recruitment remained difficult. The Fulbe chiefs of Mampata, Kitoli, and Moliti also asked for exemption from 1936–37 tax payments, and when they were denied this request they refused to make their fighters available.[29]

The Fulbe chiefs of Sonako and of Pitji also refused to provide fighting men, but for a different reason: they demanded that during the war campaign their men be accompanied on the front lines by regular Portuguese soldiers. Citing the heavy losses incurred by Fulbe auxiliaries during the 1925 expedition, the chiefs made clear that they would not send more young men off to Canhabac unless European soldiers assumed the same risks as the Africans. The Portuguese recruiters did not accommodate them—and they did not provide auxiliaries.[30] Other Fulbe, Biaffada, and Mandinka chiefs relented, however, and 1,474 African auxiliaries were made available for the war campaign.[31] As in previous expeditions, their compensation would be the opportunity for pillage, not salary.[32] Fulbe chiefs and fighters went along with this, but they were displeased; they regarded it as inadequate remuneration, despite the Portuguese provision of large quantities of kola nuts.[33]

By the end of the first week of January 1936, these auxiliaries plus 133 regular soldiers began a war campaign from the Inorei military base.[34] The governor's column fought guerrilla ambushes step by step and suffered significant losses of auxiliary soldiers, including the Mandinka chief of Bolama, Mamadu Canté.[35] On 26 January, the column defeated a Canhabac defense contingent and killed a local chief, Amanhã, and other resistance leaders. The following day, Canhabac fighters responded with a flurry of ambushes, killing several dozen auxiliary fighters, including three Fulbe chiefs. During the rest of that week, the African auxiliaries continued to suffer heavy losses—at least forty-five dead plus hundreds wounded.[36]

Peace talks were initiated by the Portuguese, and on 15 February most Canhabac chiefs agreed with Portuguese negotiators to end the fighting, although a small number of holdouts among the chiefs refused this accord.[37] The African auxiliaries were sent back to the mainland.[38] Many Fulbe chiefs who had participated and survived, such as Sidia El Kébir, were deeply embittered at what they felt was inadequate compensation for their heavy losses.[39] Following the accord, a tax was collected. However, subsequently it became evident that Canhabac villagers had no intention of acceding to further tax demands made by Portuguese commanders posted at Inorei, Bine, or Meneque. In May–June 1936, when the government announced that the hut tax was to be raised to 62 escudos, the Canhabac chiefs made clear that they would not pay it.[40] On 27 June 1936, the Portuguese sent a small military contingent (consisting almost entirely of African auxiliaries, headed by Noumou Kanté, a Bolama district official) to collect taxes. Kanté and his men were attacked soon after arrival on the island; Kanté and many others were killed, and the contingent was driven off the island.[41]

The governor next assigned the task of organizing a punitive expedition to district chief Bouram Diammé (a Fulbe).[42] Diammé organized a column of Fulbe troops and placed at their command his son Abdou Diammé. Diammé and his men fought on Canhabac for more than two months in mid-1936, with many casualties on both sides. Diammé was killed, along with Ouro N'Ballo, the brother of the district chief of Corubal. However, the Canhabacers, having themselves suffered heavy losses, sent word to the Portuguese that they would pay their taxes. But when Portuguese troops arrived on Canhabac to collect the taxes, they found that the Canhabacers had destroyed all bridges and blockaded all access to the larger villages.[43] The Portuguese soldiers returned to the mainland and made clear to the governor that a larger expeditionary force was required.

In the fall, the colonial government yet again sought to recruit Fulbe fighters for an expedition against Canhabac, but this time all Fulbe chiefs refused to participate.[44] Recruitment efforts among Biaffada and Mandinka chiefs similarly failed.[45] Agents of the Portuguese colonial government were sent clandestinely to Fulbe communities in French Guinea (and possibly Senegal) in a desperate effort to recruit "volunteers."[46] The results were minimal: the Portuguese were simply unable to raise a large enough army to send to Canhabac. There were at that point only 170 regular soldiers at the disposal of the government of Guinea. This was regarded as inadequate for a successful campaign.[47] The Guinean chief of staff requested Portuguese troop reinforcements from Lisbon, but with these not forthcoming, no campaign took place.

Through the rest of 1936, Canhabacers allowed various Guinean traders to travel to the island, but they displayed clear signs of hostility to Portuguese and Fulbe would-be travelers.[48] In February 1937, peace talks involving twenty of Canhabac's most powerful chiefs produced an agreement. They would accept Portuguese sovereignty on the following conditions: the Portuguese would replace their military posts with administrative posts (there would be no soldiers); all Fulbe and Biaffada auxiliaries would leave Canhabac; there would be no extra taxation or war indemnity. Both sides abided by the terms of the accord: as of February 1937; the Portuguese began to replace their military commanders with civilian administrators. All soldiers—including all Fulbe and Biaffada—had departed by July 1937, and war indemnity was forgiven (but that year's annual tax was paid).[49] This certainly did not represent a victory for the colonialists: it was more of a stand-off, for the accord implied that Canhabac villages would remain self-ruling, the Portuguese retaining control over only their three outposts of Inorei, Bine, and Meneque and the roads linking those posts. In effect, the Canhabacers, via the agreement that there would be no colonial troops on the island, had forced the Portuguese to compromise aspects of their political sovereignty.[50] Indeed, afterward, little changed on Canhabac, as villages were quickly repopulated, trade links between Canhabacers and other Bijagós islands as well as the mainland were reestablished, and they remained largely outside the rubric of colonial officialdom.

It may also be noted that warfare with the Canhabacers exhausted the administrative and economic resources of the colonial state. Due to a lack of funds, during the 1935–37 period all bureaucratic services suffered a "near paralysis" of action and activity.[51] Moreover, in subsequent years, the Canhabacers and other Bijagós islanders asserted de facto autonomy in various ways.[52] An administrator at one point tried to force Canhabac villagers to work for the state, but the villagers simply refused him.[53] In general, Canhabacers continued largely to ignore the few colonial officials assigned to the island's outposts.[54] And they did not provide taxes to Portuguese officials.[55]

By the time of the December 1946 conference of administrators in Bissau, it was decided that the Bijagós islands would be exempted from the hut tax and would be accorded a "special" type of head tax — apparently one whose collection would be loosely enforced, if at all.[56] By that point, for the central state, it was simply not worth the political and economic cost to perpetually reenact military campaigns. This represented a virtual admission of the relative autonomy of the Bijagós people, essentially won by way of their tenacious resistance through the wars of 1925 and 1936–37.

Local Attacks and Other Social Resistance, 1920s, 1930s, and 1940s

The Canhabac wars were by far the most significant acts of open rebellion against colonial overrule, but there were also other, smaller resistance efforts during the 1920s, 1930s, and 1940s. The armed forces of Portuguese Guinea during this period proved slow and inefficient in mobilizing responses to uprisings.[57] To be sure, in the face of a genuine threat to colonial sovereignty, the state was able to marshal sufficient forces to carry out a severe repression. At the same time, however, Portuguese fighting forces remained perpetually undermanned. They were heavily dependent upon poorly paid and understaffed African police contingents.

Many rural communities were aware that although the state could unleash a wave of violent terror, it could not do so everywhere all at once, and it might be unable to do so in a given instance. Thus, despite its capacity for brutal repression, Portuguese Guinea was a relatively weak colonial state, and peasants occasionally sought to take advantage of the particular unreliability of its rural police.

Nhacra, 1924

Nhacra, located about 20 kilometers northeast of Bissau, served as a nodal point of Balanta resistance during the late nineteenth and early twentieth centuries.[58] One of the first "troubles" following the conquest occurred in this area.

Early in August 1924, the Balanta of Nhacra and of five other villages refused to accede to demands by the Portuguese-appointed military administrator of Nhacra for "voluntary" laborers. In response, forty colonial soldiers were sent to the area, and in the course of their tour they were fired on by local fighters. Approximately three thousand Balanta from the villages of Bube, Cuméré, and Nhacra congregated to meet colonial reinforcements, but these Balanta decided not to pursue further violence. The troops returned to their bases.[59]

Bolama, Farim, and Gabu

In 1927, a French official observed that Guineans near Bolama were preparing for armed struggle. They were arming because, he said, they sought "to put an end to a domination which they find unbearable."[60] Also in 1927, another observer wrote that the Mandjack and Balanta of Farim region were frequently displaying "hostility" toward the colonial authorities.[61] Further north, at Tchemara (near the Casamance border with Senegal), in 1939, Diola fired at and wounded a Portuguese customs official who had tried to arrest them.[62]

On 12 September 1939, Mandjack inhabitants of Bolama island refused to pay colonial taxes[63] — defiance provoked by a tax increase.[64] Three hundred colonial soldiers and auxiliaries were dispatched to suppress them.[65] And in late 1945, many people in Farim, Gabu, and Bafatá, reacting against heavy taxation and forced labor, sought weapons and gunpowder from illegal traders. That October, in Bafatá, five machine guns, illegally transported to Guinea from the Gambia, were seized. As a result of these occurrences, troops were sent to Farim, Gabu, and Bafatá.[66]

Southern Balanta Rice-growing Areas

In May 1934, Balanta villagers near Bolama refused to pay a colonial tax and wounded seven soldiers sent to collect it.[67] The colonial authorities then decided not to attempt to collect taxes from the Balanta during that year. In June 1934, the governor of Guinea wrote that he had been told of a "rebellion" in the district of Kam'Baky (between Bissau and Katilvo); this apparently was a reference to an agent of a Portuguese company having been killed.[68]

In 1939, the colonial hut tax having been increased, the Balanta throughout the southern ricelands refused to pay it. A procolonial Fulbe chief, Binko Sagna, the head of Fulacunda, agreed to enforce tax collection among the Balanta "and to subdue them definitively."[69] However, Sagna "lost a lot of men" —

apparently in battle—and failed to suppress and collect taxes from the Balanta.[70] The colonialists had to await a larger mobilization of African auxiliary police before they could enforce tax payments; however, by then, thousands of Balanta had temporarily migrated into Senegal specifically to avoid those payments. In Bolama region as well, the hut-tax increase sparked protests by Balanta in an area known as Balantakunda.[71] Eventually, the taxes were collected, but again not until after large-scale emigration to Senegal.

Tensions over taxes remained palpable in many predominantly Balanta areas through the early 1940s. According to information provided to French officials by African informants, a "revolt" took place among Balanta near the border with French Guinea in June 1940, instigated by Portuguese colonial officials' efforts to recruit forced labor.[72] In September 1940, Balanta again voiced hostility to the forced-labor policy, killing several Europeans to demonstrate their opposition.[73] In May 1944, resistance to tax collection led to violence in Balanta-dominated areas of Catió region; when colonial troops from Bolama were brought in by boat and truck, resistance ceased.[74]

Migration as Resistance

From the 1920s to the 1940s, tax collection and forced-labor recruitment increasingly provoked large numbers of rural Guineans who were unable to resist militarily to defy the central state authorities by temporarily migrating to neighboring countries.[75] A turn toward migration as social resistance to economic exploitation had for many years been undertaken in Guinea-Bissau by those fleeing the predations of larger kingdoms. For example, the flight of the Balanta from regions being taken over by invading Fulbe in the 1880s is well etched in the Balanta collective memory.[76] To be sure, Balanta migration patterns in both the nineteenth and early twentieth centuries also reflected internal economic pressures such as the search for new rice fields. This helped to produce what Hawthorne refers to as a "fissioning" of Balanta communities through different parts of Portuguese Guinea.[77] But it was precisely because of their ability to "fission"—to seek out and develop new *bolanhas* (terrains amenable to wet-rice cultivation)—that when colonial policies such as taxation or forced labor were implemented with some regularity, many Balanta proved capable of relocating to areas (such as Catió in the south) where the colonialists had little presence or impact.

The turn toward migration specifically as a response to colonial exploitation began at the early stages of the "settled" colonial period—in 1924, following the repression of a Balanta uprising, when twenty thousand peasants traveled to Casamance.[78] Between 1924 and 1926, forced labor provoked large-scale flight among the Balanta from throughout the colony into the southern regions, especially Catió.[79]

It was not only the Balanta who proved capable of resisting colonial predation through migration. In 1924, entire Felupe villages departed en masse from Portuguese Guinea into Casamance as a consequence of high taxation and the confiscation of their crops.[80] Large-scale migration in 1936 of Fulbe from Portuguese Guinea into Casamance occurred as a consequence of tensions resulting from Fulbe reluctance to participate in the Canhabac war. The Mandjack of Cacheu region frequently emigrated in large numbers in order to evade colonial state predation.[81] Thus, the Cacheu village of Katama in 1921 housed more than 600 people; by 1986, the population was only 350.[82] Mandjack emigration had become "a way of life" in Cacheu region during the "settled" colonial period, with approximately 2,500 Mandjack temporarily migrating into Senegal each year by the 1940s.[83] Between 1948 and 1950, 4,879 Mandjack were emigrating from Cacheu region to Senegal and to the Gambia annually.[84] In addition, many Mandjack emigrated "internally" (i.e., to other regions in Portuguese Guinea, outside Cacheu region), specifically to escape forced-labor assignments. According to interviews conducted by anthropologist Eve Crowley, the Mandjack of Pantufa village emigrated to areas controlled by Balanta, such as Mansoa, Mansabá, and Bambadinca.[85]

These waves of migration by Balanta, Mandjack, Felupe, and some Fulbe represented substantial acts of resistance against the authority of the colonial state.[86] Although taxes were generally collected from most communities and forced labor was implemented in many areas, this extensive migration helped to sustain a social context of protest against colonial rule and helped to hinder the establishment of a more thoroughgoing form of bureaucratic state domination.

State Terror and the Felupe of Suzana-Jufunco

Finally, we complete this section on localized acts of social resistance by reference to a series of events in São Domingos, in northwestern Guinea-Bissau, that culminated in open rebellion by the Felupe people of that region. In June 1933, a small plane carrying a French pilot disappeared over southern Senegal; in July and August, searches by French investigators in Senegal from Dakar to the Gambia proved unsuccessful.[87] The religious leader of the Felupe of Suzana, Chief Apaim-Ba (called Alfredo by the Portuguese), claimed not to have seen the plane. However, Chief Mamadu Cissé, a long-time colonial collaborator and now head of the Suzana district, took the Frenchmen aside, told them he had seen the plane traveling south, and advised them to proceed on to Jufunco, where the plane had landed.

In October 1933, the governor ordered the arrest of Chief Apaim-Ba and a dozen Felupe notables of Jufunco, Igim, and Varela. At Suzana, a Portuguese official interrogated and tortured (using a *palmatoria*—a flat, indented wooden object) various Felupe leaders, including Chief Apaim-Ba, who while being beaten admitted that the plane had landed at Jufunco. However, this chief changed the details of his story several times over the next four days. The beatings and torture continued through 30 October 1933.[88]

On 1 November 1933, Captain Velez Caroço, his troops, and eight hundred auxiliaries departed Suzana, arriving at Jufunco the next day.[89] Their intent was clearly to destroy the village; here, the terror policy was to be definitively revived. But the defenders of Jufunco, forewarned, were well prepared, and in a fierce battle (2 or 3 November) the colonial forces could not break through the defenses.[90] The Portuguese did, however, capture the Jufunco chief, who was tortured to death.[91] Meanwhile, Apaim-Ba escaped his captors at Suzana and fled to the village of Oussouye, in Casamance, where he would recover from his wounds. Thousands of Felupe—including many Jufunco—similarly made their way out of Portuguese Guinea and into Casamance.[92] The Portuguese then launched an attack on Jufunco and on the neighboring villages of Igim and Yal.[93] They burned down all three villages (Jufunco had already been evacuated). The Portuguese, having failed to find the plane, were intent on maximum application of their terror-based policy of repression. This state violence involved not only the razing of the three villages but also the unearthing and destruction of symbolic religious representations that were important to the Felupe.[94]

By April 1934, many of the Felupe of Jufunco, Igim, and Varela who had taken refuge in Casamance returned home. Soon afterward, the governor of Guinea decided to construct an administrative post in Suzana (at Basseor).[95] The local Felupe, despite their defeat, expressed opposition to the installation of a post there. In response, a local administrator, Vasconcelos da Fonseca, and the town administrator of São Domingos, Arrobas Martins, organized a small party of police and with them marched into Basseor. One of the policemen was attacked, killed, and beheaded.[96] Many Felupe in the area immediately fled to Casamance, where they obtained weapons and returned to confront a military column sent from Bissau. Five hundred or so Felupe fighters sustained an assault despite relentless machine-gun fire; eventually, however, they were defeated, although some were able to flee back to Casamance.

According to official Portuguese accounts, the colonialists were subsequently able to construct their administrative post at Basseor.[97] However, according to long-time administrator António Carreira, this post was in fact never completed.[98] Later accounts suggest that the post was built but soon afterward was burned down. It was not rebuilt.[99]

Ten years later, in 1945, colonial officials became aware of a black-market trade in weapons and gunpowder, with Felupe in the Gambia selling weapons to the Felupe of Suzana district in Portuguese Guinea.[100] Several kilos of illegally imported gunpowder had been seized at Cassolol, Iatène, Kahème, and Youtou, and in January 1946 three gunpowder traffickers were arrested in Suzana district, one of them a citizen of Senegal.[101] The three traffickers were prosecuted by a military tribunal and condemned to be deported; in April they were sent to Angola.[102] Clearly, the Felupe of Suzana remained politically defiant, to the point of seeking to obtain arms and gunpowder for use against the Portuguese.

———

During the 1923–50 period, colonial political authority was often challenged by rural rebels who had not accepted the political sovereignty of the Portuguese colonial state in Guinea. Repression of armed oppositionists on the mainland did occur, but only spasmodically: typically, no more than a hundred to three hundred European troops were stationed in Portuguese Guinea at one time, and they were spread out among a number of outposts. Enforcement of colonial decrees was carried out by Cape Verdean, mestiço, or Fulbe appointees, but their effectiveness often depended on their access to an unreliable local police force. Local acts of resistance to specific tax collections or forced-labor efforts were still common. These acts helped to keep alive the social memory of rural praetorian capacity that precolonial indigenous combatants had demonstrated and that conquest-era fighters had sustained.

The responses of the state to acts of resistance varied: in the case of the Felupe, the state met resistance with repression; in the case of the Fulbe, there virtually was bargaining over the creation of forced-labor gangs. This variability reflected a frequently changing institutional/military context of state power. To be sure, the colonial state usually found a way to reactivate its policy of state terror when its political sovereignty was seriously challenged. But it was not always able to do so: the de facto autonomy of Canhabac meant that colonial leaders, unable to achieve an absolute victory over the islanders, essentially desisted from further aggression. State fragility was also suggested by the impact of (sometimes) collaborationist Fulbe chiefs in responding defiantly to colonial recruitment campaigns. Extensive resistance by many of these chiefs against participation in the Canhabac war campaigns limited what could be done in the Bijagós archipelago and prevented the assertion of full sovereignty there.

Overall, this chapter has suggested that localistic military defiance of colonial state authority occurred in various parts of Portuguese Guinea during the "settled" colonial period. I thereby diverge from Pélissier, who asserted that by 1925 this land had truly become a controlled colony since the Fulbe and Biaffada were by that point firmly in the colonial political camp, while the rebellious animists (Balanta, Baïote, Felupe, Soninké, Papel) had been conquered.[103] I have suggested that even many of the Fulbe and Biaffada chiefs, despite their often procolonial status, represented unsteady, occasionally noncompliant footings upon which colonial leaders sought to build a military underlayer of state power. This indeed helped to assure the relatively "soft" institutional character of the colonial state.

At the same time, the depiction above of acts of resistance by the Balanta, Felupe, and Mandjack, ranging from open challenges and armed attacks to migration, suggests that these peoples were not fully conquered. At Farim, Gabu, Bafatá, Nhacra, and in the south, tax increases and forced-labor recruitment gave rise to persistent collective actions. This rural defiance helped to assure a social subtext of anticolonial fervor that endured through the 1920s to 1940s. In repeatedly manifesting their resistance, rural-based communities helped to reinvigorate a praetorian social memory that would later contribute to the reemergence of full-scale national resistance during the liberation struggle of the 1960s.[104]

In sum, this chapter emphasized the fragile, although violent, nature of "settled" colonial rule, despite the success of the government in collecting taxes in many areas and in reviving its terrorist mode of repression on select occasions. Chapter 7 suggests that the dynamic evolution, adaptability, and endurance of the sociocultural structures and social formations that make up rural civil society also substantially contributed to the relatively superficial character of colonial state domination.

CHAPTER 7
Sociocultural Aspects of a Strong Rural Civil Society, 1920–1960

WE HAVE SEEN THAT DURING the "settled" colonial period, a subculture of anti-colonial resistance was sustained in the countryside. In this chapter, I suggest that rural civil society remained strongly constituted in that locally preferred power structures were able to determine the directional flow of social resources. Autonomous decision-making practices, popular sources of authority, and inter-village interactions collectively represented social and political spaces outside the purview of the colonial state.

In a number of cases, the reshaping of local structures occurred in reaction to the administrative system of ethnic authority used by the colonialists to establish a Lusophone version of indirect rule, based on chiefs, in Portuguese Guinea. This system (similar to what Mahmood Mamdani has described for colonial systems in eastern and southern Africa),[1] was based on the allocation of specific leadership roles to elites from selected ethnic groups in order to create local authority networks that effectively imparted state power into rural society. Portuguese and Cape Verdean officials from Bissau were appointed to serve as regional administrators, and they supervised *chefes de povo* (community heads) and *rege-dores* (colonially appointed chiefs)—mostly Fulbe, but also some Biaffada and Mandinka—to rule over specific communities or groups of communities. However, in contrast to what occurred in other African countries (per Mamdani), these community heads and appointed chiefs in most of Guinea-Bissau proved largely ineffective; where already existing local rulerships or collective authority arrangements were especially strongly entrenched, communities simply ignored the appointed chiefs.

In regions such as Cacheu and Mansoa, where state-appointed officials demonstrated a determination to interfere with local political and economic affairs, local actors created or expanded various nonstate social formations and institutions, then transferred their political and economic resources into them. In some of these cases, the appointment of centrally approved authorities at the local level in fact stimulated this expansion. In other regions, such as much of Fulacunda and Gabu, the Portuguese created many mini-chiefships during the early colonial period. The result was that the older, large Fulbe and Mandinka chiefships that had existed up through the conquest period became administratively fragmented. In these cases, through the decades of the colonial era some appointed chiefs were able to retain the support of their communities despite their loyalty to the colonial state; others increasingly came into conflict with locally selected village leaders. The end result was a complex mixture of local tensions—and by the 1960s, an internal fracturing of leadership structures that would not reflect state interests.[2]

Throughout most of the rural areas during the 1920–60 period, colonial officials proved unable to rearrange the social configurations of power; hence, indigenously determined forms of political and social association predominated. There were several results: political structures reflected a widening rejection of appointed chiefs; landholding arrangements were agreed upon by local actors rather than by state officials or appointees; and socioreligious systems of authority and social organization were strengthened in a way that assured the avoidance of state institutions. As a consequence of the relative vigor of these social formations, it was rural civil society rather than the state that retained control over the most critical elements of community-level powerholding in most of the countryside.

Below, it is made clear that in many areas aspects of this rural civil societal strength reflected traditions or changes that were particular to a specific ethnic community. There was, however, also a complementary, critically important dimension: the multiethnic and ethnically malleable character of many of Portuguese Guinea's most important nonstate social formations. The most significant example was the expansion of indigenous spirit forces— *irãs*. These originated in Mandjack areas but attracted tens of thousands of followers from various ethnic groups throughout Portuguese Guinea. In this and in other cases, the incorporative traditions established during the precolonial period were reproduced during the "settled" colonial period. Modified in ways that reflected the changed macro-level political context, they enabled local actors to create expanded nonstate institutions in which they housed their political and economic resources.

This chapter is devoted to understanding the nature of these grassroots forms of rural civil societal power during the 1920–60 period. In order to appreciate the general context of the emergence of these structures, I first provide an overview of the three principal patterns of state/rural civil society relations that characterized the Guinean countryside.

POLITICAL RELATIONS BETWEEN STATE AND RURAL CIVIL SOCIETY

The three general patterns of political relations that evolved between the state and rural civil society were (1) community defiance of colonial state appointees and retention of existing political forms of self-rule; (2) accommodation or co-optation by community leaders to the system of colonial administration — often accompanied by a decline in those leaders' social power and influence; and (3) transformation of centralized traditional authority structures in ways that led to stronger village-level autonomy.

In the first pattern, particularly common among peoples with long histories of anticolonial resistance and acephalous political traditions such as the Oinka and the Balanta of the southern rice-growing regions,[3] the Portuguese appointed Fulbe and other chiefs to rule at the village level.[4] However, the majority of these Oinka and Balanta communities did not heed the decrees of these externally appointed chiefs.[5] Where village-level decrees were concerned, Fulbe chiefs lacked the means to coerce the compliance of Balanta peasants. This affected matters such as social behavior, dispute resolution, land allocation, and political decision making. Community-based authority structures remained responsible for these matters. The state appointees did enjoy a degree of success in dealing with annual tax payments and forced labor because police units from the central state sometimes accompanied the labor overseers and tax collectors.[6] However, Balanta and Oinka peasants were often able to avoid forced labor and tax payments, either by migrating to isolated regions[7] or, where appointed chiefs lacked enforcement capacity, as was often the case, by simply ignoring them.[8]

This first pattern of defiance also appeared in other historically resistant regions such as the Bijagós archipelago, where the colonial authorities did not recognize the traditional matrilineal leadership structure.[9] The state officially denigrated the status of traditional councils and indigenous queens and instead appointed "administrative chiefs" to serve the colonial interest. However, colonial officials typically had great difficulty in finding Bijagós willing to serve as an appointed chief. And when they did appoint such a chief, he often ended up serving as a spokesperson for the indigenously legitimate ruling council, rather than for the colonial administration.[10] This Lusophone version of indirect rule thus failed to achieve its goal of deepening the state's power on the archipelago.

The second pattern—where traditional chiefs or groups of respected elders were co-opted or accommodated themselves to the state's decision-making powers—was to be found among some (but by no means all) Fulbe, Biaffada, and Mandinka notables.[11] In a number of cases, the local leaders, having decided to work with the Portuguese authorities, were able to retain control of their communities, but in most cases they ended up losing favor with their own people and, subsequently, proved unable to render socially significant decisions such as resource allocation or land-tenure dispute resolution.

In the third pattern of political relations between the state and rural civil society, the older, traditional political structures did not survive the colonial period, or they survived in an impotent, skeletal version of the precolonial hierarchy. Some of them succumbed to competition from new administrative appointees of the colonial state—that is, from new village chiefs and community heads whose power was grounded solely in the colonial state.[12] Other traditional leaders' centralized authority declined because of the humiliation of having ceded power to the colonial authorities over the course of the four decades from the 1920s to the 1950s. Such decline occurred in various ethnic communities. Sometimes it led to a vacuum of political power at the local level or, as noted above, to internally contested leadership struggles.[13] However, in many cases, as older chieftainships declined in political importance, they were transformed or replaced in ways that produced a new mode of indigenously controlled local-level rulership, as we will see with regard to the Mandjack of Cacheu region. The great Mandjack kingship of Basserel, having declined in the period from 1920 to 1960, was replaced by socioreligious institutions that functioned as nonstate alternative authority structures.

Thus, in this third pattern, in the wake of the considerable weakening of many historical kingships and traditional political systems, rural civil society adapted by fortifying and expanding alternative forms of politics and authority building. This constituted a separate social universe from that dominated by state officials, and it provided many rural people with alternative structures of decision making and resource accumulation that were independent of colonial institutions. These new forms of social organization—notably, a reenergized

Mandjack religiosocial system—generated significant interethnic contacts as members of other groups were incorporated into a revivified, inclusivistic rural power structure.

In both the first and the third patterns, one factor that facilitated the ability of locally respected leaders to counter or ignore state authority was that in many of the rural areas, the Portuguese did not know the identity of these leaders.[14] In the first pattern, this lack of knowledge helped make it possible for local communities to circumvent or openly reject the authoritative decisions of state appointees. This was particularly the case when the appointees bore an ethnic identity different from that of the villagers (e.g., where Fulbe or Biaffada chiefs were appointed to rule over Balanta). In the third pattern, the fact that many communities demonstrated greater respect for local religious figures than for political authorities made it possible for rural civil society to shift social power outside the colonial domain. More generally, the colonialists' lack of knowledge about rural social formations worked in favor of local political autonomy: it signaled the relative superficiality of the colonial implantation. Portuguese Guinea was characterized by the diversity of indigenous social and political structures and intercommunal interactions, and this enabled rural civil society to remain strongly anchored, sociologically and institutionally positioned in opposition to the colonial state.

Balanta Communities

In that their ancient, indigenous political system was not substantially modified during this 1920–60 period, and despite the colonial state's appointment of regedores, most Balanta communities fit the first pattern of the political relationship. The Balanta political system remained defined by age-based categories and gerontocratic leadership structures. At the same time, important decision-making processes remained collectively organized; the political leadership was relatively participatory.

Among the Balanta-Bungue subgroup, communities coalesced around founder-clans, successfully preserving their cultural and social identity.[15] Even when some of these Balanta-Bungue communities migrated to new areas (usually to evade colonial policies), they retained close ties with and a strong commitment to their villages of origin.[16] Similarly among the Balanta-Brassa, the majority Balanta subgroup, community power structures continued to be based on segmentary lineage and age-related divisions.[17]

Power differentials reflected the influence of those specific elders descended from founder-lineages, rather than simply the oldest males per se. At the same time, control over specific land areas, especially rice fields, remained central to the power base of Balanta-Brassa political leadership groupings, and this control was not altered during the "settled" colonial period. Territorial allocations generally corresponded to particular clan-based or lineage-based links to land areas.[18]

Balanta-Brassa economic activity, ranging from rice cultivation to the harvesting of palm products, was determined by peasant clans or family groups, who were deemed responsible for given terrains (usually descendants of the original settler of that terrain). Moreover, sociopolitical power was recognized through a series of traditional rice cultivation and harvesting ceremonies that were held regularly through the 1920–60 period. While fundamental land-allocation powers were accorded to Balanta elders *(balanta badā)*, it was up to a religious official, a *balouberu,* to assure the spiritual protection of specific territories and the collective religiosecular well-being of village communities within those territories.[19]

While age-group divisions remained central to the Balanta power structure of civil society, some changes among those strata did occur.[20] In general, a broad division within all Balanta clans was found between the *blufos,* young men (usually below the age of thirty) who had not yet undergone the rite of passage known as *fanadu* (which includes circumcision); and the elders.[21] However, beyond this broad framework, the more specific divisions of age groupings, which varied by Balanta clan, in fact expanded through the duration of the "settled" colonial period as the population increased and the process of internal differentiation became magnified.[22] By the 1950s, between nine and twelve male age groups were identifiable in the Kuntohe Balanta clan, and Bungue males were divided into eight to fifteen age groups. The females in each of these clans were divided into between four and seven age groups.[23]

A key function of these age grades was to assure the coordination of economic, social, and political activity among villages located across wide distances. These activities included intervillage marriages, decision-making councils, and the extensive labor coordination that was required for mangrove rice farming. Similarly, funerals and circumcision rituals attracted large numbers of Balanta from dispersed locales. These continued to be performed without the knowledge of the state-appointed chiefs (the *regulos*).[24] As noted in chapter 1, intraethnic cross-cutting ties among widespread Balanta communities had been originally developed prior to the period of the Atlantic slave trade; during the period of colonialism under discussion, councils of elders, marriages, circumcision rituals, and labor tasks through which specific age grades were mobilized across widely dispersed villages helped to preserve and reinforce idiosyncratic Balanta social structures.[25] In doing so, such cross-cutting institutions formed powerful rural-based social foundations of civil society in Balanta areas.

At the same time, the colonial period was marked by mutually beneficial, synergistic exchanges between the Balanta and other rural peoples. For example, from the late 1910s, due to internal population pressures and the quest for more rice fields (and to some extent to escape forced labor),[26] groups of Balanta-Brassa began migrating from central locales to Nalu-dominated areas of Tombali region.[27] Since these Nalu specialized in palm-product exploitation, the Balanta rice farmers complemented this economic activity, and the Nalu welcomed their arrival.[28] In the new locale, however, the Balanta preserved their own social and political institutions and economic and religious practices.[29] This phenomenon of Balanta migrating southward[30] and being accommodated by the Nalu continued throughout the colonial period (up to the early 1960s, when it was interrupted by the national-liberation struggle).[31]

Thus, at community level, the Balanta were able to maintain their political and social independence from colonial institutions, typically migrating when necessary to assure their relative autonomy and the independent structures of civil society.

The Mandjack Kingdom: Political Change and Continuity

Mandjack political structures generally reflect the third pattern noted above — large-scale political systems changing significantly through the 1920–60 period in a way that augmented independent self-rule at the local level. This was especially the case in regard to the Basserel kingdom, where rural civil society previously had consisted of landowners beholden to the king, but subsequently was altered to reflect a more representative and popular structure of young "usurpers" lacking loyalty to Basserel.

During the nineteenth century, eighteen communities with separately demarcated lands formed the greater Basserel kingdom. However, this large-scale kingdom was reduced during the terror campaigns of 1913–15. In 1917, while making preparations for the colonial state's subdivision of Cacheu region, administrators found that only twelve communities remained affiliated with Basserel. Through subsequent decades, the core of the Mandjack kingdom remained based in Basserel, but the power of the king became increasingly limited, with his rule depending on the approval of federated chiefs. The prestige and status of the Basserel kingdom had declined severely by the 1930s and 1940s, with independent Mandjack chiefs previously committed to Basserel

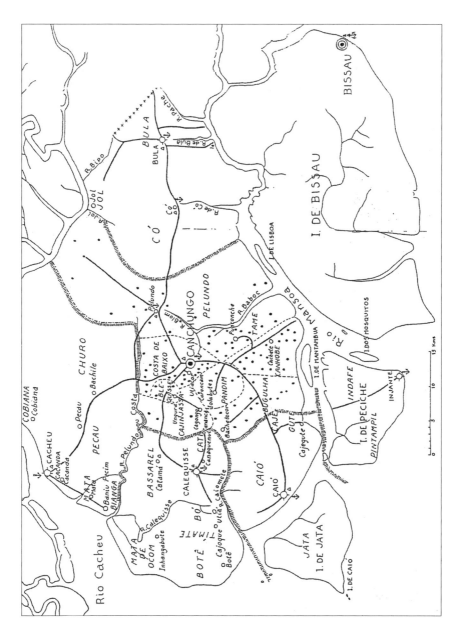

Map 5 Cacheu Region

Important areas, villages, administrative posts, roads, and ports in Cacheu region. Location relative to Bissau. Bassarel (Basserel) site of declining kingdom, rising spiritual center.

Source: Reproduced from António Carreira, *Vida social dos Majacos* (Lisbon: Centro de Estudos da Guiné Portuguesa, 1947), 23.

breaking away and becoming more autonomous.[32] By the 1960s, the rump Basserel kingdom consisted of a mere six communities.[33]

But throughout the colonial period, the Basserel king and his federated chiefs and associated aristocrats continued to wield some authority. Mandjack chiefs in the royally affiliated Cacheu villages continued to be installed by the Basserel king and to pay tributes to him through the 1940s and early 1950s, and even up to national independence in 1974.[34] These included the chiefs of the villages of Cajinjassá, Costa da Baixo, Blequisse, Cati, Calequisse, Bó, and Timate.[35]

Moreover, during the early portions of the colonial period, Mandjack chiefs could purchase or lease lifetime rulerships from the Basserel king if they could pay the relatively high usufruct costs of such a purchase. They could even possess multiple fields if they provided sufficient payments to the king.[36] These land-rights payments *(blee)* were generally substantial, often costing as much as forty head of cattle, dozens of cloths, gunpowder, rum, and other items. These *babosin* (chiefs, or as the Portuguese called them, "aristocrats") benefited from fees paid to them by their communities for officially opening and closing the weekly markets.[37] Lesser political figures could lease lands from babosin, which further enriched these village-level authority figures.

However, aggressive young upstarts in many Mandjack villages increasingly proved capable of manipulating this system to their own benefit, defying the king of Basserel and usurping new lands for their own use without the king's approval. This was particularly the case as of about the 1940s with regard to primogeniture: young men defied the king's right to decide the fate of lands that had been utilized by the sons' fathers, and, contrary to custom, asserted their right to inherit those lands directly. Their ability to do so signaled a gradual but steady breakdown of the titled land system toward the latter stages of the colonial period: lands in effect became privatized, while the political authority of the older rulers — those who remained committed to the Basserel king — degenerated into near irrelevancy. For example, between 1946 and 1952, the Basserel king, Joku, nominated seven vassal chiefs to take charge of titled lands, but none of the seven was able to assume his position, and some were driven off those titled lands by Mandjack already tilling them — the sons of the previous land titleholders.[38]

Anthropologist Eric Gable emphasizes that undergirding this diminution of kingly power in Cacheu region was the reemergence of an ancient Mandjack emphasis on local autonomy. Gable argues that, in precolonial times, the kingdom was relatively large and powerful and that some titled landholding positions were in fact determined by the king, but that for the most part the kingdom was much less hierarchical than previously assumed. This reflected the strong emphasis on the sharing of political responsibility and mutual respect within Mandjack political culture. Furthermore, in concert with the increasing economic independence of the titleholders, the long-held emphasis on personal independence,[39] political accountability, and respect for the input of village chiefs developed into an even greater emphasis on village autonomy and anticentralism in the 1920–60 period.[40] The Basserel king was eventually unable to appoint community political leaders; each community came to select its own leaders, producing a veritable democratization of rural civil society. Thus, many communities previously associated with Basserel were placing members of their own familial grouping, rather than members of the king's family, in ruling positions within their communities.

Some villages became politically autonomous more rapidly than others, which was the case in the village of Caboi, where the position of chief fell into disuse within a decade of the conquest period.[41] Other Mandjack villages (e.g., Churo) had never been associated with the Basserel kingship and did not have any tradition of chieftainship. In such instances, a colonial official often appointed as "chief" anyone of substantial wealth willing to serve in that post. Both the first chief of Churo to be selected by the Portuguese, Balencante, and his son who succeeded him, Luís Balencante, held virtually no influence over the crucial issue of land-tenure decision making.[42]

Within most villages in Cacheu region, the Portuguese had no pull regarding the chiefly selection process; chiefs were locally chosen by popular "chiefmakers." These leaders wielded considerable influence;[43] in Caió, for example, both the chief and chiefmaker were able to distribute power and political office—that is to say, assignment of compound headmanships and land-use rights.[44] At the same time, however, these powers were moderated by the coexistence of multiple patterns of land-use succession and matrilineal inheritance rights (the ability to make land bequests to maternal relatives) that provided ordinary villagers with different customary means of acquiring land and wealth. In these ways, as the Basserel kingdom shrunk in size and influence, village-selected Mandjack leaders and individual peasants managed to expand the locally determined nature of their social structures.

When necessary to preserve their recently attained autonomy, chiefs who were locally popular took advantage of the corruption that was commonplace among lower-level administrators in the region. Mandjack would in these cases bribe a corrupt official in order to assure that a young man—rather than the king's choice—would assume control of titled lands. In this way, younger Mandjack men proved able to defy the Basserel king. Manipulating colonial officials through illegal pay-offs, rather than seeing lands revert to control by the Basserel king, as had been the practice, meant that the son would retain control of his father's land. Through these pay-offs—and the further difficulty for the colonialists that they simply did not have the staff to wield power in most villages—by the 1940s, and often earlier, Mandjack communities' popular choices of new titled landholders were assured.[45]

It is important to emphasize that in fundamentally altering the pattern of land primogeniture these Mandjack usurpers reasserted the importance of specific land tracts and reestablished a fundamentally autonomous form of political authority. The Mandjack often referred to themselves as the people of the "ancestor post" in order "to emphasize their rootedness to a particular land," as each land tract was demarcated by spiritually significant wooden posts.[46]

In sum, by the conclusion of the "settled" colonial period, the Mandjack remained committed to particular land areas, but rural civil society had become significantly altered, as the former macrolevel political power of the Basserel king had reached virtually nominal status by the late 1950s: young usurpers were able to control community power structures and resources.

Given that the Basserel king remained a loyal supporter of the colonial state and functioned as the state's indirect ruler in Mandjack areas, the augmentation of de facto autonomy and the usurpation of political power by local young men meant that most Mandjack villagers had successfully avoided any meaningful degree of control by the colonial state and were able to reconstruct rural civil society on their own terms.

POWER SHIFT TO RELIGIOUS LEADERS

While the reconstruction of Mandjack social structures in large part involved the assertion of political and economic power by new landholders, an alternative sociopolitical system also emerged during the "settled" colonial period that formed part of the structure of civil society. This alternative system was grounded in a Mandjack religious order headed by a "king of the below"—in effect, the head of an underground spirit world that directly affected social and political processes occurring in the world of the above (the living world).[47] The underworld and living-world kings may be thought of as sharing power, yet performing different functions. But during the course of the 1920–60 period, the diminution of the power of the king of the living world left the "king of the below" and associated spirit entities, more influential than his above-world counterpart.

Eve Crowley's anthropological research in Cacheu region exposes with particular clarity the greater social implications of local religion. Crowley writes that—consistent with Gable's notion of dual sovereignty—the spiritist commitment of the people of Cacheu region was complementary to, rather than competitive with, the secular (living world) king of Basserel. At the same time, she makes clear that the chiefs whose authority was undermined during the period under discussion were displaced by certain shrine-based secret societies. These irã societies became the central political forces in many villages—and also became the major source of social unity in the region.[48]

One particularly powerful shrine, known as *kaboi,* was brought to Basserel soon after the end of the Portuguese military conquest of the region in the 1910s. It was used in subsequent decades as a source of power to undermine witches.[49] By the 1930s, according to anthropological research carried out at that time, the village of Caboi lacked a popularly legitimate secular chiefly authority: only the irã religious leaders served as authority figures at the local level.[50] Caboi had no association with the Basserel kingdom during those decades.[51]

The most powerful shrine spirit of kaboi that emerged was known as Mama Djombo, which achieved particular influence and popularity due to its geospiritual proximity to a deity believed to be active in northwestern Guinea-Bissau. Mama Djombo became a source of spiritual strength especially for those commoner peasants who were not able to attain privileged positions within the Basserel-controlled political world.[52] The Mama Djombo shrine—and, more broadly, the entire world of the below—did not contribute directly to Basserel's weakening as a secular kingdom. However, the shrine and spiritism did become an increasingly important and influential source of decision-making authority as the Basserel kingship's power continued to decline. These spirit shrines came to wield more influence on social and political life in the living world than did the colonially created administrative structures. For this reason, we may consider these spirit shrines to represent a central component of the newly reconstructed rural civil society.

Spirit Provinces

The twenty-nine administrative chieftainships and territories into which the Portuguese had subdivided Cacheu region during the settled colonial period were presumed (by the Portuguese) to have been based on control by a single chief over a specific land area or community. However, for the Mandjack of Cacheu region, these twenty-nine areas represented "spirit provinces" (*usák,* in Mandjack; lit., "homeland"), and each was controlled by one or more spirits. The social, political, and economic life of each village community was (and to an extent still is) based in large part on their commitments to these separate spirits and the shrines constructed to represent them in sacred sections of forestland.[53]

These spirit provinces often coincided with chieftainships that predated the colonial period. However, the displacement of secular chiefly authority was such that, by 1951, eighteen of the twenty-nine real-world provinces had no secular chief.[54] These often had already been superseded by the spirit-based secret societies. The spirit societies provided a sense of political and social coherence to the various subgroups and lesser spirit shrines contained within each province; they were a basis of local group identity.[55] Three examples of the thirty larger groupings based on the spirit provinces are the Baboi of Caboi spirit province, the Baió of Caió spirit province, and the Pantufa of Pantufa spirit province.[56]

Each secret society acted to define legally acceptable rules and social order within each spirit province and performed key political and social functions, including dispute resolution and the establishment of new legal rules. Furthermore, through their cyclically repeated initiation ceremonies, they provided opportunities to determine who was to hold the key authority and power-determining positions in the above-world society.[57] To be sure, secular chiefs or landed title-holders held significant power in some villages of Cacheu region. But even in those cases, secular chiefs were usually themselves members of shrine-based secret societies, and their roles had been obtained in part as a consequence of the allocation of power within those secret societies. Overall, then, it was the shrine protectors or spirit intermediaries who commonly held the greatest political power in a given community.[58] In all these ways, these shrines reinforced the localistic, autonomous, indigenously controlled character of rural civil society in Mandjack areas and made clear the de-linkage of most rural power structures from both the Basserel kingship and colonial authority.

Finally, we may also note that contributing to the spread and strengthening of spiritism in Cacheu region was the growth of a prophet-based revitalization movement known as *kasará*.[59] The movement proved distinctive and enduring because of its ability to provide ordinary people access to its high god, who in turn could contact local spirit forces. Kasará attracted many adherents not only among the Mandjack, but also among the Felupe, Banhun, and Papel, thereby contributing to spiritism's multiethnic and incorporative character.

The Multiethnic Character of Cacheu Spirit Provinces

In general, because they facilitated the incorporation of "outsiders" (i.e., people from outside the immediate area of a given shrine), spirit shrines encouraged a multiethnic clientele. This was possible because the basis of acceptance into a contract with a spirit shrine was a commitment to the rules and understandings particular to that shrine, not one's ethnic background. As a result, people from throughout Portuguese Guinea were able to—and did—become members of Cacheu region spirit shrine communities. In consequence, while the majority of shrine founders and shrine community leaders were of Mandjack ethnic origin, over the passage of time many shrine communities in Cacheu region—core components of rural civil society—incorporated members from an exceptionally diverse variety of ethnic groups, displaying the relatively malleable character of spirit-shrine communities.

Non-Mandjack migrants to Cacheu region were historically incorporated into spirit provinces at special rites through which the newcomers became committed to specific shrines. Although founding families were given precedence when positions of power were allocated, there were ways for newly incorporated members to be given politically and socially significant positions such as shrine priest or head of an age group.[60] And shrine affiliation provided outsiders not only with ways of joining the most intimate of Mandjack religious groupings—the secret societies—but also with a vehicle for advancement in the secular world. Social bonds were created through the secret societies.

It is important to emphasize this aspect—the provision of social cohesion for outsiders—since it demonstrates the inclusivistic practices of host families. In Caboi, for example, nearly one-fourth of founding residential lineages were of Mancanya ethnic origin.[61] The colonial administrative head of Cacheu region in the 1930s, António Carreira, emphasized in his writings the multiethnic attraction of Caboi's Mama Djombo spirit shrine. In particular, he noted pilgrimages made to that shrine by—in addition to Mandjack—Papel, Balanta, Cassanga, Banhun, and Brame, largely to take advantage of Mama Djombo's healing powers.[62] Churo, too, was a multiethnic community: the Mandjack populace incorporated into their fold numerous Papel and Balanta, and many of these Papel and Balanta intermarried with Mandjack and adapted Mandjack customs and social practices.[63] The spirit-shrine belief system also came to be shared by Banhun residing in predominantly Diola areas.

In various villages along the Cacheu River (and in nearby areas of Casamance region, Senegal), the Baboi, Cassanga, and Banhun engaged in a collective oath-taking ritual known as *simini*.[64] This was observed by the Portuguese colonial administrator and ethnographer Teixeira Mota in the late 1940s and early 1950s.[65] The *simini* ritual performed a particularly interethnic linkage role in familiarizing young men with their lands of origin north of Cacheu region—

an area inhabited by several different ethnic groups. Crowley suggests that the spread of spiritist affiliation with Mama Djombo among the Mandjack, Banhun, and Cassanga peoples of northwestern Guinea-Bissau and parts of Casamance in part reflected the long-term trading ties and social and cultural linkages among these groups.[66]

The multiethnic appeal of Mama Djombo was strengthened because the place at its spiritual core—Caboi—was located at the geographic margin of the Basserel kingdom, far removed from the king's secular grasp. This had already been the case when Basserel's power was at its height (eighteenth and nineteenth centuries), but Basserel's dramatic decline during the twentieth century helped to further consolidate Mama Djombo's geopolitical position as separate from that of Basserel. Caboi's isolated locale in a dense forest zone made it possible for people from different groups to converge without interference from centralized secular political authority. At Caboi, they could cohabit, form complex social bonds, and generate the power structures that undergirded rural civil society—and as they did so, the state-affiliated Basserel kingdom became increasingly marginalized.[67]

In sum, the ethnic commingling of Caboi's heterogenous population and the leadership structures associated with Mama Djombo's spirit shrine represented notable aspects of the emergence of a community-based rural civil society in Cacheu, marked in part by a relatively flexible notion of ethnic identity and the encouragement of multiethnic incorporatism.

Other Religion-Based Alternatives

In this successful competition with the colonial state rulers in the allocation of power in Portuguese Guinea, the irã shrines were not unique: there were other politico-religious-social components of rural civil society. It is important to mention the social impact of the baloubeiros—the spiritual authorities influential among a variety of ethnic groups—although they tended to reflect locally specific beliefs (we noted Balanta baloubeiros above). For example, the colonial authorities in the 1940s and 1950s were aware of and concerned about the power of baloubeiros functioning in the Papel area of Bandim. Covert community meetings were organized at night during which baloubeiros would render decisions regarding local-level justice, sometimes involving the use of violence directed against specific individuals (occasionally Europeans). Portuguese officials were frustrated at being unable to curtail the influence of these baloubeiros in Bandim and elsewhere.[68]

The supraethnic authority of a number of Islamic marabouts in Gabu and other regions also, for the most part, stood apart from the colonial rubric. During the 1920s and 1940s, Islamization made significant advances among the Biaffada, with most of the remaining animist Biaffada being converted to Islam.[69] This added to the large numbers of already-Islamized Fulbe and Mandinka peoples. To be sure, it was precisely Islamic chiefs (Fulbe and, to some extent, Mandinka and Biaffada) who, after lengthy nineteenth-century battles, eventually collaborated with the colonial state and who then served as administrative appointees. Nonetheless, officials never quite became comfortable with the fact that Islam represented a foreign religious belief system that they could not control or incorporate into the colonial world. Thus on 20 November 1947, in a speech to the Superior Colonial School in Lisbon at a conference on Islam, the governor of Guinea, Sarmento Rodriguez, decried what he called a "paradox": While the animist groups in Guinea had offered the most resistance to colonial rule, it was the Fulbe and Biaffada Muslims about whom the colonialists had to be the most concerned over the long term.[70] Again in 1958, a colonial report expressed serious concern regarding the possible cohesion of Islamic peoples in a way that could "overcome tribal divisions," which may, in turn, represent a long-term "threat" to the stability of the colony.[71]

The spread of Islam, like the power of the baloubeiros, constituted an important sphere of social and religious life that was outside the rubric of colonial state domination. In many regions, these elements bolstered the self-direction of rural civil society.

––––

Throughout the 1920–60 period, the spiritual and secular worlds intersected in a way that made possible the rise of meaningful and influential alternative authority sources for a significant percentage of Guineans. Shrine societies, the baloubeiros, Islam, and a variety of indigenously directed belief systems influenced the flow of ideas, social power, and resources in the countryside. Most of these belief systems represented expansions of socioreligious forces that originated in precolonial times. I thus concur with Eric Wolf's assertion that it is, in part, the conservative determination of peasants to retain control over historically legitimated social practices that radicalizes peasant communities in the face of challenges posed by would-be hegemonic states.[72] It was not that the social practice of spiritism, by itself, constituted social resistance that led to the self-directed reconstruction of Mandjack social structures: it was because the spirit shrines represented an alternative to the macropolitical power of the colonial state that they assumed their particular political significance.

In this sense, the spirit shrines, like the balouberu belief system in Bandim, acted as a "folk religion" that functioned, in James C. Scott's terms, as a "weapon of the weak" utilized as a "form of everyday resistance" against state power.[73] Through such resistance, villagers were able to create a "peasant subculture" and "autonomous social space" for the "assertion of dignity."[74] We may point out that in the upper Kasai region of the Congo (former Zaire), a similar peasant subculture was found predicated on (spirit) chiefs "of the below," viewed positively as peacemakers, in contrast to the (living) chiefs "of the above," who were more selfish and predatory.[75]

The Africanist historian T. O. Ranger has described the role played by indigenous "spirit mediums" and "priests" in Tanzania and Rhodesia in creating new forms of mobilization and cooperation *between different ethnic groups* that generated "anti-authority militancy" structured through local religious systems.[76] Indeed, in Guinea-Bissau's Cacheu region, spirit-society members constructed an alternative system of authority that determined the direction of political and economic resources, directly or indirectly challenged the ideological and social hegemony of the state, and attracted members from a variety of ethnic groups.

At the same time, these spirit-shrine societies represented a sociopolitical pillar of rural civil society. In regard to land use, a critically important economic resource in any predominantly rural society and an essential source of civil societal power, locally respected rural social actors in Cacheu region were able to outmaneuver both the Basserel kingship and colonial-state officials so as to wrest control over their respective lands. In doing so, young Mandjack leaders were able to detach themselves from the secular Basserel kingdom while also steering clear of the authority of the colonial state—erecting a self-selected structure of rural civil authority.

Thus, this was not simply a case of a subordinated peasantry seeking alternative resistance techniques but rural-based popular leaders who in fact succeeded in retaining local political and social control at the grassroots level. It is important to emphasize that this was the case not merely with regard to the spirit forces but also in regard to the impact of these spirit forces in the secular world and the ability of locally legitimate leaders to retain control of their political and economic resources in that secular world. It is in these senses that actors supported by the Guinean peasantry proved able to sustain a "strong" rural civil society that mediated against predation by the colonial state.

Finally, let us recall that not only many Mandjack in Cacheu region but also rural people in Oio region, the southern Balanta regions, the Papel in Bandim, the Felupe areas of northwestern Guinea-Bissau, and the Bijagós islands proved largely able, most of the time, to ignore or circumvent colonial officials and their appointed community chiefs. As a consequence, those appointed chiefs could not control local-level social, economic, or political life; at most, appointed chiefs could in some cases provoke contested leaderships, a point further explored in chapter 9.

Thus, throughout the "settled" colonial period, the central strengths of rural civil society would be reflected in indigenous political and social structures that represented independent alternatives to colonial authority. Within that separate civil societal sphere, age-based authority systems reemerged, local claims over specific land areas were reinforced, economic production activities remained in local hands, and, in some areas (e.g., Oio, Catió), social institutions such as marriage tied together families from common ethnic origins (as was the case with the Balanta). None of this, however, precluded the development of interethnic cooperation and ethnically malleable social processes, including the friendly incorporation of newcomers from other ethnic groups and the expansion of multiethnic spirit-shrine-based leadership groupings. These processes manifested relative boundary flexibility regarding ethnic group identity, which in turn harks back to precolonial practices. Through the colonial period, these ethnically interactive dynamics in fact helped to strengthen the behavioral independence of peasant-based civil society.

In chapter 9 it is suggested that this widening rural social space would help make it possible for Guineans to make independent choices regarding which side to support in the national-liberation struggle of the 1960s and 1970s, and that those choices would in large part reflect the particular character of rural civil society in a given locale. Meanwhile, it is important to make clear that — in addition to social power remaining locally vested, thus inhibiting political "penetration" by the state — a vibrant, informal trading sector in rural Guinea-Bissau further strengthened the independent character of social formations in the countryside. As the next chapter indicates, this deprived the central state of key resources.

CHAPTER 8

The Colonial State and the Informal Economic Sector

DESPITE THE REPEATED CHALLENGES to state sovereignty posed by rural Guineans during the 1920–60 period, the colonial state was able to accumulate some resources and sought to carry out policies that aimed at further increasing revenue flows. However, state-led institutional and economic development in Portuguese Guinea remained substantially hindered by an informal sector of the economy that enabled peasants and traders to carry out much of their business outside the purview of government regulation. This chapter makes clear the implications of the social strength of rural civil society for the overall power of the state. I depict the impact of the widening of the informal rural sector of the economy and of peasants' ability to dispense their resources on clandestine markets.

One important impact of the predominance of the informal sector was the failure to construct a nationally integrated framework of economic administration, which also contributed to internal policy problems for the government. The economic ability of rural civil society to retain control over agricultural resources and the ability of producers to trade in "hidden" markets represented a central roadblock in the path of state building, despite the ability of the national government to collect annual taxes and to construct a system of roads.

While the economic activity of Africans in Guinea-Bissau that was not aimed at the export sector was regarded as "backward" and was of little consequence to colonial governors, most producers and traders, rather than becoming dependent on colonially controlled trade, in fact made a living off this uncaptured market. Thus, while some cash crops—especially groundnuts in Fulbe-dominated Gabu province—were sold through state-approved channels, a substantial amount of economic produce, both food crops and cash crops, was being sold and traded on illicit circles outside the bounds of state officialdom. The state could not achieve greater economic control because most traders ignored or avoided pecuniary bureaucratic oversight and there were inadequate numbers of trained personnel to patrol market exchanges.

The government of Portuguese Guinea, especially as of the 1930s, did try to implement certain programs aimed at generating more efficient rural/urban economic ties, such as a rice-based urban food-supply program. However, most of these programs proved unsuccessful. This was not simply because the colonial bureaucracy was not sufficiently staffed to implement such national policies, but also because in most areas, as already noted, land tenure was allocated through internal processes specific to rural civil society, rather than by the state or state appointees; the means of agricultural production remained in the hands of the producers and the state could not control the outflow of harvest surpluses. Government leaders were unable to locate the key members of rural civil society in most areas, to build ties with them and to incorporate them into a state-run system of indirect rule, so that, on the ground, economic production, harvesting, and trading activities remained under the control of local rural actors who were not tied into the state's system of administration.

Indeed, the only two economic policies that were implemented on a comprehensive, national basis in Portuguese Guinea were tax collection and road building that involved forced labor. Officials were able to carry out these policies in most regions because they relied on the mainstay of colonial rulership in Portuguese Guinea—the use of extreme state violence. This violence was viewed as fundamental to state logic in regard to officials' effort to collect taxes and to build roads precisely because the state was faced with a deeply embedded rural civil society that was often invisible to the colonialists. In what was a reflection of state leaders' inability to construct a viable intermediary segment of reliable rural leaders throughout the colony, the state could act effectively across regional parameters only insofar as its actions were accompanied by severe acts of violence, although it normally had the capacity to employ such violence only on an episodic, selective basis.

To be sure, another central factor was the relationship between metropolitan Portugal and the colony: Lisbon, while absorbing much of the foreign-exchange earnings from groundnuts, insisted that its colonies cover their own costs;[1] Lisbon failed to provide funding for major economic and state-building projects or for a larger and better-staffed colonial administration. However, this, alone, does not explain the inability of state leaders to build workable social ties with rural civil society in most regions; nor does it explain the extreme violence—why only thus could officials collect annual taxes and oversee road construction.

Apart from this general context, it is important to acknowledge the locationally specific case in which producers and traders became partially incorporated into the colonial sector of the economy: in the mostly Fulbe areas of Gabu and (to a lesser extent) Mandinka areas of Farim, some compliant chiefs were able to exert a substantial influence over their communities;[2] these chiefs were able to convince peasants to grow groundnuts aimed at an export-oriented market that brought foreign revenue earnings to the state. This was supplemented by the produce of the *ponteiros* (Cape Verdean or European private traders), a small number of whom—between fifty and seventy-five—had established farms worked by neighboring Balanta along riverine areas in Cacine and Catió.[3] In total, groundnut production levels fluctuated between 5,000 tons and 25,000 tons per year from the late 1920s through the 1930s, and then averaged 30,000 to 35,000 tons per year in the 1940s and 1950s.[4]

However, most peasants in most regions (Cacheu, Catió, Mansoa, Fulacunda, Oio, Bafatá, São Domingos) were neither inextricably incorporated into nor dependent on a state-controlled, export-oriented production sector.[5] This was the case even with many agriculturalists in Gabu and Farim: we know this because groundnut producers from those areas often sold their harvests in neighboring Senegal or French Guinea, rather than to Portuguese state firms.[6] In Guinea-Bissau as a whole, an estimated 87 percent of the arable land was devoted to raising crops for local consumption or cash sale in informal markets.[7]

In most regions, the fact that in large measure the "formal" sector of trade represented a relatively narrow spectrum of the broader rural economy reflected the enduring autonomy and adaptability of independent rural markets, as was manifested through the expansion of informal local-level as well as long-distance trade networks.

THE INFORMAL SECTOR

In precolonial times, trading among the various peoples within what became Portuguese Guinea was carried out throughout the interior dryland as well as the coastal areas. Such trading dates back beyond the ancient Gabu empire, although Gabu's markets expanded the exchanges between ethnic groups. In subsequent centuries, the preponderance of exchanges that took place among indigenous merchants and producers in the countryside was not regulated or monitored by Portuguese officials.[8] This informal trade continued through the "settled" colonial period, being carried out by rural producers and traders who traveled to various parts of the colony and beyond. They carved out a sphere of market trading that benefited peasants and provided an economic support structure for an independent rural civil society despite the predations of the central state.

Much of the trade that took place within Portuguese Guinea reflected exchanges among rural African producers, with peasants carrying their own crops and handicraft products to local or regional markets. Balanta in the southern regions, for example, produced massive rice surpluses—much of which was either circulated within Balanta communities[9] or was bartered or sold directly to people who did not grow rice, such as the Mandjack and Brame of Cacheu region.[10] Meanwhile, Biaffada, Mandjack, Papel, Nalu, and Bijagós maintained regional, weekly markets dominated by women traders at which such products as palm oil, palm wine, poultry, salt, fish, pottery, and medicinal herbs were exchanged.[11] Within Cacheu region, trading—mostly barter exchange—was carried out in local markets in Blequisse, Bugulha, Cajinjassá, Canhobe, Costa de Baixo, Pandim, Pelundo, Tame, and other towns, as well as in regional market fairs that grouped together agriculturalists, handicraft producers, and merchants from different ethnic groups.[12] Bijagós islanders canoed to markets on the mainland to offer their cattle, coconuts, palm oil, animal skins, chickens, and oranges in return for rice, salt, cloths, crockery, and alcohol. It is worth mentioning here that the Bijagós preferred barter over cash: they often did not store metallic money pieces, but remolded them into artifacts.[13]

Beyond these interpeasant trading activities, the djula and the Lebanese both played notable roles in sustaining the vibrancy of the informal sector. The djula, professional mobile traders, were usually of Mandinka ethnic origin, and generally Islamic.[14] During precolonial centuries, most notably during the period of the Gabu empire, they had traded with groups throughout the interior of Guinea-Bissau, exchanging grain, cloths, salt, mirrors, slaves, and gold (the gold in the form of small bars or powder).[15] The djula built up important trading links and networks throughout most of Guinea-Bissau. The principal source of new goods for indigenous villagers, it was to them that agriculturalists sold much of their surplus produce.[16] Dyed cloths were one example of an important trade item that was sold to djula by local fabricators—mostly Papel, Mandinka, and

Fulbe, who generated a total of between fifty thousand and sixty thousand units of cloth per year. The djula resold those cloths to Balanta, Biaffada, Mandjack, and other purchasers in villages along a Cacheu-Mansoa-Bissau informal trade route.[17] The djula, who knew the local languages, had created strong informal ties with rural people, and they would continue to ply their trade through the period of "settled" colonial rule.[18] Such trade took place largely outside the framework of Portuguese monitoring and regulation and helped to assure dynamic informal market links within rural areas among a variety of ethnic groups.

Lebanese and Syrian immigrants also assumed a noteworthy role in rural circuits of trade. There were 178 such traders in 1928, and individually they had set up mercantile venues in villages throughout Portuguese Guinea.[19] In 1930, Syrian traders were reported to have outnumbered their European counterparts in Bafatá, a major commercial center, and in most villages in the interior they had no European competitors.[20]

CROSS-BORDER CLANDESTINE TRADE AND SECTORAL DISARTICULATION

Throughout the 1920–60 period, while informal trading characterized inter-village and interregional relations, economic linkages between Senegalese and rural Guineans in the north and the east of the colony were consolidated through the expansion of interborder trading circuits. These economic linkages assumed the form of

(1) Guinean peasants transporting, usually by foot, sacks of their own agricultural produce for resale across the Senegalese border

(2) Guinean peasants selling their produce to clandestine traders (djulas and others) specializing in moving Guinean produce from the Lusophone colony to Senegal, where this produce would be resold

(3) Guineans traveling to Senegalese farms during the agricultural off-season to work temporarily for wages.

In 1929–30, according to French colonial officials, people traveled from Portuguese Guinea to Senegal or to French Guinea specifically in order to obtain cotton to weave into clothing.[21] In December 1931, despite a Portuguese Guinean governmental effort at border patrols, a groundswell of temporary emigration out of Portuguese Guinea and into French Guinea took place immediately following that year's harvests.[22] In 1937, an observer noted a continuing, "incessant coming and going" of people from and to Portuguese Guinea and

French Guinea.[23] And in 1938, peasants were again temporarily traveling into Senegal or French Guinea in order to sell their products there.[24]

A 1939 report made clear that many Guineans moved seasonally to Casamance in order to cultivate groundnuts.[25] Some arrived with their livestock or other possessions, others empty-handed. Still others carried rice or palm oil to sell for cash.[26] Peasants took their produce to Sansalé (Boké district) to sell because they received higher prices in French-controlled territory, after which they returned to Portuguese Guinea.[27] It was evident that this cross-border practice had been occurring for many decades.[28] A French colonial official stationed near the Senegal-Portuguese Guinean border estimated that while official government figures showed that 500 tons of groundnuts had been exported from Portuguese Guinea to Senegal, the actual total was closer to between 2,000 and 3,000 tons.[29] This meant that approximately four-fifths of the cross-border groundnut trade was taking place clandestinely. As for the (mostly Balanta) rice producers, of the 43,800 to 182,251 tons of rice harvested per year in the 1940s and 1950s, much of it, as noted above, circulated within Balanta communities; but most of the remainder was sold on unmonitored, clandestine markets, often outside the colony. A maximum of only 7,305 tons of rice per year was sold to state-monitored outlets during this period—a mere fraction of that in the informal sector.[30]

One result of the widespread extent of the extraordinary economic interchange between residents of Portuguese Guinea and of Senegal (and to a lesser degree French Guinea) described above was the large-scale use of the French West African franc, rather than Portuguese currency. An early indicator was seen in June 1913, when after the victory of colonial forces in Oio a tax was imposed: no Portuguese currency was found, but French currency was plentiful, so the tax was collected in francs.[31]

In the 1930s and 1940s, despite virulent efforts on the part of colonial officials to ban the use of non-Portuguese currencies in Guinea, the predominance of the French CFA franc in trade, exchanges, wage payments, and other transactions was scarcely diminished in much of the countryside. Thus, a 1947 report made clear that CFA francs were in widespread use in Farim, where one official observed that "the majority of economic transactions are conducted with French currency."[32] That May, the France's consul in Bissau estimated that indigenous Guineans had accumulated a total of 30 million CFA francs through underground trading.[33]

The continuing economic importance of French West African currency in Portuguese Guinea was made evident in 1948 by an event in the colony's financial sector. In that year, Bissau-based traders (mestiços, Lebanese, Cape Verdean immigrants, and a handful of African merchants) sought to organize an officially approved export business. In order to do so, they were required to establish commercial bank accounts with Portuguese currency. As a consequence of their large-scale, mostly illicit transactions with the Senegalese economy, the traders had accumulated a significant amount of CFA francs. However, they possessed an insufficient number of Portuguese escudos: the banks would not accept their French-African currency.[34] This makes clear that CFA-based currency trading pervaded even the transactions of those merchants (mostly in Bissau and the other large towns) who sought to be part of the colonial trading sector, as well emphasizing the extent to which the colony's monetary policy could not adapt to the basic reality that major flows of capital were occurring within the informal sector.[35]

This is further confirmed by a report that Lebanese traders in Portuguese Guinea had accumulated "millions of French CFA."[36] In 1934, Lebanese merchants who dominated trade in Pitchi charged prices in CFA francs equivalent to prices on the Casamance side of the border.[37] Throughout rural Portuguese Guinea, until nearly 1947, Lebanese-Syrian contraband traders exchanged their currency against gold, which was then passed through the border surreptitiously. However, since gold had fallen in value considerably on the underground market of French West Africa (FWA), this contraband traffic with Portuguese Guinea declined.[38] By March 1947, the "Lebanese-Syrians prefer[red] to re-export French currency as contraband."[39] Furthermore, some of the wholesale products sold at Lebanese-owned stores made their way directly out of the country and onto the international market, often bypassing state agencies and the formal trading sector. For example, products purchased in large quantities from three Lebanese stores in Pitchi were frequently taken by truck to Bafatá, where they were sent abroad by ship.[40] This informal export trade benefited not only Lebanese merchants but also the rural people who purchased, resold, and transported the goods. There was also a degree of trade between Guineans and merchants in the Gambia; in addition to CFA francs, British currency was used in parts of Portuguese Guinea. This, too, contributed to sectoral disarticulation between the rural economy and the Bissau-based colonial sector.[41]

Another example of cross-border exchange was the clandestine trade in gunpowder among Felupe in the Suzana district, who were obtaining weapons from the Gambia.[42] In addition, rural people near Farim, Gabu, and Bafatá were soliciting informal traders who had links in the Gambia and Senegal in order to obtain arms and gunpowder. This arms trading was discovered by French colonial observers in the 1940s;[43] it is likely that a great deal more, undiscovered and unrecorded, arms trading was occurring at that time.

Several large rural areas were not integrated into urban-oriented markets—a further sign of sectoral disarticulation. Particularly in parts of Cacheu, São Domingos, Catió, northern Bafatá, and northern Gabu, there was no evidence of European intervention in market relations.[44] Most rural people there were not reliant on urban goods: by trading with djulas, they could obtain a variety of finished products from Senegal or French Guinea.[45]

URBAN FOOD SUPPLY

Sectoral disarticulation contributed significantly to the problem of assuring a steady supply of food to the populace of Bissau, Portuguese Guinea's largest urban area. As was noted early in the twentieth century (1908), Bissau had already become reliant on Balanta rice producers in the southern part of Portuguese Guinea;[46] the inability of state regulators to control the marketing direction of peasant produce meant that the state was in effect dependent on these economically autonomous Balanta rice cultivators. During the late 1930s, the colonial government felt that it did not have the resources to raise the producer price above 10 escudos for a bushel of raw rice (considered a very low price). As a result, Balanta decided to sell more of their rice in French Guinea, where they received higher-valued CFA for their rice bushels.[47] In consequence, nearly empty markets in Portuguese Guinea were reported by mid-1939, along with a lack of activity in the urban commercial trading centers.[48] This depressed the availability of foodstuffs in general in Bissau, and in 1941 the standard of living deteriorated significantly as basic food products such as flour and sugar became scarce.[49] In the late 1940s, the decline in the food supply to the capital city and the resultant dearth of meat, fish, eggs, fresh vegetables, and other produce provoked consumers to turn to the clandestine market for these products. Urban residents increasingly ignored the government-regulated central market in Bissau in favor of underground trade in food. The municipal council of Bissau, which had formally banned unauthorized, ambulatory exchanges, sought to, but could not, locate and regulate this clandestine urban food network.[50]

In addition, an "intense black market in rice trading" was reported during the mid-1940s.[51] Indeed, the extensiveness of informal rice trading, both within Portuguese Guinea as a whole as well in regard to rice exporting, was so great that the colony's governor felt compelled, in 1946, to enact two decrees of consequence. The first declared illegal the export of rice.[52] In the second, approximately two-thirds of all rice producers were told that they could not plant or harvest rice that year. Both decrees were enacted specifically in order to diminish clandestine rice trading. However, the fact that the state had not achieved direct control of, or monitoring over, production or of the direction of most rural market exchanges meant that bureaucrats in Bolama and Bissau were unable to enforce these decrees. Moreover, by April 1948, Bissau's city officials became preoccupied by the issue of supplying the capital with additional foods — especially meat and fish.[53] A key problem, according to the municipal president, Commander A. A. Peixoto Correia, was that when people took their cattle to the government market, a veterinarian inspected them, frequently finding diseased cows, which the government then refused to purchase. Thus cattle owners did not receive adequate purchase orders to render it worthwhile to transport their herds to the municipal markets; they preferred to keep their cattle as stored wealth or to trade them on intrarural markets.[54]

To improve the quality of formal urban-rural economic exchanges, a government official proposed that farmers should be provided with bank credit and extension services. However, these were rejected as overly ambitious programs, reflecting inadequate funds and lack of government access to rural producers.[55]

THE BUREAUCRACY: PROBLEMS WITH ADMINISTRATIVE SCOPE

Problems such as those of assuring food supply to Bissau were indicative of a broader lacuna: the inadequacy of administrative structures extending into most rural regions. We have made clear the extent to which most rural Guineans were able to carve out their own autonomous political and social domains, despite the appointment of a number of cooperative chiefs.[56] In terms of numbers alone, the rural colonial administration was modest indeed. The rural administrative hierarchy, on paper, consisted of a head administrator (normally a European) in each region *(circumscrição)* or district *(concelho)*, with chefes de posto (often Cape Verdeans) serving as officials in the field. When possible, these chefes de posto appointed village-level chiefs, called *regedores*.[57] But even by the late 1940s, the totality of state officialdom outside the capital consisted of only eleven administrators and thirty-two chefes de posto (along with eleven secretarial aids to the administrators).[58] Thus, the European and Cape Verdean administrators oversaw vast regions and districts that were simply too large for them to monitor regularly.[59]

This explains the inordinate dependence on Fulbe local leaders, who often proved unreliable and ineffective outside of Gabu and who were unable to stem the constant internal and external migration of Guineans.[60] Moreover, the state simply did not have the infrastructural capacity to provide an adequate number of outposts. In fact, from 1927 to 1931, the government, in the midst of a period of fiscal and administrative retrenchment, abandoned a significant number of administrative posts in northern and eastern parts of the colony.[61] Through the 1940s and 1950s, many of those posts remained unstaffed, leading a Portuguese analyst to observe, in 1958, that "a certain gap exists between administrators and indigenous residents" in the rural areas.[62]

But what of the central state administration? In the 1930s, the government bureaus were staffed by a total of 359 functionaries — including clerical workers — divided into fourteen ministries (called services).[63] However, these administrative services suffered a "near paralysis" of activity due to a lack of funds, which in turn fed a certain lethargy within many offices.[64] A governor of Portuguese Guinea himself described the "latent state of undiscipline" that characterized the bureaucracy and that produced "a lack of productivity" and "moral bankruptcy."[65] In general, according to former Governor Viegas, "the [human] elements of execution — still largely deficient — do not have the slightest understanding of what bureaucratic implementation actually means, or how to carry it out."[66] As a result, bureaucratic efficiency was "more theoretical than actual."[67]

A small number of Portuguese functionaries lamented the technical and administrative inability of the government even to provide rudimentary health care or economic assistance to the rural populace.[68] These complaints had little impact, however, nor were they widely shared. The state was simply not in a position to grapple effectively with the scope of the infrastructural inadequacies in the colony.

Government departments faced enormous infrastructural difficulties, including a poor resource base and inadequate communication and transport links among the regions.[69] A lack of trained personnel meant that officials had to rely on a growing number of men brought in from the Cape Verde islands specifically to serve as low-level Guinean government officials, along with local creoles (mestiços) who were given a tiny remittance.[70] In 1936 half the mid-level functionaries and 70 percent of civil servants as a whole were Cape Verdean.[71] Very few of these administrators had strong motivation to fulfill their tasks effectively in light of their poor pay, the state's poor resource base, and the lack of support provided by Lisbon. In 1944, an observer noted that most colonial functionaries' job efforts reflected their low pay.[72] The Department of Public Works was described in 1946 as "a veritable abyss" in which administrators allowed their duties to "lie sleeping."[73]

COLONIAL STATE MALFEASANCE AND POLICY PROBLEMATICS

It is important to emphasize that the narrow administrative reach of the state (outside greater Bissau) affected the character of the central state bureaucracy, as well as its policy capacity. The problem of lack of control over a formidable rural civil society frequently left administrators frustrated, contributing to a general sense of malaise within the bureaucracy. To be sure, the low salaries and inadequate support from Lisbon also helped to define the fundamental infrastructural problems of the Guinean state. However, the problem of state administration went beyond funding levels: it must be understood that the nature of colonial rule in Portuguese Guinea also reflected the social bases of this predominantly rural society. For some four and a half centuries, extending into this "settled" colonial era, functionaries had been dealing with indigenous political leaders who simply could not be molded to serve colonial purposes. In some quarters of the bureaucracy, the problems of dealing with *"a gente"* (rural populace) had produced an atmosphere of complacency and apathy[74]—to such an extent that a number of officials in fact succumbed to the temptation of fiscal malpractice.[75]

Fourteen military officers were found in June 1927 to have collected taxes for their personal use; state funds were found missing during the 1930s;[76] and a former governor noted repeated transgressions in his administration.[77] In 1934, a Senegalese by the name of Abu Camara, who was traveling through Portuguese Guinea on his way back to Senegal, was stopped numerous times by officials who demanded monetary "exactions."[78] Albino d'Oliveira, an administrator of Farim (which borders Senegal), demanded from all people leaving the colony and traveling on to Senegal that they had to pay for an exit visa despite the fact that they had already paid for one in Bissau.[79]

The extent of this internal corruption in the 1930s-1950s period led the anthropologist Eric Gable to refer to Portuguese Guinea as a "pecuniary state,"[80] signifying that the state administration tolerated internal sleights-of-hand. In the sparse rural outposts of the state, corrupt practices were so common that for example, people in Cacheu region who lived near a chefe de posto were able to engage in petty bribery such as passing a pack of cigarettes "under the table" to secure certain favors.[81] Eve Crowley similarly found that colonial officials in Cacheu were easily bribable and that potential colonial intervention into local affairs, albeit relatively rare, was readily staved off through graft.[82]

Fiscal improprieties also apparently occurred on a routine basis within the colonial treasury department: in 1944, it was standard practice for a positive fiscal balance sheet to be produced by Portuguese Guinea even though the actual fiscal balance was negative.[83] Fiscal misrepresentations in the accounting statements of the colony's budget in turn meant that there was a perpetually inadequate supply of money to pay for annual government expenses. Part of the problem was that imported goods did not remain within the colony but rather were sold illegally by colonial officials abroad.[84]

Beyond the issue of officials' malfeasance, the state also committed a number of policy errors that in part reflected a lack of communication between officials in the field and those in the capital, as well as a lack of familiarity with the economic ways of life in rural areas. For example, administrators attempted to build roads during a time of year when the laborers needed to farm their croplands—even though officials would later try to collect those laborers' crops as taxes.[85] In the 1940s, the government, frustrated at its inability to control the flow of rice out of the southern regions and seeking to better assure Bissau's food supply, sought to build its own wet-rice fields near Bissau. However, this project did not achieve its intended purpose because the dams built by the government all lacked canal locks and were unable to restrict the riverine flow of saltwater into the rice fields.[86]

STATE VIOLENCE, TAX COLLECTION, AND FORCED LABOR

The problems described above at least in part reflected an internally troubled bureaucracy—one not able to overcome the various obstacles in the way of the economic and administrative integration of the colony. In the face of this state fragility, the only nationwide policies that could be implemented with reasonable consistency were those that involved the use of extreme state violence—tax collection and forced labor—and even there, only partial success would be realized.

Forced Labor and Road Building

As of the late 1920s, forced-labor teams, generally organized by the local chefe de posto, were created on a piecemeal basis. These teams were principally requisitioned for road building or road repair, but occasionally for construction of a government building.[87] Conscription drives often involved the use of violence and torture. By these means, military police, directed by a chefe de posto, forced communities to make available young people for the work teams (a conscripted laborer was normally obligated to remain on a work team for two weeks). However, people commonly fled during corvée recruitment, and chefes de posto faced enormous difficulties in organizing the labor teams.

In June 1931, forced-labor requisitions provoked out-migration by Papel, Mandjack, and Brames.[88] Balanta youth typically fled into the forest when labor recruiters approached.[89] By 1935, colonial officials even sought to recruit Fulbe men who had previously served as soldiers in Portuguese conquest armies and had declared their allegiance to the colonial state.[90] Many Fulbe chiefs resisted the taking of their young men and women for road building, and those chiefs were commonly imprisoned; resistance continued nevertheless. In 1935, the extent of forced-labor evasion drove chefes de posto to recruit growing numbers of women and children, which in turn provoked more large-scale temporary migration.[91] Recruiters countered by ordering that some women be raped, and others were brutally beaten.[92] On 2 March 1935, a Portuguese administrator known as Suzannah fired on villagers who had refused to work on the construction of an official building;[93] resistance continued, however, and seven days later a fire, apparently set by the villagers, burned down two other government buildings. On 23 March, in revenge, Suzannah and his men burned down huts and fired on villagers. As a result, many residents relocated to a Casamance border area. In Cacheu region in the 1930s, when Mandjack men from Basserel were conscripted to construct a road from Canchungo to Calequisse and plant shade trees alongside it, some of the men returned during the night and chopped down the newly planted trees so that the Portuguese would not later be able to order them to harvest fruit from the trees.[94]

Despite resistance, corvée labor did construct 2,771 kilometers of roads and 698 kilometers of telegraph lines.[95] However, only 61 kilometers of the roads were tarred; the rest were dirt roads, and during the extensive rainy season, many remained impassable for months at a time. Officials normally made no effort to travel to rural areas during those months, and peasants, aware of this, took advantage of the lull to trade by barter.

Overall, forced labor, as an economic development strategy, was slow-going and inefficient. The difficulty in securing workers and the disruption caused by migration led to delay or cancellation of numerous projects. In 1947, the governor of Guinea, Captain Sarmento Rodgriguez, abolished forced labor and replaced it with regulated labor codes that forbade corporal punishment.[96] To an important extent, peasant avoidance had helped to render untenable a long-time state policy.

Tax Collection

The collection of taxes in Portuguese Guinea was a one-time annual event that involved roving police squads: the squads' mission was to locate all families and to force them to pay a levy in cash or in kind. The collectors faced the technical problem that the administration did not carry out a population census until 1928, and even then it was only in the form of an estimated (or guestimated) head count. A more thoroughgoing inventory of the populace had to wait until 1947.[97] In the meantime, the state treasury in Bissau sought to assess taxes on each family's physical abode: thus, the "hut tax" became the most common form of taxation through the 1920s and 1930s.[98]

Problems with the administration of the hut tax soon arose. In 1927, it was noted by tax officials that the Fulbe of Gabu region inhabited small huts—only two to three people to each—whereas Mandinka huts housed ten to twelve beds, with from twenty to fifty people to a hut.[99] Since both the Mandinka and the Fulbe had been paying 50 escudos per hut, it was determined that the Mandinka were paying many fewer taxes; hence, it was decided that they would pay a bed tax instead of a hut tax. The Mandinka response was to reduce the number of beds per hut from ten or twelve to two or three. Some of the inhabitants would sleep on mats during the day and hide the mats at night.[100]

In the Cacheu region, some Mandjack were named in each village to make certain that the appropriate amount of hut tax was delivered.[101] However, many Mandjack developed techniques for avoiding payments, the most common of which was to destroy huts when a tax official was approaching.[102] Another technique was to enlarge the size of a hut, fitting into it more people so that payments would be decreased. This was practiced not only by the Mandjack but also by the Balanta in various parts of the colony. Many huts were torn down and rebuilt in order that tax payments would be reduced.[103] On the Bijagós islands, tax collectors had enormous problems due to the islanders' ability to hide their stored goods; tax police would then aim to confiscate cattle instead, but, unable to identify which villagers owned which cattle, they often abandoned their efforts.[104]

Between 1928 and 1937, the official hut tax was assessed at 60 escudos per hut.[105] Taxes were also imposed on possessions, but these were rarely collected since, usually, police units were mobilized only once a year, for the collection of the hut tax.[106] Taxes in 1927 (in addition to the hut tax) were

1 escudo per sheep or goat

5 escudos per bull or cow

5 escudos per big game animal

15 escudos for the confinement of a donkey

40 escudos for the possession of a gun

5 escudos for the right to collect palm oil

20 escudos for the right to harvest palm wine.[107]

To facilitate collection of the hut tax, which might be in cash or kind, farmers were frequently beaten with whips.[108] Collection proceeded only with great difficulty and was not successful in many regions.[109] The imposition of the tax, along with the forced-labor requisitions, provoked high levels of temporary migration; whole villages would hide out until the tax collectors passed by. This was especially common in the general area of Bissau, where taxation provoked the Papel into moving temporarily to Felupe lands in Casamance. The Mandjack and Brame also migrated to Casamance.[110]

To counter such evasion, colonial officials increasingly relied on the *palmatória,* a form of corporal punishment, to punish those who refused to pay taxes.[111] The palms of the resister's hands were struck with a bludgeon, the number of blows varying from ten to twenty on each hand.[112] In addition to causing extreme pain, such brutality deprived the person beaten of the use of the hands for at least several days.[113]

The colonial authorities pursued tax collection "with a rare energy" in 1932 and 1933. There was extensive violence, but people continued to try to avoid payments.[114] In 1934, near Casamance, villagers' refusal to pay taxes provoked the Portuguese colonial authorities to resort to arresting women en masse, periodically striking them until their families paid a tax.[115] Many Guineans continued to live together in large numbers, commonly a dozen in a single small hut, in order to be able to pool resources and decrease the per-person contribution.[116] In 1935, when the Portuguese replaced the hut tax with a per-bed tax, the hiding of mats and temporary evasion still problematized the collection process.[117] It was in large part as a result of the collection problem that the financial situation of the colony remained precarious in 1936.[118] In 1939, tax-collection units had become so desperate that police or military temporarily occupied selected villages in order to seize recently harvested produce.[119] Soldiers were encouraged to consider this a battle campaign, even though armed resistance to these invasions was rare (one exception was Fulacunda, where in 1939 Balanta organized resistance against the tax-collection drive).[120]

Official figures record government tax receipts for the 1930s and 1940s, although it is not possible to verify to what extent they reflect the sums that were actually collected. The following list gives the recorded totals, in escudos, for the hut and poll taxes collected in the years 1930 to 1935 (for a breakdown of the 1947 figures, by administrative unit, see the table).

1930–31	6,682,000	1933–34	7,700,000
1931–32	8,883,000	1934–35	9,034,000[121]
1932–33	7,592,000		

The 1947 Hut Tax and Head Tax (escudos)

Treasury Receipts for Bissau Concelho	Taxes	Additional	Total	# of Contributors
Admin. of Bissau Concelho	727,790	103,970	831,760	10,397
Admin. of Bafatá District	1,404,970	200,710	1,605,680	20,071
Admin. of Gabu District	1,265,600	180,800	1,446,400	18,080
TOTALS	3,398,360	485,480	3,883,840	48,548
Treasury Receipts for Bolama Concelho	**Taxes**	**Additional**	**Total**	**# of Contributors**
Admin. of Bolama Concelho	54,850	5,590	60,440	952
Admin. of Catió District	778,610	111,230	889,840	11,123
Admin. of Fulacunda District	693,910	99,130	793,040	9,913
Admin. of Bijagós District	260,440			
TOTALS	1,787,810	215,950	2,003,760	28,499
Treasury Receipts for Bissorã Concelho	**Taxes**	**Additional**	**Total**	**# of Contributors**
Admin. of Mansoa District	2,231,460	318,780	2,550,240	31,878
Admin. of S. Domingos Dis.	357,350	51,050	408,400	5,105
Admin. of Cacheu District	1,246,770	178,110	1,424,880	17,811
Admin. of Farim District	1,334,410	190,630	1,525,040	19,063
TOTALS	5,169,990	738,570	5,908,560	73,857
	Taxes	**Additional**	**Total**	**# of Contributors**
GENERAL TOTALS	10,356,160	1,440,000	11,796,160	150,901

Source: "Managerial and Administrative Accounts of 1947: Republic of Portugal—Colony of Guinea," 15, in "Bolama (Portuguese Guinea)," 1948, ANS 2F 13, file 14.

Despite the sums collected, substantial evasion continued in most regions through the mid-1940s.[122] To facilitate more efficient tax collection, it was decided to carry out a full population census over a three-year period, to be conducted by military brigades.[123] This coincided with continued use of extreme violence and what an analyst referred to as "extortion" by police, especially in rice-producing areas,[124] followed by new waves of internal migration toward less intensively monitored zones.[125]

By the 1950s, tax collection apparently became somewhat more regularized, but it still provoked a massive outflow of temporary emigrants to Senegal, Guinea-Conakry, and elsewhere. In 1960, sixty thousand Mandjack temporarily moved to Senegal.[126] In some villages (e.g., Caboi and Churo) villagers continued to destroy beds just before the arrival of a colonial official. This technique was used to such an extent in Caboi that often only the elderly men paid taxes because they were the only ones who lacked the strength to destroy and rebuild their beds.[127] It is evident that throughout the "settled" colonial period, such techniques significantly reduced the amount of taxes collected by colonial officials and enabled rural communities to dispose of their harvests on unregulated rural markets.

The colonial state in Portuguese Guinea was characterized both by internal infrastructural weaknesses and by the ability of rural producers and merchants to avoid government oversight and control. Most villagers—despite suffering predation and brutal violence from tax collectors and from forced-labor recruiters—retained extensive control over their farmlands and harvests. To a significant degree they determined the direction of their crop sales. Tens of thousands of producers relocated for a short time or employed other means of evasion to avoid tax collectors.

The colonial state was predicated largely on the logic of annual pecuniary absorption, and there was little attention to productive local reinvestment or development programs. Moreover, enormous problems pervaded the state machinery; for example, colonial officials at the regional and local levels were too removed from infrastructural resources in the capital to prove effective; some frequently pocketed money collected as taxes—imitating higher-level malfeasance on the part of a number of their superiors. In regard to public policies, the colonial state in Guinea was unable to create a nationally integrated system of economic administration that operated in the interests of the central government. Although roads were built, some groundnut earnings were accumulated, and a semblance of tributary political authority emerged in the Gabu district during this "settled" colonial period, the problematics of implanting a more formidable colonial-state edifice remained overwhelming, proved repeatedly by the degree and extent of temporary migration, peasant elusiveness, the breadth of the informal sector, and regional disarticulation. Moreover, peasants retained control over land-tenure arrangements, the forces of production, and marketing outlets.

Faced with the widespread informal sector and a rural civil society it could not dominate, the state was forced to turn to officially condoned extreme violence to achieve success in tax accumulation. But terror-based policy processes are limited in regard to their broader social and economic implications; they are able to achieve very narrow goals for a brief time. The government was not able to take advantage of its cash collection to construct an administrative state that rendered most villagers dependent on an officially regulated economy. On the contrary, producers and traders retained control over the greater portion of their economic resources, and this, in turn, contributed to the fragile fiscal basis of colonial rulership.

The extent of this fragility would become particularly manifested once an intercommunal struggle for national independence was launched in the early 1960s: the relative autonomy enjoyed by rural civil society would make possible a massive liberation movement that would outfight and outmaneuver the colonial rulership in Portuguese Guinea. We will explore this struggle with particular regard to interethnic mobilization.

PART 4

~ ~

War and the
Postcolonial State

CHAPTER 9

Rural Civil Society's Multiethnic Mobilization for Independence

IN THE EARLY 1960s, a nationwide anticolonial uprising challenged the entire edifice of Portuguese rule in Guinea. During the rebellion, the relative autonomy of rural civil society in Guinea-Bissau helped to serve as a social springboard for political and military mobilization against an economically and institutionally fragile colonial state. I do not mean to claim that the idea of a nationalist war originated in rural social structures: this war was in fact launched by a highly organized group of urbanized intellectuals who had become strongly committed to the idea of nationalism and who initiated their struggle within Bissau itself. The story of those nationalists who led the independence struggle and who organized themselves into the political party that directed that struggle (the PAIGC—the African Party for the Independence of Guinea-Bissau and Cape Verde) is adequately analyzed elsewhere.[1] I am here suggesting that the independence movement evolved into an effective nationwide struggle that generated a widespread, interethnic commitment to nationalist success and expanded to incorporate most of the peasant populace—and that this was possible in large part as a consequence of the multiple social and political spaces that had been created by rural civil society during the period of "settled" colonial rule.

This chapter makes clear that once the PAIGC had launched the anticolonial national-liberation movement, peasant communities proved able to decide for themselves which side they would ally with and to which side they would devote their resources. The colonial state, weakened by a problematic infrastructure and an enormous informal economy, was not deeply enough embedded in rural civil society to structure the decision-making process within village communities. Taking advantage of their relative decisional autonomy, most social leaders and ordinary peasants chose either to support the liberation struggle or not to take sides, while a relatively small segment of chiefs and peasants chose active alliance with the Portuguese.

Both of the first two choices — liberation support and neutrality — functioned to favor the nationalists because both choices meant that the colonialists would not be able to control substantial portions of the populace. It also signified that the colonialists could not rely on sufficient numbers of indigenous allies to keep the nationalists at bay. The central state's already relatively fragile hold over the countryside made it possible for peasants to resist the state with increasing effectiveness as the anticolonial struggle gained momentum.

I suggest that a wide range of factors helped to determine peasants' choices over whether to join the resistance movement, to remain neutral, or to ally with the colonialists. One such factor was the attitude of local leaders such as chiefs and age-group heads toward the state. Whether the attitude of local chiefs became politically important depended significantly on whether those local chiefs were locally respected and were regarded as legitimate leaders. As indicated in chapter 7, where local chiefs were appointed directly by the colonial state, their popular appeal often diminished and their control over rural civil society was preempted by younger, nonchiefly leaders. In such cases, during the course of the national-liberation movement (MLN), peasants would often ignore their chiefs' attitudes. In other cases, however, chiefs retained the support of their local communities and their attitudes did help to determine peasants' choices.

In pursuing this examination of rural political decision making, the extent to which the ethnic configuration of rural civil society was important in the choices peasants made toward the nationalist rebels is queried. Can specific patterns of ethnic political mobilization be identified — or did nationalist mobilization assume a more complex social logic that reflected specific local power configurations, rather than an ethnic political logic? Is it possible to predict or understand peasants' political choices (whether to support the PAIGC, remain neutral, or ally with the colonialists) from their ethnic identity, or do peasants' choices reflect factors more particular to the political context of rural civil society in their specific community? This chapter also examines what the answers to these queries tell us about the significance of historical patterns of rural politics during wartime in Guinea-Bissau. Is it possible to identify specific impacts of the pre-colonial and "settled" colonial periods on an ethnic basis? Here again, do ethnic categories help us to understand these impacts, or do various political divisions within rural civil society assert a more determining effect?

Prior to discussing these key aspects of the national-liberation struggle, I briefly consider the broader political context—the PAIGC's turn toward clandestine guerrilla violence and the commonly shared underlying reasons that helped to provoke increasing numbers of peasants to ally with the rebels and to share their nationalist commitment.

THE PAIGC AND PEASANT MOBILIZATION

The PAIGC was the central (although not the only) nationalist political organization in Guinea-Bissau in the 1950s and 1960s. Although I will not here provide a comprehensive analysis of the PAIGC's formation and development,[2] it may be pointed out that the PAIGC was created by a handful of well-educated urban activists and intellectuals from Guinea-Bissau and Cape Verde.[3] In 1959, PAIGC organizers instigated a large-scale strike by dockworkers in Bissau that ended in disaster for the strikers: several dozen were massacred by Bissau police. Why, we may ask, did the colonial state respond to this peaceful strike by gunning down fifty-nine unarmed strikers? As indicated in chapter 6, during the "settled" colonial period, the policy of state terror was reactivated in response to overt challenges to state authority—meaning that specific resistance acts were met with brutal violence. Thus, the response of the colonial police to the 1959 strike would be nearly instinctive. The colonial authorities were already familiar with the PAIGC: they were aware of its efforts to mobilize the urban working-class populace in Bissau peacefully—to demonstrate for greater labor rights and African political participation. When the colonial police opened fire on the strikers, the intention was to create terror—to intimidate Guineans into abandoning any thought of anticolonial political or labor activity. The period of "settled" colonialism having been relatively brief (forty years), the reactivation of a policy of state terror (which had been instituted on a massive basis during the conquest wars of 1913–15) represented almost a gut response to the challenge posed by the PAIGC. But it is worth underlining that the colonial state renewed its terrorist policies long before the PAIGC adopted violence as its chief anticolonial strategy, and when the PAIGC sought to organize a peaceful labor movement, it was virtually automatic for the government to answer with a rain of bullets.

In a subsequent meeting, the PAIGC leaders decided—like the Chinese Communist Party following the massacre of Shanghai workers in 1927—to relocate their mobilization effort to the more isolated sectors of the countryside.[4] Even more significantly, the PAIGC now abandoned its peaceful methods of anticolonial activism and embarked on a violent struggle.[5]

Some villagers were quick to join the movement; many others were initially hesitant but, as it became evident that the PAIGC was both serious and organizationally capable of sustaining an anticolonial war effort, Guinean peasants gravitated toward supporting the mobilization in growing numbers. Several overarching factors help to explain why the peasantry increasingly chose to support the MLN. In the first place, it remained the case that the central state authorities had been able to implement, at least in part, certain widely despised administrative and economic policies, especially tax collection and forced labor. Although many peasant communities had succeeded in avoiding, circumventing, or obviating these administrative and economic policies and created relatively wide spheres of locally controlled space, those policies still represented significant burdens on the lives of rural people in most of Guinea-Bissau. To remove the entire edifice of the colonial state would thus benefit rural actors throughout the Guinean countryside. The extent of this macrolevel incentive varied, but in most instances it represented a major stimulus for peasant communities to support the anticolonial liberation struggle. We may note, however, that in contrast to Mamdani's description of peasant rebellions in Uganda being stimulated in part by reaction against despotic chiefs,[6] in Guinea-Bissau appointed chiefs were not normally able to wield despotic power; the struggle was aimed principally at the central state itself.

A second generic factor provoking the Guinea-Bissau peasantry to support the liberation struggle was the chance for historical revenge, or what T. O. Ranger, speaking generally of the connection between primary anticolonial resistance wars and modern nationalist movements in Africa, more politely terms a "continuity of mass emotion."[7] Regarding Guinea-Bissau, I refer specifically to the desire on the part of the sons and grandsons of the resistance fighters of the state terrorist period of 1913–15 to avenge the losses their forefathers suffered. Thus, for some peasant fighters, the MLN represented an opportunity "to prove that their fathers had only been vanquished temporarily."[8]

This signals attention to a third factor, also historical in nature, that helps to explain peasant participation in the national-liberation struggle: what we may term *praetorian social memory,* in particular referring to the historical precedent of praetorian success. In many peasant communities, the collective memory of military success against the Portuguese armed forces was still very much alive in the 1960s. People recalled not only the instances of defiance discussed in chapter 6 but also the sustained success of anti-Portuguese resistance in the decades of the late nineteenth and early twentieth centuries that preceded that conquest. This historical memory functioned to provide some rural communities with the sense that, given an opportune set of circumstances, they did have a chance to succeed against the Portuguese military. Indeed, interest in the MLN expanded significantly in some peasant communities when it appeared that the PAIGC would be able to acquire modern military weapons in sufficient quantities that they would not be at a major technological disadvantage.[9] The collective memory of Guineans regarding their potential to challenge the Portuguese colonial army successfully served as a psychological factor undergirding their participation in the struggle.[10]

Fourth, building on the djula pattern of long-distance trade and clandestine barter, the PAIGC began to offer people finished products (bicycles, soap, sandals, paper) in return for agricultural products. During the 1960s, they established barter-based "People's Stores" in various parts of the countryside, and growing numbers of Guineans participated in this PAIGC alternative economy. Although those stores ended up failing to provide the quality of goods that was promised,[11] they demonstrated to many peasants a sense of goodwill and a commitment to ending government economic exploitation.

A fifth factor became especially relevant as the liberation struggle developed through the 1960s: peasant counterreaction to colonial state terror in the countryside. The colonial state's response to the PAIGC challenge proved increasingly terrorist in nature, involving mass assaults against unarmed villagers, torture campaigns, and the bombing of villages and crops with chemical weapons.[12] The attitude of Portuguese officials in Bissau had changed little from the conquest period of the 1910s: in effect, the state turned back toward a policy of anticivilian terror similar to that used during the Injai-Pinto war campaigns. Portuguese jets dropped napalm on fields and livestock; air and land attacks by *caçadore* (hunter) units trained in rapid mass murder were launched against refugee camps near the Senegalese border; antipersonnel mines were laid on paths frequently used by peasants to cross into Senegal or Guinea-Conakry.[13]

The heavy reliance on "dirty" violence was the signature of an infrastructurally and militarily weakening state. Desperately turning toward terrorism in the face of the state's failure to create a legitimate domestic political authority structure, state leaders remained entrenched in a colonial political culture defined by zero-sum, no-compromise reasoning. The terror campaign proved unsuccessful, both politically and militarily. It generated such widespread enmity toward the colonial authorities that ever greater numbers of villagers joined up with PAIGC fighting forces.

These, then, represented generic factors that helped provoke peasants to sympathize with or actively support the PAIGC, and more broadly, gradually convinced a large segment of rural people to participate in the nationalist struggle. However, many peasants instead chose neutrality, while others sided with the Portuguese. To understand these choices, it is crucial to examine the social dynamics of the mobilization process.

THE ROLE OF POLITICIZED ETHNICITY IN THE NATIONALIST STRUGGLE

In the 1970s, an argument emerged from two different analytic quarters suggesting that rural peasants in Guinea-Bissau were motivated principally by the desire to "prove" themselves, politically and culturally—to satisfy their ethnic imperatives and culturally based political norms. The most comprehensive treatment of this argument was presented by José Manuel de Braga Dias, a Portuguese dissertation scholar who spent two years interviewing chiefs and ordinary peasants throughout rural Guinea-Bissau.[14] Braga Dias emphasizes the ethnic orientation associated with the specific political choices made by particular groups of peasants and their chiefs during the war. From a different perspective, Carlos Lopes, a Guinea-Bissauan scholar, suggests that chiefs in particular were in part motivated by an "ethnic logic" to defend and uphold the identity of their respective ethnic communities.[15] Lopes argues that the more hierarchical societies— Mandinka, Biaffada, Papel, Fulbe—succeeded in conserving their own respective political values, ideologies, and modes of social organization through the colonial era and that these helped to shape their wartime political choices.

I make clear below that ethnic identity, while significant in several instances, was in most cases not determinative of a given peasant community's choice of political allegiance during the independence struggle. Whether peasants chose to remain neutral, ally with the PAIGC, or express loyalty to the Portuguese often depended on a variety of factors. Communities of the same ethnic identity commonly made different choices. Thus, for most ethnic groups, "ethnic logic" per se does not adequately explain peasant participation (or failure to participate) in the armed struggle and their embrace of Guinea-Bissauan nationalism.

Here we may note that even as the colonial state unleashed massive violence against the PAIGC rebels and their peasant supporters, the state also pursued a strategy of ethnic collaboration with the perceived leaders of rural civil society. Thus, colonial state leaders sought to identify chiefs who had collaborated with the state in the past or who appeared politically ambivalent and possibly amenable to state influence. Different chiefs reacted differently to this pressure, regardless of their ethnic identity. In many cases, where chiefs were still in place, peasant communities often did *not* rise coherently in defense of an "ethnic" logic.

Moreover, increasingly through the 1960s, the colonial state's policy of ethnic collaboration backfired as peasants increasingly rejected the authority of those chiefs who did elect to collaborate with state officials. As we have seen, chiefly authority diminished significantly in much of the country through the colonial period, and chiefs often no longer had the power to control villagers' behavior by the time the liberation struggle broke out. Portuguese officials were often wrong to assume chiefly control over rural civil society—and this would be a major reason why their ethnic collaboration strategy would fail. This diminution of chiefly influence helps to account for the lack of common "ethnic" responses.

Other reasons also contributed to the failure of the colonialists' collaborationist policy. In much of the rural sector, colonial officials did not know the identity of the rural civil society leaders whose local influence had not weakened—sometimes older chiefs, sometimes young usurpers, sometimes shrine protectors. This was particularly the case with the Balanta (in whose villages decisions tended to be made collectively by elders and age-group leaders rather than by a single chief) and the Mandjack (whose village-level powerholders were selected through irã-based societies).

PAIGC ETHNIC MOBILIZATION

In analyzing the extent to which the Guinean peasantry became mobilized on an ethnic basis, it is important to take into account the PAIGC leadership's targeting of certain ethnogeographic locales once the party's rural-based organization drives were launched. PAIGC leaders were aware of the historical predisposition of the Balanta and the Oinka[16] toward anti-Portuguese resistance, and their strong praetorian capacity that long predated the colonial period. This awareness provoked PAIGC leader Amílcar Cabral to conclude that the "animist" groups would be most likely to favor revolutionary partisanship.[17] PAIGC

cadres consequently fanned out across southern Guinea-Bissau (Catió and Quinara); the response of the southern Balanta was almost immediate. State-
appointed chiefs in these regions wielded little influence; several (in Nhacra,
Encheia) were in fact assassinated, while Balanta peasants in the south as well as
in Oio region became quickly mobilized as fighters or in supporting roles such
as suppliers of food.[18]

Two of the three largest PAIGC military bases, Morés and Moké, would be
constructed in Oio region, and the second-largest base of the Forças Armadas
Revolucionárias do Povo (FARP) was positioned at Cabelel, in the Balanta-
dominated southern zone.[19] In a further historical parallel, we may note that Morés
and Moké had similarly served as centers of resistance in previous centuries.

The Balanta would in fact serve as the main fighting force in the anticolonial
struggle: they comprised the vast majority of the foot soldiers in the PAIGC liberation army and did most of the actual combat.[20] Their involvement reflected a
combination of territorial defense, social traditions (age-group leaders proving
themselves), and patterns of historical resistance. The anthropologist Hans
Schoenmakers makes the point that in its mobilization drive, the PAIGC often
targeted Balanta old men—respected elders within rural civil society—
specifically because of their influence in their villages.[21] According to British observer Basil Davidson, many Balanta periodically returned to their home villages
to receive a blessing from their ancestors through a ceremonial rite controlled
and performed by village elders.[22] In a recent study, Roy van der Drift emphasizes the centrality of the role of Balanta family elders in recruitment, and the
extent to which this indicated how deeply the armed struggle had become embraced by Balanta society (to such a degree that Balanta considered the independence struggle to have become a part of their own "tradition.")[23]

At the same time, it should be underlined that throughout the eleven-year
war it was the younger age groups who proved the most eager to participate in
the PAIGC fighting forces. Schoenmakers identifies in particular the n'haye, a
subgroup of the blufos; the n'haye were young men who traditionally acted as
"freebooters" in society, individually seeking ways to prove themselves.[24] The
researcher Diana Lima Handem similarly ascribed to specific blufo categories
(men in their teens and twenties who had not yet undergone the Balanta rites
of passage) the traditional blufo role of physically proving themselves, of establishing their independence from their elders, and of defending the community
against external aggression. Handem underlines these age-based roles as having
been central to the PAIGC mobilization success.[25]

The PAIGC's recruitment and incorporation patterns thus benefited from a combination of the continuing influence of Balanta respected community elders, on the one hand, and the customary independence-seeking of the younger age-group leaders, on the other. In both respects, the age-group-based character of Balanta social formations contributed to Balanta mobilization in support of the liberation struggle. In addition, a long history of combat with the Portuguese and a strong praetorian social memory of territorial defense that dates far into the precolonial period help to explain their participation. Our historical perspective enables us to appreciate how this praetorian social memory generated powerful local focal points for rebel military mobilization in Catió and Oio regions. And it is clear that, for the Balanta, the correspondence between political mobilization and ethnic identity was direct and overwhelming.

PAIGC Recruitment of Non-Balanta

Despite their large-scale recruitment of Balanta and Oinka, the PAIGC leadership did not want the party to become ethnically segmented. They were interested, to the extent possible, in creating a multiethnic corps of cadres. The PAIGC's success in this regard varied significantly, but they proved more successful than is generally acknowledged. The majority of Fulbe and Mandinka chiefs remained allied with the Portuguese; however, in some areas, such as Geba region, the PAIGC did make significant inroads among both Fulbe and Mandinka chiefs.[26] In other regions as well, some Fulbe and Mandinka chiefs rejected Portuguese rule and openly allied with the PAIGC. In addition, a number of Fulbe and Mandinka chiefs, while rejecting collaboration with the PAIGC, sought a more nationalist, anticolonial program. These Fulbe and Mandinka nationalists generally perceived the PAIGC to be dominated by Cape Verdeans, Papel, Brame, and Balanta and they did not want to become a minor faction within the PAIGC. Thus, a number of Fulbe activists created a separate political party, the União para a Libertação da Guiné (UPLG—the Union for the Liberation of Guinea), and a group of Mandinka politicos similarly created a separate political party, the Rassemblement Démocratique Africain de la Guinée (RDA—the African Democratic Union of Guinea).[27]

In general, the PAIGC's political mobilization in areas dominated by the Fulbe and Mandinka proved problematic,[28] but not nearly as much as has generally been presumed. Also with regard to other ethnic groups: the political reaction of chiefs and peasants to the MLN was complex, diverse, and often ambiguous. I suggest that factors particular to the character of rural civil society within each community make it difficult or impossible to generalize about the political mobilization of most ethnic groups.

THE AMBIVALENT ROLE OF ETHNIC CHIEFS

As the fighting intensified through the 1960s, civil society in rural Guinea-Bissau became increasingly divided on the basis of political choice making by local leaders regarding the MLN. For some groups of elders, age-group leaders, and local chiefs, the decision about which (if either) side to support was oriented by four decades of exploitation and by an unenlightened and uninspired colonial rulership. They chose to back the MLN. On the other side of the political order, some chiefs had already invested so much of their power base and leadership identity with the Portuguese authorities that they perceived no choice but to collaborate as they had been doing since the turn of the twentieth century. This included collecting taxes and providing the colonial army with auxiliary soldiers recruited from villages in, especially, Gabu region.

However, a third strand of local leaders or chiefs, significant in number, felt that, for both practical and political reasons, it would be in their best interests to avoid making a clear commitment to either side. These middle-of-the-road chiefs were commonly found in Biaffada and Mandinka villages, and in some predominantly Fulbe and Mandjack communities. The impact of such chiefly indecision was often to augment the level of individual choice among the peasantry: peasants who normally respected the suggestions of their chiefs were, in the face of such indecision, essentially left to decide on their own whether to support, oppose, or remain indifferent to the PAIGC. At the same time, it is important not to overemphasize the role of these local chiefs and elders; in many cases, villagers defied the warnings and advice of elders and chiefs, choosing to join up with the MLN fighters. By doing so, they often ignored their local leaders. This in part reflected the fact that in many rural areas the very institution of chieftainship had degenerated; for example, at the administrative posts of Benanto, Beado, Maninhã, Seicuró, Farincó, and Caninó (all located in Farim), the absence of legitimate chiefs among the Fulbe, Mandinka, and Balanta-Mané allowed peasants to select their political options independently. Most fled to Senegal or the Gambia; some chose to ally with the PAIGC; others elected to support pro-Portuguese chiefs.[29]

Another example from Farim region illustrates how the diminution of chiefly authority combined with internal factional bickering to produce a division of political loyalty. In the area of Bubo, near the Senegalese border, the

Fulbe-ribê populace had chosen a Mandinka chief by popular acclamation, but as the fighting began he was accused (by his opponents in Bubo) of providing aid to the PAIGC; the chief and some of his supporters fled to Casamance.[30] The Portuguese replaced him with a Fulbe-ribê chief, but this chief, not having obtained his title through popular acclamation, lacked popular legitimacy and, as a Fulbe-ribê, did not have immediate influence over the local Mandinka or Balanta-Mané. This leadership confusion encouraged peasants throughout this area to reject the solicitations of the new chief in deciding whether to support the nationalist movement. Situations similar to this, I suggest in the sections below, were typical of the political complexities throughout much of the Guinean countryside.

Papel

During the precolonial era and the anticonquest struggles, ancient Papel chieftainships mobilized powerful military forces. By the 1960s, however, traditional Papel kingships had long been weakened through their dependency on the colonial state.[31] Nonetheless, the collective Papel memory of anticolonial activism and praetorian success remained strongly entrenched. Through the "settled" colonial period, their military accomplishments would be recalled with pride as confirmation of their historical right forcefully to secure control over the lands of greater Bissau.[32]

Thus, it was logical that Tchon do Papel (Papel land) would be the first site of Cabral's organizing efforts once PAIGC forces had established bases near the outskirts of the capital city. These predominantly Papel areas would soon serve as the third principal center of resistance, after Oio and Nhacra.[33] In the late 1960s to early 1970s, many Papel fighters joined with their Balanta PAIGC compatriots to wage war against the Portuguese. Papel villagers, many of whom were infuriated over Portuguese bombings of their rice fields, provided significant support to anticolonial fighting units.[34] By 1971–73, massive local support for the PAIGC enabled the rebels to impose a military siege around the city of Bissau, similar to the events of 1907–8 (see chapter 4). That a second twentieth-century siege of Portuguese Guinea's principal city could occur, six and a half decades after the first siege, surely dramatizes the extent of the bureaucratic and infrastructural fragility of the colonial state.

Many Papel also played leadership and coordinating roles within the PAIGC. In fact, it became evident to Papel young men, especially those who lived near Bissau (the Papel homeland is located within greater Bissau), that their chances for upward mobility, or simply the opportunity to demonstrate their leadership ability, would be best achieved by adhering to the PAIGC. As the older chieftainships had declined in prestige and influence, it was the new, modern, more forward-looking appeal of the PAIGC that would serve as an attractive anticolonial social pull for these Papel. Younger Papel were aspiring toward upward mobility but with a sociopolitical vehicle that represented neither the colonial state nor traditional leadership structures. Thus, the adherence of Papel to the PAIGC's nationalist cause reflected the historical precedent of anticolonial activism, territorial defense, a tradition of praetorian success, and a new social influence of upward mobility among the more urban-focused younger generation.

Brame

Urbanized Brame (also called Mancanha), who like Papel youth were interested in upward mobility and assuring their place in the national political order that would eventually be established by the PAIGC, were similarly motivated to join that party,[35] especially in the area of Bissau. However, on the island of Bolama (in Bolama region), traditional Brame village chiefs were pressed by the Portuguese to convince the populace to support the colonial state. But these chiefs' prestige had diminished and they wielded little influence. The Portuguese had recognized the traditional Biaffada chieftainship on São João but had denigrated the Brames' chieftainship, and these Brame chiefs thereby became especially strongly motivated to support the PAIGC-led liberation struggle — as did the local Biaffada peasantry, despite their chief's collaboration with the Portuguese.[36]

On Bula and Có, according to oral history taken in 1970, all Brame chiefs had been members of either the Bami or Medu families (the majority were Bami; only six were Medu).[37] Through the colonial period, a Medu chief was appointed by the Portuguese authorities to rule over the Brame of Bula and Có. After his death, the Portuguese allowed the residents of there to elect their own chief, and they chose a member of the Bami family, Marcelo António dos Santos. However, this election occurred after most Brame residents of Bula had fled to PAIGC-held areas or to Senegal, and significant numbers of Balanta voters participated in this election (dos Santos, although of Brame origin, was raised by Balanta). His right to rule was questioned not only by Medu family elders but even by members of his own Bami family, due in part to the participation of Balanta in the election and due to dos Santos's embrace of Islam. By late 1970, dos Santos was actively participating in artificial, short-lived ethnic "congresses" organized by the Portuguese,[38] and popular anger against him in Bula was thus augmented.[39] Continuing internal discord alienated most ordinary peasant families from the traditional Brame leadership; their support turned toward the PAIGC.

Thus, despite Portuguese intervention, the majority of Brame favored the PAIGC, although for a complex mixture of reasons that included the fracturing of rural civil society (there was internal discord among the ruling elders as well as well between traditional leaders and the peasantry). Overall, it would be largely inaccurate to analyze the Brames' allegiance to nationalism as essentially reflecting an ethnic logic or ethnically defined historical experiences.

The Mandjack of Cacheu

The political choice making of the Mandjack in regard to the nationalist movement defies any singular generalization. Many preferred a neutral status; some played an ambivalent role, shifting warily toward one side or the other. As the anticolonial struggle unfolded, an increasing number actively supported the PAIGC. Others created their own nationalist political party, the Movimento Político da Guiné;[40] this party, however, diminished in popularity through the 1960s.[41] Still other Mandjack, also a relatively small number, who had collaborated with the colonial state during the "settled" colonial period continued to do so during the nationalist struggle.[42]

Eve Crowley's anthropological study of the Mandjack emphasized that "most individuals in Cacheu region were non-aligned."[43] Crowley and Gable concur that of those who adopted a neutral position, many migrated to Senegal or the Gambia, usually temporarily.[44] Despite the declining influence of the Basserel kingdom, the political attitudes of chiefs in a number of villages proved an important factor in determining the reaction of Mandjack peasants. But in villages such as Caboi and Churo, political chiefs and other authority figures bore no particular influence on the political decision making of Mandjack peasants.[45]

We have seen earlier that the social memory of the Mandjack of Cacheu region, like that of the Oinka and the Balanta, harks back to military success during the precolonial period and in combating the conquest efforts of the colonialists. However, the weakening of the Basserel kingship during the "settled" colonial period had enormously complicated the potential for a unified Mandjack response. Certainly, armies could no longer be organized by the now widely disrespected monarch. Peasants in Cacheu region who chose to ally actively with the PAIGC were generally able to travel to PAIGC bases. However, the choices of Mandjack peasants would largely reflect local village contexts, defying any single, collective ethnic political direction.

Especially in the early phases of the war, the role of Portuguese state terror partly explains the pragmatic ambivalence of many peasants in Cacheu region. As Crowley emphasizes, the risks of aligning with the PAIGC included imprisonment or beatings by the Portuguese secret police (the PIDE), while alignment with the colonialists often meant the loss of respect by one's neighbors. This no-win situation made the choice of alignment especially painful.[46]

But specific contexts were also important. For example, village leaders who were closely aligned with the Basserel kingship tended to support the colonialists. In Basserel itself, King Vincinte Nai certainly remained loyal to the Portuguese.[47] Mandjack chiefs who supported the king—and thereby the Portuguese— included the village chiefs of Cajinjassá, Costa de Baixo, Blequisse, Cati, Calequisse, Caió, Pecixe, Bó, and Timate.[48] In addition, although most villagers in Cacheu region engaged in repeated conflicts with the colonialists, a small number of them enjoyed close commercial bonds with European or mestiço traders in Euro-dominated towns. The historical evolution of trade between some Mandjack villagers and Europeans or mestiços reflected the geographic proximity of particular villagers to Portuguese towns and helped to provoke those villagers' support for the colonialists (especially in Caió, Pecixe, and the Costa de Baixo).[49]

Such procolonial villages were relatively few in number; most villagers were strongly committed to the PAIGC.[50] This in part reflected the nature of rural civil society in Cacheu region: the independent Mandjack chiefs and ruling councils of elders previously committed to Basserel had become more autonomous of this weakening kingdom, and they tended to support the PAIGC. Furthermore, not only chiefs but also commoner Mandjack peasants and local notables from non-aristocratic lineages were able to make individual choices. Most peasants, having become disenfranchised from the Basserel kingship (and smaller centralized chieftainships in Cacheu region), chose neutrality or elected to support the PAIGC.[51]

The alienation of ordinary villagers from the Basserel kingship was consolidated by the king's dealings with the Portuguese: throughout the war, King Nai provided the garrison at Basserel with meat, even though the Portuguese paid only a very low price for it.[52] This widened the disrespect for the kingship among both ordinary peasants and unaffiliated chiefs; he quickly became "more a reviled than revered figure."[53] Even in Basserel itself, some peasants backed away from overt support for the king and preferred to remain neutral.[54] Similarly, in villages whose chiefs remained loyal to Basserel, such as Costa de Baixo, Bó, and Timate, many peasants defied their chief and actively supported the PAIGC-led struggle, migrating to PAIGC-controlled areas. Others, usually but not always a minority, respected their chiefs' favoring of the colonial state.[55]

In a number of Cacheu region villages, rural civil-societal conflicts were defined by power struggles: aspirants or sitting leaders would seek to remove a competitor from the field of politics by collaborating with the Portuguese authorities. This occurred at Caió, for example, where Chief Mangu was accused by a competitor, Batican, the chief of Costa de Baixo, of working with an anticolonial Mandjack political party (FLING). Batican, a long-time colonial state collaborator, informed the Portuguese of Mangu's purported activities, and Mangu was promptly arrested by the PIDE, who banished him to a Bijagós island. He died there several years later.[56] In Bugulha and Cajegute, local chiefs remained strongly supportive of the colonial authorities, but many elders were reluctant to support this position. This led to much political ambivalence on the part of peasants.[57] In Caió, a divided chieftainship emerged when some elders decided to withdraw their support for the existing chief, Uol Gomes, who was popular with many young people, and to support his opponent, António Sapateiro. In Churo, the peasantry not only distrusted the Portuguese-appointed chief but assassinated him.[58]

Thus, a number of villages were characterized by bifurcated political positioning. In contrast, in the villages of Blequisse, Cati, and Cajinjassá, the local chiefs were personally popular. These chiefs' choice to support Basserel's commitment to the colonial state was backed by most villagers.[59]

Meanwhile, the Mandjack communities of Tame and Canhobe were characterized by a recent leadership disarticulation, with traditional authorities bereft of political influence. This meant that Portuguese officials had no means of politically influencing the peasantry at local level; this proved typical of many villages in Cacheu region. The colonial state's dependency on pliant chiefs revealed its ultimately fragile character since, without loyal chiefs, the colonialists found that they could not prevent the peasants from finding ways to support the PAIGC.[60]

In sum, most Mandjack either opted out of the struggle or ended up actively supporting the PAIGC. This reflected the fundamental independence of rural civil society: Mandjack chiefs had become autonomous of Basserel or peasants had created their own authority structures in defiance of those chiefs who had remained supportive of Basserel and the colonial state. In communities that had for many years been autonomous of Basserel, local elders and ordinary peasants rejected any chiefly association with centralized kingship, and many peasants chose to join the PAIGC forces or fled to PAIGC-held safe zones.[61] In other cases, the "cynicism for statist authority" was reflected by an effort on the part of Mandjack villagers to avoid involvement or interaction with either the PAIGC or the colonial authorities.[62]

Fulbe Chiefs

Since by the first decade of the 1900s, most Fulbe chiefs (not all) were actively collaborating with the Portuguese state builders, many of them serving as direct appointees, it would seem reasonable to assume that the role of the Fulbe in the liberation struggle could be clearly predicted and would follow a pro-Portuguese direction. However, Fulbe chiefs' political behavior at grassroots level reveals a complex multidirectionality of political affiliation.

To be sure, most Fulbe chiefs did support the colonialists, and several thousand Fulbe served as auxiliary soldiers for the Portuguese. However, a large number of Fulbe chiefs struck a middle ground and sought to avoid active support for either side.[63] And some chiefs allied with PAIGC. Thousands of ordinary Fulbe peasants, in many cases defying their chiefs, either remained neutral (by temporarily migrating to Guinea-Conakry) or supported the PAIGC-led nationalists. Thus, Fulbe political choices could not be clearly predicted from their ethnic identity alone.

Political divergences among the Fulbe may be accounted for by considering the particular ways that rural civil society in Fulbe areas had evolved. Even though Fulbe chiefs represented the most privileged group of rural leaders, in many cases—as also occurred with the Mandjack—their authority had diminished significantly through the "settled" colonial period. This in large part reflected their direct service to the colonial administration; in some cases, they appeared to be de facto vassals of the Portuguese.[64]

A second factor explaining their diversity of reactions to the struggle was the long-term division between the Fulbe-ribê (formerly, ruling elites) and the Fulbe-djiábê (former slaves)—harking back to the slave rebellions and internal wars of the nineteenth century, especially those related to the rise and fall of the state of Fuladu. Even though most Fulbe chiefs later accommodated themselves to Portuguese overrule, this intra-Fulbe tension persisted through the colonial period. When the national-liberation struggle broke out, whereas most Fulbe-ribê supported the Portuguese, many Fulbe-djiábê actively backed the PAIGC rebels.[65] There were major exceptions to this general model of intra-Fulbe politicization, however, and this relates to a third explanatory factor: community-level power struggles among Fulbe chiefs. Many power struggles took place *between different Fulbe-ribê chiefs,* with one or the other choosing to ally with the PAIGC in response to his rival's commitment to the Portuguese.[66] These rivalries within rural civil society helped to account for the particular political choices of some Fulbe chiefs regardless of their subethnic identity.

A fourth factor explaining the unpredictability of Fulbe political choices was the growing multiethnic diversity of many majoritarian Fulbe communities. Indeed, in regions such as Gabu and Bafatá, despite the predominance of Fulbe populations, a relatively large number of other ethnic group members, including Biaffada, Mandjack, and even Balanta and Papel, had migrated into and settled parts of these areas. Also, many Mandinka communities were already indigenous to these areas.

In all these respects, the multiethnic character of eastern Guinea-Bissau, despite Fulbe predominance, produced a variety of political alliances. For both chiefs and peasants, the direction of their political choices was especially unpredictable. The political position of a particular chief or group could not be unilaterally predicted from ethnic identity alone.

In the all-Fulbe communities of Mancrosse and Mansoná, local political structures were defunct. The officially approved chiefs lacked respect in their communities—but the populace nonetheless supported the colonial state against the PAIGC.[67] In Corubal, the existing Fulbe chief proved incapable of organizing local resistance to counter PAIGC raids, but local Fulbe-ribê leaders organized their own private militia groups to defend the area against such raids. This eventually led to a proliferation of mini-chieftainships and internal disorder. In Ganado, the local Fulbe-djiábê chief distinguished himself as a powerful opponent of the PAIGC rebels, countering the more common Fulbe-djiábê decision to ally with the Mandinka, who favored the nationalists.[68] In Sancorlá, the authoritarian style of rule on the part of the local Fulbe-ribê chief provoked both local Fulbe and Mandinka peasants to flee the area and join up with the PAIGC. In contrast, the Fulbe-djiábê peasantry of Joladu and Manganã migrated in order to distance themselves from both the colonialist and PAIGC forces.

Most Fulbe-djiábê leaders who proclaimed opposition to the PAIGC nonetheless proved unenthusiastic about supporting the colonialists. In fact, this concern provoked the Portuguese to undertake an administrative reform in Bafatá region in the mid-1960s, producing an entirely new administrative district: Cansonco. Cansonco was effectively delinked from Sancorlá so that a new layer of Fulbe chiefly authority could be appointed that would be more pliable than the Fulbe chiefs of Sancorlá.[69] In Pachana (based on the former Gabu kingdom province by that name), the creation of a fictitious chieftainship by the Portuguese resulted in disinterest on the part of the local populace in being associated with or responding to those who assumed that position. This, in turn, produced a multiplication and division of chiefly power in Pachana in the 1960s and 1970s; the local peasantry allied with the PAIGC.[70]

Overall, political loyalties in Bafatá region, in Gabu, Fulacunda, and other

Fulbe-populated areas, were cast in a number of different directions, reflecting the particular character of rural civil society in each area. Many Fulbe chiefs and peasants remained procolonial, but many others chose neutrality or pro-PAIGC support.[71] Political loyalty decisions reflected the contour of local power struggles, and in some communities peasants were openly anxious to take advantage of an opportunity to challenge the colonial authorities militarily.[72] The altered structure of rural civil society in predominantly Fulbe areas was marked by a factionalization of chiefly power, and this assured that ethnic identity would prove a fallible prognosticator of the direction of political mobilization.

Biaffada

Following the defeat of Biaffada chiefs by, initially, the Fulbe in the late nineteenth century and then Portuguese colonial forces in the early twentieth century, the previously hierarchical structure of the Biaffada political order largely dissipated from the 1920s to the 1950s. As in a number of Mandjack and Fulbe communities, although to a much greater extent, popular respect by the Biaffada peasantry for their chiefs diminished, while the rate of intermarriage with members of other ethnic groups (particularly Mandinka) grew substantially.[73] By the 1960s, the Biaffada had declined into a very small ethnic group dispersed through such areas as Forria, Quinara, Cubisseco, Corubal, Contabanem, Xime, Badora, Cuor, and Gussara (these areas stretched through the regions of Fulacunda and Gabu). Most of these areas became ethnically mixed and, as this process occurred, Biaffada often became strongly associated with Mandinka chiefs and communities in those areas. Because of these close ties, most Biaffada reacted toward the national-liberation struggle as did the Mandinka: with ambivalence, some favoring and some opposing the struggle, but most preferring neutrality.[74] As rural civil society in these areas was characterized by a weakening of Biaffada chieftainship and a convergence with Mandinka leaders, many peasants chose to ally with the PAIGC. But some did not, so that, as with the Fulbe, Biaffada ethnic identity did not prove a determining influence on their direction of political mobilization.

Mandinka

If any ethnic group defies generalization regarding their political loyalty during the liberation war, it is the Mandinka. To be sure, they had inherited the strong legacy of their centuries-long empire building of Gabu. However, the defeat of the Gabu empire by Fulbe armies initiated the political dismemberment of the Mandinkas' previously hierarchical authority structure. This process was exacerbated by Portuguese colonial overrule; colonial state administrators sought out Mandinka chiefly collaborators but never fully trusted them, preferring to lend primary support to Fulbe appointees, while former Gabu became divided into a number of small districts.

By the start of the independence struggle in the 1960s, Mandinka were spread out in villages throughout central, northern, and eastern parts of the colony. The generally ambivalent attitude of their chiefs in part reflected underlying distrust of both the Portuguese and the PAIGC. Moreover, in some cases, the political position of Mandinka chiefs became especially complicated as a consequence of longstanding grievances against Fulbe chiefs who had been appointed by the Portuguese to rule over what had been Mandinka-controlled areas. Most Mandinka adopted a neutral political stance, but as the nationalist war dragged on, intravillage arguments over who to support intensified, and internal chiefly competition drove an increasing number of chiefs and peasants to ally with the PAIGC.

Moreover, by the time of the nationalist struggle a large number of Mandinka families had either intermarried with members of other ethnic groups or had migrated away from their original home areas. One such example was the Mandinka village of Maqué, located in an ethnically mixed area between the towns of Bissorã and Farim. Because of its strategic location between those two towns, the Portuguese established a military outpost early in the independence war, and soldiers from that outpost frequently stole cattle from the villagers.[75] Mandinka villagers had already become sympathetic with the PAIGC due to their close social and economic ties with Balanta in that area; the theft of cattle by Portuguese soldiers subsequently assured the Mandinka villagers' full political allegiance to the PAIGC. In fact, by 1964, the ruling elders of Maqué agreed "to evacuate the village and move deep into the forest to establish a new provisional settlement."[76] This was quickly carried out, and for the next ten years the Mandinka of Maqué, now transplanted to denser terrain north of their home village, lent active support to the PAIGC, including providing PAIGC fighters with direct back-up reconnaissance.[77]

Similar situations provoked other Mandinka to affiliate with the PAIGC, but, depending on the nature of intravillage politics (chiefly power struggles), most preferred neutrality. For the Mandinka as a whole, political choice making regarding the MLN varied, was provoked by a variety of factors, and belied the emergence of a coherent ethnic response.

MULTIETHNIC GUINEAN NATIONALISM AND RURAL CIVIL SOCIETY

While there was a diversity of responses to the nationalist movement on the part of the Mandinka, Fulbe, Biaffada, and Mandjack, it is evident that large numbers of each of these groups participated actively in the national-liberation struggle. The interethnic character of the PAIGC fighting forces was thereby assured. This interethnic coordination represented an oft-repeated and deeply embedded historical tradition. As we saw in chapters 3 and 4, for example, pre-colonial and conquest-era warfare was characterized by interethnic military coordination. As in previous decades and centuries, so in this more recent war: the impetus toward local autonomy in many regions did not preclude, and in fact often helped to motivate, the creation of strategic alliances with actors from most ethnic groups. Thus, the independence struggle represented only the latest incarnation of rural Guinea-Bissau's historical turn toward interethnic mobilization to counter an imperial, European military onslaught. The historical tradition of intercommunal coordination had laid the sociopraetorian groundwork for the modern anticolonial nationalist struggle.

Centuries of successful military alliances ranged from ancient Gabu's pan-ethnic field generals to modern Fuladu's common construction by Fulbe and Biaffada; from coordinated defenses of territories against centralized kingdoms by disparate acephalous communities in the nineteenth century to the anticolonial primary wars waged by both decentralized and centralized societies early in the twentieth century. These experiences all helped to consolidate a political culture geared toward heterogenous, intergroup praetorian collaboration. When the PAIGC raised the clarion cry of anticolonial combat in the 1960s, some groups responded more rapidly than others, but eventually substantial numbers from all groups participated. In doing so, rural civil society in Guinea-Bissau helped to produce a national-scale fighting force predicated on the forcible ending of Portuguese rulership.

One historically embedded social tradition in particular facilitated this consolidation of a cooperative political culture: the incorporative character of spiritism (see chapter 7). Cacheu-based spiritism was popular among participants from different ethnic groups throughout the 1960s and 1970s. The spiritism belief system in and outside Cacheu region helped to provide Mandjack, Balanta, Papel, Felupe, Mandinka, and others with the social strength to endure the personal hardships of war during the course of the liberation struggle.[78] Peasant fighters as well as pro-PAIGC noncombatants relied heavily on contracts established with spiritist protectors to ensure their survival.[79] Mandjack, Balanta, Papel, Felupe,

Mandinka, and other villagers from various regions sought out shrine societies for assistance during the war.[80] Most of the PAIGC/FARP fighting forces were believers in spiritism, and they were convinced that Cacheu-region spirits significantly contributed to their military successes.[81] T. O. Ranger similarly refers to the mobilizational role of the spiritual officers of religious societies in coordinating and motivating mass participation in nationalist movements in Rhodesia and Tanzania.[82]

In chapter 10, I indicate that the achievement of national political power by the PAIGC generated continued growth of spiritism in postcolonial Guinea-Bissau. Here it is important to emphasize that the spiritual beliefs of the PAIGC fighters reflected a commitment to a political culture oriented toward interethnic cooperation that harks back to the precolonial era. This commitment served as an important source of strength for thousands of pro-PAIGC peasants; it represented a crucial social pillar of rural civil societal power that helped enable the general populace to combat the centralized state effectively. The anticolonial mobilizational success proved a major factor in Lisbon's 1973 decision to abandon its attempt to retain power in Guinea-Bissau, which led to the PAIGC's rapid takeover of central state control following the departure from Bissau in 1974 of the last colonial troops.

HISTORICAL LINEAGES OF PEASANT AND ETHNIC RESISTANCE

In most of rural Portuguese Guinea, the overall decline of chiefly power in rural civil society remains central to understanding both the populist embrace of nationalism and the failure of the colonialist ethnic collaboration strategy. But the weakening of chiefly power did not occur everywhere; nor, where it did develop, did it do so at the same pace: in some cases, the continuing influence of chiefs bore significantly on the political choices of peasant populations. As a consequence of this variation, the impact of the history of particular communities' relations with the Portuguese-controlled state were rendered especially complex. Precolonial kingdoms such as the former Gabu and Fuladu had hardly retained more than a facsimile of authoritative status: their remnants had been compartmentalized into appointed mini-chieftainships. This helped to exacerbate the internal political fracturing of Fulbe, Mandinka, Biaffada, and (to a lesser extent) Mandjack communities.

As a consequence of the varied (and changing) patterns of relationships between state and rural civil society, the direction of ethnic political mobilization during the liberation struggle would prove largely unpredictable. The state's superficial hold over politically disarticulated communities opened the door to internal factionalism, chiefly power struggles, and successful peasant defiance of chiefly preferences. Among the Mandjack, Biaffada, Mandinka, and Fulbe, local politics and the internal character of rural civil society proved more significant factors than identity. Community-level discord and the multiethnic fabric of many communities led chiefs to ally with either the PAIGC or the Portuguese for reasons particular to their sociopolitical context. Interethnic relations among the Biaffada, Mandinka, Balanta, and Fulbe-djiábê, and intermarriage among members of these groups, further exacerbated the decline in chiefly pull and contributed to the growing phenomenon whereby colonially loyal chiefs were ignored by the local peasantry. As a result of these factors, for most groups, political mobilization did not occur—and could not have been predicted—along the lines of an ethnic logic.

It was those ethnic groups and communities whose elites and peasants had persistently refused to collaborate with colonial state officials during the "settled" colonial period that most fully reproduced precolonial patterns of praetorian success during the war for independence. Indeed, among the Balanta and Oinka, their long-standing difficulties with the Portuguese, magnified by the colonial state's appointment of non-Balanta chiefs to rule over Balanta communities, did, in fact, help to produce a relatively coherent intraethnic response. At the same time, their acephalous political structure meant that they would largely be unaffected by the decline in chiefly authority that had occurred elsewhere in the colony. This, in turn, facilitated the rapid rekindling of a praetorian social memory as well as a strong commitment to territorial defense, which clearly had not been snuffed out during the "settled" colonial period. Still, the ethno-territorial motivation did not preempt the ability of the PAIGC to forge a powerful interethnic movement in terms of both military and political logistics. Nor did this localistic defensive motivation inhibit these same Balanta, Oinka, and Papel from joining the expanding spirit societies that further consolidated multiethnic ties.

The above analysis diverges from Mamdani's thesis that peasant rebellions in Africa originated in conflicts between "strangers" and "migrants." Mamdani asserts that such rebellions often reflected collective efforts on the part of peasants who had migrated to established villages and who resented being treated as outcasts in those villages.[83] In Guinea-Bissau, the majority of Guinea-Bissauans (Mandinka, Biaffada, Balanta, Mandjack, Fulbe) migrating to established peasant communities (Mandjack, Nalu, Mandinka, Papel, Balanta) were successfully incorporated and integrated into those communities, reflecting a long-standing tradition of "hosts" accommodating migrants.[84] As a result, both migrants and hosts were active PAIGC allies, and the PAIGC was able to consolidate interethnic unity and coordination, which helped to account for their growing military success and ultimate achievement of national power.

One impact of this effective cross-group social, political, and military cooperation during the armed struggle was the intensified use of crioulo—a combination of Portuguese and African languages that had until then been used by a relatively limited number of people connected to town-centered trading circuits.[85] The pragmatic need for people from various ethnolinguistic origins throughout the countryside to communicate effectively helped to assure the expansion of crioulo during the armed struggle. It represented a noteworthy aspect of cross-group cooperation.[86]

Finally, a word about the series of "ethnic congresses" that were organized as a last-ditch effort to rally the remnants of the chiefly supporters of the Portuguese within each ethnic group. They were organized toward the end of the nationalist war, with the colonialists in retreat.[87] However, by that point (1970–73), the leadership structures within rural civil society had become highly fractured: the majority of popularly legitimate community leaders favored the rebels; others preferred neutrality. The interethnic collaboration taking place along social, religious, and political lines functioned in direct contrast to the logic of ethnic compartmentalization that guided the congresses. Thus, the puppet-like ethnic congresses proved short-lived and politically irrelevant, bearing no significant impact on rural political sentiment.

During those congresses, the Portuguese did not waver from their state terrorist policies. They showered selected rural areas with napalm, conducting murderous raids and torturing peasants. It was precisely this continued redeployment of sustained terror (along with other factors enumerated earlier) that was so crucial in provoking the mobilization of rural civil society. The state terror policy proved a major strategic error since it helped to set the political and military stage for colonial collapse. Ultimately, the widespread deployment of terror as a sustained policy in reaction to the growing rejection of colonial rule signaled the fatal internal dysfunction of the Guinean colonial state. The state lacked the infrastructural capacity and political commitment to build up more legitimate modes of authority and linkages with rural civil society. The political bankruptcy of the "ethnic congresses," based on an outdated presumption of chiefly loyalty, made this especially clear.

The response in the countryside to the colonial state's reliance on terror and the state's inability to craft workable social institutions depended in large part on the changes particular to rural civil society within each community. In the end, the combination of a shared and historically embedded defense of sociopolitical autonomy, variegated community-level leadership structures, the interethnic nature of most communities, and the interlinked social formations within rural civil society as a whole would favor the rebels "against" the colonial state.

CHAPTER 10

Postcolonial Legacies

Weak State, Strong Civil Society

THE PAIGC SET AN IMPOSING challenge for itself upon assuming national power. As we have seen, the sociopolitical strength and autonomy of rural civil society and the evolution of a widespread informal economy had helped to undermine the institutional capacity of the colonial state, and ultimately these factors contributed to the mobilizational ability of the anticolonial rebels. I have suggested in particular that the national-liberation struggle was successful, in part, as a consequence of the relative independence of rural civil society's entrenched social formations. In this chapter I argue that the consequences of this civil societal strength would prove problematic for the postcolonial state. This is because the state took upon itself the task of reconstructing a national administrative framework in a context in which the social basis of political power in the rural areas remained essentially intact. Although the now-ruling PAIGC had entered into power with a high degree of postwar popularity, rural civil society remained structurally positioned "against" central state institutions.

Indeed, it would soon become clear that the postindependence state could not easily overcome the overriding legacy of the colonial period: namely, the fragile social basis of centralized state administration. We have seen that the appointment of unpopular chiefs by the colonial administration had represented a weak source of political hegemony. After independence, once the popular exuberance of nationalist victory and celebration over colonial departure had subsided, the country's leadership was faced with the fact that an administrative implantation within rural Guinea-Bissau had not been attained and that the state's policy capacity was thereby circumscribed. Political and social control over rural civil society, including decision making, remained essentially in the hands of community-based authorities, peasant-selected councils, age-group leaders, popular chiefs, religio-spiritual leaders, and various other social groupings.

In response to this challenge, the state immediately sought to expand a system of "village committees" originally established on a skeletal basis during the national independence struggle in PAIGC-controlled zones. In effect, the post-independence state sought to consolidate a new politico-administrative structure with firmer social roots in rural civil society. The aim was what Mahmoud Mamdani, in his analysis of postindependence radical states such as Tanzania and Mozambique, referred to as the convergence of political and administrative local power into centrally approved party-cadre hands—the latter in effect replacing the fused power of colonially loyal chiefs and assuring state-party domination of villages.[1]

However, in the case of Guinea-Bissau, the state, in its quest to spread bureaucratic power, would not make substantially greater progress than its colonial predecessor. As I suggest below, this lack of progress points to the enduring social formations with which the state would have to contend—formations that were, in fact, expanding. Legitimate village chiefs, age-group heads, community elders, and religious authorities did generally respect the macrolevel sovereignty of the national state and of the PAIGC. But the real-world political power of civil society at grassroots level remained in the hands of these representative, component parts of the communities. The central state did not successfully achieve a structural interference in and reworking of rural local economic and political power arrangements.

The continuing strengths of rural civil society reflected processes that had been taking place throughout the "settled" colonial period as well as during the independence struggle. These included, especially, a strengthened commitment to local political control, manifested by local political arrangements that either reflected specific, group-based political practices (although these often changed over time) or multiethnic political formations. Indeed, the nature of the local assertion of political power did not preclude the evolution of complex social formations across territorial and ethnic boundaries. Thus, a significant source of postcolonial civil societal strength would be manifested through various inter-ethnic movements and religio-political sources of authority that were shared by members of different groups. As increasing numbers of communities had become multiethnic, ethnic identity proved to be of decreasing significance as people invested their social allegiances in spiritist, socioreligious groupings.

However, it was also the case that interethnic social movements were populated by people who retained a strong sense of their own ethnic identity, especially where that identity was linked to territorial domains. Precisely because many power arrangements in rural Guinea-Bissau remained largely locally determined, in certain sectors of the countryside political structures were "ethnically" identifiable in the sense that members of the same group were devoted to a common framework of authority. This included the revival of several localized Mandjack kingships in Cacheu region. But at the same time, because other locales—including those in Cacheu region, as elsewhere—manifested political power in a way that included various ethnic groups, the social basis of rural civil society came to include both those that were definable in terms of ethno-locales as well as those that were essentially multiethnic within the same locale. In both cases, it was these local arrangements, rather than the state, that determined the structuring of political power in rural Guinea-Bissau.

This represented a fundamental continuity with important political values prioritized during the precolonial and "settled" colonial periods, especially regarding a generally shared determination to assure a decentralized political order. The capacity of rural communities to select their own sources of political power and social authority was not overturned by the new postindependence state leadership, despite the state's monopoly of macrolevel (national) political power. The state's broad political sovereignty was established, but the state proved unable to implement social policies effectively at the regional level, as social formations managed to carve out their own real-world political and policy autonomy, as they had during the precolonial and colonial periods.

THE VILLAGE COMMITTEE SYSTEM

The village (tabanca) committees established initially in PAIGC-held areas during the independence struggle were expanded by the government, after independence, to most of the countryside. Through the 1970s and 1980s, in practice there was significant divergence in the way these tabanca committees functioned, reflecting the wide variety of political and social structures in rural Guinea-Bissau as well as differing levels of commitment to the PAIGC.[2] In Oio, Mansoa, and Tombali regions—which had been key centers of peasant resistance during the anticolonial war—a substantial number of village committees had been established during the independence struggle, and the committees continued to proliferate, village by village, after the war. However, this did not mean that the state was being effectively implanted within rural civil society so much as that villagers had decided to embrace the tabanca structure without abrogating their own control over local politics. The multiplication of village committees (in these regions as well as others) did not signify an expansion of administrative capacity so much as a strong, peasant-controlled rural civil society proving capable of wielding power either within the committees or in ignorance of them. For example, the village of Kandjadja, in Oio region, near the Farim River in Mansabá sector, was principally composed of Mandinka but also incorporated Balanta and Fulbe communities. The five-person village committee was dominated by representatives of Mandinka families that had historically wielded local power[3]—power embedded in the local authority system rather than the village-committee framework. They, not the state, were in control of village decision making.[4]

Immediately after independence in the Balanta village of Infandre, in Mansoa region, the PAIGC held a regional-level meeting that included Infandre representatives, but the locally respected male elders did not attend. An Infandre village committee was elected at the meeting, but thereafter the elected committee became entirely ostracized from the villagers—ineffective, since "Power still remains vested in the elders."[5]

In the Mandjack villages of Caboi and Caió (Cacheu region), the members of the village committees were locally respected figures, but they did not meet in the villages—rather, they served as representatives at the regional administrative level. Meaningful social power was in fact held by shrine priests and lineage heads. Their power was exercised during problem-solving meetings held in sacred forest clearings. It was at these meetings that key local policy issues were debated and resolved, including issues related to development projects, conflicts between competing lineages, and local agricultural issues.[6] Neither the "village" committee nor the state's regional administrator had influence in the crucial local policy matters.

Indeed, locally vested authority in rural civil society in postindependence Guinea-Bissau remained in the hands of village-preferred leaders, and the state was largely unable to exert a meaningful policy role. Key social policies at the community level were normally not within the domain of the committees, and when committees sought to render decisions that significantly affected the distribution of local power and wealth (e.g., landholding or cattle ownership) the impact of such decisions depended on whether local people accorded with them and on the degree of local legitimacy of the committee in question. However, most village committees did not brazen into these crucial social and economic domains. Few committees effectively served their intended purpose of bridging the gap between state and rural civil society;[7] state officials rarely visited tabanca committees, and despite pretenses to the contrary, there was no effective mechanism for transmitting tabanca committee views to state-level decision makers.

LOCALISM AND ETHNIC IDENTITY

The interethnic social, religious, and political linkages that were formed throughout the countryside in many cases did not obviate a sense of in-group ethnic identity, but rather coincided with local-level configurations of power. The continuing impact of group-specific ethnolocal consciousness was an element signifying the strength of rural civil society vis-à-vis the central state, despite the rise in multiethnic villages and the fact that intraethnic political mobilization was a factor only among a minority of groups during the nationalist struggle.

Particularly telling at community level was the issue of land control and the association between territory and identity. According to Carlos Lopes, some peasant communities in Guinea-Bissau supported the land-nationalization decree announced shortly after independence because they interpreted it as guaranteeing protection of their ethnically defined identity (the intent of the law implied the opposite, however).[8] The locally determined power formations that comprised rural civil society continue to determine land-tenure arrangements, and in some areas people associated their ethnic identity with geographic locales.

Recent research among the Mancanha (or Brame)[9] makes clear that despite several different migrations within Guinea-Bissau, today they continue to remain closely attached to their chão (indigenous land, or homeland) of origin in Có and Bula. Indeed, this territorial link provides the Mancanha with an especially powerful sense of intragroup ethnic coherence.[10] A similarly strong ethnic/territorial relationship evolved among the Nalu, among the original settlers of precolonial Guinea-Bissau (they arrived in the late 1400s), whose very identity as an ethnic group is grounded in their five-century-long effort to retain control over their ancient lands (located between the Tombali and Company rivers).[11] Today, individual Nalu villagers trace their descent directly to founding (first-arriving) families, with intravillage territorial divisions and control over particular soils being predicated on ancestor-spiritual ties between founders and their descendants.[12]

For the Balanta, the overriding commitment to local control over specific territories and rice fields remains especially central to their worldview. Power is accorded to the descendants of founder-lineages, who are responsible for decision making regarding the control of space and specific terrains.[13] Balanta elders who determine land usage reinforce, through their decision making, believed links with the supernatural world in a way that strengthens the territory/identity connection.[14] Community-based governing institutions are determined by Balanta peasants themselves and reflect an ongoing concern for the respective political autonomy of each community.[15] At the same time, the councils of elders and age-grade groupings are manifestations of a macrolevel affiliation to a common ethno-political identity;[16] in fact, Handem refers to the Balanta as a vast, self-run "federation" of large-scale, extended households.[17]

Rice farming facilitated the consolidation of this macrolevel identity because labor demands required the mobilization of interhousehold and intercommunity linkages, which in turn assured the maintenance of large-scale networks among villages. Specified units of young people were responsible for upholding these networks. Their effectiveness (in such labor-extensive tasks as dike building and rice transplantation) was accomplished through multiple cross-village ties created by the Balanta age-grade system.[18] Linkages across widespread communities were reinforced through such social mechanisms as intervillage marriages (as we saw when discussing the precolonial and colonial periods), which often served to help resolve disputes. A long-distance communication system was maintained by the passing of information through complex, village-to-village networks operating through hollowed-out tree trunks[19] — the communication system previously used to mobilize vast armies. In the postcolonial period, marriages, communication networks, councils of elders, and rice-farming techniques all continued to reflect the impact of "cross-cutting institutions" and helped to define Balanta identity. This provided intraethnic continuity to Balanta social practices, while also making clear their adaptability to the contemporary context.[20]

Moreover, while Balanta "cadets," or juniors (young men, usually blufos), had played key political and military roles during the liberation struggle, Balanta elders successfully reprised their traditional community leadership roles after independence. This helps to provide historical meaning to the fact that gradually through the postindependence period, most tabanca committees were eventually either controlled by local elders or became marginalized from village decision making, with the elders retaining control in either case.[21] Crucially, these elders (balanta badã) were responsible for performing ritualistic ceremonies associated with land use and cultivation, thereby tying together their own power with the Balanta religious-belief framework.[22] This framework emphasizes "the non-appropriation and inalienability" of Balanta land areas[23] and it materially contributes to the Balanta achievement of de facto economic autonomy.[24]

The badã elders do not rule unilaterally but rather in extensive consultation with other elders—in a council called *beho*, or *ko*—and with age-group leaders. Decision making tends to occur relatively openly; those directly affected by specific decisions participate. There is, to be sure, differentiation of political tasks into age-related groups, but this is moderated by the value given to common discussion of important issues in Balanta political culture.[25]

The postindependence period also witnessed a revival of the practice of fanadu, the male rite of passage (suspended during the independence war), involving from two to three months of ceremonies. This rite was especially significant because it reinforced ancient Balanta social expectations for specified age groups, combining religious and judiciary sanctification for entry into a set of task responsibilities for the initiated.[26] The restoration of fanadu ceremonies in effect meant the establishment of a new beginning for the next generation of balanta badã.[27]

More generally, it is evident that rural civil society in Balanta areas reflected durable aspects of their precolonial political culture, while adapting to recent challenges in a way that assured grassroots political autonomy.[28] Handem describes postindependence Balanta territories in both the northern and southern regions as "totally liberated" from external interference in village-level affairs, with village politics serving as "the sole theatre for the elaboration of local political relations."[29]

The Mandjack of Cacheu Region

Another important example of this localism in rural Guinea-Bissau is Cacheu region, where, despite the expansion of multiethnic spirit societies, the Mandjack shared a common communal framework while constructing strong local subidentities linked to specific land areas marked by ancestor posts and defined by reference to local rivers.[30] In much of Cacheu region, rivers served as de facto boundaries between Mandjack territories and subethnic identity patterns. This territorial, identity-based system in Cacheu region has been reinforced through a system of land inheritance that the Mandjack believe dates back to founder-agreements forged with local spirit protectors.[31] Further contributing to the consolidation of in-community ties is a high rate of intravillage endogamy: in approximately three-quarters of the marriages taking place in the six villages of Basserel, both parties to a couple hail from the same village.[32]

At the same time, as we have seen, the Basserel kingship—formerly associated with the state—was in decline, and rural civil society, fundamentally and popularly rooted in each village community, was being consolidated. By the postindependence period, each of the six communities that had been affiliated with the kingship had become independent of Basserel (see chapter 7).[33] Important chiefs made decisions in consultation with other elders and respected individuals who served in a council that was essentially delinked from the Basserel kingship. Thus, rural civil society in Mandjack areas reflected a more locally specific basis of decision making than had been the case in the past.

Moreover, in 1975, in one of the few instances of central-state involvement in local affairs, the newly installed PAIGC government legally mandated the abdication of the Basserel king ruling at the time—Vincinti Nai—and forbade the payment of royal tributes to him and other kings.[34] However, Nai's dethronement accorded with the preferences of most Mandjack peasants, who roundly abhorred him for his collaboration with the Portuguese during the independence struggle.[35] To a large extent, the abdication reflected processes already occurring on the ground. The king had essentially already lost his political mandate in the former kingdom, and the official abdication in effect only rubberstamped a decentralization of authority that had already taken place.

The increasingly inclusivistic structure of political decision making facilitated changes in social and cultural practices. The extent of these changes was reflected in a 1986 meeting of Mandjack men, which agreed, by consensus, to abolish rituals that were felt to be outdated (e.g., groom service and the custom of declaring the kin of witchcraft practitioners to be guilty by association).[36] These changes represented the continuing evolution, rather than demise, of a distinct Mandjack ethnic identity. It is important to note that these changes were initiated by Mandjack peasants themselves. The association between ethnic identity and territorialism remained operational: it was precisely Mandjack peasants' control over their own territories, and the consolidation of political power in rural civil society by representative community leaders, that made it possible for cultural, social, land-related, and political decision making to assume a more participatory character.

Land tenure was another indication of the popularization of political power at village level. In 1975 and 1980, the government passed laws intended to prevent titled Mandjack landowners from continuing to lease their fields; the laws insisted that landowners could retain only those lands that they personally tilled. However, the state proved unable to implement these laws, and locally legitimate Mandjack titleholders continued their practice of leasing lands to peasants of their choosing.[37] In chapter 7 we saw that land titles were now re-garded as legitimate because the old practice of allowing the king to appoint titleholders had fallen into disuse during the colonial period; now the new titles were inherited by the sons of tillers, rather than reverting to the kingship. This system was maintained in the postcolonial period. The sons of land tillers car-ried out a virtual privatization of the lands under their control, which is what made their titleholding locally legitimate.[38] By 1986, "virtually all the titled fields in Basserel were being farmed by sons who were 'sitting where their fa-thers sat.'"[39] The postcolonial state's effort to abolish the system of titled fields proved unsuccessful. These "sons of tillers' became the titleholders and contin-ued to lease out their lands to other peasants.

Thus, peasants in Cacheu region themselves determined exactly how their identity would be defined, decided on the village structure of rural civil society (especially regarding their own selection of village powerholders), and deter-mined how the process of agricultural land allocation and land use was to occur. Their control over their own lands, defined by rivers and ancestor posts, helped to assure a correlation between territorial autonomy and political self-direction.

THE REESTABLISHMENT OF MANDJACK KINGSHIPS

By 1987, the state's presence in the countryside had diminished to the point where the central government felt that it had no choice but to recognize tradi-tional authorities as legitimate political entities.[40] The state began to legalize local kingships, signifying governmental acknowledgment that the national administrative system of village committees was not functioning in any policy-relevant capacity and that de facto power was held by popular local leaders.[41] With regard to our previous discussion of the declining political influence of village committees, it is important to underline that this process was already oc-curring in the wake of de facto state withdrawal.[42] Kingship recognition repre-sented a last-ditch effort by the national leadership to establish a political and administrative tie of some kind—however undesirable and tenuous—between the central state and rural civil society.

In several Cacheu areas—not including Basserel—villagers proceeded to re-constitute, by popular acclamation, a number of distinct kingships.[43] Lengthy rituals of enthronement took place at Caió, the isle of Jeta, and the isle of Pecixe, where new kings were reinstated in 1987, 1992, and 1993. Through these rituals, participants voiced pride in the fact that they were renewing their own "customs" and "traditions"; in doing so, they effectively established social control over the process of kingship restoration.[44] Because of their symbolic power and real-world implications, these rituals enabled local actors to assure that the new kingships would act in their own communities' cultural and political interests.

How is the diminution of the Basserel monarchy, 1973–86, to be reconciled with the return of kingships in parts of the region in 1987–93? In the first place, it is crucial to understand that precisely because these new kingships were not constructed in order to reinforce state structures, they contrasted starkly with those erected under colonialism. Their emergence in fact signified the fact that state power had withered significantly in much of rural Cacheu: there was—both in practical administrative reality and in terms of the perspectives of villagers—no alternative to the revivification of the monarchies.

Second, these monarchies no longer possessed widespread economic powers, and they were rendered more representative as institutions, the very process of kingly selection reflecting strong participation by villagers. The central government had no influence over or oversight of the selection process. Ordinary Mandjack recreated these kingships in their own locally specified ways; it was they who defined the "king's" new responsibilities. Thus, these kingship restorations were not imposed by descendants of former kings or by the state. According to anthropologist Clara Carvalho, "these enthronements . . . were conscious political acts on the part of populations that intended to reconfirm their local identity and their own power and signify their autonomy and independence."[45]

The communities that restored kings intended, among other things, for the new royalists to serve as a locally selected layer of authority protecting the community from external intervention[46]—exactly the opposite of what the central government had intended. At the same time, the new kings were able to mediate between "cosmic and natural forces," thereby providing a unifying cultural and symbolic motif for Mandjack villagers.[47] The new kingships represented another instance of local empowerment "from below," an "affirmation of local wishes and interests," and a deepening of the community orientation of political authority.[48] While state leaders wished eventually to incorporate these kingships into the national administrative system, this was not politically or bureaucratically feasible. These new Mandjack kingships reflected above all the locally determined and decentralized character of rural civil society in the Caió, Jeta, and Pecixe areas of Cacheu region.

Kandjadja, Oio Region

At the same time that this "politics of localism" was taking place in Cacheu region and in predominantly Balanta areas of the south and north, the increasingly multiethnic makeup of villages in a variety of regions provided for substantial interaction among peoples who had originated from many different areas. The synergistic functionality of ethno-territorial identity and interethnic interaction can be seen especially in the village of Kandjadja, in Oio region, as described by Lars Rudebeck.

Kandjadja had three components: Kandjadja-Mandinka, the central village; Kandjadja-Fulbe, some three kilometers away; and Kandjadja-Balanta, "a village of several hundred inhabitants with a completely different culture, language, religion, eating and drinking habits" from the other two Kandjadja villages.[49] In essence, these constituted three separate microworlds based on distinct ethno-territorial consciousness, behavior, and residency. However, there was at the same time substantial interchange among the three communities. Although they did not intermarry in significant proportions, these communities did engage in extensive commercial and barter transactions, and they participated in common, village-wide health programs.[50] At the same time, the three ethnic communities all respected the historically legitimated system of common authority in the form of a local council and a chief.[51]

The case study of Kandjadja presents two pillars of rural social strength: local-level community control and interethnic cooperation. Attachment to ethnic and local identity did not preclude broader, intercommunal, cross-regional engagements of a social, economic, and political nature.

The Growth of Spirit Shrines: Cacheu Region

Interethnic social formations that characterized the precolonial, colonial, and nationalist war periods further proliferated and expanded after independence. The local articulation of political authority and the ethno-territorial affiliations did not inhibit the increasingly free flow of interchange among differing groups, and this interchange provided a diverse social subtext for the emergence of synergistic social formations, as is made especially clear by the spirit-shrine (irã) socioreligious belief system.[52] While certain elements of this system reflected geographical and social characteristics of Cacheu region, the system at the same time explicitly functioned to incorporate Guinea-Bissauans from many different ethnic groups.

In other regions as well, these spirit societies are multiethnic and inclusivistic. They are a fundamental part of rural civil society because they are pivotal, stabilizing social institutions that contribute to the accumulation and distribution of power, authority, and resources. Independent of any government link, they captured the loyalties of thousands of members and produced leadership structures and norms that conditioned their adherents' activities.

In Cacheu region, spiritism operates on the basis of contracts agreed upon at shrine sites in specified wooded areas.[53] The contracts function as "an enforceable promise made to a spirit": failure to fulfill the contract results in serious misfortune for the supplicant; fulfillment of the contract, on the other hand, brings success in secular life.[54] The success can take the form of the ending of drought or disease or more personal problems such as sterility. Contract fulfillment can also produce the advancement of career or job prospects.[55]

The contracts often necessitate that regular payments be made to the spirits in the form of rum, rice, sacrificed livestock, and other valuable items.[56] Relatively large sums of money, often sent by emigrant family members working abroad, were spent by Cacheu region villagers to provide gifts to the irã during the 1980s. The emigrés were aware that their money was being used for this purpose—and in fact the provision of gifts to the irã serves as a significant motivating factor for sending the funds in the first place.[57] In consolidating these contracts, the irã provided adherents with a mechanism of distinctive social identity, common interest, and inclusiveness.[58] This, in turn, enabled spirit shrines (the home base of a particular spirit) to function as powerful, behind-the-scenes spheres of social organization and as de facto community-based authorities and problem solvers.[59]

According to Eve Crowley, "province-wide secret societies have now become the active force that incorporates dispersed villages into a common unit."[60] Each spirit was located in a specific, geoterritorial locale. There were thirty such locales,[61] and as seen earlier (chapter 7) these spirit provinces were important geopolitical entities. The leading members—those who headed the secret societies and who served as intermediaries with the irã—were either themselves the respected secular village leaders or were enormously influential in the selection process of the village leaders. These shrine leaders were popular members of the spirit societies: they assumed responsibility for day-to-day decisions and served as final judicial arbiters and political decision makers.[62] Contemporarily, as in the past, they function as socioreligious authority figures. Their power base lies outside the purview of any state institution and they are central to the direction of decision making in Cacheu region.

We have already come across the deity who is directly linked to these spirit societies and who is known as the "king of the below." The power and influence of this deity grew during the colonial period and remained strong after independence. This "king of the below" acts through his real-world mediators—priests and loyal village chiefs.[63] In 1986, male devotees of this "king of the below" held a rare initiation ceremony in the forest site of Penau—his sacred site. This ceremony, *kambatch,* is held once every quarter-century.[64] The extent of the continuing importance of this ceremony—and of the power of the spirit king and associated shrine spirits—was demonstrated when virtually all Mandjack men (not only those living in Guinea-Bissau but also elsewhere in sub-Saharan Africa and even overseas, in Europe and the United States) found a way to return home to Cacheu region for this ceremony.[65] In support of the ceremony, emigrants sent or brought a total of US$23,000 to Cacheu region.[66]

The "king of the below" functions essentially as a symbolic unifier of the spirit societies. At the same time, the affiliated shrine societies incorporate an unusually wide variety of ethnic group members from throughout Guinea-Bissau. Crowley calculated that, in a twelve-month period (1987/88), approximately 10,000 spiritual supplicants visited Mama Djombo, averaging 830 clients per month.[67] Approximately 32 percent were from Cacheu region (including Caboi, the home site of Mama Djombo); 47 percent were from elsewhere in Guinea-Bissau.[68] These supplicants represented no fewer than twenty-five different ethnic groups. The most prominent (two-thirds of the total) were Mandjack, Papel, and Brame, but also included were notable numbers of Balanta, Biaffada, Banhun, Cassanga, Nalu, Mansoanca, Felupe, and Bijagós (each comprising 2 to 6 percent of the pilgrims).[69]

Thus, the social/spirit world of Cacheu region represents a fundamental alternative to state power. More broadly, spiritism has captured the social allegiance of a significant portion of the peasantry of Guinea-Bissau. Spiritism, in its distinct combination of geoterritorial religiosity and multiethnic incorporatism, has evolved into an important social formation that constitutes a central strand of rural civil society and helps to determine the configuration of social and political power in much of the countryside.

Independent Social Indicators

The above examples show how local power was structured so as to assure the independent authority of village-level social, religious, political, and economic

arrangements. I now briefly note several linguistic, cultural, educational, and religious indicators of the extent to which rural Guineans managed to steer clear
of government institutions and created nonstate social space.

Linguistic Indicators

Figures from the 1979 population census revealed that crioulo, after expanding
in use during the armed struggle, had become the language of choice in the urban areas and among those who work for the national government. It is not
difficult to find crioulo speakers in parts of the countryside, but there are major
limitations to its further expansion. This is suggested by the fact that local languages held sway in substantial portions of the rural areas. Whereas in the urbanized regions of Bissau and Bolama crioulo speakers comprised 86 percent
and 79 percent of the populations, respectively, in the predominantly rural regions of Oio, Gabu, and Bafatá only 3 percent, 31 percent, and 18 percent, respectively, spoke crioulo.[70] The principal languages of these rural regions were
Balanta in Oio and Fulbe and Mandinka in Gabu and Bafatá, although other
languages, too, were spoken in these regions, especially in villages of mixed ethnic identity. In the region of Tombali, Balanta was the predominant language;
crioulo was not widely spoken there.

Thus, despite the expansion of crioulo as a means of practical intergroup
communication, a wide spectrum of rural inhabitants was not integrated into a
uniform, nationwide linguistic nexus. State leaders confronted a language barrier in their effort to absorb the countryside into their administrative rubric. Local languages may here be considered to represent a social defense mechanism,
helping to preserve relative rural autonomy vis-à-vis state domination and incorporation into a singular national culture.

The Basserel Culture Club

After independence, a "club for the development of culture in Basserel"—the
Basserel Culture Club—was formed in Cacheu region. It consisted of young villagers seeking to promote what they determined to be in the best interests of the
villages they came from. Although initially "the Club," as it was known in
Basserel, was linked to the government's National Youth Organization, the links
were broken because members felt that village interests could be best preserved
by acting independently.[71] In the mid-1980s, the members of the club insisted
on a "democratic" internal structure oriented toward collective decision making

because they felt it to be more in keeping with the communitarian principles of Cacheu region than the centralist authority structure of the government.[72]

The club, according to its members, favored promoting the abolition of destructive traditional practices such as witchcraft curses. At the same time, however, the club wanted to uphold some historically Mandjack economic practices (e.g., cooperative labor) and established a fund to do so.[73] What is important from the perspective of this study is that this club represented an important social group whose decisions remained independent of the centralized state.

Islamic Private Education

A further example of rural autonomy from state institutions was the expansion of private Islamic education. The percentage of school-aged children attending state-run schools declined from a high of 60–70 percent in the late 1970s to 37 percent by 1988.[74] In contrast, among Islamized groups (Fulbe, Mandinka, and most Biaffada), there was a substantial proliferation of private (or voluntary) Koranic schools. Furthermore, these schools were better attended, better staffed, and in better physical condition.[75]

Comments from people in Kandjadja illustrate the cultural gap that existed between the state-run and the Islamic schools: because the state school taught along the lines of European education, they disparagingly called it "the school of the whites," whereas the Koranic school was more respectfully called the "school of the marabu" (the local religious leader). Rural people in Kandjadja, disappointed by the central state's relative lack of interest in their development, decided "to fall back upon their Mandinka identity and traditions in order to manage their lives." Thus, there was "virtual withdrawal" of their children from the state-run school.[76]

Ki Yang-Yang

In Catió region during the 1980s, a unique promodernization movement arose. Known as Ki Yang-Yang, it was set in motion by Balanta youth who juxtaposed themselves against traditional Balanta social values and leadership practices, particularly the empowerment of elders.[77] To a large extent, the movement benefited from a long tradition of Balanta youth rebellion against the local elders: members of the younger generation had to demonstrate their independent spirit.[78] At the same time, however, Ki Yang-Yang openly counterposed itself to the irã societies. In effect, Ki Yang-Yang members believed that the Balanta god

(N'Ghala) and the irã were battling for the souls of young Balanta. Thus, although rejecting elderly authority, this was a deeply spiritual movement led by a female prophet (Ntombikte). For its members, it represented a source of social strength that was independent of official institutions.[79]

Although Ki Yang-Yang adherents did not explicitly articulate antigovernment statements, their behavioral autonomy led to state repression as the movement gained appeal through the 1980s. Members were arrested, mistreated, tortured, and, allegedly, killed.[80] The "problem" (from a statecentric perspective) was that although it did not directly challenge governmental authority, the movement represented, for national leaders, the "backwardness" of Balanta peasant society.[81] The repression suggests the breadth of the gap between the central state and the rural populace. In the end, Ki Yang-Yang did not involve more than a small percentage of Balanta youth: most remained preoccupied with their age-group responsibilities, especially with regard to economic activities.[82] Also, many Balanta, despite the admonitions of Ki Yang-Yang, were in fact attracted to the irã shrines. The movement did not displace elders as community leaders, and Ki Yang-Yang in fact lost much of its appeal by the late 1990s, decreasing in visibility and impact. Nonetheless, this movement still exists in some Balanta areas, and it does make clear the continuing ability of movements at grassroots level to generate alternative sources of social authority and legitimation.

Overall, we may conclude that Ki Yang-Yang, the Basserel Culture Club, the proliferation of private Islamic schools, and the continuing strength of rural-based local languages represent examples of the more general phenomenon of withdrawal from state-dominated orbits—cultural, educational, social, linguistic, and political. The rising popularity of alternative community organizations and movements represents the continuing reassertion of local autonomy and of an independent rural civil society, along with widespread rejection of government-initiated alternatives.

The "settled" colonial period bequeathed a dual legacy characterized by: (1) potent and adaptable institutions within rural civil society and (2) their counterpart, a tenuous and weakly constituted national administrative framework. Despite the change of political regimes at independence, this legacy would not undergo significant transformation. Indeed, as this chapter has made clear, in Guinea-Bissau, rural social power rested on two powerful pillars: community-centered authority structures, in some cases expressed ethnically, and interethnic interchanges occurring in various social and religious formations.

As a consequence of the socially and historically embedded character of rural civil society, state-created village committees failed to provide an effective institutional and policy link between the state and villagers; the committees were either taken over from within by locally legitimate leaders or were marginalized from community-level decision making. In some cases, this local rooting of autonomous social formations reflected group traditions that were tied to specific land areas; they may be considered ethno-territorial in nature. In other cases, rural civil societal power was manifested on a cultural plane, with the formation of "clubs" that in essence assumed responsibility for an ever-larger component of social and political decision making. This "withdrawal" of authoritative social formations from state-controlled social orbits was dramatized in parts of Cacheu region by the emergence of locally selected popular kingships. In Islamic areas of the country, private Koranic schools flourished in the wake of the decline of state-run schools. Linguistically, while the use of crioulo had increased during the armed struggle and dominated in urban/state milieus, some rural-based groups resisted incorporation into this speech mode. At the same time, religious and spiritual movements with strong political impacts increasingly captured the loyalties of rural Guinea-Bissauans.

In all these ways, the postcolonial state's social and political authority in the rural areas was effectively subverted by peasants and popular community leaders. The countryside asserted a grassroots de facto autonomy. Rural civil society remained strongly positioned vis-à-vis the institutional girders of Guinea-Bissau's relatively weak state, and the national government consequently failed to make rural political forces conform to or became integrated into its administrative structures. To a large extent, this rural social strength reflected the continuity of a lengthy and historically rich legacy of local self-rule in the Guinea-Bissauan countryside—a legacy that had been repeatedly and emphatically reasserted on various fronts—praetorian, religious, political, social, community-based, and intercommunal. The end result was an ever-widening institutional and policy gap between state and rural civil society. The next chapter makes clear that this gap would be reinforced by the expansion of the informal sector of the economy and would have important implications for the politics of the central state.

CHAPTER 11

The Postcolonial State, the Economy, and Renewed War

ONE IMPLICATION OF THE tenuous nature of the postindependence state's national influence was that the state's bureaucratic staff for the most part functioned within the confines of a relatively narrow base of power. Through the postcolonial period, this staff became ever more isolated and "inward" oriented. Rural social control over agricultural production systems and the growth of the informal sector of the economy contributed to a weakening of the center's power since rural trading networks and economic production systems remained largely outside the purview of government regulation. As this chapter shows, in combination with the administrative, social, and political aspects of rural civil societal autonomy and state weakness, marketing spheres that operated apart from state-monitored circuits of capital ensured that the fiscal basis of state rulership would remain fragile indeed.

The government's internal weakening was increasingly manifested by growing factionalism and institutional paralysis. State leaders reverted to ever more authoritarian strategies to hold onto power. Eventually, internal divisions led to a total division of state power—with the president on one side and the bulk of the armed forces on the other—at which point rural civil society assumed a pivotal role. At this moment of crisis, the central state, similarly to the zero-sum approach of its colonial predecessor,[1] chose all-out war, but would be very quickly confronted with the combined forces of the rural populace and the major

222

portion of the armed forces. But before further discussion of the new outbreak of national war, it is important to establish the economic and institutional context of state fragility in the postcolonial years from 1974 to 1998.

ECONOMIC ISOLATION OF THE STATE

After independence, the government had to confront an agricultural economy whose production systems and marketing structures to a large extent had re-mained, as we have seen, under the control of independent economic actors. These "uncaptured" producers and traders were not unwilling to trade with "official" outlets (i.e., with state trading companies or merchants who had regis-tered with the state and whose business the state was able to tax), but only to the extent that it was in their economic interests to do so.[2] The problems for the state (in the postindependence period as in the colonial era) were twofold: First, producers' land-tenure and land-use systems remained largely in the hands of rural communities and reflected the ways in which rural civil society was locally configured. The members of the various village-level decision-making bodies, chiefly structures, religious institutions, and shared-power arrangements that made up rural civil society carried out land-use decisions that they felt were in the best interests of their communities, regardless of state preferences. Second, the principal rural marketing channels remained for the most part outside the domain of state agencies. Producers and traders found alternative markets that offered more favorable barter or cash values.

These two aspects of the informal sector of the Guinea-Bissauan economy generated a fundamental disarticulation between the rural socioeconomic order and the national government. The overall impact was to hinder the incorporation of rural agriculture into the official economy and to deprive the state of a significant tax base. This substantially limited the state's potential for resource ac-cumulation and accentuated its de facto institutional isolation and pecuniary crisis.

Land Tenure

The single most dramatic and clear-cut example of local economic control was with regard to land tenure and land use. Throughout the postcolonial period, agricultural production systems remained in the hands of villagers, without regulation by state agencies or intervention by private companies. Thus, for ex-ample, in the predominantly Balanta Tombali region, the organization of rice fields and their maintenance was controlled by individual households, coordinated teams of rice growers, respected elders who were presumed to be able to exert spiritual influence over the harvest outputs, and designated community members responsible for mobilizing work forces.[3] The profoundly decentralized, shared-power arrangement among heads of households, age-group leaders, and elders that characterized rural civil society in that region meant that their decisions would continue to reflect their particular social priorities. The mobilization of group labor for large-scale projects (e.g., dike construction; wet-rice harvesting) was organized by household heads and age-group leaders and the distribution of harvest fields was on a per-household basis.[4]

In Papel areas of Biombo and greater Bissau, chiefs with a strong spiritual reputation were expected not merely to indicate which rice fields belonged to whom and to bless fields during planting season, but also to redistribute their own surplus harvests to especially needy villagers.[5] On the Bijagós islands, not only land distribution and land use, but also fishing was at the disposition of the four principal clans.[6]

In the predominantly Mandjack Cacheu region, community consultation regarding land distribution and use enabled titleholders to pass on their lands to their sons; and in Basserel, money was used for the purchase of expensive gifts to irã spirits (see chapters 7 and 10).[7] In Fulbe areas of Gabu region, local chiefs played an especially important role in land use: "common area" harvests accrued to these chiefs, who in turn assigned cultivable land to families. Similarly, in Islamized Biaffada villages chiefs who were accorded *imam* status were able to influence land-related decision making. Villagers voluntarily gave a small percentage of their crops as tribute to these chiefs.[8]

Overall, local control over land use and exploitation of the local environment benefited the existing framework of rural civil society. The fundamental distribution of political and economic power at village level remained unchallenged by state forces. No overarching state administrative structure monitored, regulated, or supervised these multiple, complex agricultural production systems.[9] Land tenure and the distribution of harvests followed rules particular to each community; hence, rural civil society continued to organize the ways in which crops were cultivated.

Informal Trade: A Widening Sector

The fundamental independence of economic production was also largely replicated in the area of barter and cash exchanges.[10] "Informal" rural trade among groups of producers, as well as between producers and local merchants or specialized djula traders,[11] remained the bedrock of the Guinea-Bissauan rural economy.[12] Thus, for example, Balanta intervillage economic exchanges followed long-term reciprocity agreements: rice—the country's staple food—was offered in return for other food crops, livestock, compensation for help with harvesting, and for use in religious ceremonies.[13] Throughout the country, interethnic trading characterized exchanges between producers of different foods, between agronomic and cattle farmers, and between producers and handicraft specialists. Thus, Balanta rice producers exchanged rice for iron tools and cloths fabricated by Papel blacksmiths and weavers; Mandjack women bartered palm products for Balanta-produced rice.[14] Balanta rice producers were also able to obtain tobacco from Fulbe producers in Gabu and dried fish from Mandjack and Balanta fishermen.[15] Biaffada women exchanged rice from Balanta in return for dried fish.[16] Fulbe cattle herders in Gabu sold milk and meat in return for Balanta-produced rice and palm oil produced by Mandjack in Cacheu region.[17] And Mancanha women migrated temporarily from the north of the country to Papel farming areas near Bissau, where they cultivated vegetables in Papel gardens known as *quintais;* Papel families were given a portion of the proceeds, the rest being sold for profit by the Mancanha.[18]

The state did establish a chain of rural trading sites (People's Stores) as points of exchange with producers. The idea was to provide the cultivators with imported goods or cash in return for cash crops (groundnuts; palm products; rice);[19] however, government policy errors led to low prices being offered, and the peasants took their products to informal exchange points, often controlled by djulas, who paid more than the official price.[20] As much as 65 percent of agronomic surpluses (rice, manioc, millet, corn) was bartered informally—in peasant-to-peasant exchanges (in return for palm oil, baskets, salt, cooking pots) and with djulas outside the narrow official circuit (the djula offering finished products such as iron tools, soap, clothing, watches, whisky, and bicycles).[21]

A significant portion of informal-sector trade took place across the Senegalese or Guinea-Conakry border. The extensive cross-border trading described in chapter 8 did not diminish after independence.[22] Fish, groundnuts, coconuts, and palm oil—the principal cash products of Cacheu region—were routinely taken to Casamance for sale there, and much of the rice produced in Tombali and Quinara were transported to either Senegal or to Guinea-Conakry.[23] Smuggling networks crisscrossed the border region between Gabu and Casamance and between Gabu and Guinea-Conakry.[24] On the whole, taking into account cross-border trading and intervillage transactions, nearly three-quarters of groundnuts and rice produced in Guinea-Bissau was either exchanged locally in producer-to-producer transactions or traded on djula-based rural markets.[25]

In 1986, in a desperate effort to stimulate the "formal" trading sector (where product exchanges would be recorded and taxed), the government privatized most of the Peoples' Stores and approved an expansion in the number of private firms registered with the state. And official prices were boosted several times in the mid-to-late 1980s (172 percent for groundnuts, with similar increases for other crops), but the prices still could not match those offered in Senegal or by the djulas. Producers continued to sell on informal markets, often located just across the national border, where superior prices and a wider diversity of goods were available.[26] Throughout the postcolonial period, the state-managed, state-regulated sector continued to suffer. Barter and cross-border trade predominated.[27]

Segmentation of the economy was further reflected in the fact that prices for some products were established locally, without any involvement or oversight by state officials. An example can be found in the palm-wine trade in Cacheu region. The trade as it existed in Basserel before the 1980s is described by an observer as follows: "[N]ormally a two-tiered pricing system [for palm wine] is agreed upon. Palm-wine tapsters can sell to outsiders at a higher price than they can to members of the community. Women (mostly Mandjack) from the market center in Canchungo contract with tapsters in 'bush' communities like Basserel either to buy their product or to sell it on consignment."[28] But in the mid-1980s, after extensive discussion among producers, tapsters, sellers, consumers, and elders, this two-tiered system was replaced by a single-price structure. The two-tiered system was felt to have been used too arbitrarily by sellers and village market women. The uniform price was agreed to be set relatively low so as to ensure maximum availability, and public announcements were then made to inform merchants outside Basserel of the new single price.[29] All of these decisions were rendered without input or oversight by state officials.

We also have seen that there was use of multiple currencies by traders during the colonial period;[30] this expanded after independence. The high value of the CFA franc vis-à-vis the Guinean peso—despite several upward valuations of the peso in the late 1980s—assured that the franc remained the standard currency of rural trade.[31] Indeed, for this reason, the price of groundnuts in Senegal exerted a greater influence on cash-based trading circuits in rural Guinea-Bissau from 1974 through the 1990s than did pricing policy set by the Bissauan government. There was also a substantial amount of cross-border migratory labor. During Guinea-Bissau's agricultural off-season, many young rural Guinea-Bissauans temporarily left the country to work at cash-paying jobs (e.g., weaving, shoemaking, farm work),[32] and this, too, suggests segmentation of the rural economy.

To be sure, the national government did accumulate some resources from its control over the tiny privatized segment of the agricultural sector — officially recognized merchants who had rejuvenated a growing number of the old privately owned pontas (agricultural farms) and established new ones, growing cashew nuts and palm kernels that were exported along state-regulated channels.[33] However, most of Guinea-Bissau's farm products continued to be cultivated on village lands, controlled, as indicated above, through locally structured land-tenure arrangements. Moreover, the government-recorded agricultural exports (93 percent of all officially recorded exports in the 1990s)[34] were not enough to offset the extent of poor economic planning and government overspending. Through 1996, the national debt (US$910 million) remained four times greater than GDP.[35] Consumer price increases provoked by structural-adjustment reforms further encouraged people to seek alternative marketing sources.[36] The 1990s were marked by popular retreat into informal-sector trading circuits — including some of the harvested produce from the ponta farms.[37]

In 1997, the national government, trying to come to grips with the extent of disarticulation between the official and informal sectors, boldly decided to abandon the national currency, the Guinean peso, and to replace it with the franc CFA.[38] However, this did not occur quickly enough to produce a notable effect on the scale of informal trade before mounting political turmoil within the government exploded into national warfare in 1998.

STATE FRAGMENTATION AND STATE VIOLENCE

The combination of a strong rural civil society, a national administration that was politically fragile and disconnected from the major social formations in the rural areas, and a vibrant informal economic sector all diminished the ability of the state to consolidate its power, to tax its populace, and to implement macrolevel policies on a national basis. Instead, state leaders turned "inward," toward a focus on ministerial factionalism, manifested through microlevel disputes among public-service departments.[39] Policy making and implementation were increasingly characterized by a general disorganization of public-sector programs, while the political process was marred by coups d'état, attempted coups, and purported coups.

As the political, social, and economic isolation of the central state from the rural social order grew more acute, there was a growing reliance on authoritarianism and state violence as the sole remaining means of enforcing central authority. In this regard, the postindependence Guinea-Bissauan state would replicate aspects of the political behavior of its colonial predecessor.

Institutional Problems

A number of observers characterized the national leadership as having entered into de facto "total seclusion, cut off from national realities."[40] Within the sixteen new ministries virtually devoid of influence outside the capital city, officials tended to consolidate their own particular circle of confidants rather than concentrating on economic development programs.[41] This factionalization of power generated not only rising tensions within the government, but also an increasing emphasis on internally directed public-sector spending: 59 percent of overall government expenditure was allocated to civil servants' salaries during the 1980s.[42]

Ministerial policy capacity, too, was problematic, as it had been during the colonial period. The Ministry of Social Infrastructure was unable to perform basic tasks such as the transportation of road materials;[43] its construction sector was considered "paralyzed" (an exception was the repair of several government buildings).[44] The Ministry of Economic Coordination and Planning operated as a separate enclave and drew up unrealistic plans oriented toward industrial growth despite the nonviability of an industrial sector.[45] The Ministry of Rural Development and Fishing was hampered by an overbalance of high-level officials who lacked professional qualifications, producing an "absence of planning" and an inability to improve farming techniques or productivity;[46] the living and working conditions of midlevel officials in this ministry were so poor as to negatively affect their motivation and productivity.[47] Two development programs that the latter ministry did pursue — the Rice Production Project, involving several dozen families in Bafatá region, and the ambitiously named Integrated Rural Development Program, in Cacheu region — were both characterized by inappropriate inputs, managerial incompetence, and a fundamental lack of understanding of the farming techniques used in each region.[48]

The internal disarray of the state administration and multiple policy errors were compounded by extensive and growing corruption, repeating a pattern of official misbehavior established by the colonialists. Officials were found to have illegally marketed food aid provided by international donors.[49] Some government ministers transferred official funds to personal accounts abroad; a minister of natural resources falsified records in order to appropriate others' salaries for himself.[50] Corruption also plagued government-controlled merchandising: employees diverted goods toward illegal sales.[51] The exchange department of the National Bank, natural-resource officials, other high-level functionaries, and police officers were found to have committed serious violations of fiscal rules for personal gain.[52] Corrupt practices that expanded through the 1990s included the misappropriation of development aid.[53] The extent of internal corruption led one analyst to refer to the central government as a "kleptocracy."[54]

Coup after Coup

Early in the initial six postcolonial years of internal government feuding, Guinea-Bissau's first president, Luiz Cabral,[55] became enclosed in a very narrow, intragovernmental power base. He soon began arresting and executing accused regime opponents,[56] the Commissariat of National Security carrying out these acts of repression. Mass graves containing approximately five hundred victims of the security forces were later found.[57]

Cabral was especially concerned over what he perceived to be the ambitions of his second in command, João Bernardo ("Nino") Vieira, the principal commissioner (and an army general). Cabral dismissed him in 1979. Within a year, however, Vieira had rounded up enough supporters in the army to stage a successful coup d'état, forcing Cabral to flee to Portugal. Vieira then assumed the presidency. However, this did not diminish the extent of intragovernmental factionalism or challenges to the presidency: coup attempts and purported coup attempts took place in 1982, 1983, and 1985.[58]

As president, Vieira responded as Cabral did before him: he used the state security agencies to augment the level of state violence. Arrests and executions of ministerial officials and army officers took place in 1986 and 1987.[59] In the 1990s, behind-the-scenes factional conflicts intensified, leading to more killings.[60] The government's secret-police activities included arrests of hundreds of accused coup plotters, and the police generated an atmosphere of political fear in the capital city throughout the late 1980s and the 1990s.

This strategy of state violence in large part reflected the extreme isolation and paranoia of the national government. The victims of Vieira's violence were those closest at hand—those appearing to represent direct threats to the regime. These were mostly people within Bissau's political circles presumed (often wrongly) to harbor violent political intentions. Before the end of the 1990s, state-provoked conflicts would explode into full-scale war.

NATIONAL WAR—AND ANOTHER VICTORY FOR RURAL CIVIL SOCIETY

The hostilities of 1998–99 followed a falling out between President Vieira and his military chief of staff, Ansumane Mané. Vieira's distrust of high military officials contrasted starkly with Mané's strong popularity among the soldiery. It was this popularity that made Vieira fearful of Mané's ambitions.[61] Vieira eventually accused Mané of providing arms to a Senegalese separatist army in Casamance region (it is unclear whether this was the case).[62] On that pretense, on 5 June 1998 the president dismissed Mané from the army—after which most armed-forces units withdrew their support from Vieira's government and backed Mané.[63]

Mané subsequently organized a rebellion: the larger portion of the Guinea-Bissauan armed forces (nearly two-thirds) asserted independent control over various military bases.[64] The president asked for, and was granted, military assistance from the Senegalese government, while the "rebel" armed forces of Guinea-Bissau received strong and growing popular support from ordinary Guineans.

Foreign troops (mostly Senegalese, but also some from Guinea-Conakry) were sent to Bissau to support the president's loyalists. Fighting initially took place within the capital city, but it intensified and broadened through May–August 1998. By then, the rebels controlled the national airport and had spread out into parts of the countryside.[65] Senegal, which already had shipped approximately three thousand troops to Bissau, then sent several convoys of troops from Casamance region of Senegal over the Guinea-Bissauan border in order to attack Mané's troops from the north. By this point, observers estimated, 90 percent of the populace of Guinea-Bissau were in support of the rebels.[66] Indeed, across the countryside, veterans of the anticolonial nationalist war of the 1960s joined with Mané's forces, some of them with weapons stored for three decades.[67]

This round of fighting did not produce a decisive outcome, and in late August 1998 a peace accord was signed. But between August and November, the accord was twice broken by both sides. Intensive fighting resumed for several weeks at a time.[68] During the battles, with substantial popular support, the rebels gained control of almost the entire countryside, as well as most major towns, including Bafatá, Guinea-Bissau's second largest city. Another peace accord was signed, promising shared power between the rebels and the Vieira government, but fighting recommenced by April 1999. This time, there would be no further accords.[69]

When the rebel army besieged the capital city, the government loyalists could leave Bissau only by boat. The rebels launched a "final assault" in April–May 1999, engaging loyalist soldiers and Senegalese troops in all-out street fighting. After several weeks of intensive combat, the Vieira government and all of the Senegalese troops were defeated on all fronts; hundreds were captured and killed.[70] The president fled to the Portuguese embassy (and later to Lisbon), and other leaders of the government went into hiding. A transitional government headed by Ansumane Mané was formed soon afterward,[71] with power subsequently being transferred to a new regime that the rural populace hoped would prove more sensitive to the political and economic interests of the peasantry.

What is important to note is that this 1998–99 warfare emerged out of a social context in which the state had functioned in virtual isolation of rural civil society. To be sure, this war was different from previous struggles in that it did not initially involve rural social forces but, rather, breakaway elements of the government's army. But once the war was fully engaged, the rebels did receive extensive backing from rural communities from throughout the country. In effect, the rebellion may be regarded as a popular war against the sitting government, and it succeeded in overthrowing that government—despite significant military support from external states—in large measure as a consequence of the popular embrace of the rebels. This war was not simply the outcome of a general's coup attempt: it reflected the ultimate impact of the government's internal fragmentation and the state's profound political alienation from rural civil society.

—-

The postindependence state in Guinea-Bissau continuously suffered economic, institutional, and political crises. These crises in large measure reflected the strength of the country's independent social formations, the control of productive resources by agriculturalists and traders who were independent of central monitoring, and fundamental disarticulation of the national economy.

The political and economic isolation of the central state did not begin with the departure of the Portuguese, but had evolved out of the colonial state's prior inability either to dominate rural civil society or to establish constructive ties with it. The postindependence state could not overcome this legacy. Increasingly, it turned "inward," producing a growing factionalism—a zero-sum struggle by officials for access to ministerial and other high-level posts, including the presidency. This was compounded by an insufficient appropriation of domestic resources and failure to rejuvenate the economy.

Rising state dysfunctionality ultimately reflected the historical dilemma of an institutionally underdeveloped national government faced with a rural civil society that was strongly positioned vis-à-vis the central administration. When the state finally broke apart and most of the military abandoned the central-state leadership, the stage for a broader struggle had already been set: the prior evolution of entrenched social formations helped to make possible the mobilization of rural support for the rebels.

For the third time in the twentieth century, the rural populace of Guinea-Bissau coordinated their efforts to help force the ouster of a central-state government. This time, as during both the first decade of the 1900s and the anticolonial struggle of the 1960s and 1970s, the central state, politically isolated, could hope to survive only by seeking help from an external source—the neighboring government of Senegal. The 1998 call for assistance was a virtual reenactment of the desperate plea of the Portuguese Guinean government in 1908: on that occasion, the colonial government, besieged by twenty thousand indigenous fighters, begged the French stationed in Senegal to send a naval vessel to Bissau to support what remained of the Lusophone army.[72] Ninety years later, the central state in Bissau, now postcolonial but again devoid of institutional resources, remained so alienated from rural civil society that it again turned to a Franco-phone regime in Senegal for military support. In 1908, the sending of the French naval vessel saved the Portuguese; this time, however, the Senegalese support was not enough: the Lusophone regime in Bissau was outfought by rebel troops supported countrywide.

As the twentieth century came to a close, praetorian drama had again revealed the depths of state fragility in Guinea-Bissau. More broadly, this reflected the lengthy historical evolution of entrenched social formations that served as the foundation for a formidable rural civil society.

CHAPTER 12

Conclusions: Guinea-Bissau in Comparative Perspective

I HAVE DEPICTED THE HISTORICAL evolution of the political, military, social, and economic underpinnings of a strong rural civil society in Guinea-Bissau—the counterside to a relatively weak state. The particular manifestations and impacts of rural autonomy have shifted repeatedly, commensurate with various social and political changes occurring through the precolonial, colonial, and postcolonial periods and in reaction to the changing nature of challenges counterposed to rural social formations. The underlying creative force and adaptability of rural civil society would help to hinder the creation of a powerful colonial state, and this state–v.–rural civil society conundrum would persist through the postcolonial period. In these respects, the historical lineages of state fragility in Guinea-Bissau to a large extent may be found in the endurance, malleability, and local rootedness of rural social, political, and economic power.

Overall, the findings of this book support Joel Migdal's observation that the ability of pluralistic, overlapping units of society to struggle successfully for "social control" is a central factor in understanding the sources of state weakness, particularly where social structures are multiplex and "weblike."[1] In various parts of the developing world, these social formations have effectively blocked the ability of the centralized state "to govern the details of most people's lives in the society," which explains why universalistic state policies tend to fail in such cases.[2]

The present study has made clear that it is, indeed, especially at the local level that the manifestations of rural civil societal strength are most clearly revealed. The widespread distribution of historically embedded social formations— located especially in Africa's rural heartland, where the greater portion of the continent's population and sources of social power and wealth are found—represent the political underpinnings of a strong civil society and of state fragility. In Guinea-Bissau, the internal social formations that evolved apart from government structures are central to understanding why a state fundamentally lacking in policy capacity emerged in the postcolonial period. As occurred elsewhere in Africa, contemporary social fragmentation may in part be traced to rural reactions to strategies adopted by the colonial state, such as the establishment of artificial chieftainships.[3] In some cases, this altered the terrain of social authority from the precolonial period, but in doing so this authority was subdivided in a way that set the stage for internal conflicts that further weakened the capacity of the colonial and postcolonial state to effectuate policy decisions. Meanwhile, social formations had been created "from below" that served as more locally legitimate centers of civil authority.

The colonial state's overrule in rural Guinea-Bissau proved unusually and distinctly incomplete. The Portuguese, like other colonial elites, relied heavily on the appointment of stooled chiefs in a conscious effort to prevent the emergence of pan-ethnic politics.[4] But this effort proved unsuccessful, as Guinea-Bissau's praetorian, political, and social defiance rendered unworkable the Portuguese version of indirect rule. Peoples from an acephalous political tradition engaged in armed confrontations and bolstered village-based systems of authority, while previously hierarchical systems became disarticulated to the point that the colonial state lacked a viable support base on which to construct its intended administrative system. The flawed effort to achieve political and social hegemony over rural civil society eventually culminated in the successful, rural-based movement for national liberation, but the very basis of this movement's success—entrenched social, economic, and political structures at the village level—sowed the seeds for state fragility after independence. The state's existential quagmire was intensified by the expansion of an "informal" economy defined by clandestine production and trading activities that the state, despite sustained efforts, was unable to control and exploit sufficiently to bankroll the national government's institutional growth.

The postcolonial rulership of Guinea-Bissau shared with its continental counterparts a determination to carry out a more effective consolidation of state power, particularly with regard to the creation of a viable administrative system

of authority within the countryside. Mahmood Mamdani has described this process in postindependence Africa as a centralizing effort to establish party-state
institutions that sought to restructure the previous system of appointed chieftainship. In doing so, postcolonial states sought to impose revamped forms of top-
down control over peasant political and economic structures.[5] Crawford Young
refers to this as an effort to create "integral states," characterized by "an enhanced
hegemony" and a more direct, unrestricted, and thoroughgoing control over civil
society.[6] In essence, this represented an effort to carry out, in the case of postindependence Guinea-Bissau, what the colonial state could not; namely, the political and economic penetration of the social formations comprising rural civil
society.[7]

However, in Guinea-Bissau, this effort, manifested (in part) through an expanded system of state-sanctioned village committees, was stymied through the
multiplication of locally legitimate sources of political and social authority.
Economically, the postcolonial state found itself isolated—as had the colonial
state earlier—in the face of continued control by rural civil society over the
forces of production and as a consequence of the widening circuits of informal
trade that captured the bulk of both agronomic and cash-crop outputs. The end
result was an increasingly brittle bureaucratic infrastructure that was easily fractured as internal tensions arose; the subsequent outbreak of national war that
led to defeat for the central state's forces both symbolized and reflected the enduring potency of deeply ingrained rural social formations.

Our understanding of state-policy blockage abjures a deterministic "political geography" approach that would emphasize weakly populated rural "hin-
terlands" or point to a lack of willpower on the part of state leaders to secure
political control at the village level.[8] On the contrary, Guinea-Bissau's political
leaders—in the precolonial, colonial, and postcolonial periods—sought to assert their authority to the fullest imaginable extent, resorting, in the case of the
colonial governors, to state terrorism on repeated occasions. At the opposite
end of the analytic spectrum, we similarly found Mamdani's presumption of the
success of indirect rule and Young's description of the carrying out of African
states' hegemony mandate inadequate to explain the contours of the relations
between state and rural civil society in Guinea-Bissau.[9]

Rather, I have suggested that an understanding of state fragility can best be
achieved by turning toward an investigation of the historical origins of indigenously crafted sources of rural civil-societal autonomy. In doing so, we locate
our analysis within the African rural heartland, with particular regard to local
social formations that reflect the logic of ethnic and interethnic relations.

LINEAGES OF RURAL CIVIL SOCIETY

The development of rural civil society through the precolonial, colonial, and independence eras was strengthened through the construction of ethnically diverse and interlinked social and political institutions. While in some cases local authority structures evolved within a distinct intragroup frame, in many instances locally determined political leadership assumed more complex, intercommunal, and ethnically malleable forms. As effective counters to macrolevel political overrule during the "settled" colonial period, both locally distinct as well as intergroup social and religio-political formations evolved that provided safe refuge from government institutions and served as alternative sources of legitimate authority and social power.

Social formations persistently countered both the broad administrative plans and the specific policy goals of colonial and postcolonial national governments, carving out a wide space of de facto political and social self-rule in the countryside. At the same time, the informal economic sector, building on ancient traditions of interethnic barter, long-distance networks controlled by specialized djula traders, and extensive cross-border transactions, provided an alternative framework of trade that allowed peasants to control the direction of their sales and purchases. Land-tenure arrangements administered locally reinforced the existing power structure of rural civil society and, in combination with the proliferation of hidden trade networks, helped to defeat state efforts at organizing a nationwide system of economic administration.

It is essential to emphasize that the origins of Guinea-Bissau's rural social-authority structures and local control over political, social, and economic processes hark back to precolonial times. During those early centuries, "strong" and adaptable social formations were established in the rural areas of what is today called Guinea-Bissau. Despite repeated migrations, people struggled to defend their respective territories (whether ancient or newly established), and in this sense politics was in part group-specific and land-based. At the same time, we must note that Guinea-Bissauan ethnic groups were not then and are not today static or uniform entities: they were, and are, heterogenous groupings that commonly incorporate members from different localities through intermarriage and immigration. Thus, for example, both the Mandjack Basserel kingdom and the Papel kingdoms of Bissau island were multiethnic in origin. Extensive intermingling between Balanta and Mandinka, Mandinka and Biaffada, and Balanta and Biaffada produced new ethnic and regional groups—such as the Oinka—as well as the decline of older groups and their absorption into others (e.g., the Biaffada into the Mandinka).

Ethnically pluralistic regional market fairs, along with other economic exchanges and barter transactions, became defining features of intersocietal relations. As trade evolved, extensive mercantile circuits developed throughout and beyond what later became Guinea-Bissau. Over the centuries, political-system change was characterized by the rise and decline of great kingdoms and decentralized polities. Interethnic political alliances, intermarriage, and economic exchanges helped to define the relative success of these societies during peacetime. This was especially true of the multiethnic (although predominantly Mandinka) Gabu empire.[10] Precolonial kingdoms elsewhere in sub-Saharan Africa were similarly incorporative. As Richard Roberts wrote regarding Segu Bambara, in the Middle Niger valley: "In the process of reproducing the [Bambara] state, members of many different ethnic groups were forged into the Bambara warrior group."[11]

During periods of warfare in Guinea-Bissau, an especially noteworthy pragmatic alliance was that formed by Fulbe, Biaffada, and Mandinka chieftains who held sway in Forria and Gabu in the last decades of the nineteenth century. These wars gave rise to an unusually fluid military context and in turn encouraged a trend toward frequent alliance formation among chiefs from different ethnic backgrounds. This pragmatic approach to chiefly alliance making in war would again be manifested during the national liberation movement of the 1960s and 1970s.

Contrary to Peter Mendy and René Pélissier, who assert that Guinea-Bissau's history of resistance was not characterized by multiethnic common fronts,[12] I have made clear that this pragmatic alliance formation produced interethnic linkages throughout the duration of precolonial as well as anticolonial warfare. This pragmatism brought Fulbe-ribê and Fulbe-djiábê chiefs together with Biaffada, Mandinka, and Soninké; the Mandjack of Cacheu provided substantial support to the Papel kingdoms of Bandim, Safim, Bor, and Enterramento; Balanta fighters crossed the Geba River to support Biaffada villagers many times in the 1880s and 1890s; and Balanta, Mandinka, and Soninké repeatedly created common military fronts in Oio region (the combined forces ranged from three thousand to twenty thousand fighting men). The defensive assertion of local territorial control was often a prime motivating factor in provoking the coordinated participation of these various groups — as it would be again, later, in the success of the intercommunal struggle for national independence.

Luso-dependency and Indigenous Praetorian Power

A key theme developed in this book has been the relative peripheralization of Portuguese influence until near the end of the nineteenth century. During the precolonial period, the battles and great internal kingdom shifts were for the most part little affected by the dispersed lançados and the small Lusophone settlements that dotted the Guinea-Bissauan coast and inland rivers. And even when, during the period from the sixteenth to the nineteenth centuries, administrators assigned to the Rivers of Guinea succeeded in wresting from the Portuguese monarchy sufficient resources to support fort building (in Cacheu, Bolama, Bissau, and Farim), these projects were completed only after Portuguese military defeats made it necessary for the Europeans to return to their practice of providing tributes and gift giving to African kings.

Historians have well depicted how, elsewhere in West and East Africa, the conquest phase of European implantation was marked by relatively scant European forces who relied heavily on deceptive treaties and African auxiliary forces to subdue anticolonial resistance efforts.[13] However, in Guinea-Bissau the indigenous combatants were unusually successful in resisting the conquest effort.[14] Not only did Papel-Balanta fighters impose the Great Siege on the fort town of Bissau, nearly expelling the entire European populace,[15] but the Portuguese governors over the decades regularly complained that the entire country was in revolt—meaning that the Portuguese had been defeated in virtually every region. The colonials pleaded with Lisbon for more troops and military resources.[16]

The Portuguese did attain the backing of most Fulbe chiefs during the first decade of the twentieth century, but this largely reflected the coincidental fact that indigenous wars were resolved in ways that favored local Fulbe chiefs' linkage to the Lusophone colonialists. In this respect, the colonial military efforts in "Portuguese" Guinea differed from the experience of the British, who were able to employ an "ethnic recruiting strategy" to select what they termed "martial races" to support their war efforts and supply local police forces in India, Nigeria, Uganda, and Kenya.[17] The Portuguese in Guinea-Bissau were unable to recruit and rely consistently on a particularly martial "race."

A key factor undergirding the indigenous praetorian capacity in rural Guinea-Bissau was the ability of communities to obtain and make effective use of rifles that were equivalent, or nearly equivalent, in technological quality to those used by European soldiers. Cannons and Gatling and Maxim machine guns were introduced during the colonial period, but these were not widely available to Portuguese soldiers, and when they were, soldiers often were not able to replace broken parts or otherwise maintain them. The French, British, Belgians, and Germans, by contrast, were able, despite sustained and cleverly waged resistance efforts in the late nineteenth century, to subdue their territories largely because of their more extensive and effective deployment of modern military hardware.[18]

By 1910, despite their repeated efforts, the Portuguese had not succeeded in breaking through the powerful praetorian defenses of Guinea-Bissau's rural civil society.[19] In desperation, the colonial administration turned to a policy that historically has been associated with infrastructurally weak states: the systematic use of all-out terror against the civilian populace. Led by the infamous marauder Adbul Injai, mercenaries used torture and public murder to establish permanent military outposts throughout the countryside between 1913 and 1915, thereby completing the conquest mandate on behalf of the Portuguese.

Still, during the "settled" colonial period, acts of rural defiance repeatedly punctured the formal veneer of state political control: those years saw open rebellion, local violence against tax collectors, and attacks on police. Passive but assertive forms of defiance included a variety of political, social, and economic autonomy-enhancing behind-the-scenes efforts. For example, despite some colonial-state success at taxation and the creation of forced-labor crews, in vast portions of the colony peasants avoided the state's efforts; they utilized many strategies of evasion, including sometimes temporarily migrating, sometimes bribing corrupt junior colonial officials.

At the same time, land use and other key aspects of rural economic life remained in peasant hands throughout most regions, while the use of multiple currencies and reliance on djula trade networks all weakened the ability of the state or state-approved agencies to "capture" peasant produce. The consequence was similar to that of the Middle Eastern nation of Yemen, where multiple currencies and a disarticulated economy assured continuing state fragility.[20] In Guinea-Bissau, as in Yemen, the impact was to limit the fiscal development of the state, contributing to internal state factionalism and an administrative environment defined by bureaucratic malaise.

RURAL AUTONOMY, STATE TERROR, AND LOCAL RESISTANCE

The relative success of rural civil society in preserving community-based political autonomy during the "settled" colonial period was made clear by the fact that locally legitimate authorities, rather than those that were state approved, held power in most communities. In Balanta areas, appointed chiefs were ignored and age-group leaders were accorded specific responsibilities. In Cacheu region, Mandjack village leaders succeeded in usurping the power of chiefs who remained loyal to the Basserel king—a collaborator. At the same time, there was an expansion of interethnic spirit societies, and peasants invested substantial resources in irã shrines. Village leadership groups and chiefs emerged directly out of (and were chosen by) the spirit societies—a process similar to that in colonial Zimbabwe, where spirit mediums usurped the political influence of appointed chiefs.[21] Meanwhile, in Fulbe, Mandinka, and Biaffada areas of Gabu and other northern parts of Guinea-Bissau, rural civil society became gradually fragmented: many peasants lost respect for colonially appointed chiefs, choosing instead to support alternative, more popular local chiefs.

A consequence of this de facto local control was that in the early 1960s when the PAIGC-led liberation movement became active, rural civil society throughout Guinea-Bissau was well positioned to support the rebels. Meanwhile, however, state terror, which had been employed relentlessly during the conquest phase and periodically from the 1920s to the 1950s, saw an emphatic and full revival. The colonial state's terrorist response in the 1960s to popular resistance—bombings, torture, antipersonnel mines, and destruction of crops—was a consequence of state leaders' zero-sum mind-set and its narrow policy perspective.

The massive violence unleashed by the Portuguese served to hasten the end of colonial rulership, since the number of rural social actors motivated to take up the mantle of nationalist warfare expanded as the intensity of state terror increased. During the course of the nationalist war, the fractured nature of authority structures within communities enabled much of the Fulbe, Mandinka, and Biaffada peasantry to make political choices autonomously (i.e., independently of their chiefs). Political options for these peoples, as for the Mandjack, depended more on their political juxtaposition within rural civil society, as determined by rapidly changing intravillage power configurations, than on chiefly influence or ethnic solidarity.

To be sure, the territorial effort of some ethnic groups—the Balanta, Oinka, and Papel, in particular—to defend specific land areas represented a crucial historical resistance pattern that reemerged during the liberation movement. But ethnically coherent choices were more the exception than the rule. Reproducing an ancient historical pattern of hosts accommodating migrants,[22] many peasants had relocated to villages dominated by a different group. The increasingly multiethnic and intermarried character of village communities added to the complexity of factors influencing political decision making, which subsequently became multidirectional (although increasingly pro-PAIGC).

Overall, then, a combination of factors collectively proved conducive to the eventual success of the anticolonial rebels. There was, in most communities, control over rural social space by legitimate leaders of civil society, with a consequent localistic structuring of rural political power; there also was the predominance of the informal marketing sector, plus the peasantry's control over most agricultural resources; and there was the colonial state's own fundamental institutional fragility. This broad sociopolitical and economic context is central to appreciating both the achievements of the liberation movement and the demise of the colonial state.

Bifurcated Civil Societies and Peasant Liberation Struggles

Marshall S. Clough's informative study of chiefs in colonial Kenya shows that while some chiefs sought out the new opportunities presented by the colonial state, others held to older traditions in large part because their followers insisted that they do so.[23] As a result, a complex bifurcation within rural civil society emerged, with some Kenyan chiefs gravitating toward modern political parties and others reinforcing locally controlled councils that were not under the watch of the state. In Guinea-Bissau, particularly during the course of the war for independence, a number of chiefly disputes and divisions took place that reflect a similar bifurcation: some chiefs had been artificially appointed to their posts, while others, popularly chosen, remained committed to precolonial modes of decision making and rulership.

This being the case, we are compelled to consider Mahmood Mamdani's point that contested power at the local level in Africa in fact reflected a division between local and "stranger" (migrant) groupings, typically emerging in the course of nationalist movements.[24] According to Mamdani, the local groups tended to defend colonially endowed chieftainships, while the "strangers" were rebelling precisely against the colonially created system of indirect rule. The present study suggests that in Guinea-Bissau the predominant pattern was one of interethnic collaboration within communities in Oio, Cacheu, Bafatá, and other regions. To some extent, this may suggest, in contrast to the pattern in South Africa, Uganda, and Kenya that Mamdani describes, the extent of Guinea-Bissau's exceptionally weak state status. Those stronger states succeeded in controlling rural civil society by strengthening pliant chieftainships and usurping indigenous control over the land, with colonially appointed chiefs benefiting immensely from their collaborative status:[25] the resulting power struggles within rural civil society that emerged in subsequent years reflected this state-provoked bifurcation. However, in Guinea-Bissau the state had not obtained the penetration to consolidate the power of collaborative chiefs.

In Guinea-Bissau, the most that was accomplished in this regard was the weakening of the grand kingships and strong chieftainships, but the colonial appointees who replaced these authorities were not typically provided with the institutional resources to achieve effective political and economic domination over the social formations and leadership groupings that comprised rural civil society. At the same time, local peasants' resentment against appointed chiefs was not as significant a motivating factor as it was for peasant rebel movements in Uganda, Kenya, and South Africa. In Guinea-Bissau, appointed chiefs had not achieved the type of deep restructurings of community power relations and resource appropriation that Mamdani describes as occurring in relatively stronger colonial-state contexts. Even in the Guinea-Bissauan districts of Gabu and Fulacunda, where appointees did succeed in creating substantial political divisions at the community level, this must be appreciated in the larger context of the overall decline of chiefly authority, rather than reflecting an exacerbation of "decentralized despotism," as discussed by Mamdani.[26] As a result, the choices in Guinea-Bissau—to join the national-liberation struggle, to remain neutral, or to support the colonialists— tended to reflect the relative independence of peasant decision making.

Peasants' political choices were not based on a clear-cut dichotomy between "strangers" and local indigens or between those who supported colonial appointees and those who opposed them. The movement to end colonial rule reflected a broad range of motivations and factors and cannot be accurately interpreted as essentially a communitarian effort to confront a system of decentralized despotism. What was truly significant in Guinea-Bissau was the extent to which the relative social, political, and religious autonomy of rural civil society—taking into account the variation in form and structure of social formations from one community to the next—made it possible for ordinary peasants to make political choices that reflected their perceived self-interest.

External Conditions

Ultimately, those peasant choices, and, more generally, the relative autonomy of rural civil society, proved favorable to the PAIGC and help to account for the success of the anticolonial struggle. At the same time, it must be noted that, beyond these internal, domestic dynamics, the external conditions in the 1960s and 1970s represented an important aspect of the PAIGC's final triumph in achieving independence for Guinea-Bissau. The Portuguese were experiencing growing international isolation, and there was expanding worldwide support for the PAIGC, along with the April 1974 overthrow of the Salazar dictatorship in Lisbon by junior military officers.[27] There was no need for a full-scale PAIGC military victory: the new regime in Lisbon would decide to terminate all efforts to retain control over not only Guinea, but also Mozambique and Angola.

Despite the importance of the external factors, they are not fully explanatory; the combination of a strong rural civil society and a relatively weakly entrenched colonial state is also crucial to understanding the success of the rebels. Had the colonial state done a more effective job of overturning local power structures and consolidating state overrule throughout the countryside, the nationalist war effort would either not have arisen or, if it had, it would have been quickly defeated. Furthermore, the ouster of Portuguese troops from nearly 90 percent of the territory of Guinea-Bissau by indigenous anticolonial forces had produced dissension within the Portuguese military of such intensity that it directly contributed to the 1974 coup in Lisbon and the subsequent reversal of Lisbon's overseas policy. In this regard, the praetorian power of African social formations wielded a determining impact on imperial politics, rather than the reverse. Thus, while international circumstances were important in understanding the outcome of Guinea-Bissau's resistance struggle of the 1960s and 1970s, ultimately the cumulative impact of rural civil societal strength over the long term must also be accorded substantial explanatory weight.

STATE VIOLENCE AND WEAK STATES

In assessing the terminal phase of colonialism in Guinea-Bissau in the context of a strong rural civil society and bureaucratic decay, it is particularly important to suggest the comparative implications of state terror as the national government's policy of choice. It has been a central argument of this book that both in 1913–15 as well as during the independence struggle of the 1960s and 1970s, the state's failure to institutionalize a system of local administrative authority convinced officials that terror was the only option available to them. Elsewhere as well, political elites operating within weakened state infrastructures faced with strongly constituted social forces have opted to pursue systematic terror against their civilian populaces.[28] An example can be seen in the Central American case of El Salvador, where state reaction to mass mobilization reflected an elite subculture historically committed to massive violence; the peasant massacre of 1932 served as "a model response to the threat of rebellion" for the following fifty years.[29] The same response in Portuguese Guinea similarly reflected the underlying institutional disarray of the central state, as well as a profound gap between the state and rural civil society. This comparison can be extended to Guatemala regarding the government's repression of the Ixil Indians, which was, like that in colonial Guinea-Bissau, set in a context marked by sharp ethnic/

racial divisions between the state elites and the rural populace.[30] To some extent, a parallel can also be drawn with the militarization of politics in Nazi Germany, where an internally fractured bureaucratic infrastructure encouraged political leaders to link the use of terror to the state's very existence.[31]

These comparisons may be contrasted with most of the other states of colonial-era Africa. By the 1940s and 1950s, most colonies had embarked on administrative and political reforms that began to shift power toward electorally based institutions and provided educated youths with avenues for upward mobility.[32] The colonial state in Portuguese Guinea, however, continued to operate with de facto political blinders: state leaders vainly sought to grasp onto decaying sources of domestic political support such as pliant chieftainships.

Ultimately, in Portuguese Guinea as in El Salvador and Nazi Germany, the turn toward state terror proved dysfunctional: an overemphasis of attention and resources on the mechanics of violence undermined the state's ability even to wage war (the ultimate irony) and diminished its ability to administer large numbers of civilians.[33] In Portuguese Guinea, the colonialists found themselves on the losing side of military campaigns against the PAIGC through the late 1960s and early 1970s even as their terror campaigns intensified. In El Salvador, the peasant-backed rebellion similarly enjoyed its greatest success at the peak period of the military terror campaigns.[34] In Nazi Germany, even as the mass terror of the "final solution" annihilated millions of Jews in the closing months of 1944 and early 1945, the German bureaucracy became decreasingly effective in regard to both civilian administration (which was overstretched throughout Nazi-occupied Europe) and its war-making capacity.[35]

However, unlike the postauthoritarian government of El Salvador or post-war Germany, the government of postcolonial Guinea-Bissau was not able to turn toward the United States or another superpower for political and economic sustenance. Guinea-Bissau's postcolonial state would remain institutionally fragile, ultimately dependent on a recalcitrant rural civil society capable of defending and strengthening its fundamental political and social autonomy.

Indeed, the self-strengthening of rural civil society became especially evident in the postindependence period, when popularly authentic social formations and sources of community-level authority were dynamically reconstituted. Peasants ignored officially established village committees and directed their loyalty toward local community leaders, meanwhile expanding vibrant informal trading networks. Limited-rule popular kingships were revived in the face of the virtual withdrawal of the national system of administration. There was an expansion of crioulo as a lingua franca, but this did not provide the social glue

sufficient to forestall conflict between the state and rural social sectors,[36] and crioulo's embrace was itself resisted by a large segment of the rural populace. Shrine
societies continued to increase in size and influence and exerted significant social
and political power in much of the countryside. It was through these societies
that community decision-making structures were accorded social and political
power, whereas postindependence state-preferred political officials were largely
ignored. A similar process occurred in Zimbabwe, where spirit mediums directly
or indirectly greatly influenced the village committees, assuring a historic continuity of ancestor-based political authority and spiritual influence in these postindependence political units.[37]

In Guinea-Bissau's Cacheu region, each spirit-shrine society was based on
a given land area and thus consolidated a link between Mandjack identity and
territorial location. At the same time, these same spirit shrines encouraged a
multiethnic clientele by facilitating the incorporation of "outsiders" (i.e., people
from outside the immediate area of a given shrine). There is here a dialectic that
has characterized the social foundation and development of rural civil society
in precolonial, colonial, and postcolonial Guinea-Bissau: a dual commitment
by community leaders and peasants to locally controlled land areas,[38] balanced
against a symmetrical emphasis on incorporating ethnic outsiders and engaging
in substantive interethnic social and economic exchanges. Peasants from a variety of group-specific and regional backgrounds have demonstrated a powerful
allegiance to a politics of territorially defined localism; at the same time, they
engage in multidirectional barter exchanges and participate in heterogenous social institutions.

The combination of ethnolocalistic political and social arrangements and incorporative, collaborative, interethnic social formations represent twin, reflective
sources of social power in rural Guinea-Bissau, contemporarily as in the past.
These social pillars of rural civil society obviated what Rothchild and Foley refer
to as a "bureaucratic centralist" pattern of rule wherein the state seeks to consolidate government control rather than engage in reciprocal bargaining with rural
actors.[39] In Guinea-Bissau, this "bureaucratic centralist" effort, manifested especially in the system of village committees, failed to displace already existing local
power structures. At the same time, the expansion of the informal sector of the
economy played a key role in inhibiting a fuller extraction of revenue from rural
communities by the government.

Meanwhile, intrastate compartmentalization and factionalism were dramatized by a series of coups d'état (1980s and 1990s), and in 1998 produced a
falling out between the president and the armed forces. The subsequent rebellion

by the major portion of Guinea-Bissauan soldiers was strengthened through the support of the general populace, which helped to assure success for the rebels. In retrospect, it must be recognized that the central state had been constructed on an unstable social foundation, lacking institutional, organizational, or social roots in the rural civil society that surrounded it. As a result, popular forces in the countryside were well positioned to help assure the success of the rebellion.

The Politics of Social Autonomy

We may conclude with a comparative observation that calls into question Mamdani's assertion that not only colonial states but also postcolonial states have succeeded in instituting village-level decentralized and/or centralized "despotism" in Africa.[40] The present study suggests that Mamdani confuses state intention with social reality; in rural communities in Guinea-Bissau, strong social forces have ignored or manipulated state-created institutions so as to favor locally popular actors. Mamdani assigns more success to the postcolonial state than it has merited, at the expense of underappreciating the extent of peasant success in fortifying locally legitimate rural civil society.

Similarly to Mamdani, Jean-François Bayart has suggested that politics in Africa reflect the absence of an "organizational principle" that has the potential to unify social units in a meaningful way, although he does recognize that popular social formations have impeded central state rule. Bayart's argument is that while antistate actors can "chip" at state authority, they do not produce a redistribution of power—"not even in Guinea-Bissau, Angola, Mozambique, Ethiopia, Madagascar or Congo, where the subordinated social groups have apparently reaped little benefit from their investment in revolts, nationalist or agrarian struggles."[41]

However, this book has made clear that the goal of most rural communities in Guinea-Bissau was not to "redistribute power" so much as to conserve legitimately based local control over community-level social-authority structures. Thus, peasants have indeed benefited from their investment in revolts and "agrarian struggles," not because they merged their interests into a common "organizational principle," but because they successfully defended and preserved their political and social space, assuring the autonomy of the leadership groups and social formations that constitute rural civil society.

In Guinea-Bissau, as in other parts of Africa, the various manifestations of rural civil societal authority have preserved their relative autonomy from state-centric forces. Lineages, chiefdoms, secret societies, and local communities have constructed, altered, and reconstructed their own authority and leadership structures. As Chazan has eloquently pointed out, it is especially in the rural areas that communities have proven capable of defending their institutional forms and the "organizational modes" that predominate in village settings.[42] Indeed, a recent study of Angolan politics emphasizes the continuing de facto reality of village-level autonomy, made possible through the determination, guile, and skill of locally legitimate community leaders.[43]

Victor Azarya's distinction between incorporation and disengagement further helps to underline the broader implications of the relative autonomy of rural social formations, in Guinea-Bissau as elsewhere in Africa. Azarya defines incorporation as "the process whereby large segments of the population associate with the state and take part in its activities in order to share its resources."[44] Disengagement, by contrast, occurs when "people increasingly disassociate themselves from values attributed to the state . . . authority and prestige are differentiated from [state-controlled] political power."[45]

It is clear that the rural populace of Guinea-Bissau increasingly chose—and was able to assure—its relative disengagement from the state nexus during the colonial and postcolonial periods. At the same time, it has been my argument that the sources of this relative peasant success, along with the deleterious impact on state fragility in Guinea-Bissau, may in large measure be traced to enduring indigenous legacies and the multiple incarnations of strongly embedded and dynamic precolonial social and political traditions, including interethnic exchanges as well as autonomous territorial localism. In this respect, this book calls particular attention to the broader political impact of rural civil society and its historically generated community-based social formations as central to understanding the domestic lineages of state fragility in sub-Saharan Africa.

Notes

PREFACE

1. For earlier syntheses of aspects of this research, see Joshua B. Forrest, *Guinea-Bissau: Power, Conflict, and Renewal in a West African Nation* (Boulder, Colo.: Westview Press, 1992); Richard Lobban and Joshua Forrest, *Historical Dictionary of the Republic of Guinea-Bissau,* 2d ed. (Metuchen, N.J.: Scarecrow Press, 1988); and Joshua B. Forrest, "State, Peasantry, and National Power Struggles in Post-independence Guinea-Bissau" (Ph.D. diss., University of Wisconsin-Madison, 1987).

2. The reader seeking comprehensiveness is urged to consult studies by René Pélissier, Gérard Gaillard, Philip J. Havik, Walter Hawthorne, and Joye Bowman. See the selected bibliography.

3. Mamadou Mané, "Contribution à l'histoire du Kaabu, des origines au XIXe siècle," *Bulletin de l'Institut Fondamental d'Afrique Noire* 40, no. 1 (1978): 97; Joye Bowman, "Conflict, Interaction, and Change in Guinea-Bissau: Fulbe Expansion and Its Impact, 1850–1900" (Ph.D. diss., University of California Los Angeles, 1980), 34–35.

4. In this regard, I follow Joye Bowman in *Ominous Transition: Commerce and Colonial Expansion in the Senegambia and Guinea, 1857–1919* (Brookfield, Vt.: Avebury, 1997).

INTRODUCTION

1. Malyn Hewitt, *Portugal in Africa: The Last Hundred Years* (London: Longman, 1981); A. I. Asiwaju, Michael Crowder, and Basil Davidson, eds., "Portugal in Africa," *Tarikh* 6, no. 4 special issue (1980); R. J. Hammond, *Portugal and Africa* (Stanford: Stanford University Press, 1966); James Duffy, *Portugal in Africa* (Cambridge: Harvard University Press, 1962).

2. Patrick Chabal, "Revolutionary Democracy in Africa: The Case of Guinea-

Bissau," in *Political Domination in Africa: Reflections on the Limits of Power,* ed. Patrick Chabal (Cambridge: Cambridge University Press, 1986), 108.

3. Insightfully, Chabal urges a broader than usual interpretation of "civil society" in Africa, suggesting that it should refer to virtually all elements of powerless nonstate actors (villagers, fishermen, nomads, age-group members, village councillors, as well as disenfranchised politicians, military officers, and intellectuals): Patrick Chabal, "Thinking about Politics in Africa," introduction to *Political Domination in Africa: Reflections on the Limits of Power,* ed. Patrick Chabal (Cambridge: Cambridge University Press, 1986), 15.

4. Joel S. Migdal, *Strong Societies and Weak States: State-Society Relations and State Capabilities in the Third World* (Princeton, N.J.: Princeton University Press, 1988).

5. Ibid., 32.

6. Ibid., 33-34.

7. Naomi Chazan, "Patterns of State-Society Incorporation and Disengagement in Africa," in *The Precarious Balance: State and Society in Africa,* ed. Donald Rothchild and Naomi Chazan (Boulder, Colo.: Westview Press, 1988): 121-48.

8. Ibid., 122.

9. Ibid., 124.

10. Martin Doornbos, "The African State in Academic Debate: Retrospect and Prospect," *Journal of Modern African Studies* 28, no. 2 (1990): 197.

11. Ibid., 191.

12. Ibid.

13. Elke Zuern, "The Changing Roles of Civil Society in African Democratisation Processes," in *Consolidation of Democracy in Africa: A View from the South,* ed. Hussein Solomon and Ian Liebenberg (Aldershot, U.K.: Ashgate, 2000), 97, 108-9.

14. Naomi Chazan et al., *Politics and Society in Contemporary Africa* (Boulder, Colo.: Lynne Rienner, 1988), 198.

15. Jean-François Bayart, "Civil Society in Africa," in *Political Domination in Africa: Reflections on the Limits of Power,* ed. Patrick Chabal (Cambridge: Cambridge University Press, 1986), 113.

16. Ibid.

17. Ibid., 114.

18. Ibid., 115.

19. Jane I. Guyer, "The Spatial Dimensions of Civil Society in Africa: An Anthropologist Looks at Nigeria," in *Civil Society and the State in Africa,* ed. John Harbeson, Donald Rothchild, and Naomi Chazan (Boulder, Colo.: Lynne Rienner, 1994), 215-29.

20. James Coleman, "The Concept of Political Penetration," in *Government and Rural Development in East Africa: Essays on Political Penetration,* ed. Lionel Cliffe, James S. Coleman, and Martin Doornbos (The Hague: Martinus Nijhoff, 1977), 3.

21. B. Guy Peters, "The Machinery of Government: Concepts and Issues," in *Organizing Governance: Governing Organizations,* ed. Colin Campbell and B. Guy Peters (Pittsburgh: University of Pittsburgh Press, 1988), 31.

22. Joshua B. Forrest, "Asynchronic Comparisons: Weak States in Post-colonial Africa and Mediaeval Europe," in *Comparing Nations: Concepts, Strategies, Substance,* ed. Mattei Dogan and Ali Kazancigil (Oxford, U.K.: Basil Blackwell, 1994), 260-96; Joshua B. Forrest, "The Quest for State 'Hardness' in Africa," *Comparative Politics* 20, no. 4 (1988): 427.

23. Forrest, "Quest," 427–30.

24. Jeffrey Herbst, *States and Power in Africa: Comparative Lessons in Authority and Control* (Princeton, N.J.: Princeton University Press, 2000).

25. Goran Hyden, *No Shortcuts to Progress* (Berkeley: University of California Press, 1983), 60, 63, 71, 72.

26. Crawford Young, *The African Colonial State in Comparative Perspective* (New Haven: Yale University Press, 1994); Mahmood Mamdani, *Citizen and Subject: Contemporary Africa and the Legacy of Late Colonialism* (Princeton, N. J.: Princeton University Press, 1996).

27. Young, *African Colonial State,* 35.

28. Ibid., 217. This point was initially articulated in two concisely written articles that remain especially valuable; see Crawford Young, "The African State and Its Political Legacy," in Rothchild and Chazan, *Precarious Balance,* 28; Crawford Young, "The Colonial State and the Post-colonial Crisis," in *Decolonization and African Independence: The Transfers of Power, 1960–1980,* ed. Prosser Gifford and William Roger Louis (New Haven: Yale University Press, 1988), 9.

29. Young, *African Colonial State,* 139.

30. Ibid., 118.

31. Ibid., 139.

32. Ibid., 141.

33. Mamdani, *Citizen and Subject.*

34. Ibid., 37–58.

35. The terror aspect of soft states is discussed below.

36. Young, *African Colonial State,* 35. See also Hyden, *No Shortcuts;* Forrest, "Asynchronic Comparisons"; Rothchild and Chazan, *Precarious Balance.*

37. Herbst, *States and Power.*

38. See Hyden, *No Shortcuts;* Forrest, "Asynchronic Comparisons"; Donald Rothchild and Michael W. Foley, "African States and the Politics of Inclusive Coalitions," in Rothchild and Chazan, *Precarious Balance,* 233–64.

39. Herbst, *States and Power,* 4, 11, 71, 145–46, 253.

40. This term is used repeatedly throughout Herbst, *States and Power* (e.g., pages 16, 46, 167).

41. Victor Azarya, "Reordering State-Society Relations: Incorporation and Disengagement," in Rothchild and Chazan, *Precarious Balance,* 9.

42. Ibid., 19.

43. Young, *African Colonial State,* 101.

44. As indicated at the front of the book, the term *Guinea,* unless otherwise specified, refers to Portuguese Guinea. Although there are occasional references to French Guinea or Guinea-Conakry, *Guinea* standing alone refers to the Portuguese colony.

45. The quotation marks around "settled" are meant to suggest *so-called,* or *less than fully settled.*

46. Herbst, *States and Power,* 3, 25, 44, 175.

47. As made clear in Young, *African Colonial State.*

48. Leaders' incentives and geography are Herbst's central factors: *States and Power,* 4, 36, 41, 43, 103, 253.

49. Young, *African Colonial State,* 100.

50. Ibid., 100–101; Young, "The Colonial State," 12.

51. Young, *African Colonial State,* 152; Young, "The Colonial State," 9.

52. Thomas P. Callaghy, *The State-Society Struggle: Zaire in Comparative Perspective* (New York: Columbia University Press, 1984).

53. Basil Davidson, "Colonialism on the Cheap—the Portuguese in Africa up to c. 1921," *Tarikh* 6, no. 4 (1980): 3.

54. Young, *African Colonial State,* 93.

55. Michael Crowder, ed., *West African Resistance: The Military Response to Colonial Occupation* (New York: Hutchinson, 1971), 16.

56. Young, *African Colonial State,* 94.

57. Ibrahim K. Sundiata, "The Structure of Terror in a Small State: Equatorial Guinea," in *African Islands and Enclaves,* ed. Robin Cohen (Beverly Hills: Sage Publications, 1983), 81–100; Sundiata, *Equatorial Guinea: Colonialism, State Terror, and the Search for Stability* (Boulder, Colo.: Westview Press, 1990); Rhoda E. Howard, "Repression and State Terror in Kenya: 1982–1988," in *State Organized Terror: The Case of Violent Internal Repression,* ed. P. Timothy Bushnell et al. (Boulder, Colo.: Westview Press, 1991), 77–91.

58. Human Rights Watch/Africa, *Mauritania's Campaign of Terror: State-Sponsored Repression of Black Africans* (New York: Human Rights Watch, 1994). However, this descriptive analysis does not include a conceptual discussion of state terror.

59. Sundiata does note, however, that the state relied on extensive violence during the colonial period in Equatorial Guinea: Sundiata, *Equatorial Guinea,* 34.

60. See especially Bushnell et al., *State Organized Terror;* Michael Stohl and George Lopez, eds., *The State as Terrorist: The Dynamics of Governmental Violence and Repression* (Westport, Conn.: Greenwood Press, 1984).

61. Stohl and Lopez, *State as Terrorist,* 7–8.

62. Alex P. Schmid, "Repression, State Terrorism, and Genocide: Conceptual Clarifications," in Bushnell et al., *State Organized Terror,* 28, 31.

63. Ibid., 31.

64. P. Timothy Bushnell et al., "State Organized Terror: Tragedy of the Modern State," in Bushnell et al., *State Organized Terror,* 9.

65. Ibid., 11–13.

66. Manuel Antonio Garretón, "Fear in Military Regimes: An Overview," in *Fear at the Edge: State Terror and Resistance in Latin America,* ed. Juan E. Corradi, Patricia Weiss Fagen, and Manuel Antonio Garretón (Berkeley: University of California Press, 1992), 20–21.

67. Malyn Hewitt makes a similar point regarding Portugal's choice of military conquest over economic and religious penetration in deciding to embark on prolonged wars of pacification in Africa: *Portugal in Africa,* 50.

68. René Pélissier, *Naissance de la Guiné: Portugais et Africains en Sénégambie, 1841–1936* (Orgeval, France: Pélissier, 1989), 212; and see 411.

69. Peter Karibe Mendy, *Colonialismo Português em Africa: A tradição de resistência na Guiné-Bissau, 1879–1959* (Bissau: Instituto Nacional de Estudos e Pesquisas, 1994).

70. Carlos Lopes, *Kaabunké: Espaço, território, e poder na Guiné-Bissau, Gâmbia, e Casamance pré-coloniais* (Lisbon: Comissão Nacional Para as Comemorações dos Descobrimentos Portugueses, 1999), 101, 111, 125, citation from 246. Lopes's study is discussed in chapter 1.

71. See chapters 2, 3, and 4.

72. Crowder, *West African Resistance,* 8.

73. Ibid., 9–11.

74. Ibid., and see Mendy's discussion of leaders of African resistance in *Colonialismo Português,* 38–46.

75. Crowder, *West African Resistance,* 15.

76. Ibid., 13.

77. See also Mendy's Portuguese-language discussion of the extended duration of Guinea-Bissau's "tradition of resistance" in Mendy, *Colonialismo Português,* 107–50. While Mendy emphasizes the similarity between primary resistance efforts in Guinea-Bissau and those in other African colonies, I more forcefully emphasize the inability of the Portuguese to interfere with wars occurring within the Guinea-Bissauan interior during most of the eighteenth and nineteenth centuries.

78. T. O. Ranger, "Connexions between 'Primary Resistance' Movements and Modern Mass Nationalism in East and Central Africa," parts 1 and 2, *Journal of African History* 9, no. 3 (1968): 437–53; no. 4 (1968): 631–41.

79. Ibid., part 1: 439, 444, 449; ibid., part 2: 634, 638.

80. Mendy, *Colonialismo Português,* 343, 425. Contrary to the argument presented here, Mendy argues that ethnic groups did not collaborate in the long history of Guinea-Bissauan resistance.

81. David Lan, *Guns and Rain: Guerrillas and Spirit Mediums in Zimbabwe* (London: James Currey, 1985), 56–57, 106, 146–47.

82. See chapter 9.

83. I am grateful to Crawford Young for his comments on this.

84. For an exceptionally informative study of "landlord-stranger reciprocities" among the peoples of the Guinea-Bissau area in the preceding period (i.e., up to the 1600s), see George E. Brooks, *Landlords and Strangers: Ecology, Society, and Trade in Western Africa, 1000–1630* (Boulder, Colo.: Westview Press, 1993), esp. 38–39. Brooks highlights various types of peaceful exchanges, including intermarriage, between migrants and settled West African societies, including, in the Guinea-Bissau area, the Mandinka, Biaffada, Banhun, and Papel. The present study, in discussing the later precolonial, colonial, and postcolonial periods, is consistent with Brooks's argument.

85. Janet MacGaffey, *The Real Economy of Zaire* (Philadelphia: University of Pennsylvania Press, 1991), 12.

86. Ibid., 154.

87. Ibid., 34.

88. Daniel dos Santos, "The Second Economy in Angola: *Esquema* and *Candonga,*" in *The Second Economy in Marxist States,* ed. Maria Los (New York: St. Martin's Press, 1990), 157–74.

89. Ibid., 162.

90. The term *uncaptured* is suggested for this context by Goran Hyden in *Beyond Ujamaa in Tanzania: Underdevelopment and an Uncaptured Peasantry* (Berkeley: University of California Press, 1980).

91. Richard L. Roberts, *Warriors, Merchants, and Slaves: The State and the Economy in the Middle Niger Valley, 1700–1914* (Stanford, Calif.: Stanford University Press, 1987), 154–58.

92. Ibid., 160–61, 173.

93. Ibid., 171.

94. Ibid., 212.

95. Hewitt, *Portugal in Africa;* Duffy, *Portugal in Africa;* Asiwaju, Crowder, and Davidson, "Portugal in Africa."

96. Richard L. Roberts, *Two Worlds of Cotton: Colonialism and the Regional Economy in French Soudan, 1800–1946* (Cambridge: Cambridge University Press, 1996), 10, 286–89.

Chapter One

1. A detailed historical portrait of precolonial peoples in Guinea-Bissau may be found in Brooks, *Landlords and Strangers;* see also Bowman, *Ominous Transition,* 8–18.

2. For a penetrating examination of these Lusophone European settlers *(lançados)* and their interactions with local peoples in the area of Guinea-Bissau during the fifteenth and sixteenth centuries, see Brooks, *Landlords and Strangers.*

3. Ibid.; Lopes, *Kaabunké.*

4. For details on these early migrations into the Guinea-Bissau region, see Gérald Gaillard, ed., *Migrations anciennes et peuplement actuel des côtes guinéennes* (Paris: L'Harmattan, 2000).

5. Brooks, *Landlords and Strangers,* 33. See also Richard Andrew Lobban and Peter Karibe Mendy, *Historical Dictionary of Guinea-Bissau,* 3d ed., 1996.

6. Walter Rodney, *A History of the Upper Guinea Coast, 1545–1800* (New York: Monthly Review Press, 1970).

7. António Carreira, *Os Portuguêses nos rios da Guiné* (Lisbon: Author, 1984), 80. This contrasts with Brooks's hypothesis regarding their arrival in the fifteenth century (*Landlords and Strangers,* 111).

8. Carreira, *Os Portuguêses,* 80.

9. Bowman, "Conflict, Interaction, Change," 53.

10. Carreira, *Os Portuguêses,* 80; Bowman, *Ominous Transition,* 13; Bowman, "Conflict, Interaction, Change," 13.

11. Untitled letter, António Vás de Araujo, regimental major *[sargento-mor]* of Farim, 1783 [day illegible], in Arquivo Histórico Ultramarino (AHU), box 13, doc. 1.

12. António Carreira, *Panaria Cabo-Verdiano-Guineense: Aspectos históricos e socio-económicos* (Lisbon: Museu de Etnologia do Ultramar, 1968), 17, 31, 38.

13. Eve Lakshmi Crowley, "Contracts with the Spirits: Religion, Asylum, and Ethnic Identity in the Cacheu Region of Guinea-Bissau" (Ph.D. diss., Yale University, May 1990), 76.

14. George Brooks, "Historical Perspectives on the Guinea-Bissau Region," in *Vice-Almirante Avelino Teixeira da Mota, in Memoriam* (Lisbon: Academia de Marinha, 1987): 277–304.

15. Brooks, *Landlords and Strangers.*

16. Report, Carbou, French consul in Bissau, to gov.-genl., French West Africa (FWA), Dakar, 11 Aug. 1945, Bissau, ANS 2F 12, file 14, #328. See also Bowman, *Ominous Transition,* 8.

17. Bowman, *Ominous Transition.*

18. António Carreira, interview by the author, Lisbon, 12 Feb. 1984.

19. António Carreira, *Vida social dos Manjacos* (Lisbon: Centro de Estudos da Guiné Portuguesa, 1947), 25.

20. Bertrand Bocandé, "Notes sur la Guinée Portugaise ou Sénégambie Meridonale," *Bulletin de la Société de Géographie* (Paris), 3d ser., no. 11 (May/June 1849): 340.

21. As the size of the Brame polity diminished, the number of people identifying themselves as Brame was also reduced. By the 1940s, most Brame lived in only two villages, Có and Bula. Crowley, "Contracts," 287, 298 n. 39.

22. Carreira, *Os Portuguêses,* 15.

23. Crowley, "Contracts," 79.

24. Carreira, *Vida social dos Manjacos,* 15.

25. Carreira, *Os Portuguêses,* 15.

26. António Carreira, interview by Joye Bowman in *Ominous Transition,* 11.

27. Edward Eric Gable, "Modern Manjaco: The Ethos of Power in a West African Society" (Ph.D. diss., University of Virginia, 1990), 12.

28. Bowman, *Ominous Transition,* 11.

29. Ibid.; Crowley, "Contracts," 287.

30. António Carreira, noted in Bowman, *Ominous Transition,* 11.

31. Eve Crowley, "Institutions, Identities, and the Incorporation of Immigrants within Local Frontiers of the Upper Guinea Coast," in *Migrations anciennes,* ed. Gaillard, 118.

32. This is further discussed in chapter 7.

33. Carreira, *Os Portuguêses,* 15.

34. Gable, "Modern Manjaco," 13–15.

35. Ibid., 19.

36. Pélissier, *Naissance,* 21.

37. Crowley, "Contracts," 116–17, 287.

38. Ibid., 234, 238.

39. Ibid., 238.

40. "Memória sobre Bissau," Duque Collaio da Veiga Vidal, chefe do estado maior e secretario, n.d., AHU, box 25, doc. 77.

41. José Manuel de Braga Dias, "Mudança socio-cultural na Guiné Portuguesa" (Ph.D. diss., Universidade Técnica de Lisboa, Instituto Superior de Ciências Sociais e Política Ultramarina, Lisbon, 1974), 192.

42. Pélissier, *Naissance,* 114 n. 149.

43. Crowley, "Contracts," 76.

44. Pélissier, *Naissance.*

45. Diana Lima Handem, "Nature et fonctionnement du pouvoir chez les Balanta Brassa" (thèse de 3ème cycle, Ecole des Hautes Etudes en Sciences Sociales, Centre d'Etudes Africaines, Paris, 1985), 7, 32.

46. The other being the Fulbe, also with one-quarter of the populace, as indicated by the 1992 population census. Handem, "Nature," 16.

47. Walter Hawthorne, "Nourishing a Stateless Society during the Slave Trade: The Rise of Balanta Paddy-Rice Production in Guinea-Bissau," *Journal of African History* 42, no. 1 (2001): 1–24.

48. Hawthorne, "Migrations and Statelessness: The Expansion of the Balanta of Guinea-Bissau, 1900–1950," in *Migrations anciennes*, ed. Gaillard, 139–50; Handem, "Nature," 33.

49. Handem, "Nature," 27; Walter Hawthorne, "The Interior Past of an Acephalous Society: Institutional Change among the Balanta of Guinea-Bissau, c. 1400–c. 1950" (Ph.D. diss., Stanford University, 1998), 323–39. The data is further analyzed by Hawthorne in a book-length study of stateless societies in Guinea-Bissau that he is currently completing for Heinemann's Social History of Africa series.

50. A. J. Dias Dinis, "As tribos de Guiné Portuguesa na história," *Congresso comemorativo do quinto centenário do descobrimento da Guiné,* vol. 1 (Lisbon: Sociedade de Geografiia, 1946): 241–78, at 252. Handem, "Nature," 4; Hawthorne, "Nourishing," 5.

51. Avelino Teixeira da Mota, "Les relations de l'ancien Cabou avec quelques états et peuples voisins," *Ethiopiques* 28, special issue (Oct. 1981): 158.

52. Handem, "Nature," 40.

53. Lopes, *Kaabunké,* 150.

54. Handem, "Nature," 14.

55. Hawthorne, "Migrations and Statelessness," 141–42; idem, "Interior Past," 263–65, 323–24.

56. Handem, "Nature," 14, 40–42.

57. Ibid., 14.

58. Ibid., 36, 41, 44.

59. Ibid., 42–43, 256.

60. Carreira, *Panaria Cabo-Verdiano-Guineense,* 20; Hawthorne, "Interior Past," 72, 98, 229–30; Hawthorne, "Nourishing."

61. Handem, "Nature," 42, 44.

62. Ibid., 41.

63. Ibid., 19; Hawthorne, "Interior Past," 60, 62.

64. Handem, "Nature," 20.

65. Ibid., 39.

66. Ibid., 13, 184; Hawthorne, "Interior Past," 60.

67. Hawthorne, "Interior Past," 43. Age-grade societies are institutions that group together people from the same age group into social units that span a multiplicity of villages. Each age-grade society performs specific economic, social, and political tasks, such as young men who help one another to tend crops.

68. Ibid., 201, 212; Handem, "Nature," 159, 161.

69. Mota, "Les relations," 155.

70. Hawthorne, "Interior Past," 194, 203; Handem, "Nature," 160.

71. Hawthorne, "Interior Past," 188; 200; 229; 325.

72. Fernand Rogado Quintino, "Os povos da Guiné Portuguesa," article in *Boletim Cultural da Guiné Portuguesa* [hereafter, *BCGP*] 24, no. 96 (1969): 883–84.

73. Mota, *Guiné Portuguesa,* 159. See also Bowman, *Ominous Transition,* 16.

74. A. Teixeira da Mota, "Actividade marítima dos Bijagós nos séculos XVI e XVII," in *In memoriam António Jorge Dias* (Lisbon: Junta de Investigações Ciêntíficas do Ultramar, 1974), 243–44. See also Bowman, *Ominous Transition,* 8–10, Brooks, *Landlords and Strangers,* 86.

75. Brooks, *Landlords and Strangers,* 267.

76. Ibid., 82–86; Hawthorne, "Interior Past," 93, 96.

77. Mota, "Les relations," 158.

78. Ibid., 159.

79. André Alvarès de Almada, *Tradado breve dos Rios de Guiné do Cabo Verde* (Lisbon: Luis Silveira, 1841), cited in Mota, "Les relations," 160.

80. Sékéné Mody Cissoko, "De l'organisation politique de Kaabu," *Ethiopiques* 28, special issue (Oct. 1981): 198.

81. Brooks, *Landlords and Strangers,* 89.

82. Mota, "Les relations," 157–58.

83. Gérald Gaillard, "Présentation," in *Migrations anciennes,* ed. Gaillard, 14–15.

84. Carlos Lopes, "Relações de poder numa sociedade Malinké: O Kaabú do séc. XIII ao séc. XVIII," *Soronda: Revista de Estudos Guineenses* 10 (July 1990): 18; name of king provided by Philip J. Havik — personal communication.

85. Mota, "Les relations," 243–44.

86. Brooks, *Landlords and Strangers,* 262–63.

87. Carreira, *Os Portuguêses,* 49.

88. Christiano José de Senna Barcellos, "Guiné Portugueza: Memória" (Lisbon, 9 Dec. 1908); ANS 2F 12, #132. Barcellos was an administrative deputy for Cape Verde and Guinea, from the late 1800s to the early 1900s.

89. Carlos Lopes, "A transição histórica na Guiné-Bissau: Do movimento de libertação nacional ao estado" (thesis, Institut Universitaire d'Etudes du Développement, Geneva, Switzerland, 1982), 31–32.

90. See chapter 6.

91. Some historians believed Fulbe groups to have settled at Gabu in the fourteenth or even the thirteenth century, but the current consensus supports their arrival in the fifteenth century; see R. P. Mveng, "Considérations générales sur le colloque," *Ethiopiques* 28, special issue (Oct. 1981): 14, and Yves Person, "Problèmes de l'histoire du Gaabu," in ibid., 70.

92. Mané, "Contribution à l'histoire du Kaabu," 116–17.

93. Ibid., 116.

94. Bowman, *Ominous Transition,* 17; Carreira, *Panaria Cabo-Verdiano-Guineense,* 54; Mendes Moreira, *Fulas do Gabú* (Bissau: Centro de Estudos da Guiné Portuguesa, 1948). Fulbe-ribê were called Red Fulbe by the Portuguese, reflecting their relatively elite status; Fulbe-djiábê were called Black Fulbe — a reference to their slave origins.

95. Carreira, *Os Portuguêses,* 87; António Carreira, "Organização social e económica dos povos da Guiné Portuguesa," *BCGP* 16, no. 64 (1961): 647–713, at 673.

96. Mané, "Contribution à l'histoire du Kaabu," 118; Bowman, *Ominous Transition,* 17, 40–41.

97. Bowman, *Ominous Transition,* 52; Carreira, *Os Portuguêses,* 81. This is discussed more fully in chapter 3.

98. Gabu was the typical pronunciation of the Fulbe; Kaabu was the generalized pronunciation of the Mandinka. Although Gabu was predominantly Mandinka, the name Gabu was used by Portuguese administrators and ethnographers; the French pronounced

it Kaabu. The analysis below of the Gabu kingdom is based largely on the works of the Senegalese historians Mamadou Mané, Nouha Cissé, and Sékéné Mody Cissoko and the Portuguese historian (and former colonial administrator and ethnologist in Guinea-Bissau) Teixeira da Mota; see citations below. For a complementary analysis of Gabu that is rich in historical description and insight, see Lopes, *Kaabunké,* 82–98; Bowman, *Ominous Transition,* 32–41; and Bowman, "Conflict, Interaction, Change," 52–98. Briefer treatments may also be found in Lobban and Mendy, *Historical Dictionary of Guinea-Bissau,* and in Forrest, *Guinea-Bissau.*

99. André Donelha, *Description de la Sierra Léone et des rivières de Guinée du Cap-Vert* (1625), Junta de Investigaçoês Cientificas do Ultramar, Centro de Estudos de Cartografia Antiga (Lisbon, 1977), 119–21.

100. Mané, "Contribution à l'histoire du Kaabu," 95, 97, 100; Sékéné Mody Cissoko, "De l'organisation politique du Kabu," *Ethiopiques* (1981), 199; Bowman, *Ominous Transition,* 35; Lopes, *Kaabunké,* 109, 179.

101. Mané, "Contribution à l'histoire du Kaabu," 106; Bowman, *Ominous Transition,* 35, 37; Lopes, *Kaabunké,* 179.

102. Brooks, *Landlords and Strangers,* 109–11; Crowley, "Contracts," 73.

103. Mané, "Contribution à l'histoire du Kaabu," 96–101; Bowman, *Ominous Transition,* 13. The relationship of the Gabu rulers with the already settled Fulbe is described below.

104. Lopes, *Kaabunké,* 103–4, 149–54.

105. Mané, "Contribution à l'histoire du Kaabu."

106. Lopes, *Kaabunké,* 151, 154. The ancient Mandinka extracted salt from these wetlands.

107. Crowley, "Contracts," 90–91.

108. Bowman, *Ominous Transition,* 34.

109. Cissoko, "De l'organisation politique," 197; Cornelia Giesing, "Fari Sangul, Sankule Faring, migrations et intégration politique dans le monde mandé selon les traditions des guerriers koring de la Sénégambie Méridionale," in *Migrations anciennes,* ed. Gaillard, 243, 249, 289.

110. Cissoko, "De l'organisation politique," 197.

111. Lopes, *Kaabunké,* 173, 181; Giesing, "Fari Sangul," 290.

112. Cissoko, "De l'organisation politique," 198.

113. Crowley, "Contracts," 91–92; Lopes, *Kaabunké,* 177.

114. Djibril Tamsir Niane, "Les sources orales de l'histoire du Gabu," *Ethiopiques* 28, special issue (Oct. 1981): 129–31.

115. Mota, "Les relations," 153. Cissoko, in "De l'organisation politique," 202, points out that the actual number of provinces may have ranged between twenty-four and forty-seven, reflecting, in part, provincial border changes over time. See also Lopes, *Kaabunké,* 175–77.

116. Lopes, *Kaabunké,* 102; 132–34; 168; Cissoko, "De l'organisation politique," 204.

117. Sékéné Mody Cissoko, "Introduction à l'histoire des Mandingues de l'Ouest," *Ethiopiques* 28, special issue (Oct. 1981): 84.

118. Lopes, *Kaabunké,* 125, 127, 173, 233, 246.

119. Ibid., 99.

120. Carreira, *Panaria Cabo-Verdiano-Guineense,* 11, 40, based on descriptions from explorers in the 1450s.

121. Lopes, *Kaabunké,* 101. The djula were in part autonomous in that some of their trading networks were directly tied to those of Gabu.

122. Mota, "Les relations," 151.

123. Mané, "Contribution à l'histoire du Kaabu," 128; Lopes, *Kaabunké,* 135.

124. Abdoulaye Ly, *La Compagnie du Sénégal* (Paris: Présence Africaine, 1958), 287; Mané, "Contribution à l'histoire du Kaabu," 128.

125. Mané, "Contribution à l'histoire du Kaabu," 128.

126. Walter Rodney, *A History of the Upper Guinea Coast, 1545 to 1800* (Oxford: Clarendon Press, 1970), 103.

127. Lopes, *Kaabunké,* 77.

128. Mané, "Contribution à l'histoire du Kaabu," 130.

129. Lopes, *Kaabunké,* 144.

130. Carreira, *Os Portuguêses,* 15; Crowley, "Contracts," 238.

131. Carreira, *Os Portuguêses,* 15.

Chapter Two

1. Brooks, *Landlords and Strangers,* 38–39.

2. Ibid., 189; Crowley, "Contracts."

3. Brooks, *Landlords and Strangers,* 180, and Crowley, "Contracts," 102.

4. Letter, Salvador Correadeiao Benarud, to his superior in Lisbon, 26 Sept. 1670, AHU, box 2, doc. 48.

5. Ibid.

6. Rosemary E. Galli and Jocelyn Jones, *Guinea-Bissau: Politics, Economics, and Society* (Boulder, Colo.: Lynne Rienner, 1987), 14–15; Brooks, *Landlords and Strangers,* 137; Mendy, *Colonialismo Português,* 109.

7. See Philip J. Havik's discussion of Sephards and others who were expelled, in Havik, "Missionarios e moradores na costa da Guiné: os padres da Companhia de Jesu e os tangomãos no princípio do século XVII," *Revista Studia* [Lisbon] 56, no. 7 (2000): 223–62.

8. See esp. Crowley, "Contracts," 99, 102.

9. Brooks, *Landlords and Strangers,* 189.

10. Ibid., 136; Galli and Jones, *Guinea-Bissau,* 15–17.

11. Brooks, *Landlords and Strangers,* 189; Galli and Jones, *Guinea-Bissau,* 15–17; Bowman, *Ominous Transition,* 159 n. 27; Crowley, "Contracts," 99.

12. They were generally given the most difficult jobs, which in times of war could mean supply carrier or front-line foot soldier.

13. Crowley, "Contracts," 99–101; Hawthorne, "Interior Past," 119, 123.

14. Crowley, "Contracts," 240.

15. Ibid.; Brooks, *Landlords and Strangers,* 189.

16. Crowley, "Contracts," 241; Brooks, *Landlords and Strangers,* 189; Hawthorne, "Interior Past," 199, 121–22.

17. Crowley, "Contracts," 241.

18. Brooks, *Landlords and Strangers,* 136; Hawthorne, "Interior Past," 120.

19. Note [unsigned], 13 Nov. 1687, AHU, box 3, doc. 40.

20. "Baptism of the King of Bissau," letter from Bernandim Areivede Anárada, 27 Oct. 1694, AHU, box 3, doc. 95.

21. Crowley, "Contracts," 119.

22. Ibid.

23. Letter [unsigned], Cacheu, 24 Mar. 1697, AHU, box 4, doc. 18.

24. Letter [unsigned], 10 Nov. 1698, AHU, box 4, doc. 31.

25. Reports from António dos Barros Beurra, Cacheu, 30 Jan. 1719, AHU, box 4, doc. 95; João Baptista e Machado, 1 Aug. 1731, AHU, box 5, doc. 108; João Baptista e Machado, 1731 [no day specified], AHU, box 5, doc. 112.

26. Carreira, *Os Portuguêses,* 38.

27. Quotations from letter by António de Barros Bezerra, administrator (capitão-mor) of Cacheu, 13 June 1721, reproduced in Carreira, *Os Portuguêses,* 61.

28. Joaquim Veríssimo Serrão, *História de Portugal VI* [1750-1807] (Lisbon: Editorial Verbo, 1982), 148.

29. Using different source material, Mendy places the date of the fort's destruction at 1707. Mendy, *Colonialismo Português,* 121-27, provides further details on decision-making regarding the fort's dismantling.

30. Letter, Joaó Pereyra de Carvalho, captain of Cacheu, 31 Mar. 1733, AHU, box 6, doc. 24.

31. Letter, Joaó Baptista e Machado, Cacheu, 1 Aug. 1731, AHU, box 5, doc. 108.

32. Note [unsigned], Cacheu, 1 June 1734, AHU, box 6, doc. 33.

33. Carreira, *Os Portuguêses,* 61.

34. Letter [unsigned], Cacheu, 24 Mar. 1697, AHU, box 4, doc. 18.

35. Letter, Joaó Pereyra de Carvalho, captain of Cacheu, 31 Mar. 1733, AHU, box 6, doc. 24.

36. Report [unsigned], 29 Jan. 1737, AHU, box 6, doc. 90.

37. Letter, Fran. Rog. Sottomayor, 27 Dec. 1751, AHU, box 8, doc. 11.

38. That letter is reproduced in Carreira, *Os Portuguêses,* 62.

39. Note [unsigned], Cacheu, 15 May 1763, AHU, box 9, doc. 40.

40. Note [unsigned], 1774, AHU, box 25, doc. 57.

41. Letter, José Antonio Pinto, Cacheu, 30 Apr. 1806, AHU, box 17, doc. 84.

42. On this point, see also Mendy, *Colonialismo Português,* 126-34.

43. Letter, Ignaçio Xer Bayaoff, 4 July 1777, AHU, box 11, doc. 43.

44. Ibid.

45. Letter, José Antonio Pinto, Cacheu, 30 Apr. 1806, AHU, box 17, doc. 84.

46. Letter, Jozé Felix de Azevedo Costa e Silva, 11 June 1782, AHU, box 13, doc. 5.

47. Note [unsigned], June 1782, AHU, box 25 [no doc. no].

48. Letters, José Antonio Pinto, Cacheu, 30 Apr. 1806, AHU, box 17, doc. 84, and Luiz Pedro de Araujo e Silva, commander, Cacheu, 25 Dec. 1786, AHU, box 13, doc. 53.

49. Report, naval sergeant Pascoal Pereira da Silveira, Farim, 25 Aug. 1802, AHU, box 16, doc. 63.

50. Note [unsigned], Cacheu, 7 June 1803, AHU, box 16, doc. 89.

51. "Report on That Which His Majesty Sends to the King of Bissau," c. 1752, AHU, box 25, doc. 29.

52. "Report on That Which Is Necessary to Continue Work on the Fort in Bissau," 1752, AHU, box 25, [no doc. no.].

53. Serrão, *História de Portugal,* 178.

54. Letter [unsigned], Bissau, 16 May 1753, AHU, box 25, doc. 78-A.

55. Serrão, *História de Portugal,* 148.

56. Portugal. Bulletin de Renseignements Politiques, Economiques et Littéraires, 29 Feb. 1936, Lisbon, Secretariat of National Propaganda, ANS 2F 4 12.

57. Ibid.; Serrão, *História de Portugal,* 148.

58. Serrão, *História de Portugal,* 372.

59. Letter, Ignaçio Xer Bayaoff, 2 June 1777, Praça de Guerra de S. José de Bissão, AHU, box 11, doc. 30.

60. Letter, João Gonçalves, Bissau, n.d., AHU, box 25, doc. 41.

61. Report, navy sergeant Pascoal Pereira da Silveira, Farim, 25 Aug. 1802, AHU, box 16, doc. 63.

62. Carreira, *Os Portuguêses,* 64.

63. Note, António Vás de Araujo, 24 Jan. 1776, AHU, box 11, doc. 1.

64. Report, navy sergeant da Silveira, 25 Aug. 1802; letter, Bernadino de Senna, Farim, 9 May 1781, AHU, box 12, doc. 9; letter, José Antonio Pinto, Cacheu, 30 Apr. 1806, AHU, box 17, doc. 84.

65. Letter, António Vás de Araujo, regimental major of Farim, 1783 [day illegible], AHU, box 13, doc. 1.

66. Ibid.

67. Letter, Joze Pedro da Costa, 29 Mar. 1784, AHU, box 14, doc. 1-A.

68. Letter, João Pereira Barreto, interim commander, Cacheu, 28 Apr. 1785, AHU, box 13, doc. 38.

69. Note, Joaquim Jozê Barbosa, 1 Apr. 1791, AHU, box 14, doc. 33.

70. Note [unsigned], c. 1775, AHU, box 25, doc. 22.

71. Letter, Luiz e Pedro e Araujo e Silva, commander, Cacheu, 17 Sept. 1787, AHU, box 14, doc. 5.

72. Letter, Francisco de Borja Garção Hockler, 6 Oct. 1802, AHU, box 17, doc. 43.

73. Note, Domingos da Viega Escorcio, 24 June 1792, AHU, box 14, doc. 41.

74. Carreira, *Os Portuguêses,* 18.

75. Ibid., 21, 29, 30.

76. Barcellos, "Guiné Portugueza," 1908, ANS 2F 12, #132.

77. Carreira, *Os Portuguêses,* 53–54.

78. Ibid., 53–54.

79. Barcellos, "Guiné Portugueza," 1908, ANS 2F 12, #132.

80. Carreira, *Os Portuguêses,* 106.

81. Ibid., 30, 60–61.

82. "Information," Berthet, French consul to Portuguese Guinea, Bissau, 20 Nov. 1940, ANS 2F 12, file 14, #119.

83. Mané, "Contribution à l'histoire du Kaabu," 128.

84. Carreira, *Os Portuguêses,* 52–53.

85. "Memória sobre Bissau," Duque Collaio da Veiga Vidal, chefe do estado maior e secretario, n.d., AHU, box 25, doc. 77.

86. Letter, Lourenço Ant . . . [illegible], state sec. of the navy, 9 Sept. 1815, AHU, box 21, doc. 49.

87. Carreira, *Os Portuguêses,* 100.

88. Christiano José de Senna Barcellos, *Subsídios para a história de Cabo Verde e Guiné: Memória,* vol. 5 (Lisbon: Imprensa Nacional, 1911), 119.

89. Carreira, *Os Portuguêses,* 30.

90. Barcellos, *Subsídios para a história,* vol. 5, 12.

91. Carreira, *Os Portuguêses,* 106.

92. Barcellos, "Guiné Portugueza," 1908, ANS 2F 12.

93. Pélissier, *Naissance,* 103, n. 107.

94. Barcellos, "Guiné Portugueza," 1908, ANS 2F 12.

95. Pélissier, *Naissance,* 47.

96. Ibid., 78.

97. Bowman, *Ominous Transition,* 124–32, and Joye Bowman, "'Legitimate Commerce' and Peanut Production in Portuguese Guinea," *Journal of African History* 28, no. 1 (1987): 87–106.

98. Pélissier, *Naissance,* 120.

99. Letter, unidentified official, Portuguese Guinea, 12 Dec. 1879, AHU, 2d sec., file 387, doc. 100. This issue is further discussed in chapter 3.

100. Report, Joaquim L. Thiago, 15 Jan. 1885, Bolama, AHU, file 387, [no doc. no.].

101. Letter, Fernando Aug.o Lis de Sant'Anna, governor of Guinea, to minister and sec. of state, naval and overseas affairs, Bolama, 7 Nov. 1899, AHU, 2d sec., [no doc. no.].

102. António Carreira, interview by author, Lisbon, 12 Feb. 1984.

103. Letter, Hostains, French vice-consul, Portuguese Guinea, to minister of foreign affairs, Paris, 26 June 1919, ANS 2F 14, #1.

104. This is discussed in chapter 3.

105. Letter, Honório Barreto, governor, Portuguese Guinea, to French commander at Gorée, 25 Mar. 1856, ANS 20, no. 3, subset 2F 3, #20.

106. Pélissier, *Naissance,* 203.

107. Ibid., 237–38.

108. Letter, Jozé e António Pinto, Cacheu, 28 May 1809, AHU, box 19, doc. 65; "O Prezídio de Cacheu foi atacado," letter, António Tavares da Veiga Santos, mayor, Plaza of Cacheu, 6 Aug. 1830, Cacheu, to sec. of state of affairs of the navy and foreign dominions, AHU, box 24, doc. 18.

109. Ibid.; letter from state sec. of the navy, 9 Sept. 1815, AHU, box 21, doc. 49.

110. Carreira, *Os Portuguêses,* 77–79.

111. Pélissier, *Naissance,* 110.

112. Letter, João Pereira Barretto, regimental major at Cacheu, 18 Nov. 1814, AHU, box 21, doc. 42.

113. Luís António de Carvalho Viegas, *Guiné Portuguesa* (Lisbon: Freitas Mega, 1936), 1:68; Barcellos, *Subsídios para a história,* 110, 124.

114. Letter, French officer Limamuis, to his commander, 17 Sept. 1861, ANS no. 2, F3, subset 2F, #66/4.

115. Letter, Carlos Aug.o Franco, gov.-genl., Cape Verde, 8 Aug. 1862, AHU, box 24, doc. 328.

116. Letters, French consul [to Bissãu], 25 June 1866, ANS subset 2F/2F3, #51.

117. Letter [unsigned], 7 Feb. 1871, ANS subset 2F3, #65. See also Pélissier, *Naissance,* 110, incl. n. 136.

118. Pélissier, *Naissance,* 111.

119. Barcellos, *Subsídios para a história,* 287.

120. Ibid., 163–64.

121. Ibid., 164–65.

122. Note, Domingos da Viega Escorçio, commander of the Plaza of Bissau, 24 June 1792, Bissau, AHU, box 14, doc. 34.

123. Letter, José da Silva Maldonado de Eça, to Luiz Pinto de Souza, Bissau, 9 May 1795, AHU, box 15, doc. 20; letter, Jozé Joaquim de Souza Trovão, Cacheu, 24 Apr. 1802, AHU, box 16, doc. 49; report, navy sergeant da Silveira, 25 Aug. 1802.

124. Report, navy sergeant da Silveira, 25 Aug. 1802.

125. Letter, Jozé de Araujo Gomes, infantry captain of the Praza of S. Jozé de Bissão, 20 Apr. 1804, Bissau, AHU, box 17, doc. 48.

126. Letter, Thomas da Costa Ribeiro, to Antonio Xavier [a Lisbon businessman], Bissau, 5 Apr. 1805, AHU, box 18, doc. 13.

127. Letter, Manoel Pinto de Gouvêa, Bissau, 24 Jan. 1809, AHU, box 19, doc. 70; letter, Jozé Antonio Pinto, Bissau, 20 Mar. 1809, AHU, box 19, doc. 76.

128. See chapter 1.

129. "Memória sobre Bissau," Duque Collaio da Veiga Vidal, chefe do estado maior e secretario, n.d., AHU, box 25, doc. 77.

130. Ibid.

131. Pélissier, *Naissance,* 54. Through the nineteenth century, the Portuguese increasingly came to rely on Cape Verdeans with educational or military experience to assume government positions in Guinea-Bissau. Until 1879 Cape Verde and Guinea were part of the same Portuguese administrative jurisdiction.

132. Carreira, *Os Portuguêses,* 68.

133. Crowley, "Contracts," 113.

134. Pélissier, *Naissance,* 68.

135. Ibid.

136. Crowley, "Contracts," 115.

137. Pélissier, *Naissance,* 116.

138. Ibid.; Handem, "Nature," 325.

139. Telephone analogy from a Balanta interviewed by Hawthorne. See "Interior Past," 203.

140. Pélissier, *Naissance,* 159; Handem, "Nature," 325.

141. Handem, "Nature," 325–26.

142. Letter, Honório Barreto, governor, Portuguese Guinea, to the French commander at Gorée, 25 Mar. 1856, ANS 20, no.3, 2F2, subset 2F, #20.

143. Barcellos, "Guiné Portugueza."

144. Pélissier, *Naissance,* 125.

145. "Report to the Delegates of the Commission against Direct Taxation," Durème, 6 Feb. 1885, Bolama, AHU, file 387, [no doc. no.].

146. Pélissier, *Naissance,* 124.

147. Report, Fernando Aug.o Lis de Sant'Anna, governor of Guinea, to sec.-genl., provincial government, 11 Dec. 1899, AHU, [no doc. no.].

148. Barcellos, *Subsídios para a história,* 295–300; Mendy, *Colonialismo Português,* 144–45.

149. Pélissier, *Naissance,* 125–26.

150. Ibid., 119.

151. See the introduction.

Chapter Three

1. See chapter 1.

2. Lopes, *Kaabunké,* 197–218.

3. Bowman, *Ominous Transition.*

4. The Fulbe-djiábê were known as Fula joon or Fula djon by the Mandinka, but as Matchudô (slaves) by the Fula-Forro and Fulbe-Futa ruling classes. The Fulbe-Futa originated in Futa-Jallon (in what later became French Guinea), although some Fulbe from Quebo and Boé were also considered Fulbe-Futa. The Fulbe-Toro consisted of another separate group, smaller in number (within Guinea-Bissau), that had migrated from the Toro Fulbe kingdom in Senegal periodically over the eighteenth and nineteenth centuries.

5. The Fulbe-Toro and Fulbe-Futa were generally associated with Fulbe-ribê.

6. This figure is provided by René Pélissier; see *Naissance,* 20.

7. Carreira, *Os Portugueses.*

8. Bowman, *Ominous Transition,* 107–14.

9. Pélissier, *Naissance,* 49–50 nn. 91 and 92.

10. Chapter 1 gives an overview of Gabu's political system.

11. Cissoko, "De l'organisation politique," 205.

12. Mané, "Contribution à l'histoire du Kaabu," 133–34; Cissoko, "Introduction à l'histoire," 90–91.

13. Lopes, *Kaabunké,* 189; idem, "Relações de poder numa sociedade Malinké," 23.

14. Bowman, *Ominous Transition,* 34–40.

15. Lopes, *Kaabunké,* 23.

16. Mané, "Contribution à l'histoire du Kaabu," 134; Bowman, *Ominous Transition,* 40.

17. Cissoko, "Introduction à l'histoire," 90; Bowman, *Ominous Transition,* 40.

18. Mané, "Contribution à l'histoire du Kaabu," 133.

19. Ibid., 134; Lopes, *Kaabunké,* 205.

20. Mané, "Contribution à l'histoire du Kaabu," 135; Lopes, *Kaabunké,* 199–204.

21. Bowman, *Ominous Transition,* 41, 49.

22. Nouha Cissé, "La fin du Kaabu et les débuts du royaume du Fuladu" (thesis, University of Dakar, 1977–78), 25.

23. Mané, "Contribution à l'histoire du Kaabu," 137; Bowman, "Conflict, Interaction, Change," 88.

24. Thierno Diallo, "Le Gaabu et le Fuuta-Jalon," *Ethiopiques* 28 (Oct. 1981): 194.

25. Ibid., 186; Cissé, "La fin du Kaabu," 56.

26. Cissé, "La fin du Kaabu," 26. The discussion in the following paragraphs of the growing conflict between Futa Jallon and Gabu would be enhanced by reference to Bowman's particularly nuanced treatment (*Ominous Transition,* 54–58).

27. Jorge Vellez Caroço, *Monjur. O Gabu e a sua história* (Bissau: Centro de Estudos da Guiné Portuguesa, 1948), 117.

28. Ibid.; Pélissier, *Naissance,* 51 n. 96.

29. Caroço, *Monjur,* 118; Mané, "Contribution à l'histoire du Kaabu," 141.

30. Caroço, *Monjur,* 118; Mané, "Contribution à l'histoire du Kaabu," 142; Cissé, "La fin du Kaabu," 59.

31. Cissé, "La fin du Kaabu," 28.

32. Mané, "Contribution à l'histoire du Kaabu," 142.

33. Bowman, "Conflict, Interaction, Change," 95; Pélissier, *Naissance,* 51 n. 96; Caroço, *Monjur,* 121.

34. Mané, "Contribution à l'histoire du Kaabu," 142–43.

35. Ibid., 144. He eventually arrived at Farim.

36. Pélissier, *Naissance,* 51 n. 96.

37. Mané, "Contribution à l'histoire du Kaabu," 142; Cissoko, "Introduction à l'histoire," 91; Cissé, "La fin du Kaabu," 61.

38. Bowman, *Ominous Transition,* 56–57; Lopes, *Kaabunké,* 214.

39. Mané, "Contribution à l'histoire du Kaabu," 144–45; Pélissier, *Naissance,* 51 n. 96.

40. Carreira, *Os Portugêses,* 83 n. 1.

41. Pélissier, *Naissance,* 51 n. 96.

42. Bowman, *Ominous Transition,* 104–5.

43. Bowman, "Conflict, Interaction, Change," 193. Fuladu was located mostly within the boundaries of today's Guinea-Bissau.

44. Bowman, *Ominous Transition,* 105; Carreira, *Os Portugêses,* 82.

45. Fuladu also reached into Casamance.

46. Bowman, *Ominous Transition,* 74–75, 103, 105; Carreira, *Os Portugêses,* 81, 83.

47. Bowman, *Ominous Transition,* 105, 132; Carreira, *Os Portugêses,* 81–82.

48. Cissé, "La fin du Kaabu," 72–73.

49. Bowman, "Conflict, Interaction, Change," 203.

50. Ibid., 203–4; Bowman, *Ominous Transition,* 55.

51. Bowman, "Conflict, Interaction, Change," 204, 205.

52. Mané, "Contribution à l'histoire du Kaabu," 147.

53. Cissé, "La fin du Kaabu," 78–79; Bowman, *Ominous Transition,* 74.

54. Cissé, "La fin du Kaabu," 79.

55. Bowman, *Ominous Transition,* 105; Carreira, *Os Portugêses,* 84.

56. Mané, "Introduction à l'histoire du Kaabu," 145.

57. Ibid., 148; Bowman, "Conflict, Interaction, Change," 114.

58. Mané, "Introduction à l'histoire du Kaabu," 148.

59. Carreira, *Os Portuguêses,* 85.

60. Mané, "Introduction à l'histoire du Kaabu," 148.

61. Pélissier, *Naissance,* 159 n. 100, 174.

62. Bowman, *Ominous Transition,* 78.

63. Ibid., 102–3; Carreira, *Os Portuguêses,* 83.

64. "Relatório de [report by] Joaquim Pedro Vieira Judice Biker," Lisbon, 12 Oct. 1903, AHU, doc. 260. See also Mota, "Les relations," 161.

65. Bowman, "Conflict, Interaction, Change," 144.

66. Bowman, *Ominous Transition,* 87–88; Pélissier, *Naissance,* 217.

67. Bowman, *Ominous Transition,* 89.

68. Ibid., 108–9, 124.

69. Carreira, *Os Portuguêses,* 86. For further discussion of the rise and decline of groundnut farming along the Rio Grande, see Bowman, "'Legitimate Commerce,'" 87–106.

70. Letter signed by Julio Antonio Pereira and twenty-six other "traders and proprietors," Bolama, 12 Feb. 1885, AHU, file 387, doc. 1282/210.

71. Ibid. This letter describes repeated appeals made in the 1882–85 period.

72. Barcellos, "Guiné Portuguesa," 1908, ANS 2F 12, #132. The date of separation was 18 Mar. 1879.

73. "Declaration to the Commission," Bolama, 13 Jan. 1885, AHU, file 387, [unsigned; no doc. no.].

74. Letter, 4 May 1883, AHU, file 387, doc. 100.

75. Carriera, *Os Portuguêses,* 84.

76. Bowman, "Conflict, Interaction, Change," 172.

77. "Declaration to the Commission," 13 Jan. 1885.

78. Pélissier, *Naissance,* 142–44.

79. Bowman, *Ominous Transition,* 131; Pélissier, *Naissance,* 146.

80. Bowman, "Conflict, Interaction, Change," 177.

81. Pélissier, *Naissance,* 147.

82. Carreira, *Os Portguêses,* 85.

83. Ibid., and see Pélissier, *Naissance,* 148 n. 56, for his remarks on his differing interpretation with Carreira; for the text of the actual Fulbe-Portuguese accord, see Carreira, *Os Portguêses,* 173–75.

84. Carreira, *Os Portuguêses,* 85.

85. Pélissier, *Naissance,* 149, incl. n. 60.

86. Ibid., 151.

87. These 1882 events are indicated in "Report to the Delegates of the Commission against Direct Taxes," Durème, 6 Feb. 1885, Bolama, AHU, file 387, [no doc. no.].

88. Bowman, *Ominous Transition,* 108.

89. Bowman, "Conflict, Interaction, Change," 176.

90. Letter [unsigned], 4 May 1883, AHU, file 387, doc. 100.

91. Mendy, *Colonialismo Português,* 163–64; Bowman, "Conflict, Interaction, Change," 225.

92. Bowman, *Ominous Transition,* 81–82; Pélissier, *Naissance,* 159, 169; Mendy, *Colonialismo Português,* 164.

93. Letter, Portuguese governor, Bolama, 29 Nov. 1883, AHU, 2d sec., file 387, doc. 22.

94. A. H. de Oliveira Marques, *História de Portugal* (Lisbon: Palas Editores, 1976), 177; Mendy, *Colonialismo Português,* 156.

95. Pélissier, *Naissance,* 128.

96. Barcellos, "Guiné Portuguesa," 1908, ANS 2F 12, #132.

97. Letter, Julio António Pereira and twenty-six others, Bolama, 12 Feb. 1885, AHU, file 387, doc. 1282/210.

98. Pélissier, *Naissance,* 177.

99. Bowman, *Ominous Transition,* 84.

100. Pélissier, *Naissance,* 178; Mendy, *Colonialismo Português,* 174–75.

101. Bowman, *Ominous Transition,* 84–85.

102. Report, Biker, AHU, box 12, doc. 167, no. 460.

103. Bowman, *Ominous Transitions,* 85, 88; Pélissier, *Naissance,* 195, 214.

104. Pélissier, *Naissance,* 197.

105. Pélissier, *Naissance,* 195, 213–14; Bowman, *Ominous Transition,* 88.

106. Pélissier, *Naissance,* 214–15, 219.

107. Bowman, *Ominous Transition,* 88. See Bowman, ibid., 89–90, for details on French involvement in these wars.

108. Pélissier, *Naissance,* 217–19.

109. Bowman, *Ominous Transition,* 89–94.

110. Molo and his followers later peacefully became British subjects. Molo died in the Gambia in 1931.

111. Carreira, *Os Portugêses,* 87–88.

112. Bowman, *Ominous Transition,* 115.

113. Report, Biker, Lisbon, 12 Oct. 1903, AHU, doc. 260.

114. Carreira, *Os Portugêses,* 90; Pélissier, *Naissance,* 283.

115. Letter, Treillard, to gov.-genl., FWA, 20 Mar. 1908, Dakar, ANS 2F 12, #37.

116. Bowman, "Conflict, Interaction, Change," 184.

117. Carreira, *Os Portugêses,* 91.

118. Bowman, *Ominous Transition,* 167.

119. Pélissier, *Naissance,* 195, incl. n. 257.

120. Robert S. Smith, *Warfare and Diplomacy in Pre-Colonial West Africa* (London: Methuen, 1976), 47.

121. Bowman, *Ominous Transition,* 107. Bowman also emphasizes the impact of the interference of the Europeans.

122. Ibid., 133, 143.

Chapter Four

1. Marques, *História de Portugal,* 177; Mendy, *Colonialismo Português,* 188–211. Animist Biaffada groups may be contrasted with Islamized Biaffada, who were increasingly allied with the procolonialist Fulbe.

2. Carreira, *Os Portugêses,* 107.

3. See chapter 2.

4. Carreira, *Os Portuguêses,* 91.

5. Pélissier, *Naissance,* 263.

6. These recently arrived Balanta had emigrated from Geba and Mansoa areas during the nineteenth century in search of rice-farming land; Hawthorne, "Interior Past," 256, 261–62.

7. Report, Biker, Lisbon, 12 Oct. 1903, AHU, doc. 260. For further discussion of the Soninké, see Bowman, *Ominous Transition,* 62 n. 12; regarding their early interethnic origin, see Giesing, "Fari Sangul," 247–50.

8. Handem, "Nature," 13.

9. Report, Biker, 12 Oct. 1903, AHU, doc. 260.

10. Pélissier, *Naissance,* 235; Mendy, *Colonialismo Português,* 194.

11. Report, Biker, 12 Oct. 1903, AHU, doc. 260.

12. Pélissier, *Naissance,* 237. Islamic Mandinka were sometimes enemies of the non-Islamic Soninké.

13. "Documents Regarding Occurrences in Farim and Oio," Moura Cabral, interim governor, Guinea, 25 Sept. 1897, AHU, doc. 247.

14. Pélissier, *Naissance,* 238.

15. Handem, "Nature," 34.

16. Cabral, "Farim and Oio," 25 Sept. 1897, AHU, doc. 247.

17. Letter, governor of Guinea, to minister and sec. of state, naval and overseas affairs, Bolama, 25 Mar. 1897, AHU, doc. 77; Cabral, "Farim and Oio," AHU, doc. 247.

18. Letter, governor of Guinea, 25 Mar. 1897, AHU, doc. 77.

19. Letter, Biker, Bolama, 4 Feb. 1902, AHU, [no doc. no.].

20. Pélissier, *Naissance,* 239.

21. Hawthorne, "Interior Past," 212, 264.

22. Pélissier, *Naissance,* 239.

23. Ibid., 202, 239.

24. Letter, Bolama, 27 Apr. 1897, AHU, doc. 111. Also, report, Biker, Lisbon, 12 Oct. 1903, AHU, doc. 260.

25. Report, Biker, 12 Oct. 1903, AHU, doc. 260.

26. Ibid.

27. Ibid.

28. Report, Alfredo Cardoso de Soveral Martins, governor of Guinea, to minister and sec. of state, overseas and naval affairs, Bolama, 8 Sept. 1903, AHU, doc. 261.

29. Pélissier, *Naissance,* 263–64.

30. Ibid., 264.

31. Ibid.

32. Barreto, *História da Guiné,* 348–49.

33. Ibid. This indigenous trade with Senegal was due to the higher prices obtained for agricultural products in the Casamance region; see chapter 8.

34. "Note to the Lieutenant Governor of Senegal at Saint-Louis," n.d. [c. 1908], Brocard, ANS 2F 7, #165.

35. Pélissier, *Naissance,* 265–66.

36. Unsigned cable, French colonial official, Paris, 11 Oct. 1907, ANS 2F 12, #31.

37. Note, Brocard, Bissau, 28 June 1908, ANS 2F 13, #90.

38. Ibid.

39. "Note to the Lieutenant Governor of Senegal," Brocard, ANS 2F 7, #165.

40. Ibid.

41. Letter, Guyon, office head, Casamance, to lieut. gov., Senegal, Sedhiou, 28 Nov. 1907, ANS 2F 12, #24.

42. Note, Dessaille, government of French Guinea, to gov.-genl., FWA, 17 Oct. 1907, Conakry, ANS 2F 12, #8.

43. Telegram, lieut. gov., Senegal, to gov.-genl., FWA, 20 Nov. 1907, Dakar, ANS 2F 12, #18.

44. Telegram, administrator of Kadé, to French Guinea, 29 Nov. 1907, ANS 2F 12, #19.

45. "Note to the Lieutenant Governor of Senegal," Brocard, ANS 2F 7, #165.

46. Ibid.

47. Note [unsigned], Bolama, 2 Dec. 1907, AHU, doc. 136.

48. Pélissier, *Naissance,* 268 n. 269.

49. Note [unsigned], Bolama, 2 Dec. 1907, AHU, doc. 136.

50. Letter, Robert Arnanes, based on information received from M. Merliné, to gov.-genl., FWA, 30 Dec. 1907, Dakar, ANS 2F 12, #23.

51. Mendy, *Colonialismo Português,* 201.

52. Letter, Hostains, French vice-consul, Portuguese Guinea, 26 June 1919, ANS 2F 14, #1; letter, Arnanes, to gov.-genl., FWA, 30 Dec. 1907, Dakar, ANS 2F 12, #23.

53. Letter, Poulet, Conakry, 6 Jan. 1908, ANS 2F 12, #26.

54. Pélissier, *Naissance,* 269.

55. Letter, Hostains, 26 June 1919, ANS 2F 14, #1.

56. In the official bulletin, no. 7, 22 Feb. 1908, para. 39, Governor João Aug.o d'Oliveira Muzanty.

57. Pélissier, *Naissance,* 269–70.

58. Handem, "Nature," 34–35.

59. Ibid., 34–35.

60. Letter, Treillard, to gov.-genl., FWA, 20 Mar. 1908, Dakar, ANS 2F 12, #37.

61. Pélissier, *Naissance,* 270.

62. Telegram, Poulet, to governor, FWA, 28 Mar. 1908, Conakry, ANS 2F 12, #35.

63. Letter, Treillard, 20 Mar. 1908, Dakar, ANS 2F 12, #37.

64. These figures are from "Note for the Lieutenant Governor of Senegal in Saint-Louis," Brocard, ANS 2F 7, #165.

65. Ibid. Injai is more fully discussed in chapter 5.

66. Pélissier, *Naissance,* 273.

67. Correspondence, governor of Guinea, to minister of colonies, Bolama, 3 July 1913, AHU, 2d sec., [no doc. no.]; relatório [report], Abdul Injai, Praia, National Press of Cape Verde, 1920, ANS 2F 14, #9.

68. "Note for the Lieutenant Governor," Brocard, 1908, ANS 2F 7, #165. This garrison is referred to in French as Garankey-Kounda.

69. Pélissier, *Naissance,* 273.

70. Ibid.

71. "La Révolte en Guinée," in *Século* [Portuguese newspaper], 30 May 1908, ANS

2F 12, #84; "Summary Report of Administrator Brocard: Situation in Portuguese Guinea until 26 May 1908," ANS 2F 12, #40.

72. Report, Biker, 12 Oct. 1903, AHU, doc. 260.

73. Summary report, Brocard, ANS 2F 12, #40.

74. "La Révolte en Guinée." Bissau is further discussed below.

75. Summary report, Brocard, ANS 2F 12, #40.

76. Crowley, "Contracts," 140.

77. Summary report, Brocard, ANS 2F 12, #40.

78. "Coluna d'operações na Guiné — 1908," n.d. [June 1908?], AHU, Gerais.

79. Letter, division head [of the military], Bissau, 26 Sept. 1908, AHU, Gerais.

80. Letter, Ponty, to director of political and administrative affairs/Africa desk [Paris], Dakar, Jan. 1909, ANS 2F 13, #10.

81. "La Révolte en Guinée."

82. Note, commander of the *Cassard,* to gov.-genl., FWA, Dakar, 10 June 1908, ANS 2F 12, #51; "Notice on the Situation of the French in Portuguese Guinea, Political and Commercial," [unsigned], Bissau, 27 June 1908, ANS 2F 12, #82.

83. "Notice on the Situation of the French."

84. Telegram, Falcão de Castro Nazareth, infantry captain, Bolama, 14 Mar. 1910, AHU, [no doc. no.].

85. Letter, [unsigned], from government HQ in Bolama to minister and sec. of state for foreign and naval affairs, Bolama, 16 Aug. 1908, AHU, 2d sec., [no doc. no.].

86. "Note from the Administrator Paul Brocard regarding the Events of Bissau between the First and the Fifteenth of July 1908," 24 July 1908, ANS 2F, #112, 9.

87. Many grumetes were of Papel extraction; they had gone to live within Bissau's walls because they had been integrated into the Bissauan economy as low-wage workers. When combat broke out, they often returned to their villages of origin to fight alongside the Papel attackers.

88. Pélissier, *Naissance,* 191, 200.

89. Ibid., 200–203; Mendy, *Colonialismo Português,* 191.

90. Ibid., 221.

91. Handem, "Nature," 326.

92. Pélissier, *Naissance,* 199 n. 267, 223–25.

93. Note, Brocard, 24 July 1908, Dakar, ANS 2F 12, #112, 9.

94. Report, Martins, governor of Guinea, to minister and sec. of state, 8 Sept. 1903, AHU, doc. 261.

95. Injai report, ANS 2F 14, #9.

96. Note, Robert Armanes, French official, to head, Office of FWA, 21 Jan. 1908, Dakar, ANS 2F 12, #34.

97. "Note to the Lieutenant Governor of Senegal," 1908, Brocard, ANS 2F, #165. This was also the case regarding Mandinka auxiliaries who returned to their villages after a campaign.

98. Letters: Robert Armanes to gov.-genl., FWA, 30 Dec. 1907, Dakar, ANS 2F 12, #23; and Armanes to Office of FWA, 21 Jan. 1908, ANS 2F 12, #34.

99. Information received from Chytel [a Frenchman], in telegram from Poulet, French official, Conakry, 6 Jan. 1908, ANS 2F 12, #26.

100. Note, Brocard, 24 July 1908, Dakar, ANS 2F 12, #112.

101. Summary report, Brocard, ANS 2F 12, #40.

102. Note, Brocard, Bissau, 1 July 1908, ANS 2F 12, #94.

103. "Note for the Lieutenant Governor," Brocard, ANS 2F 7, #165.

104. Pélissier, *Naissance,* 275.

105. Brocard summary report, ANS 2F 12, #40.

106. Letter, [military] division head, Bissau, 26 Sept. 1908, AHU, Gerais.

107. Note, Brocard, Bissau, 1 July 1908, ANS 2F 12, #94.

108. Note, Ponty, reporting information told to him by Brocard, 26 May 1908, Dakar, ANS 2F 12, #166.

109. Pélissier, *Naissance,* 277.

110. Note, Brocard, ANS 2F 7, #165. A key cause of malaria (and other illnesses) spreading in May was the typically heavy rainfall of April. The April rains result in the proliferation of mosquitoes and other disease-carrying insects.

111. "Portaria 121, published in the Official Journal of Portuguese Guinea, no. 19 du 16 Mai 1908," João Aug.o d'Oliveira Muzanty, governor of Guinea, Bolama, ANS 2F 12, #88.

112. Note, Brocard, 1908, ANS 2F 7, #165.

113. Ibid.

114. Summary report, Brocard, ANS 2F 12, #40; note, Ponty to minister of colonies, Paris, 26 May 1908, Dakar, ANS 2F 12, #166.

115. "La Révolte en Guinée," in *Século* [Portuguese newspaper], no. 9499, 31 May 1908, ANS 2F 12, #85.

116. Letter, Séguy, to French minister in Lisbon, 30 May 1908, Bissau, ANS 2F 12, #42.

117. Letter, Boyer, frigate captain, commander of the *Cassard,* to gov.-genl., FWA, Bissau, 30 June 1908, ANS 2F 12, #62.

118. Note, Admiral Berryer, commander, French naval forces, Morocco, to gov.-genl., FWA, 31 July 1908, ANS 2F 12, #120.

119. Note, commander of the *Cassard,* to gov.-genl., 13 June 1908, Conakry, ANS 2F 12, #53.

120. Note, commander of the *Cassard,* to gov.-genl., 26 June 1908, ANS 2F 12, #59.

121. Letter, Boyer, 30 June 1908, ANS 2F 12, #62.

122. Telegram, Peuvergne, high administrator of the Casamance, to gov.-genl., FWA, 18 July 1908, Saint-Louis, ANS 2F 12, #74. This official consequently sent an emissary to speak to the Papel immigrant groundnut harvesters in Senegal to emphasize that the French marines had no intention of becoming militarily involved in conflicts occuring in Portuguese Guinea.

123. Letter, Boyer, 30 June 1908, ANS 2F 12, #62.

124. Note, Brocard, Bissau, 1 July 1908, ANS 2F 12, #94.

125. Ibid.

126. Letter, Boyer, 30 June 1908, ANS 2F 12, #60; note, Brocard, Bissau, 1 July 1908, ANS 2F 12 #94.

127. Note, Brocard, 1 July 1908, ANS 2F 12, #94.

128. Ibid.

129. Note, Brocard, 24 July 1908, ANS 2F 12, #112.

130. Ibid.

131. Ibid.

132. Ibid.

133. Ibid; note, Durac, agent of the French West Africa Company in Portuguese Guinea, to the government, FWA, 25 July 1908, ANS 2F 7, #178.

134. Note, Brocard, 24 July 1908, ANS 2F 12, #112.

135. Pélissier, *Naissance,* 278–79, incl. n. 5.

136. Letter, Liotard, FWA official, to office of political and administrative affairs, African suboffice, Dakar, 26 Sept. 1908, ANS 2F 7, #183.

137. Pélissier, *Naissance,* 280.

138. Note, B. Vasrelle, minister of colonies, to gov.-genl., FWA, Paris, 4 Dec. 1908, ANS 2F 12, #135.

139. Letter, Ponty, Jan. 1909, to director, Africa desk, ANS 2F 13, #10.

140. Pélissier, *Naissance,* 282.

141. Report, Biker, 12 Oct. 1903, AHU, doc. 260.

142. They did so by engaging in widespread illegal trading in modern guns that was then taking place in West Africa.

143. Smith, *Warfare and Diplomacy,* 112. For other cases of West African resistance, see also Crowder, *West African Resistance.*

144. Letter, Governor Pimental, to minister and sec. of state for overseas trade, Bolama, 20 Mar. 1910, AHU, [no doc. no.].

145. "Information concerning Portuguese Guinea," Liotard to minister of colonies [Paris], Dakar, 28 Nov. 1909, ANS 2F 13, #2697.

146. Bowman, *Ominous Transition,* 158 n. 13.

147. Pélissier, *Naissance,* 400.

Chapter Five

1. Pélissier, *Naissance,* 299.

2. This concept of applying a state-terror analysis to specific periods of colonial Portuguese Guinea was initially articulated in Joshua B. Forrest, "The Terrorist Colonial Origins of Portuguese Guinea's Soft State," paper presented at the fortieth annual conference, African Studies Association, Columbus, Ohio, 13–16 Nov. 1997.

3. Ibid., 8–10; Bowman, *Ominous Transition,* 145; Hawthorne, "Interior Past," 271; Mendy, *Colonialismo Português,* 221.

4. Pélissier, *Naissance,* 305–6.

5. Ibid., 309 n. 78.

6. The five-century reference is to include the contemporary period.

7. See chapter 3 for description of the gradual incorporation of Fulbe chiefs into the colonial camp.

8. Mendy, *Colonialismo Português,* 221; Pélissier, *Naissance,* 309.

9. Pélissier, *Naissance,* 308.

10. Letter, M. Merliné, French general consul, to minister of colonies [of France], Dakar, 16 Oct. 1919, ANS 2F 14, #11; Injai report, 1920, ANS 2F 14, #9.

11. For details, see Joye L. Bowman, "Abdul Injai: Ally and Enemy of the Portuguese in Guinea-Bissau, 1895–1919," *Journal of African History* 27, no. 3 (1986): 463–79, and Injai report, ANS 2F 14, #9.

12. Letter, Merliné, 16 Oct. 1919; letter, Hostains, French vice-consul, Portuguese Guinea, to the French consul in Lisbon, 22 Feb. 1921, Bissau, ANS 2F 14, #5; Injai report, ANS 2F 14, #9.

13. Pélissier, *Naissance,* 311.

14. Hawthorne, "Interior Past," 292–93.

15. Letter, José Manuel d'Oliveira e Castro, extraordinary inspector, to director-general, colonial accounts, Bolama, 24 Nov. 1914, AHU, [no doc. no.]; also, report of gov.-genl., FWA, Conakry, 9 Oct. 1916, ANS 2F 11.

16. Pélissier, *Naissance,* 307.

17. Ibid., 308.

18. Bowman, *Ominous Transition,* 147.

19. Pélissier, *Naissance,* 309–10, 322.

20. Ibid., 310.

21. Injai report, ANS 2F 14, #9.

22. Pélissier, *Naissance,* 310.

23. Injai report, ANS 2F 14, #9.

24. Pélissier, *Naissance,* 311, 313.

25. Ibid., 311.

26. Ibid.

27. Ibid., 311–12.

28. Mendy, *Colonialismo Português,* 225.

29. Pélissier, *Naissance,* 312–13.

30. Ibid., 323. Pélissier insightfully notes that Morés was then, as it would be during the 1960s–70s war of national liberation, a center of Oinka resistance.

31. Injai report, ANS 2F 14, #9.

32. Pélissier, *Naissance,* 314.

33. Ibid., 315.

34. Injai report, ANS 2F 14, #9. The escudo replaced the milreis upon the advent of Republican rule in Portugal: *Naissance,* 315 n. 99.

35. Pélissier, *Naissance,* 314–15.

36. Mendy, *Colonialismo Português,* 226.

37. Cablegram, Ponty to gov.-genl. of the colonies, Paris, 19 Dec. 1913, ANS 2F 13, #40; letter, Daeschner, French envoy to Lisbon, to Doumergue, minister of foreign affairs [Paris], 24 Jan. 1914, Lisbon, ANS 2F 13, #34; telegram, [unsigned], Bolama, 16 Dec. 1913, AHU, [no doc. no.].

38. Telegram, governor of Guinea, Bolama, 9 Jan. 1914, AHU, [no doc. no.]; Injai report, ANS 2F 14, #9.

39. Letter, Daeschner, 24 Jan. 1914, ANS 2F 13 #34; telegram, governor of Guinea, 9 Jan. 1914, AHU, [no doc. no.].

40. Letter, Daeschner, 24 Jan. 1914, ANS 2F 13, #34.

41. Injai report, ANS 2F 14, #9.

42. Crowley, "Contracts," 151.

43. Ibid., 210 n. 51.

44. Letter, Daeschner, 24 Jan. 1914, ANS 2F 13, #34.

45. Gable, "Modern Manjaco," 16.

46. Mendy, *Colonialismo Português,* 231; Pélissier, *Naissance,* 320.

47. Pélissier, *Naissance,* 320–21; Mendy, *Colonialismo Português,* 231.

48. Pélissier, *Naissance,* 321.

49. Gable, "Modern Manjaco," 1. He was sent to São Tomé.

50. Letter, [unsigned], Lisbon, 12 Nov. 1915, AHU, [no doc. no.].

51. Telegram, Motta, Bolama, 10 Feb. 1914, AHU, [no doc. no.].

52. Telegram, Bolama, 13 Feb. 1914, AHU, [no doc. no.].

53. Letter, C. Maclaud, head administrator, Casamance, to lieut.-gov., Senegal, in Saint-Louis, 27 May 1914, Ziguinchor, ANS 2F 13, #31.

54. Mendy, *Colonialismo Português,* 235.

55. Pélissier, *Naissance,* 322.

56. Ibid.

57. Hawthorne, "Interior Past," 290.

58. Ibid., 273, 286–87, 290–91.

59. Note [unsigned], Lisbon, 12 Nov. 1915, AHU, [no doc. no.].

60. Pélissier, *Naissance,* 323.

61. Bowman, *Ominous Transition,* 148.

62. Mendy, *Colonialismo Português,* 235.

63. Pélissier, *Naissance,* 324.

64. Letter, d'Oliveira e Castro, to director-general, colonial accounts, 24 Nov. 1914, AHU, [no doc. no.].

65. Pélissier, *Naissance,* 236; Mendy, *Colonialismo Português,* 241.

66. In the official bulletin, no. 20, Bissau, 15 May 1915; letter, Governor-general Fournier, FWA, to minister of colonies, 20 June 1915, ANS 2F 13, #67; note, Portuguese official in Bissau [signature illegible, n.d.; early-to-mid 1915], ANS 2F 13.

67. Note, lieut.-gov., French Guinea, to gov.-genl., FWA, Dakar, 10 Oct. 1916, Conakry, ANS 2F 13, #4.

68. Letter, Fournier, 20 June 1915, ANS 2F 13, #67; official bulletin, no. 34, 21 Aug. 1915, Bissau, ANS 2F 13.

69. The official bulletin, no. 20, 15 May 1915, ANS 2F 13.

70. Letter, Fournier, 20 June 1915, ANS 2F 13, #67.

71. Note, Antonetti, lieut.-gov., St. Louis, to gov.-genl., FWA, 27 May 1915, ANS 2F 13, #78.

72. Letter, agent of the FWA Company, to head office, Dakar, 1 June 1915, Bissau, ANS 2F 13, #73.

73. Ibid.; letter, Fournier, 20 June 1915, ANS 2F 13, #67.

74. Letter, Fournier, 20 June 1915, ANS 2F 13, #67.

75. Letter, agent, FWA Company, 1 June 1915, Bissau, ANS 2F 13, #73.

76. Pélissier, *Naissance,* 328–29.

77. Note, Antonetti, 5 Sept. 1915, Saint-Louis, Senegal, ANS 2F 13, #57.

78. Mendy, *Colonialismo Português,* 244–45; Pélissier, *Naissance,* 329, 331 n. 165.

79. Letter, Séguy, adviser for France, to gov.-genl., West Africa, 10 Oct. 1915, Bolama, ANS 2F 13, #54.

80. Letter, Hostains, French vice-consul, Portuguese Guinea, to French consul, Lisbon, 22 Feb. 1921.

81. Note, Antonetti, 5 Sept. 1915, ANS 2F 13, #57.

82. Letter, Hostains, 22 Feb. 1921.

83. Carreira, *Os Portuguêses,* 117, incl. n. 1.

84. Telegram, Motta, Bolama, 14 Apr. 1914, AHU, [no doc. no.].

85. Crowley, "Contracts," 115.

86. Note, Santos Monteiro, Lisbon, 8 Feb. 1915, AHU, [no doc. no.].

87. "Confidential Supplementary Report," high commissioner, Casamance, to lieut. gov., Senegal, 23 May 1917, ANS 2F 14, #66.

88. "Information," Berthet, French official, 15 Apr. 1940, Dakar, ANS 2F 12, file 14, #32.

89. Bowman, "Abdul Injai."

90. Handem, "Nature," 267.

91. Hawthorne, "Interior Past," 284, 299.

92. According to France's high commissioner to Casamance, "Confidential Supplementary Report," 23 May 1917, ANS 2F 14, #66.

93. Bowman, *Ominous Transition,* 148.

94. Inauguration speech delivered by minister of Portuguese colonies at the Congress of the First Centenary of the Discovery of Portuguese Guinea, quoted in letter from the French consul in Bissau to gov.-genl., FWA, Dakar, 18 Sept. 1946, Bissau, ANS 2F 14, file [file holder] 14, #325.

95. Pélissier, *Naissance,* 291.

96. Bowman, "Abdul Injai," 471.

97. Bowman, *Ominous Transition,* 145; Mendy, *Colonialismo Português,* 250–51.

98. Examples include a letter from a Portuguese official to Teixeira Pinto, Lisbon, 28 Feb. 1916, AHU, doc. 357, no. 1382; and letter, Hostains, to French consul, Lisbon, 22 Feb. 1921.

99. This was also the case in Portugal's conquest of the interior of Mozambique and Angola: see Newitt, *Portugal in Africa,* 52.

100. Crowder, introduction to *West African Resistance,* 16.

101. Young, *African Colonial State,* 95.

102. Ibid., 1.

103. Ibid., 99.

104. Crowley, "Contracts," 151.

105. Letter, governor of Guinea to minister of colonies, Lisbon, Bolama, 16 Apr. 1915, AHU, [no doc. no.].

106. Bowman, "Abdul Injai," 472–73; Hawthorne, "Interior Past," 298–99.

107. Note, Dagenes, 22 July 1916, St. Louis, ANS 2F 14, #50.

108. Letter, d'Oliveira e Castro, to director-genl., colonial accounts, 24 Nov. 1914.

109. Bowman, *Ominous Transition,* 151; Pélissier, *Naissance,* 343 n. 228.

110. See chapters 2 and 4.

111. Letter, consul Hostains, to gov.-genl., FWA, Bissau, 28 May 1925, in ANS 2F 7, file 14, #58.

112. Letter, Gustave de Coutouly, French vice-consul, Portuguese Guinea, to French minister of foreign affairs, 19 July 1917, Bissau, ANS 2F 13, #97.

113. Ibid.; letter from Coutouly to minister of foreign affairs, Bissau, 12 June 1917, ANS 2F 14, #63.

114. "Report on the Bijagós campaign in Canhabac" by army major Joaquim Maria da Costa, Bolama, 23 Jan. 1918, AHU, [no doc. no.].

115. Report, Cipriano Pereira, military commander, to chief of staff [of Guinea], Bini headquarters [on Canhabac Island in the Bijagós archipelago], 16 Jan. 1918, AHU, [no doc. no.].

116. Ibid.

117. Letter, Gustave de Coutouly, to French minister of foreign affairs, 8 Nov. 1917, Bissau, ANS 2F 13, #98.

118. Report, Pereira, Bini, Canhabac, 16 Jan. 1918, AHU, [no doc. no.].

119. Letter, interim governor, Guinea, to minister of colonies (Lisbon), Bolama, 28 Jan. 1918, AHU, 2d sec., doc. 44/17.

120. Letter, Brunet, gov.-genl., FWA, to [French] minister of colonies, 24 Sept. 1920, Paris, ANS 2F 14, #6.

121. Pélissier, *Naissance,* 343 n. 228.

122. Bowman, "Abdul Injai," 474.

123. Letter, Hostains, to [French] minister of foreign affairs, Paris, 26 June 1919, Bissau, ANS 2F 14, #1.

124. Ibid.

125. These statistics were recorded and presented by Injai later (in 1920), after he had been captured and imprisoned; letter, Hostains, 22 Feb. 1921, ANS 2F 14, #5.

126. Letter, French consul Merliné, to minister of colonies, Dakar, 16 Oct. 1919, ANS 2F 14, #11.

127. Letter, Hostains, to gov.-genl., FWA in Dakar, 20 Apr. 1919, Bissau, ANS 2F 14, #16.

128. Note, gov.-genl., FWA, to minister of colonies, Dakar, 24 Sept. 1919, ANS 2F 14, #11; letter, Hostains, 22 Feb. 1921, Bissau, ANS 2F 14, #5. Some (a very few) slaves were still sold on clandestine markets in the Guinean interior.

129. Letter, interim gov.-genl., to French minister of colonies, based on information provided by Hostains, Aug. 1919, ANS 2F 14, #49. The political role of these activists was initiated with the Guinean League *(a Liga Guineense)*—created after 1910 and abolished in 1915. See Philip J. Havik, "Mundasson i Kambansa: espaço social e movimentos políticos na Guiné Bissau, 1910–1994," *Revista Internacional de Estudos Africanos,* nos. 18–22 (1995–99), 120–24; Bowman, *Ominous Transition,* 162 n. 55.

130. Note, Benguey, high administrator, to lieut. gov., Senegal, 24 June 1919, Ziguinchor, ANS 2F 14, #21.

131. Pélissier, *Naissance,* 344.

132. Note, Benquey, 8 July 1919, Ziguinchor, ANS 2F 14, #23.

133. Letter, M. Merliné, 16 Oct. 1919, ANS 2F 14, #11; note, Benquey, 8 July 1919, ANS 2F 14, #23; letter, Hostains, 26 June 1919, Bissau, ANS 2F 14, #1.

134. Pélissier, *Naissance,* 345.

135. Letter, Hostains, 26 June 1919, ANS 2F 14, #1.

136. Letter, Hostains, 20 Apr. 1919, Bissau, ANS 2F 14, #16; note, Benguey, 24 June 1919, Ziguinchor, ANS 2F 14, #21.

137. Letter, Hostains, ANS 2F 14, #1.

138. Bowman, *Ominous Transition,* 154; Pélissier, *Naissance,* 346.

139. Note, Hostains, 16 Aug. 1919, Bissau, ANS 2F 14, #39.

140. Letter, Hostains, 22 Feb. 1921, Bissau, ANS 2F 14, #5. According to Injai, 473 of his men were killed. Injai report, ANS 2F 14, #9.

141. Letter, Hostains, 22 Feb. 1921, ANS 2F 14, #5.

142. Letter, Brunet, gov.-genl., FWA, to French minister of colonies, 24 Sept. 1920, Paris, ANS 2F 14, #6. Injai died at Cape Verde in 1922.

143. Bowman, *Ominous Transition,* 156–57.

144. Letter, Abdul Injai, to French consul, 7 Oct. 1919, Bolama, ANS 2F 14, #3.

145. Injai report, ANS 2F 14, #9.

146. Letter, Hostains, 20 Apr. 1919, Bissau, ANS 2F 14, #16. Their names were not given.

147. Pélissier, *Naissance,* 338 n. 194.

148. Report, service of civil affairs, French Guinea, 19 Apr. 1916, Conakry, ANS 2F 11, #20.

149. Sebastião José Barbosa, arrête no. 250, Bolama, 21 Aug. 1916, Bolama, ANS 2F 11.

150. Letter, Gustave de Coutouly, French vice-consul, Portuguese Guinea, to French minister of foreign affairs, 9 May 1917, Bissau, ANS 2F 13, #96.

151. As announced by Guinea interim governor Carlos Ivo de Sá Ferreira in official bulletin no. 18, 10 July 1918, ANS 2F, #49.

152. Report, office of government, Guinea, Bolama, 15 Aug. 1917, AHU, [no doc. no.].

153. Letter, Governor Ferreiras, to minister of colonies, Bolama, 16 Aug. 1917, AHU, doc. 168/255.

154. Letter, Lieut. António Alves Fernandes, Cacheu, 12 July 1917, AHU, [no doc. no.].

155. Note, Benquey, high administrator, to lieut. gov., Senegal, 2 Aug. 1919, Ziguinchor, ANS 2F 14, #42.

156. Letter, Hostains, 22 Feb. 1921, ANS 2F 14, #5. This incident occurred sometime between 1916 and 1918.

CHAPTER SIX

1. Young, *African Colonial State.*

2. See chapter 8.

3. Mendy, *Colonialismo Português,* 66, 390–415.

4. Ranger, "Connexions."

5. Forrest, "Terrorist Colonial Origins," 33. See also Mendy, *Colonialismo Português,* 51, 390–410.

6. See also Peter Mendy, "A conquista militar da Guiné: Da resistência à 'pacificação' do arquilipélago dos Bijagós, 1917–1936," in *Stronoir* 13 (Jan. 1992): 41–52.

7. Pélissier, *Naissance,* 57. The isle of Escravos, formerly said to be part of the Bijagós, is now considered part of mainland Guinea.

8. Chapters 1, 2, and 5.

9. According to Hostains, on the basis of an on-site tour of Canhabac, Aug. 1918, discussed in Hostain's report dated 28 Nov. 1918, cited in Pélissier, *Naissance,* 357 n. 287.

10. Letter, Hostains, French consul, to gov.-genl., FWA, Bissau, 28 May 1925, ANS 2F 7, file 14, #58.

11. According to a piece written by the governor himself: Jorge Frederico Velez Caroço, "Operações a Canhabaque," article in the official bulletin, supp. to no. 9, 30 June 1925.

12. Mendy, *Colonialismo Português,* 263, 359; Pélissier, *Naissance,* 358–59.

13. Letter, Hostains, 28 May 1925, ANS 2F 7, file 14, #58.

14. Ibid.

15. Ibid.

16. Pélissier, *Naissance,* 358–59.

17. Ibid., 359.

18. Letter, Hostains, 28 May 1925, ANS 2F 7, file 14, #58.

19. Pélissier, *Naissance,* 359.

20. Letter, Hostains, 28 May 1925.

21. Mendy, *Colonialismo Português,* 267; Pélissier, *Naissance,* 359.

22. "Information on the Neighboring Foreign Colonies," 1st trimester 1936 and 2d trimester 1936, ANS 2F 11, file 14, #2.

23. Pélissier, *Naissance,* 393.

24. "Neighboring Foreign Colonies," 1st trimester 1936.

25. Letter, Hostains, to gov.-genl., FWA (in Dakar), 17 Jan. 1936, Bissau, ANS 2F 7, #2; also "Neighboring Foreign Colonies," 1st trimester 1936.

26. Pélissier, *Naissance,* 393.

27. Ibid., 393–94.

28. "Neighboring Foreign Colonies," 1st trimester 1936.

29. Ibid.

30. Ibid.

31. Pélissier, *Naissance,* 393.

32. "Neighboring Foreign Colonies," 1st trimester 1936.

33. "Extract" in "Information on Portuguese Guinea," Hostains, 14 Jan. 1936, ANS 2F 7, file 14.

34. Mendy, *Colonialismo Português,* 268.

35. Pélissier, *Naissance,* 394–95.

36. Letter, Hostains, 17 Jan. 1936, Bissau, ANS 2F 7, #2. "Information," Berthet, French administrator, 15 Apr. 1940, Dakar, ANS 2F 12, file 14, #32.

37. Pélissier, *Naissance,* 396.

38. Letter, Hostains, 17 Jan. 1936, Bissau, ANS 2F 7, #2.

39. This statement was translated from the Arab original by a French official: note [unsigned], 6 June 1936, ANS 2F 11, file 11.

40. "Information on Neighboring Foreign Colonies," 4th trimester 1936, ANS 2F 11, file 14.

41. Note, adjunct administrator Jules Surlemont, to administrator, Casamance, 7 July 1936, Ziguinchor, ANS 2F 11, file 14, #106.

42. "Neighboring Foreign Colonies," 4th trimester 1936.

43. Ibid.

44. Ibid., and see Pélissier, *Naissance,* 396 n. 127.

45. "Neighboring Foreign Colonies," 4th trimester 1936.

46. Edouard Tellier, adjunct administrator, Kolda Circle, "State of Information Regarding Portuguese Guinea," 1 Apr. 1936, ANS 2F 14, #4.

47. Pélissier, *Naissance,* 396 n. 127.

48. "Neighboring Foreign Colonies," 4th trimester 1936.

49. Newspaper article titled [in translation from the French] "The Last Rebels of Portuguese Guinea Have Surrendered," 28 May 1937, ANS 2F 11, file 14. The newspaper is not identified.

50. Pélissier, *Naissance,* 396.

51. Viegas, *Guiné Portuguesa,* 1:183.

52. "Annex II: Note on the Bijagós," report, Office of Political Affairs, government of FWA, 1938, ANS 2F 7, file 14.

53. "Information on Portuguese Guinea," police commissariat of Ziguinchor, Senegal, 20 Oct. 1938, ANS 2F 11, file 14, #6750.

54. "Annex II," ANS 2F 7, file 14.

55. "Information on the Neighboring Foreign Colonies: Portuguese Guinea," 1st trimester 1939, director of political and administrative affairs, FWA, 2 June 1939, Dakar, ANS 2F 11, file 14, #285.

56. Note, "Portuguese Guinea: On the Indigenous Tax," French consul, 30 Dec. 1946, ANS 2F 13, file 14.

57. "Military Information on Portuguese Guinea," Edouard Tellier, 3 Aug. 1935, Kolda, Guinea-Conakry, ANS 2F 11, file 14.

58. See chapters 2 and 4.

59. Pélissier, *Naissance,* 354, incl. n. 280.

60. Letter, Morel, high commissioner, Casamance, to governor, Senegal, 11 June 1927, Ziguinchor, ANS 2F 11, file 14, #28C.

61. "Note on Portuguese Guinea," French official, Conakry, 9 Mar. 1927, ANS 2F 11, file 14.

62. "Information on Neighboring Foreign Countries—Portuguese Guinea, 3d Trimester, 1939" [unsigned; probably from governor, French Guinea], to gov.-genl., FWA, Conakry, ANS 2F 11, file 14.

63. Telegram, Martine, governor, French Guinea, to gov.-genl., FWA, 30 Sept. 1939, Conakry, based on information received from French border official at Sansalé, ANS 2F 11, file 14, #480.

64. "Information on Neighboring Foreign Countries—Portuguese Guinea, 3d Trimester, 1939" [governor, French Guinea], ANS 2F 11, file 14.

65. "Information Regarding Portuguese Guinea," weekly bulletin of information transmitted by the annex service of documentation and control of information, French Guinea, 14 Oct. 1939, Conakry, ANS 2F 11, file 14, #494.

66. "Portuguese Guinea—Politics," 29 Dec. 1945, ANS 2F 13, file 14, #2224.

67. Letter, A. Vadier, governor, to gov.-genl., FWA, Conakry, 16 Aug. 1934, ANS 2F 11, file 14, #229.

68. Note, Vadier, to gov.-genl., FWA, 12 June 1934, Conakry, ANS 2F 9, #220/3218.

69. "Information on Neighboring Foreign Countries—Portuguese Guinea, 2d Trimester, 1939," governor, French Guinea, to gov.-genl., FWA, Dakar, 7 Aug. 1939, Conakry, ANS 2F 11, file 14, #401.

70. Ibid.

71. "Information on Neighboring Foreign Countries—Portuguese Guinea, 3d Trimester, 1939" [governor, French Guinea], to gov.-genl., FWA, Conakry, ANS 2F 11, file 14.

72. "Information Obtained Regarding Portuguese Guinea," weekly bulletin of information to French Guinea, ANS 2F 11, file 14, #167.

73. "Report on Neighboring Foreign Colonies—Portuguese Guinea—3d Trimester, 1940," French Guinea, ANS 2F 11, file 14.

74. "Portuguese Guinea," unidentified French official, 12 May 1944, ANS 2F 11, file 14, #596; "Portuguese Guinea," information, French official, 9 June 1944, ANS 2F 11, file 14, #748.

75. Tax collection and forced labor are discussed in chapter 8.

76. Handem, "Nature," 266.

77. Hawthorne, "Interior Past," 21–24, 263, 268–69, 272; idem, "Migrations and Statelessness," 139.

78. Pélissier, *Naissance,* 354, incl. n. 280.

79. Ibid.; Hawthorne, "Migrations and Statelessness," 144–45; idem, "Interior Past," 315.

80. Pélissier, *Naissance,* 354.

81. An additional incentive for migration was to find work: Gable, "Modern Manjaco," 109; Crowley, "Contracts," 168.

82. Gable, "Modern Manjaco," 109.

83. Ibid., 110.

84. Crowley, "Contracts," 168.

85. Ibid. See also W. M. J. van Binsbergen, "Socio-ritual Structures and Modern Migration among the Manjak of Guinea-Bissau," *Anthropologische Verkenningen* 3, no. 2 (1984): 11–43.

86. Mendy, *Colonialismo Português,* 400, 404–5.

87. Pélissier, *Naissance,* 379.

88. Ibid., 380.

89. Letter, Brevie, gov.-genl., FWA, to minister of colonies, Paris, 16 June 1934, Dakar, ANS 2F 9, #646.

90. Letter, French consul to gov.-genl., 4 June 1934, Bissau, ANS 2F 9, #20.

91. Pélissier, *Naissance,* 380.

92. Letter, Brevie, 16 June 1934, Dakar, ANS 2F 9, #646. Approximately twenty-five hundred Guinean Felupe refugees who had fled Portuguese Guinea in November

1933 were counted by a French regional official in Casamance on 15 Mar. 1934 (Pélissier, *Naissance,* 382 n. 71).

93. Letter, French consul, 4 June 1934, Bissau, ANS 2F 9, #20.

94. Pélissier, *Naissance,* 381.

95. Letter, French consul, 4 June 1934, ANS 2F 9, #20.

96. Pélissier, *Naissance,* 386.

97. Ibid.

98. Pélissier interview with Carreira, 2–3 Dec. 1986, in Pélissier, *Naissance,* 385 n. 80.

99. Pélissier, *Naissance,* 387.

100. "Portuguese Guinea—Politics," 29 Dec. 1945, ANS 2F 13, file 14, #2224.

101. Ibid.; "Portuguese Guinea—Extract Transmitted to the Governor of Senegal," French consul, Bissau, 26 Jan. 1946, ANS 2F 13, file 14, #55.

102. "Portuguese Guinea," French consul, Bissau, 1–10 Apr. 1946, ANS 2F 13, file 14, #1177.

103. Pélissier, *Naissance,* 363.

104. See chapter 9.

CHAPTER SEVEN

1. Mamdani, *Citizen and Subject.*

2. This is made especially clear in chapter 9.

3. Oinka refers to the people of the Oio region—Balanta who had migrated or fled to Oio and Soninké who had been ousted from northern Guinea-Bissau by invading Fulbe during the late nineteenth century (see chapter 4).

4. José Manuel de Braga Dias, "Mudança socio-cultural na Guiné Portuguesa" (diss., Universidade Técnica de Lisboa, Instituto Superior de Ciências Sociais e Política Ultramarina, Lisboa, 1974), 85, 86.

5. Ibid., 116, 143.

6. See chapter 8.

7. Hawthorne, "Interior Past," 321–23; Handem, "Nature," 329.

8. Dias, "Mudança socio-cultural," 143.

9. Ibid., 190.

10. Ibid.

11. The Portuguese also found a relatively small number of Balanta willing to serve as collaborative overseers; villagers called them chameleons: Hawthorne, "Interior Past," 303–4, 314.

12. Dias, "Mudança socio-cultural," 104.

13. See chapter 9.

14. Dias, "Mudança socio-cultural," 145.

15. Handem, "Nature," 37.

16. Ibid., 39.

17. Ibid., 57–60, 64; Hawthorne, "Interior Past," 20–21, 26.

18. Handem, "Nature," 57–58, 71, 75, 77, 89–90.

19. Ibid., 30, 59–60, 206–7.

20. Ibid., 64; Hawthorne, "Interior Past," 273.

21. Handem, "Nature," 66.

22. Ibid., 89–90.

23. Ibid., 65.

24. Hawthorne, "Interior Past," 16–20, 225–28, 315.

25. Ibid., 263–64, 325–28; Hawthorne, "Nourishing," 1–24.

26. Forced labor is further discussed in chapter 8.

27. Hawthorne, "Migrations and Statelessness," 142–46; Handem, "Nature," 35.

28. Handem, "Nature," 35.

29. Ibid.; Hawthorne, "Migrations and Statelessness," 146–49.

30. Hawthorne, "Interior Past," 315, 323.

31. Handem, "Nature," 36. See my chapter 9 regarding Balanta participation in the independence struggle.

32. Gable, "Modern Manjaco," 1; Dias, "Mudança socio-cultural," 124, 137; Crowley, "Contracts."

33. Gable, "Modern Manjaco," 16–17.

34. Ibid., 13, 20; Carreira, *Vida social dos Manjacos,* 131, 133.

35. Dias, "Mudança socio-cultural," 124.

36. Ibid., 276.

37. Gable, "Modern Manjaco," 13, 19, 238, 275–76.

38. Ibid., 22, 215, 279, 307.

39. On this point, see also Carreira, *Vida social dos Manjacos,* 100.

40. Gable, "Modern Manjaco," 49, 216, 293–94.

41. Crowley, "Contracts," 161.

42. Dias, "Mudança socio-cultural," 130.

43. The term chiefmaker is suggested in Crowley: "Contracts," 221.

44. Ibid.

45. Gable, "Modern Manjaco," 215, 279.

46. Ibid., 279.

47. Ibid., 2, 18.

48. Crowley, "Contracts," 273, 517.

49. Ibid., 229.

50. Carreira, *Vida social dos Manjacos,* 113–17.

51. Crowley, "Contracts," 571.

52. Ibid., 516–17; Crowley, "Institutions, Identities," 133.

53. Crowley, "Contracts," 215–17.

54. Ibid., 258, 273.

55. Ibid., 256; Crowley, "Institutions, Identities," 131.

56. Crowley, "Contracts," 281; Crowley, "Institutions, Identities," 120–21.

57. Crowley, "Institutions, Identities," 128, 131; Crowley, "Contracts," 272.

58. Crowley, "Contracts," 274.

59. Ibid., 602–4, 611.

60. Ibid., 223–24, 226, 583; Crowley, "Institutions, Identities," 128.

61. Crowley, "Institutions, Identities," 119–20, and idem, "Contracts," 276, 234.

62. António Carreira, "A etnonímia dos povos de entre o Gambia e o estuário do Geba," BCGP 19, no. 75 (1964): 233–75.

63. Dias, "Mudança socio-cultural," 130.

64. Crowley, "Contracts," 224, 279, 264.

65. Teixeira da Mota, Guiné Portuguesa, vol. 1 (Lisbon: Agência Geral do Ultramar, 1954), cited in Crowley, "Contracts," 264.

66. Crowley, "Contracts," 280, 519.

67. Ibid., 580–81.

68. J. M. Silva Cunha, "Missão de estado dos movimentos associativos em Africa: Relatório da campanha de 1958 (Guiné)," Centro de Estudos Políticos e Sociais da Junta de Investigações do Ultramar, Lisbon, 1959, 14–15.

69. "O Islamismo e o seu futuro em Guiné Português," report on speech by Governor Sarmento Rodriguez at Conference on Islam, Lisbon, 24 July 1948, ANS 2F 13, file 14. Also, "Information," French consul to Bissau, 15 Apr. 1940, ANS 2F 11, file 14, #78.

70. "O Islamismo e o seu futuro."

71. Cunha, "Missão de estado," 44. Of a total national populace of 502,000, an estimated 146,500 were Muslim.

72. Eric R. Wolf, Peasant Wars of the Twentieth Century (New York: Harper & Row, 1969).

73. James C. Scott, "Everyday Forms of Peasant Resistance," in Forrest D. Colburn, ed., Everyday Forms of Peasant Resistance (Armonk, N.Y.: M. E. Sharpe, 1989), 27.

74. Ibid.

75. Wyatt MacGaffey, Kongo Political Culture: The Conceptual Challenge of the Particular (Bloomington: Indiana University Press, 2000), 257 n. 13.

76. Ranger, "Connexions," part 1, 437–53 (quotes from 447 and 449).

CHAPTER EIGHT

1. Viegas, Guiné Portuguesa, vol. 1.

2. This chiefly influence waned significantly toward the end of the "settled" colonial period; it was by no means universal in many Fulbe and Mandinka communities. See my chapter 9.

3. Galli and Jones, Guinea-Bissau, 43. For further details on formal sector trading in which peasants sold produce to the state, see Galli and Jones, Guinea-Bissau, 37–43.

4. "Note on Portuguese Guinea," French official in Guinea Conakry, 9 Mar. 1927, ANS 2F 11, file 14; "Information on Neighboring Foreign Colonies," 1st trimester 1935, French official, Dakar, ANS 2F 11, file 14; "General Bulletin from the [French] Colonies — Special Commerce from [Portuguese] Guinea," Oct. 1946, ANS 2F 13, file 14. Also see Viegas, Guiné Portuguesa, 2:412; Galli and Jones, Guinea-Bissau, 40–41; Gervase Clarence-Smith, The Third Portuguese Empire, 1825–1975: A Study in Economic Imperialism (Manchester, U.K.: Manchester University Press, 1985), 153; Laura Bigman, History and Hunger in West Africa (Westport, Conn.: Greenwood Press, 1993), 33.

5. A small number of rice-producing peasants in other regions sold some of their

rice to Portuguese export agencies, but this represented a small proportion of these peasants' rice sales.

6. "Economy—Portuguese Guinea," 3 Mar. 1945, ANS 2F 13, file 14, #295.

7. James Cunningham, "The Colonial Period in Guinea," *Tarikh* 6, no. 4 (1980): 43.

8. Carreira, *Panaria Cabo-Verdiano-Guineense.*

9. This process of rice exchanges within Balanta communities, involving use both for consumption and as a commodity, is described in detail in Jan Douwe van der Ploeg, "Autarky and Technical Change in Guinea-Bissau: On the Importance of Commodisation and Decommoditisation as Interrelated Processes," in *Rural Households in Emerging Societies: Technology and Change in Sub-Saharan Africa,* ed. Margaret Haswell and Diana Hunt (Oxford: Berg, 1991), 99.

10. Ibid.; Hawthorne, "Interior Past," 328; Crowley, "Contracts," 157.

11. Philip J. Havik, "Female Entrepreneurship in a Changing Environment: Gender, Kinship, and Trade in the Guinea Bissau Region," in Carl Risseuw and Kamala Ganesh, eds., *Negotiation and Space: A Gendered Analysis of Changing Kin and Security Networks in South Asia and Sub-Saharan Africa* (New Delhi: Sage Publications, 1998), 207.

12. Carreira, *Vida social dos Manjacos,* 12.

13. Aug.o J. Santos Lima, *Organização económica e social dos Bijagós* (Lisbon: Centro de Estudos da Guiné Portuguesa, 1947), 134–36.

14. Carreira, *Os Portuguêses,* 80–81.

15. Ibid., and see Lopes, *Kaabunké,* 101, 144–48.

16. Lopes, "Relações de poder numa sociedade Malinké," 21.

17. Carreira, *Panaria Cabo-Verdiano-Guineense,* 141.

18. Carreira, *Os Portuguêses,* 82.

19. Pélissier, *Naissance,* 368 n. 9, 369.

20. "Information Collected regarding Portuguese Guinea," 3d trimester 1930, French consul to Portuguese Guinea, Bissau, ANS 2F 11, file 14.

21. Ibid.

22. "Information on Portuguese Guinea," 4th trimester 1931, French official, Conakry, report to the government of FWA, Dec. 1931, ANS 2F 11, file 14.

23. "Information on the Neighboring Foreign Colonies: Portuguese Guinea," 3d trimester 1937, governor, French Guinea, ANS 2F 11, file 14.

24. "Neighboring Foreign Colonies: Portuguese Guinea," 1st trimester 1938, Pierre Vivaud, director, political and administrative affairs, Dakar, 24 June 1938, ANS 2F 11, file 14, #1820.

25. "Documentation Collected regarding Portuguese Guinea," 2d trimester 1939, Bureau of the General Secretariat, report to gov.-genl., FWA, 30 July 1939, Dakar, ANS 2F 11, file 14, #479.

26. "Report on Foreign Colonies—Portuguese Guinea," 3d trimester 1939, Surlemont, 30 Sept. 1939, Ziguinchor, ANS 2F 11, file 14, #3738.

27. "Neighboring Foreign Countries—Portuguese Guinea," 2d trimester 1939, governor, French Guinea, report to gov.-genl., FWA, Dakar, Conakry, 7 Aug. 1939, ANS 2F 11, file 14, #401.

28. Letter, Goujon, commander of subdivision of Sédhiou, to commander, district of Ziguinchor, 15 Jan. 1940, Sédhiou, ANS 2F 11, file 14, #1C.

29. "Report on the Neighboring Foreign Colonies of Senegal, 1st Trimester, 1939: Documentation Collected regarding Portuguese Guinea," governor of Senegal, report to gov.-genl., FWA, Saint-Louis, Senegal, 20 May 1939, ANS 2F 11, file 14, #239.

30. Galli and Jones, *Guinea-Bissau,* 43; Forrest, *Guinea-Bissau,* 28.

31. Pélissier, *Naissance,* 315.

32. Letter, French consul, Portuguese Guinea, to gov.-genl., FWA, Bissau, 20 May 1947, ANS 2F 13, file 14, #485.

33. Ibid. One franc CFA (equivalent to two metropolitan French francs) was worth between ten and twelve Portuguese escudos in Guinea in the late 1940s; Carreira, *Panaria Cabo-Verdiano-Guineense,* 146.

34. "Situation economique et sociale en Guinée Portugaise," Bensimon, vice-consul in Bissau, report to French high commissioner, FWA (Dakar), 7 Dec. 1948, Bissau, ANS 2F 13, #646.

35. Galli and Jones, *Guinea-Bissau,* 41–42.

36. "Portuguese Guinea—Contraband with A.O.F.," French consul, 16 Mar. 1947, ANS 2F 13, file 14.

37. Letter, A. Vadier, governor, to gov.-genl., FWA, Conakry, 16 Aug. 1934, ANS 2F 11, file 14, #229.

38. "Contraband," French consul, 16 Mar. 1947, ANS 2F 13, file 14.

39. Ibid.

40. Letter, Vadier, Conakry, 16 Aug. 1934, ANS 2F 11, file 14, #229.

41. "Documentation Collected regarding Portuguese Guinea," 2d trimester 1939, report to gov.-genl., FWA, 30 July 1939, Dakar, ANS 2F 11, file 14, #479.

42. "Portuguese Guinea—Politics," 29 Dec. 1945, ANS 2F 13, file 14, #2224.

43. Ibid.

44. Letter, Chartier, high commissioner, Casamance, to governor of Senegal, Saint-Louis, 28 May 1934, Ziguinchor, ANS 2F 9.

45. "Situation economique et sociale," Bensimon, 7 Dec. 1948, Bissau, ANS 2F 13, #646.

46. "Note regarding the Events of Bissau," Paul Brocard, 24 July 1908, ANS 2F, #112, 12.

47. "Information on Neighboring Foreign Colonies, 4th Trimester, 1938, Portuguese Guinea," Office of Political Affairs, FWA, 7 Mar. 1939, Dakar, ANS 2F 11, file 14, #113.

48. "Documentation Collected regarding Portuguese Guinea," 2d trimester, 1939, general secretariat, 2d bureau, to gov.-genl., FWA, 30 July 1939, Dakar, ANS 2F 11, file 14, #479.

49. "Information on Portuguese Guinea, 18 Aug. 1941," governor, French Guinea, 30 Sept. 1941, Conakry, ANS 2F 11, file 14, #431.

50. Letter, Mario Rodrigues Pires, Arauto [Bissau], 3 Sept. 1948, ANS 2F 13, file 14.

51. "Situation economique et sociale," Bensimon, 7 Dec. 1948, Bissau, ANS 2F 13, #646.

52. Letter, Bogaers, French consul, Portuguese Guinea, to minister of foreign affairs (Africa desk), Paris, 25 Sept. 1946, ANS 2F 13, file 14, #81.

53. Letter, Bensimon, French vice-consul, Bissau, to minister of foreign affairs, Paris, 30 Apr. 1948, Bissau, ANS 2F 13, file 14, #451/92.

54. Correia's comments described in letter, Mario Rodrigues Pires, Arauto, 5 Sept. 1948, ANS 2F 13, file 14; letter, Bensimon, 30 Apr. 1948, Bissau, ANS 2F 13, file 14, #451/92.

55. José Luis Ferreira Mendes, "Considerações sobre a problemática de planificação e do desenvolvimento agrícola na Guiné," *BCGP* 26, no. 101 (1971): 217–23. See also Galli and Jones, *Guinea-Bissau,* 45–49, Havik, "Mundasson i Kambansa," 127, and Forrest, *Guinea-Bissau,* 27.

56. The compliant Fulbe chiefdoms of Gabu region proved exceptional (see chapter 7), but even these ended up factionally divided, locally popular chiefs challenging appointed ones with increasing success.

57. Viegas, *Guiné Portuguesa,* 1:268–69; Mário Zanatti, "O Indigenato da Guiné," in *Congresso comemorativo do quinto centenário do descobrimento da Guiné,* vol. 1, 389–99, at 397.

58. Gable, "Modern Manjaco," 363.

59. "Information Collected regarding Portuguese Guinea," 3d trimester 1930, French consul to Bissau, ANS 2F 11, file 14. See also Viegas, *Guiné Portuguesa,* 1:205.

60. Viegas, *Guiné Portuguesa,* 1:205.

61. Ibid., 2:58; Pélissier, *Naissance,* 368–69.

62. Cunha, "Missão de estado," 64.

63. Viegas, *Guiné Portuguesa,* 1:279.

64. Ibid., 183.

65. Ibid., 185.

66. Ibid., 169.

67. Ibid.

68. José de Oliveira Ferreira Diniz, "A política indígena na Guiné Portuguesa," *Congresso commentoritivo do quinto centenário do descobrimonto da Guiné,* vol. 1 (Lisbon: Sociedade de Geografia, 1946), 347–65, esp. 350.

69. Ibid., 202–5.

70. Cunha, "Missão de estado," 66.

71. Crowley, "Contracts," 210 n. 52; Pélissier, *Naissance,* 389.

72. "Information," Berthet, French consul, Bissau, 24 Jan. 1944, ANS 2F 12, file 14, #56.

73. "The Portuguese Bluff in Guinea," report, French consul, Bissau, 24 Dec. 1946, ANS 2F 13, file 14.

74. Ibid.

75. Pélissier, *Naissance,* 244, 297.

76. Ibid., 366–67.

77. Viegas, *Guiné Portuguesa,* 1:185–86.

78. "Annex to letter," A. Vadier, governor, to gov.-genl., FWA, Conakry, 16 Aug. 1934, ANS 2F 11, file 14.

79. "Information," Berthet, 24 Jan. 1944, ANS 2F 12, file 14, #56.

80. Gable, "Modern Manjaco," 335–36.

81. Ibid., 215, 332–34.

82. Crowley, "Contracts," 162.

83. "Information," Berthet, 24 Jan. 1944.

84. "Situation economique et sociale," Bensimon.

85. "Portuguese Guinea—Politics," note, French consul, 16 Nov. 1944, ANS 2F 11, file 14, #1318. Forced labor and taxation are discussed below.

86. Rui Ribeiro, "Barragens em Bolanhas de Agua Salgada," *Soronda: Revista de Estudos Guineenses,* no. 4 (July 1987): 38–57. The saltwater was brought into Guinean rivers from effluent undercurrents originating in the Atlantic Ocean. In contrast to the government's dams, Balanta rice growers in the south had developed hand-built dikes that effectively impeded the flow of this salty water.

87. "Information Obtained regarding Portuguese Guinea," [unidentified author], Mar. 1931, ANS 2F 11, file 14.

88. Pélissier, *Naissance,* 373 n. 41.

89. Hawthorne, "Interior Past," 311.

90. "Information on Neighboring Foreign Colonies," 2d trimester 1935, French official, ANS 2F 11, file 14.

91. "Information on Portuguese Guinea," French official, 1935, ANS 2F 11, file 14.

92. Hawthorne, "Interior Past," 313–14.

93. Note, adjunct administrator Jules Surlemont to superior administrator of the Casamance, 29 Mar. 1935, Ziguinchor, ANS 2F 11, file 14, #106.

94. Gable, "Modern Manjaco," 108–9.

95. Pélissier, *Naissance,* 367.

96. "The Portuguese Colony and the Governor of Portuguese Guinea," French consul, Bissau, 2 Dec. 1947, ANS 2F 13, file 14.

97. Carreira, *Os Portuguêses,* 118.

98. "Information on the Neighboring Colonies: Portuguese Guinea," 1st trimester 1934, confidential report, unidentified French administrator, Casamance, 1934, ANS 2F 11, file 14.

99. Letter, lieut.-gov., French Guinea, to gov.-genl., FWA, 10 June 1927, ANS 2F 11, file 14, #205/452.

100. Ibid.

101. Gable, "Modern Manjaco," 117; Crowley, "Contracts," 155.

102. Crowley, "Contracts," 155.

103. Hawthorne, "Interior Past," 307.

104. Lima, Organização Económica, 70–72.

105. Viegas, *Guiné Portuguesa,* 2:213.

106. "Conference of the Administrators of Portuguese Guinea," Arauto, 12 Dec. 1946, ANS 2F 13, file 14.

107. Correspondence, lieut. governor, French Guinea, to gov.-genl., French West Africa, 10 June 1927; ANS 2F 11, file 14, #205/452.

108. "Information Collected regarding Portuguese Guinea," 3d trimester 1930, French consul, ANS 2F 11, file 14.

109. "Information on Portuguese Guinea," 4th trimester 1931, report from French Guinea to government, FWA, Dec. 1931, ANS 2F 11, file 14.

110. Pélissier, *Naissance,* 373 n. 41.

111. Note, Vidaud, administrator of colonies, 30 May 1938, ANS 2F 11, file 14, #372.

112. Letter, lieut. gov., French Guinea, 10 June 1927, ANS 2F 11, file 14, #205/452.

113. "Information Collected regarding Portuguese Guinea," 3d trimester 1930, ANS 2F 11, file 14.

114. "Information on Portuguese Guinea," 1st and 2d trimesters 1932, French official in Conakry, to government, FWA, ANS 2F 11, file 14; "Information on the Neighboring Colonies: Portuguese Guinea, First Trimester, 1934," confidential report, 1934, ANS 2F 11, file 14.

115. Letter, A. Vadier, governor, to gov.-genl., FWA, Conakry, 16 Aug. 1934, ANS 2F 11, file 14, #229.

116. "Information on Neighboring Foreign Colonies," 1st trimester 1935, French official, ANS 2F 11, file 14.

117. "Information on Neighboring Colonies: Portuguese Guinea," 2d trimester 1935, French official, ANS 2F 11.

118. Le Bressou, "Compte Rendu du 11 Mars 1936 du Commandant de Cercle de Sedhiou," 11 Mar. 1936, ANS 2F 11, #3.

119. "Report on the Neighboring Foreign Colonies of Senegal, 1st Trimester 1939: Documentation Collected regarding Portuguese Guinea," governor of Senegal, to gov.-genl., FWA, 20 May 1939, St.-Louis, Senegal, ANS 2F 11, file 14, #239.

120. "Information on Neighboring Foreign Countries—Portuguese Guinea," 2d trimester 1939, governor, French Guinea, to gov.-genl., FWA, Conakry, 7 Aug. 1939, ANS 2F 11, file 14, #401.

121. Luís António de Carvalho Viegas, Guiné Portuguesa, vol. 2 (Lisbon: Freitas Mega, 1939), 454.

122. Letter, French consul, to governor of Senegal, 9 Apr. 1940, Bissau, ANS 2F 11, file 14, #78; "Information on Neighboring Colonies—Portuguese Guinea," 2d trimester 1941, 21 July 1941, ANS 2F 11, file 14; "Portuguese Guinea," French official, 24 Mar. 1944, ANS 2F 11, file 14, #365; "Economy—Portuguese Guinea," 26 Mar. 1945, ANS 2F 13, file 14, #416.

123. "Decisions Made during the Conference of Administrators," Arauto [Bissau], 6 Dec. 1946, ANS 2F 13, file 14; "Portuguese Guinea: On the Indigenous Tax," French consul, 30 Dec. 1946, ANS 2F 13, file 14.

124. Havik, "Mundasson i Kambansa," 129.

125. Hawthorne, "Migrations and Statelessness," 145.

126. Gable, "Modern Manjaco," 111.

127. Crowley, "Contracts," 155–56.

CHAPTER NINE

1. Comprehensive treatments may be found in Mustafah Dhada, Warriors at Work: How Guinea Was Really Set Free (Niwot: University of Colorado Press, 1993); Patrick Chabal, Amílcar Cabral: Revolutionary Leadership and People's War (Cambridge: Cambridge University Press, 1983); Basil Davidson, No Fist Is Big Enough to Hide the Sky (Baltimore: Penguin Books, 1981); Lars Rudebeck, Guinea-Bissau: A Study of Political Mobilization

(Uppsala: Scandinavian Institute of African Studies, 1974); and Gérard Chaliand, *Armed Struggle in Africa: With the Guerrillas in "Portuguese" Guinea* (New York: Monthly Review Press, 1969). For more succinct but highly informative accounts, see Lobban and Mendy, *Historical Dictionary of Guinea-Bissau;* Galli and Jones, *Guinea-Bissau;* Forrest, *Guinea-Bissau.*

2. See esp. Dhada, *Warriors at Work;* Chabal, *Amílcar Cabral;* and Rudebeck, *Guinea-Bissau.*

3. Chabal, *Amílcar Cabral;* Rudebeck, *Guinea-Bissau;* Galli and Jones, *Guinea-Bissau,* 55–71; Dhada, *Warriors at Work,* 2–5; Forrest, *Guinea-Bissau,* 6.

4. Joshua B. Forrest, "Guinea-Bissau Independence Revolt," in *Encyclopedia of Political Revolutions* (Washington, D.C.: Congressional Quarterly, 1998): 211–13.

5. Dhada, *Warriors at Work,* 4–5.

6. Mamdani, *Citizen and Subject,* 190–202.

7. Ranger, "Connexions," part 2, 631.

8. Pélissier, *Naissance,* 399.

9. Handem, "Nature," 333.

10. This aspect of the argument is consistent with Ranger's general points regarding African nationalism in "Connexions."

11. Dhada, *Warriors at Work,* 88–93.

12. Ibid., 18; E. D. Valimamad, "Nationalist Politics, War, and Statehood: Guinea-Bissau, 1953–1973" (Ph.D. diss., St. Catherine's College, Oxford University, 1984), 109.

13. Dhada, *Warriors at Work,* 18, 41, 243 n. 123.

14. Dias, "Mudanças socio-cultural," 200–202. Dias was escorted by Portuguese military patrols and his own political views were indicated by his references to the PAIGC as "terrorists," but the extensiveness of his field work and interviews — carried out during the war — is unparalleled.

15. Carlos Lopes, *Etnia, estado, e relações de poder na Guiné-Bissau* (Lisbon: Edições 70, 1982). See also Lopes, *Guinea-Bissau: From Liberation Struggle to Independent Statehood* (London: Zed Press; Boulder, Colo.: Westview Press, 1987); idem, "A transição histórica."

16. As noted earlier, the Oinka included Balanta, Soninké, and mixed Mandinka-Balanta communities located in the Oio region.

17. Dhada, *Warriors at Work,* 10.

18. Dias, "Mudança socio-cultural," 119–20, 143–47; 178–79; Hans Schoenmakers, "Old Men and New State Structures in Guinea-Bissau," *Journal of Legal Pluralism* 25/26 (1987): 99–138.

19. Dhada, *Warriors at Work,* 243 n. 123.

20. Dias, "Mudança socio-cultural," 87, 143.

21. Schoenmakers, "Old Men," 129. However, as noted, individual chiefs did not have leadership roles in this acephalous society.

22. Davidson, *No Fist,* 73–74.

23. Roy van der Drift, "Birds of Passage and Independence Fighters: An Anthropological Analysis of Balanta Migration to Southern Guinea-Bissau and Mobilisation for the Liberation War, 1890–1964," in *Migrations anciennes,* ed. Gaillard, 163.

24. Schoenmakers, "Old Men," 122, 126.

25. Handem, "Nature," 92–93, 95, 97, 335.

26. Dhada, *Warriors at Work,* 9, 11.

27. Ibid., 7, 10.

28. Ibid., 10.

29. Dias, "Mudança socio-cultural," 117. As noted in chapter 1, the term *Balanta-Mané* refers to those Islamized Balanta who had intermarried for several generations with Mandinka; by the 1960s, many resided in the areas of Tiligi and Barro (Dias, "Mudança socio-cultural," 88–89). The cultural practices of the Balanta-Mané differ from the majoritarian Balanta-Brassa. Politically, however, they also adhered strongly to the PAIGC.

30. Dias, "Mudança Socio-cultural," 118.

31. Ibid., 194.

32. Luís António de Carvalho, *Guiné Portuguesa,* (Lisbon: Freitas Mega, 1940) 3:41.

33. Lopes, "A transição histórica," 85.

34. Dias, "Mudança Socio-cultural," 94.

35. Ibid., 96.

36. Ibid., 95–96, 185–86.

37. Ibid., 131.

38. These congresses are noted below in the section "Historical Lineages of Peasant and Ethnic Resistance."

39. Dias, "Mudança socio-cultural," 131–33.

40. Dhada, *Warriors at Work,* 10.

41. Gable, "Modern Manjaco," 210.

42. Dias, "Mudança Socio-cultural," 92.

43. Crowley, "Contracts," 171.

44. Gable, "Modern Manjaco," 210; Crowley, "Contracts," 171.

45. Crowley, "Contracts," 171.

46. Ibid., 176.

47. Gable, "Modern Manjaco," 212.

48. Crowley, "Contracts," 171; Dias, "Mudança socio-cultural," 124.

49. Crowley, "Contracts," 171.

50. Dias, "Mudança socio-cultural," 91, 124.

51. Dias, "Mudança socio-cultural," 91; Gable, "Modern Manjaco," 210; Crowley, "Contracts," 171, 177.

52. Gable, "Modern Manjaco," 225.

53. Ibid., 212.

54. Ibid., 210.

55. Dias, "Mudança socio-cultural," 125.

56. Crowley, "Contracts," 177.

57. Dias, "Mudança socio-cultural," 139.

58. Ibid., 140–41, 130–31; Crowley's research in the mid-1980s further confirms the strong support of Churo for the PAIGC; see "Contracts," 171.

59. Dias, "Mudança socio-cultural," 126.

60. Ibid., 140, 139.

61. Ibid., 137–38.

62. Gable, "Modern Manjaco," 210.

63. Dias, "Mudança socio-cultural," 71, 150, 161, 179; Forrest, *Guinea-Bissau,* 121.

64. Dias, "Mudança socio-cultural," 157.

65. Ibid., 71, 76.

66. Ibid., 149–72.

67. Ibid., 150.

68. Ibid., 153–54.

69. Ibid., 156–57.

70. Ibid., 165–66.

71. Ibid., 149, 159, 161, 172.

72. Ibid., 170–71.

73. Ibid., 96–97.

74. Ibid., 97.

75. Schoenmakers, "Old Men," 128.

76. Ibid., 129.

77. Ibid., 131. The Maqué villagers returned to their home village by the end of the independence struggle.

78. Crowley, "Contracts," 179.

79. Ibid., 179, 573.

80. Ibid., 179.

81. Ibid., 575.

82. Ranger, "Connexions," part 1, 447–49.

83. Mamdani, *Citizen and Subject,* 190–202.

84. See chapter 1.

85. See chapter 2.

86. Havik, "Mundasson i Kambansa," 139.

87. Manuel Belchior, *Os congressos do povo da Guiné* (Varzim, Portugal: Arcadia, 1973).

CHAPTER TEN

1. Mamdani, *Citizen and Subject,* 107.

2. Schoenmakers, "Old Men," 133.

3. Lars Rudebeck, "The Effects of Structural Adjustment in Kandjadja, Guinea-Bissau," *Review of African Political Economy* 49 (winter 1990): 43.

4. See also Joshua B. Forrest, "Guinea-Bissau," in *Postcolonial History of Lusophone Africa,* ed. Patrick Chabal (London: Hurst, 2002), 236–63, at 246.

5. Schoenmakers, "Old Men," 132–33.

6. Crowley, "Contracts," 244–45.

7. Forrest, *Guinea-Bissau,* 52.

8. Lopes, *Etnia,* 95.

9. Brame — a minority ethnic group; see chapter 1.

10. Mamadú Jao, "Ethnical Origin and Migration among the Mancanha of Guinea-Bissau," in *Migrations anciennes,* ed. Gaillard, 215–22.

11. Odile Hanquez Passavant, "Une histoire des Nalou, ~XIVe-XIXe siècle: Naissance d'un groupe et appropriation d'un nom," in *Migrations anciennes,* ed. Gaillard, 386, 400.

12. Amélia Frazão-Moreira, "Récits de migration des Nalou de Cubucaré," in *Migrations anciennes,* ed. Gaillard, 409–10.

13. Hawthorne, "Interior Past," 61; Handem, "Nature," 71.

14. Hawthorne, "Interior Past," 62; Handem, "Nature," 77, 116.

15. See also Forrest, "Guinea-Bissau."

16. Hawthorne, "Interior Past," 194.

17. Handem, "Nature," 72.

18. Hawthorne, "Interior Past," 62, 225–28.

19. Ibid., 60, 203.

20. Ibid., 60–62.

21. Handem, "Nature," 339–40.

22. Ibid., 117, 132; Hawthorne, "Interior Past," 228.

23. Handem, "Nature," 320.

24. Hawthorne, "Interior Past," 229.

25. Handem, "Nature," 138, 140, 144, 166–67, 176.

26. Ibid., 287, 98, 139, 286.

27. Ibid., 285, 340–41; Hawthorne, "Interior Past," 193–94.

28. Handem, "Nature," 125, 131, 184, 341; Hawthorne, "Interior Past," 62.

29. Handem, "Nature," 340–41.

30. Gable, "Modern Manjaco," 9–10.

31. Clara Carvalho, "Réflexions autour des histoires d'origine à Pecixe (Cacheu)," in *Migrations anciennes,* ed. Gaillard, 228.

32. Gable, "Modern Manjaco," 17.

33. Ibid.

34. Ibid., 24.

35. Ibid., 212.

36. Ibid., 25.

37. Ibid., 213–15.

38. Ibid., 214, 303.

39. Ibid., 303; see also 213–15.

40. Clara Carvalho, "Ritos de poder e a recriaçao da tradição: Os régulos manjaco da Guiné-Bissau" (Ph.D. diss., Instituto Superior de Ciências do Trabalho e da Empresa, Lisbon, 1998), 19, 389.

41. Ibid., 42; Havik, "Mundasson i Kambansa," 149.

42. Also noted in Forrest, "Guinea-Bissau," 248–49.

43. Carvalho ("Ritos de poder," 82) notes seven new kingships in Caió sector alone.

44. Ibid., 369.

45. Ibid., 388.

46. Ibid., 389.

47. Ibid., 83, 219.

48. Ibid., 398.

49. Rudebeck, "Effects of Structural Adjustment," 44–45.

50. Ibid., 45.

51. The chief and council were of Mandinka background because the Balanta and Fulbe were numerical minorities; the Mandinka community was much larger.

52. See summary in Forrest, "Guinea-Bissau," 247–48.

53. Crowley, "Contracts," 310.

54. Ibid., 312.

55. Ibid., 627.

56. Gable, "Modern Manjaco," 47.

57. Crowley, "Contracts," 206.

58. Ibid., 370.

59. Ibid., 390.

60. Ibid., 273.

61. Ibid., 364–65 and 398 n. 2.

62. Gable, "Modern Manjaco," 47.

63. Ibid.

64. Ibid., 2, 18.

65. Ibid., 24.

66. Ibid., 94.

67. Crowley, "Contracts," 509.

68. Ibid., 510, 513.

69. Ibid., 520, 523–24.

70. Mário Santos, "Algumas considerações sobre a nossa situação sociolingustica," *Soronda: Revista de Estudos Guineenses* 4 (July 1987), 12.

71. Gable, "Modern Manjaco," 81.

72. Ibid.

73. Ibid.

74. Rudebeck, "Effects of Structural Adjustment," 47.

75. Ibid.

76. Ibid., 48, 49.

77. Carlos Cardoso, "Ki Yang-Yang: Uma Nova Religião dos Balantas?" *Soronda: Revista de Estudos Guineenses* 10 (July 1990), 3.

78. Also noted in Forrest, "Guinea-Bissau," 247.

79. Ibid., and Inger Callewaert, "Balanta Migrations Related to the Genealogy of the Prophetess and to the Origin and Spread of Kiyang-yang," in *Migrations anciennes,* ed. Gaillard, 165–82.

80. Cardoso, "Ki Yang-Yang," 5.

81. Rudebeck, "Effects of Structural Adjustment," 46.

82. For the informal sector, see chapter 11.

Chapter Eleven

1. See chapter 9.

2. As noted in the introduction, the term *uncaptured* is from Hyden, *Beyond Ujamaa.* This point that Guineans would have traded with state institutions had the terms of trade been more fair is consistent with Hyden's analysis of the Tanzanian peasantry.

3. Rui Ribeiro, "Barragens em bolanhas de agua salgada," *Soronda: Revista de Estudos Guineenses* 4 (July 1987); 46–47, 74; see also J. D. Lea, Cornelius Hugo, and Carlos Rui

Ribeiro, "Rice Production and Marketing in Guinea Bissau: A Contribution for Policy Dialogue," Food and Feed Grain Institute unpublished report, Kansas State University, 1990.

4. Ploeg, "Autarky and Technical Change," 100–101.

5. Anne-Marie Hochet, *Paysanneries en attente: Guinée-Bissau* (Dakar: ENDA, 1983), 40–41.

6. Raul Mendes Fernandes, "Nhomingas e Bidjogos—da pesca de 'subsistência' à pesca 'comercial,'" *Soronda: Revista de Estudos Guineenses* 4 (July 1987), 59; Joshua B. Forrest, "State and Peasantry in Contemporary Africa: The Case of Guinea-Bissau," *Africana Journal* 17 (1998): 7.

7. Hochet, *Paysanneries,* 40–41, 77, 82–83.

8. Ibid., 53–63, 99.

9. Ribeiro, "Barragens," 55.

10. Hochet, *Paysanneries;* Ploeg, "Autarky and Technical Change"; Philip J. Havik, "As sociedades agrárias e a intervenção rural na Guiné-Bissau: Uma revista da literatura pós-independência," *Revista Internacional de Estudos Africanos* 14/15 (1991): 279–310; Lea, Hugo, and Ribeiro, "Rice Production and Marketing"; Lobban and Forrest, *Historical Dictionary of Guinea-Bissau,* 12–13, 17, 51–52.

11. The djula are marketing specialists who had forged partially autonomous trading circuits during the precolonial period (associated with the Gabu kingdom; see chapter 1). They expanded informal trading circuits through the period of "settled" colonial rule.

12. For a discussion of both formal and informal trade that complements this section, see Forrest, "Guinea-Bissau," 241–43.

13. Ploeg, "Autarky and Technical Change," 101, 107.

14. Lea, Hugo, and Ribeiro, "Rice Production and Marketing," 12.

15. Hochet, *Paysanneries,* 79, 118, 122.

16. Ibid., 123.

17. Ibid., 138.

18. Havik, "Female Entrepreneurship," 212.

19. Rosemary E. Galli, "On Peasant Productivity: The Case of Guinea-Bissau," *Development and Change* 18, no. 1 (1987): 91–92.

20. Hochet, *Paysanneries,* 11.

21. Ibid, 16, 18–20, 24, 65, 96, 102, 114–24, 135, 141–43. Most of the remainder of the surplus was consumed or stored.

22. Ibid., 15–16.

23. Samba Ka, "Rich Entrepreneurs, Poor Economies: Smuggling Activities in Senegambia" (Ph.D. diss., Johns Hopkins University, 1994), 32.

24. Ibid., 122.

25. Galli, "On Peasant Productivity," 92.

26. Ka, "Rich Entrepreneurs," 200; Havik, "Female Entrepreneurship," 216.

27. Havik, "Female Entrepreneurship," 213; Galli, "On Peasant Productivity," 92–93; Forrest, *Guinea-Bissau,* 87–97.

28. This is Gable's description in "Modern Manjaco," 54.

29. Ibid., 55–57.

30. See chapter 8.

31. Havik, "Female Entrepreneurship," 216.

32. Forrest, "State and Peasantry," 16–17.

33. Havik, "Female Entrepreneurship," 208–9; Havik, "Mundasson i Kambansa," 165; Forrest, "Guinea-Bissau," 242.

34. "Guinea Bissau on the Reform Path," *Africa Research Bulletin* 35, no. 1 (1998): 13320.

35. Ibid.

36. Havik, "Mundasson i Kambansa," 146.

37. Forrest, "Guinea-Bissau," 242–43.

38. Ibid, 244.

39. For details, see Forrest, *Guinea-Bissau,* 55–62; Galli and Jones, *Guinea-Bissau,* 100–108; Joshua B. Forrest, "A Decade of Domestic Power Struggles," *Journal of Modern African Studies* 25, no. 1 (1987): 95–116.

40. The quote is from Momar Seyni Ndiaye, "La Guinée-Bissau, sept ans après," *Le Soleil* [Dakar] 15 Aug. 1980; see also Galli and Jones, *Guinea-Bissau,* 73–74; Forrest, "State, Peasantry, and National Power Struggles," 246–60; Lars Rudebeck, "Problèmes de pouvoir populaire et de développement: Transition difficile en Guinée-Bissau," Research Report 63, Scandinavian Institute of African Studies, Uppsala, Sweden, 1982, 40–41, 64; Jean-Claude Andreini and Marie-Claude Lambert, *La Guinée-Bissau d'Amílcar Cabral à la reconstruction nationale* (Paris: Editions l'Harmattan, 1978), 3.

41. Lopes, "A transição histórica," 224.

42. "Guinea-Bissau," *Economist Intelligence Unit Quarterly Review,* annual supplement (1983): 13; for more details see Galli and Jones, *Guinea-Bissau,* 117.

43. Until 1984 this ministry was called the Ministry of Public Works.

44. Julio D. Davila, *Human Settlements in Guinea-Bissau* (London: International Institute for Environment and Development, 1987), 73–75, 85–86.

45. Lopes, "A transição histórica," 265; Galli and Jones, *Guinea-Bissau,* 119–20.

46. José Filipe Fonseca, "A formação e a assistência técnica na agricultura e desenvolvimento rural," *Soronda: Revista de Estudos Guineenses* 4 (July 1987): 135, 142.

47. Ibid., 136.

48. Galli and Jones, *Guinea-Bissau,* 139–46.

49. *Nô Pintcha* [Bissau newspaper], 25 Feb. 1984, and 7 Sept. 1983.

50. *Nô Pintcha,* 7 Sept. 1983; *West Africa,* no. 3411, 20 Dec. 1982, 3310; *Le Soleil,* 26–27 Nov. 1983.

51. *Nô Pintcha,* 4 Sept. 1983; *West Africa,* no. 3411, 20 Dec. 1982, 3310; *Africa Confidential* 19, no. 8 (1978).

52. *West Africa,* 26 Jan. 1987, 152; *Expresso* [Lisbon], 20 Nov. 1986.

53. José Manuel Saraiva, "A Guiné é um país de Traições," *Expresso* [Lisbon], 26 Sept. 1998; Carlos Albino, "Grupo de Nino desviou ajuda humanitária chinesa," *Diário de Notícias,* 14 May 1999; "Caetano N'Tchama," *Expresso,* 19 Feb. 2000; see also Havik, "Mundasson i Kambansa," 145.

54. Mustafah Dhada, "Guinea-Bissau at the Crossroad: A Case of Capitalism in a Tight Skirt," paper presented at the African Studies Association meeting, Philadelphia, Nov. 1999.

55. Luiz Cabral was half brother of the assassinated nationalist leader Amílcar Cabral.

56. Forrest, "Guinea-Bissau since Independence"; Forrest, *Guinea-Bissau,* 57–58.

57. Personal sources, Bissau, 1983; "Guinée-Bissau, un coup d'état renverse le président Cabral," *Afrique contemporaine* 113 (Jan.-Feb. 1981): 18.

58. Galli and Jones, *Guinea-Bissau,* 94–108; Forrest, *Guinea-Bissau,* 59–61; Forrest, "Guinea-Bissau since Independence," 107–12.

59. Forrest, *Guinea-Bissau,* 60–61; Galli and Jones, *Guinea-Bissau,* 108.

60. Report on Guinea-Bissau, *Diário de Notícias* [Lisbon], 9 Oct. 1999.

61. Babacar Ndiaye, "Repères sur la crise bissau-guinéenne," *Revue de la gendarmerie nationale,* no. 195 2d trim. 2000: 123–28; Reuters report, Richard Waddington, 8 June 1998.

62. This army, the Mouvement des Forces Démocratique de la Casamance, seeks regional separation from the Dakar-based Senegalese government; see Jean-Claude Marut, "Casamance: Les assises du MFDC à Banjul (22–25 juin 1999)," *Afrique contemporaine* 191 (July-Sept. 1999): 73–79.

63. Gérald Gaillard, "Guinée-Bissau: Un pas douloureux vers la démocratie," *Afrique contemporaine* 191 (July-Sept. 1999), 54.

64. Forrest, "Guinea-Bissau," 256–57.

65. Ibid.; AP reports, Ian Stewart, 24 June and 13 Nov. 1998.

66. BBC report, Mark Doyle, Bissau, 7 July 1998, cited in Forrest, "Guinea-Bissau," 257.

67. AP report, Ian Stewart, 26 June 1998.

68. Gaillard, "Guinée-Bissau: Un pas douloureux," 47–48. This 90 percent estimate is admittedly difficult to gauge accurately.

69. Forrest, "Guinea-Bissau," 258.

70. José Pedro Castanheira, "A ultima batalha," *Revista/Expresso* [Lisbon], 22 May 1999.

71. For details, see Forrest, "Guinea-Bissau," 259–60.

72. See chapter 4.

Chapter Twelve

1. Joel S. Migdal, *Strong Societies and Weak States: State-Society Relations and State Capabilities in the Third World* (Princeton, N.J.: Princeton University Press, 1988), 36, 37, 261.

2. Ibid., 34.

3. Ibid., 110, 123–25.

4. Bruce Berman, "Structure and Process in the Bureaucratic States of Colonial Africa," *Development and Change* 15, no. 1 (1984): 186–87.

5. Mamdani, *Citizen and Subject,* 215–17.

6. Young, *African Colonial State,* 288.

7. See the introduction to this book for discussion of political penetration.

8. Herbst, *State Power,* 252–56.

9. Mamdani, *Citizen and Subject;* Young, *African Colonial State.*

10. Lopes, *Kaabunké.*

11. Richard L. Roberts, *Warriors, Merchants, and Slaves: The State and the Economy in the Middle Niger Valley, 1700–1914* (Stanford, Calif.: Stanford University Press, 1987), 7.

12. Mendy, *Colonialismo Português,* 423; Pélissier, *Naissance,* 401, 411.

13. Smith, *Warfare and Diplomacy;* Young, *African Colonial State.*

14. Crowder, in *West African Resistance,* suggests that African resistance efforts throughout the continent were more extensive and enduring than previously believed, but even from this comparative point of view, the resistance efforts in Portuguese Guinea were dramatically more successful than elsewhere in West Africa.

15. See chapter 4.

16. Barcellos, *Subsídios para a história,* vol. 5, 2–40.

17. Young, *African Colonial State,* 105.

18. Crowder, *West African Resistance,* 8.

19. Some Portuguese had hoped that their influence over the grumetes (Christianized Africans) would provide a link to rural social forces. However, as indicated in chapter 2, the grumetes played an ambivalent role, sometimes allying with the Portuguese but at other times making clear their allegiance to local peoples. In the end, the Portuguese did not trust them.

20. Kiren Aziz Chaudhry, *The Price of Wealth: Economics and Institutions in the Middle East* (Ithaca, N.Y.: Cornell University Press, 1997), 65–67, 111–16.

21. Lan, *Guns and Rain,* 143–51.

22. See chapter 1.

23. Marshall S. Clough, *Fighting Two Sides: Kenyan Chiefs and Politicians, 1918–1940* (Boulder, Colo.: University Press of Colorado, 1990), 183–89.

24. Mamdani, *Citizen and Subject,* 183–217.

25. Ibid., 52–55, 58–61.

26. Ibid., 124–25, 138–79, 194–202.

27. Forrest, *Guinea-Bissau,* 39.

28. Ted Gurr, "The Political Origins of State Violence and Terror: A Theoretical Analysis," in *Government Violence and Repression: An Agenda for Research,* ed. Michael Stohl and George A. Lopez (Westport, Conn: Greenwood Press, 1986), 66.

29. Michael McClintock, *The American Connection,* vol. 1: *State Terror and Popular Resistance in El Salvador* (London: Zed Books, 1985), 99–100; Charles D. Brockett, "Sources of State Terrorism in Central America," in Bushnell et al., *State Organized Terror,* 69.

30. Brockett, "Source of State Terrorism," 70; Michael Richards, "Cosmopolitan World View and Counterinsurgency in Guatemala," *Anthropological Quarterly* 58, no. 3 (1985): 90–107.

31. Bernd Wegner, "Violent Repression in the Third Reich: Did It Stabilize Hitler's Rule?" in Bushnell et al., *State Organized Terror,* 161–62.

32. Young, *African Colonial State,* 199.

33. On Nazi Germany, see Wegner, "Violent Repression," 160.

34. Brockett, "Sources of State Terrorism."

35. Wegner, "Violent Repression," 163, 165.

36. See also Havik, "Mundasson i Kambansa," 139, 163, 167.

37. Lan, *Guns and Rain,* 209–10.

38. This is quite different from Herbst's emphasis in *States and Power* on "political geography" (referring to lightly populated rural areas and wide geographic space) as explaining African state lack of interest or ability to pursue territorial hegemony. I am

arguing that the importance of territoriality is in fact deeply rooted within the human nodes of rural civil society itself and is reflected in social institutions that have overcome repeated state efforts at territorial conquest.

39. Donald Rothchild and Michael W. Foley, "African States and the Politics of Inclusive Coalitions," in Rothchild and Chazan, *Precarious Balance,* 251.

40. Mamdani, *Citizen and Subject.*

41. Jean-François Bayart, "Civil Society in Africa," in *Political Domination in Africa,* ed. Patrick Chabal (Cambridge: Cambridge University Press, 1986), 119.

42. Naomi Chazan, "Patterns of State-Society Incorporation and Disengagement in Africa," in Rothchild and Chazan, *Precarious Balance,* 131, 137.

43. Linda Heywood, *Contested Power in Angola, 1840s to the Present* (Rochester, N.Y.: University of Rochester Press, 2000), 36, 61, 182, 212.

44. Azarya, "Reordering State-Society Relations," 6.

45. Ibid., 8.

Sources

PRIMARY SOURCES

Arquivo Histórico Ultramarino (AHU)

Located in Lisbon, Portugal, this is the primary archival holding of original colonial documents from Portuguese Guinea. The archives are organized rudimentarily in twenty-one boxes *(caixas)* marked "Guiné Portuguesa," "Guiné," "Guiné 2e Secção," or "Guiné Gerais." Each of these twenty-one boxes contains several hundred documents stacked in a large pile, not in any particular chronological or topical order. Many documents are arranged within a *pasta,* or file. Document dates range from the late 1600s to the early 1900s.

Archives Nationales de Senegal (ANS); formerly Archives du Gouvernement Générale d'Afrique Occidentale

Located in Dakar, Senegal, these archives contain detailed firsthand accounts of events in Portuguese Guinea compiled by French colonial officials, merchants, and other observers who were stationed in or frequently spent time in Portuguese Guinea, often for years at a time.

Répertoire des Archives (de l'ANS) Série F: Affaires Étrangères, 1809-1921

    2F. Guinée Portugaise et Ile de Cap Vert (1820-1921)

    2F 2. Correspondance du Gouverneur de la Guinée portugaise reçue par le Commandant de Gorée, 1834-58

    2F 3. Relations du Gouvernement du Sénégal avec le Gouvernement de la Guinée portugaise, 1861-71

    2F 7. Réclamations particulières, 1903-14

    2F 7. Versement 14. Iles Bissagos

    2F 8. Relations avec la Guinée portugaise, 1914-16

2F 11. Exportations et importations d'armes et munitions en Guinée portugaise, 1916–20

2F 12. Troubles de Guinée portugaise, 1908

2F 13. Troubles de Guinée portugaise: Incidents d'ordre intérieur, 1909–17

2F 14. Affaire Abdul N'Diaye, 1917–20

2F 18. Incidents de frontières, 1902–9

2F 19. Incidents de frontières, 1910–19

Sous-Série 2F [subset 2F]: *Guinée Portugaise et Ile de Cap Vert 2e Partie, 1921–1947*

2F 7. Documents variés

2F 11. Documents variés

2F 13. Documents variés

2F 14. Documents variés

Secondary Sources

As noted in the preface, the principal ideas developed in this book emerge out of my study of primary documents in the Arquivo Histórico Ultramarino in Lisbon and the Archives Nationales de Sénégal in Dakar; however, during the past decade and a half (while this book was being written), the quality and quantity of published and unpublished scholarly literature concerning Guinea-Bissau has expanded considerably. These new works have helped to "round out" my documentary research and substantially broaden the empirical landscape of the study. Collectively, these new investigations, in combination with my investigation of colonial documents, make it possible to present a significantly revisionist perspective on Guinea-Bissau's state and rural civil society. Thus, while the notes and archival materials obtained from archives in Portugal and Senegal form the core source materials of my reading of Guinea-Bissauan history, this study also synthesizes recent anthropological and historical work of other scholars of Guinea-Bissau that provide special insight into crucial aspects of the dynamic between the state and rural civil society. These include, especially, René Pélissier's richly detailed, enormous masterwork; Joye L. Bowman's well-documented book on the rise and fall of Fuladu; Carlos Lopes's provocative study of Gabu (Kaabunké); Peter Mendy's comprehensive investigation of resistance; early-precolonial-era analyses by George Brooks; revealing insights into precolonial stateless societies by Walter Hawthorne; probing studies of colonial-era economic and political change by Philip J. Havik; Mustafah Dhada's definitive study of the liberation struggle; Clara Carvalho's innovative recent work on Mandjack kingships; Eve Crowley's and Eric Gable's pathbreaking studies on Mandjack society and history; Diana Hamden's illuminating sociological investigation of the Balanta; and Gérald Gaillard's multilingual, fascinating edited volume on early migration patterns.

At the same time, aspects of the present study draw in part on the work of the previous generation of Lusophone scholars of Guinea-Bissauan history, especially António Carreira, Luís Viegas, and Joaquim Veríssimo Serrão, as well as Christiano Barcellos, João Barreto, and Teixeira da Mota. Their accounts provide essential backround to an appreciation of some of the key moments of Guinean colonial politics. They also often acknowledge the fragility of the colonial state and the strength of rural Guinean social structures.

SELECTED BIBLIOGRAPHY

Barcellos, Christiano José de Senna. *Subsídios para a história de Cabo Verde e Guiné.* Vol. 4. Lisbon: Imprensa Nacional, 1910.

———. Vol. 5. Lisbon: Imprensa Nacional, 1911.

———. Vol. 6. Lisbon: Imprensa Nacional, 1912.

Barreto, João. *História da Guiné, 1418–1918.* Lisbon: Author, 1938.

Bayart, Jean-François. "Civil Society in Africa." In *Political Domination in Africa: Reflections on the Limits of Power,* ed. Patrick Chabal, 109–25. Cambridge: Cambridge University Press, 1986.

Belchior, Manuel. *Os congressos do povo da Guiné.* Varzim, Portugal: Arcadia, 1973.

Berman, Bruce. "Structure and Process in the Bureaucratic States of Colonial Africa." *Development and Change* 15, no. 1 (1984): 161–202.

Bigman, Laura. *History and Hunger in West Africa.* Westport, Conn.: Greenwood Press, 1993.

Bowman, Joye. "Abdul Injai: Ally and Enemy of the Portuguese, 1895–1919." *Journal of African History* 27, no. 3 (1985): 463–79.

———. "Conflict, Interaction, and Change in Guinea-Bissau: Fulbe Expansion and Its Impact, 1850–1900." Ph.D. diss., University of California, Los Angeles, 1980.

———. "'Legitimate Commerce' and Peanut Production in Portuguese Guinea." *Journal of African History* 28, no. 1 (1987): 87–106.

———. *Ominous Transition: Commerce and Colonial Expansion in the Senegambia and Guinea, 1857–1919.* Brookfield, Vt.: Avebury, 1997.

Brooks, George E. "Historical Perpectives on the Guinea-Bissau Region." In *Vice-almirante Avelino Teixeira da Mota, in memorium,* 277–304. Lisbon: Academia de Marinha, 1987.

———. *Landlords and Strangers: Ecology, Society, and Trade in Western Africa, 1000–1630.* Boulder, Colo.: Westview Press, 1993.

———. "A Nhara of the Guinea-Bissau Region: Mãe Aurélia Correia." In *Women and Slavery in West Africa,* ed. Claire C. Robertson and Martin A. Klein, 295–319. Madison: University of Wisconsin Press, 1983.

Bushnell, P. Timothy, Vladimir Shlapentokh, Christopher K. Vanderpool, and Jeyaratnam Sundram, eds. *State Organized Terror: The Case of Violent Internal Represssion.* Boulder, Colo.: Westview Press, 1991.

Callewaert, Inger. "Balanta Migrations Related to the Genealogy of the Prophetess and to the Origin and Spread of Kiyang-yang." In *Migrations anciennes,* ed. Gaillard, 165–82.

Cardoso, Carlos. "Ki Yang-Yang: Uma nova religião dos Balantas?" *Soronda: Revista de estudos Guineenses* 10 (July 1990): 3–15.

Caroço, Jorge Vellez. *Monjur: O Gabu e a sua história.* Bissau: Centro de Estudos da Guiné Portuguesa, 1948.

Carreira, António. "Organização social e económica dos povos da Guiné Portuguesa." *Boletim Cultural de Guiné Portuguesa* 16, no. 64 (1961): 647–713.

————. *Panaria Cabo-Verdiano-Guineense: Aspectos históricose socio-económicos.* Lisbon: Museu de Etnologia do Ultramar, 1968.

————. *Os Portuguêses nos rios da Guiné.* Lisbon: Author, 1984.

————. *Vida social dos Manjacos.* Lisbon: Centro de Estudos da Guiné Portuguesa, 1947.

Carvalho, Clara. "Réflexions autour des histoires d'origine à Pecixe (Cacheu)." In *Migrations anciennes,* ed. Gaillard, 223–29.

————. "Ritos de poder e a recriaçao da tradição: Os régulos manjaco da Guiné-Bissau." Ph.D. diss., Instituto Superior de Ciências do Trabalho e da Empresa, Lisbon, 1998.

Chabal, Patrick. *Amílcar Cabral: Revolutionary Leadership and People's War.* Cambridge: Cambridge University Press, 1983.

————, ed. *Political Domination in Africa: Reflections on the Limits of Power.* Cambridge: Cambridge University Press, 1986.

Chazan, Naomi. "Patterns of State-Society Incorporation and Disengagement in Africa." In *The Precarious Balance: State and Society in Africa,* ed. Donald Rothchild and Naomi Chazan, 121–48. Boulder, Colo.: Westview Press, 1988.

Chazan, Naomi, R. Mortimer, John Rarenhill, and Donald Rothchild, eds. *Politics and Society in Contemporary Africa.* Boulder, Colo.: Lynne Rienner, 1988.

Cissé, Nouha. "La fin du Kaabu et les debuts du royaume du Fuladu." Master's thesis, Dakar University, 1977–78.

Cissoko, Sékéné Mody. "De l'organisation politique de Kaabu." *Ethiopiques* 28, special issue (1981): 195–206.

————. "Introduction à l'histoire des Mandingues de l'Ouest." *Ethiopiques* 28, special issue (1981): 73–91.

Clarence-Smith, Gervase. *The Third Portuguese Empire, 1825–1975: A Study in Economic Imperialism.* Manchester, U.K.: Manchester University Press, 1985.

Congresso comemorativo do quinto céntenário do descobrimento da Guiné. Vol. 1. Lisbon: Sociedade de Geografiia, 1946.

Crowder, Michael, ed. *West African Resistance: The Military Response to Colonial Occupation.* New York: Hutchinson, 1971.

Crowley, Eve Lakshmi. "Contracts with the Spirits: Religion, Asylum, and Ethnic Identity in the Cacheu Region of Guinea-Bissau." Ph.D. diss., Yale University, May 1990.

————. "Institutions, Identities, and the Incorporation of Immigrants within Local Frontiers of the Upper Guinea Coast." In *Migrations anciennes,* ed. Gaillard, 115–37.

Cunha, J. M. Silva. "Missão de estado dos movimentos associativos em Africa: Relatório da campanha de 1958 (Guiné)," Centro de Éstudos Políticos e Sociais da Junta de Investigações do Ultramar, Lisbon, 1959.

Cunningham, James. "The Colonial Period in Guinea." *Tarikh* 6, no. 4 (1980): 31–46.

Davidson, Basil. "Colonialism on the Cheap—the Portuguese in Africa up to c. 1921." *Tarikh* 6, no. 4 (1980): 1–30.

————. *No Fist Is Big Enough to Hide the Sky.* Baltimore, Md.: Penguin Books, 1981.

Dhada, Mustafah. *Warriors at Work: How Guinea Was Really Set Free.* Niwot, Colo.: University of Colorado Press, 1993.

Dias, José Manuel de Braga. "Mudança socio-cultural na Guiné Portuguesa." Ph.D. diss., Universidade Técnica de Lisboa, Instituto Superior de Ciências Sociais e Política Ultramarina, Lisbon, 1974.

Dias Dinis, A. J. "As tribos de Guiné Portuguesa na histório." *Congresso comemorativo,* 241–78.

Diniz, José Oliveira Ferreira. "A política indígena na Guiné Portuguesa." *Congresso comemorativo,* 347–65.

Drift, Roy van der. "Birds of Passage and Independence Fighters: An Anthropological Analysis of Balanta Migration to Southern Guinea-Bissau and Mobilisation for the Liberation War, 1890–1964." In *Migrations anciennes,* ed. Gaillard, 151–64.

Fernandes, Raul Mendes. "Nhomingas e Bidjogos—da pesca de 'subsistência' à pesca 'comercial.'" *Soronda: Revista de Estudos Guineenses* 4 (July 1987): 58–94.

Fonseca, José Filipe. "A formaçâo e a assistência técnica na agricultura e desenvolvimento rural." *Soronda: Revista de Estudos Guineenses* 4 (July 1987): 133–43.

Forrest, Joshua B. "Asynchronic Comparisons: Weak States in Post-colonial Africa and Mediaeval Europe." In *Comparing Nations: Concepts, Strategies, Substance,* ed. Mattei Dogan and Ali Kazancigil, 260–96. Oxford, U.K.: Basil Blackwell, 1994.

———. "Guinea-Bissau." In *A History of Postcolonial Lusophone Africa,* ed. Patrick Chabal. London: Hurst, 2002: 236–63.

———. "Guinea-Bissau Independence Revolt." *Encyclopedia of Political Revolutions,* 211–13. Washington, D.C.: Congressional Quarterly, 1998.

———. *Guinea-Bissau: Power, Conflict, and Renewal in a West African Nation.* Boulder, Colo.: Westview Press, 1992.

———. "Guinea-Bissau since Independence: A Decade of Domestic Power Struggles." *Journal of Modern African Studies* 25, no. 1 (1987): 95–116.

———. "The Quest for State 'Hardness' in Africa." *Comparative Politics* 20, no. 4 (1988): 423–42.

———. "State and Peasantry in Contemporary Africa: The Case of Guinea-Bissau." *Africana Journal* 17 (1998): 1–26.

———. "State, Peasantry, and National Power Struggles in Post-independence Guinea-Bissau." Ph.D. diss., University of Wisconsin-Madison, 1987.

Frazão-Moreira, Amélia. "Récits de migration des Nalou de Cubucaré." In *Migrations anciennes,* ed. Gaillard, 403–12.

Gable, Edward E. "Modern Manjaco: The Ethos of Power in a West African Society." Ph.D. diss., University of Virginia, May 1990.

Gaillard, Gérald. "Guinée-Bissau: Un pas douloureux vers la démocratie." *Afrique contemporaine* 191 (July-Sept. 1999): 43–57.

———. "Présentation." In *Migrations anciennes,* ed. Gaillard, 7–37.

———, ed. *Migrations anciennes et peuplement actuel des côtes guinéennes.* Paris: L'Harmattan, 2000.

Galli, Rosemary E. "On Peasant Productivity: The Case of Guinea-Bissau." *Development and Change* 18, no. 1 (1987): 69–98.

Galli, Rosemary E., and Jocelyn Jones. *Guinea-Bissau: Politics, Economics, and Society.* Boulder, Colo.: Lynne Rienner, 1987.

Giesing, Cornelia. "Fari Sangul, Sankule Faring, migrations et intégration politique dans le monde mandé selon les traditions des guerriers koring de la Sénégambie méridionale." In *Migrations anciennes,* ed. Gaillard, 241–305.

Guyer, Jane I. "The Spatial Dimensions of Civil Society in Africa: An Anthropologist

Looks at Nigeria." In *Civil Society and the State in Africa,* ed. John Harbeson, Donald Rothchild, and Naomi Chazan, 215–29. Boulder, Colo.: Lynne Rienner, 1994.

Handem, Diana Lima. "Nature et fonctionnement du pouvoir chez les Balanta Brassa." Thèse de 3ème cycle, Ecole des Hautes Etudes en Sciences Sociales, Paris, 1985.

Harbeson, John W., Donald Rothchild, and Naomi Chazan, eds. *Civil Society and the State in Africa.* Boulder, Colo.: Lynne Rienner, 1994.

Havik, Philip J. "Female Entrepreneurship in a Changing Environment: Gender, Kinship, and Trade in the Guinea Bissau Region." In *Negotiation and Space: A Gendered Analysis of Changing Kin and Security Networks in South Asia and Sub-Saharan Africa,* ed. Carl Risseeuw and Kamala Ganesh, 205–25. New Delhi: Sage, 1998.

———. "Mundasson i Kambansa: Espaço social e movimentos políticos na Guiné Bissau, 1910–1994." *Revista Internacional de Estudos Africanos* 18–22 (1995–99): 115–67.

———. "As sociedades agrárias e a intervenção rural na Guiné-Bissau: Uma revista da literatura pós-independência." *Revista Internacional de Estudos Africanos* 14–15 (1991): 279–310.

Hawkins, Joye Bowman. See Bowman, 1980.

Hawthorne, Walter. "The Interior Past of an Acephalous Society: Institutional Change among the Balanta of Guinea-Bissau, c.1400–c.1950." Ph.D. diss., Stanford University, 1998.

———. "Migrations and Statelessness: The Expansion of the Balanta of Guinea-Bissau, 1900–1950." In *Migrations anciennes,* ed. Gaillard, 139–50.

———. "Nourishing a Stateless Society during the Slave Trade: The Rise of Balanta Paddy-Rice Production in Guinea-Bissau." *Journal of African History* 42 (2001): 1–24.

Herbst, Jeffrey. *States and Power in Africa: Comparative Lessons in Authority and Control.* Princeton, N.J.: Princeton University Press, 2000.

Hewitt, Malyn. *Portugal in Africa: The Last Hundred Years.* London: Longman, 1981.

Hochet, Anne-Marie. *Paysanneries en attente: Guinée-Bissau.* Dakar: ENDA, 1983.

Hyden, Goran. *Beyond Ujamaa in Tanzania: Underdevelopment and an Uncaptured Peasantry.* Berkeley: University of California Press, 1980.

———. *No Shortcuts to Progress.* Berkeley: University of California Press, 1983.

Jao, Mamadú. "Ethnical Origin and Migration among the Mancanha of Guinea-Bissau." In *Migrations anciennes,* ed. Gaillard, 215–22.

Ka, Samba. "Rich Entrepreneurs, Poor Economies: Smuggling Activities in Senegambia." Ph.D. diss., Johns Hopkins University, 1994.

Lima, Augusto J. Santos. *Organização económica e social dos Bijagós.* Lisbon: Centro de Estudos da Guiné Portuguesa, 1947.

Lobban, Richard, Jr., and Joshua Forrest. *Historical Dictionary of the Republic of Guinea-Bissau.* 2d ed. Metuchen, N.J.: Scarecrow Press, 1988.

Lobban, Richard, Jr., and Peter Karibe Mendy. *Historical Dictionary of the Republic of Guinea-Bissau.* 3d ed. Lanham, Md.: Scarecrow Press, 1996.

Lopes, Carlos. *Etnia, estado, e relações de poder na Guiné-Bissau.* Lisbon: Edições 70, 1982.

———. *Guinea-Bissau: From Liberation Struggle to Independent Statehood.* London: Zed Press; Boulder, Colo.: Westview Press, 1987.

———. *Kaabunké: Espaço, território, e poder na Guiné-Bissau, Gâmbia, e Casamance pré-*

coloniais. Lisbon: Comissão Nacional Para as Comemorações dos Descobrimentos Portugueses, 1999.

―――. "Relações de poder numa sociedade Malinké: O Kaabú do séc. XIII ao séc. XVIII." *Soronda: Revista de Estudos Guineenses* 10 (July 1990): 17–26.

―――. "A transição histórica na Guiné-Bissau: Do movimento de libertação nacional ao estado." Mémoire (thesis). Geneva: Institut Universitaire d'Etudes du Développement, 1982.

MacGaffey, Janet. *The Real Economy of Zaire.* Philadelphia: University of Pennsylvania Press, 1991.

Mamdani, Mahmood. *Citizen and Subject: Contemporary Africa and the Legacy of Late Colonialism.* Princeton, N.J.: Princeton University Press, 1996.

Mané, Mamadou. "Contribution à l'histoire du Kaabu, des origines au XIXe siècle." *Bulletin de l'Institut Fondamental d'Afrique Noire* 40, no. 1 (1978): 88–159.

Marques, A. H. de Oliveira. *História de Portugal.* Lisbon: Palas Editores, 1976.

Mendes, José Luis Ferreira. "Considerações sobre a problemática de planificação e do desenvolvimento agrícola na Guiné." *Boletim Cultural da Guiné Portuguesa* 26, no. 101 (1971): 217–23.

Mendy, Peter Karibe. *Colonialismo Português em Africa: A tradição de resistência na Guiné-Bissau, 1879–1959.* Bissau: Instituto Nacional de Estudos e Pesquisas, 1994.

―――. "A conquista militar da Guiné: Da resistência à 'pacificação' do arquipélago dos Bijagós, 1917–1936." *Stronoir* 13 (January 1992): 41–52.

Migdal, Joel S. *Strong Societies and Weak States: State-Society Relations and State Capabilities in the Third World.* Princeton, N.J.: Princeton University Press, 1988.

Mota, Avelino Teixeira da. *Guiné Portuguesa.* Lisbon: Agência Geral do Ultramar, 1954.

―――. "Les relations de l'ancien Cabou avec quelques états et peuples voisins." *Ethiopiques: Revue socialiste de culture négro-africaine* 28, special issue (1981): 149–67.

Niane, Djibril Tamsir. "Les sources orales de l'histoire du Gabu." *Ethiopiques: Revue socialiste de culture négro-africaine* 28, special issue (1981): 128–36.

Passavant, Odile Hanquez. "Une histoire des Nalou, ~XIVe-XIXe Siècle: Naissance d'un groupe et appropriation d'un nom." In *Migrations anciennes,* ed. Gaillard, 385–401.

Pélissier, René. *Naissance de la Guiné: Portuguais et Africains en Sénégambie, 1841–1936.* Orgeval, France: Pélissier, 1989.

Pinto, João Teixeira. *A ocupação militar da Guiné.* Lisboa: Agencia Geral das Colónias, 1936.

Ploeg, Jan Douwe van der. "Autarky and Technical Change in Guinea-Bissau: On the Importance of Commodisation and Decommoditisation as Interrelated Processes." In *Rural Households in Emerging Societies: Technology and Change in Sub-Saharan Africa,* ed. Margaret Haswell and Diana Hunt, 93–113. New York: Berg, 1991.

Quintino, Fernand Rogado. "Os povos da Guiné Portuguesa." *Boletim Cultural de Guiné Portuguesa* 29, no. 96 (1969): 883–84.

Ranger, Terence O. "Connexions between 'Primary Resistance' Movements and Modern Mass Nationalism in East and Central Africa." Parts 1 and 2. *Journal of African History* 9, no. 3 (1968): 437–53; no. 4 (1968): 631–41.

Ribeiro, Rui. "Barragens em bolanhas de agua salgada." *Soronda: Revista de Estudos Guineenses* 4 (July 1987): 38–57.

Roberts, Richard L. *Two Worlds of Cotton: Colonialism and the Regional Economy in French Soudan, 1800–1946.* Cambridge: Cambridge University Press, 1996.

―――. *Warriors, Merchants, and Slaves: The State and the Economy in the Middle Niger Valley, 1700–1914.* Stanford, Calif.: Stanford University Press, 1987.

Rothchild, Donald, and Naomi Chazan, eds. *The Precarious Balance: State and Society in Africa.* Boulder, Colo.: Westview Press, 1988.

Rudebeck, Lars. "The Effects of Structural Adjustment in Kandjadja, Guinea-Bissau." *Review of African Political Economy* 49 (winter 1990): 34–51.

―――. *Guinea-Bissau: A Study of Political Mobilization.* Uppsala, Sweden: Scandinavian Institute of African Studies, 1974.

―――. "Problèmes de pouvoir populaire et de développement: Transition difficile en Guinée-Bissau." Research report 63. Uppsala, Sweden: Scandinavian Institute of African Studies, 1982.

Santos, Daniel dos. "The Second Economy in Angola: *Esquema* and *Candonga*." In *The Second Economy in Marxist States,* ed. Maria Los, 157–74. New York: St. Martin's Press, 1990.

Santos, Mário. "Algumas considerações sobre a nossa situação sociolinguística." *Soronda: Revista de Estudos Guineenses* 4 (July 1987): 3–14.

Schoenmakers, Hans. "Old Men and New State Structures in Guinea-Bissau." *Journal of Legal Pluralism* 25–26 (1987): 99–138.

Scott, James C. "Everyday Forms of Peasant Resistance." In *Everyday Forms of Peasant Resistance,* ed. Forrest D. Colburn, 3–33. Armonk, N.Y.: M. E. Sharpe, 1989.

Serrão, Joaquim Verssimo. *História de Portugal VI, 1750–1807.* Lisbon: Editorial Verbo, 1982.

Smith, Robert S. *Warfare and Diplomacy in Pre-colonial West Africa.* London: Methuen, 1976.

Stohl, Michael, and George Lopez, eds. *The State as Terrorist: The Dynamics of Governmental Violence and Repression.* Westport, Conn.: Greenwood Press, 1984.

Sundiata, Ibrahim K. *Equatorial Guinea: Colonialism, State Terror, and the Search for Stability.* Boulder, Colo.: Westview Press, 1990.

―――. "The Structure of Terror in a Small State: Equatorial Guinea." In *African Islands and Enclaves,* ed. Robin Cohen, 81–100. Beverly Hills: Sage, 1983.

Valimamad, E. D. "Nationalist Politics, War, and Statehood: Guinea-Bissau, 1953–1973." Ph.D. diss., Saint Catherine's College, Oxford University, 1984.

Viegas, Luís António de Carvalho. *Guiné Portuguesa.* Vol. 1. Lisbon: Freitas Mega, 1936.

―――. *Guiné Portuguesa.* Vol. 2. Lisbon: Freitas Mega, 1939.

―――. *Guiné Portuguesa.* Vol. 3. Lisbon: Freitas Mega, 1940.

Wolf, Eric R. *Peasant Wars of the Twentieth Century.* New York: Harper & Row, 1969.

Young, Crawford. *The African Colonial State in Comparative Perspective.* New Haven: Yale University Press, 1994.

Zanatti, Mário. "O Indigenato da Guiné." In *Congresso comemorativo,* 389–99.

Index

307